A COMPENDIUM

OF

HERBAL MAGICK

A COMPENDIUM

OF

HERBAL MAGICK

PAUL BEYERL

Phoenix Publishing Inc.

By the same author:

The Master Book of Herbalism

This edition printed 2008

PHOENIX PUBLISHING, INC.
1160 Yew Avenue
PO Box 3829
Blaine, WA 98231

ISBN 978-0-919345-45-4

Printed in the U.S.A.

Contents

Part III

7

Preface

The world of herbe magick is not, generally, considered the acceptable path for an herbalist. And it can be a very strange path. I formally entered this world of herbes in February, 1976, and started a journey which will not be complete until I have spent several more lives upon this wonderful planet. My childhood was in a rural area. I was raised on a dairy farm but my memories are not of the barn and herd so much as of the wooded acreage where leeks, wild dicentra, trilliums and ferns grew. Those woods were filled with a natural magick which I was far too undeveloped to recognize. I remember listening, at night, to the two rows of venerable pines which formed a path to the birch bridge constructed by my father. I had an affinity for the family willow from which my father would cut a forked branch when my dowsing skills were put into play.

Later, when I was about eleven or twelve, we moved into town. Nature was replaced by a yard which grew back as fast as it took to cut. Our first family garden—still small by rural standards, shrunk each year by a lawn mower width or so until there was none, except a few flowers here and there. My forays into nature were taken when I would ride my bicycle into the country and wander along the streams and explore among the trees. During those years, before I graduated from high school, I learned the barest foundation of herbal gardening from our neighbor, Yetive. Tibby, as she preferred to be called, knew some herbal remedies and knew about growing herbs in her gardens. At the time, I was too unaware to realize what I was learning.

Leaving behind my parents' religion, I wandered as a "profound agnostic," as I liked to refer to myself. In my late twenties my Saturn return brought me back, face to face, with issues of my own mortality and of my own spiritual and religious beliefs. My path began with Aldous Huxley and led me through Asian religions. I hand-copied the entire Jane English translation of the *Tao*, and endless pages of notes and quotations from the *Gita*. I copied from the *Bardo Thodol* and from any related book I could put my hands on. It was fragmented study at best for I had no teacher, but I did well enough that the Universe brought me a gift.

I set aside the life I had been creating and moved to northern Minnesota where my time was spent rebuilding a farmhouse and studying the native flora, from which I established a garden of wild flowers and native herbs. I worked at meditating and becoming more harmonious with my environment and then I knew it was time. My inner voice told me that I must return to Minneapolis for it was there my teacher was waiting.

A few months later, in March 1976 (just twenty years ago this week as I put the finishing touches on this manuscript), I was seated in a suburban basement, taking my first classes in preparation for initiation into a coven of witches. I don't remember the circumstances, but one day one of my teachers commented that "what our community needs is an herbalist." Everything fell into place and I knew that becoming an herbalist was every bit as important as becoming a priest. And as they say, "the rest is history."

My original intent was to study remedial work, or the herbal study concerned with remedies for illness and herbal preparations which treat the physical body. My study of herbalism, however, grew out of my magickal training so it was inevitable that I began to collect information about the magickal properties of herbes. Initially I was, as so many students are, enamored with the idea of using herbes for spell magick. I came to see, through the wisdom of Paracelsus and of Doctor Hartmann, that the study of herbal magick provided me with tools of healing which touched the patient's soul and promoted health through a truly spiritual form of holistic work.

My work as an herbalist has continued over the years. As I celebrate my twentieth anniversary as a priest, I have been blessed with many things. My partner and I live with more than an acre of herb gardens and trees, containing ritual circles, and a proximity to nature which permeates our days. I was blessed by the Universe to have found myself in the position as founder of a Wiccan tradition (even though at the time I was so caught up in life I didn't realize it until the process was several years in the making). My spiritual beliefs which created the foundation of The Tradition of Lothloriën were greatly influenced by both Eastern and Western religious history. I am appreciative of the training I received as a child (even today the cedars by that church yard have space in my memory) and remember an early question and answer we had to memorize: "Where is God?" to which the correct answer was, "God is Everywhere."

As I made slow and painful progress on the arduous path toward wisdom, that very simple statement has proven more true than its authors may have ever realized. I have often used that simple catechism lesson to illustrate the principles of pantheism to a monotheist. To wit, if "god" permeates the entire Universe, then god is in the flowers and trees, god is in the thunder storm, god is in the creatures of the woodland and god is in the fish. But it doesn't stop there, for god is in the coal mine, god is in my computer, god is in pollution and god is in war. Everything which exists, then, is "god" and that includes the presence of the divine in your sexual ecstasy and in all which exists, including those things we wish did *not* exist. But this is not to be a treatise on theology.

There is divinity in every plant which is part of the larger divinity. And that larger divinity is the creator of the Universe. It is as if the spiritual essence is part of the DNA. It is as if every plant has its own spiritual energy or its own *deva*. What are devas? As an herbalist, I must come to terms with the spiritual nature of the world of plants. In *The Holy Books of the Devas* my text and myths speak of the devas. I first encountered the term *deva* in *The Magic of Findhorn* by Paul Hawken, and I believe the Findhorn community borrowed the term from the Sanskrit. In the Hindu pantheon, the word *deva* is the plural of *devi* and refers to those spiritual energies which arise from the Highest Consciousness of the Universe. In other words, devas are the radiant light of the Universal Divine which permeates all things.

I have met people who can see the auras of plants and are capable of recognizing different species by the differences in spiritually radiant energy. I have known people who speak to plants (well, we all do in some ways). I have known people who hear plants speak to them, sometimes very literally. Others have seen small, spritely beings which they describe as faeries. Most of us simply know that plants are much more than the sum of their physical substance and the word *deva* has come to be used as the spiritual essence, being or divine personality of a particular species.

Since the earliest of times people were aware that all of nature is divine. Great and wondrous and oftentimes frightening myths and stories were told which explained the presence of divine energy as it existed in thunder, in trees or in the sunlight. Some of this lore was the foundation of religions. But the simpler stories—such as those of a plant's energy—explored day-to-day matters, such as romance. These stories have been preserved in folklore through poems and chants and ditties and spells. We believe that, in simpler times, people lived in closer proximity to nature. Artificial lighting is a modern invention. Back in the days of old so freely romanticized by modern authors, even a trip out the door to relieve one's self would bring you into close proximity with the weather, with the dark. People were not so trapped with words for they did not read a daily paper, they did not listen to radio nor watch television. In fact, until very recent history, people as a whole were quite illiterate. There was no need to describe the spiritual magick of a plant in lovely, esoteric phrases. When lore is passed down as an oral tradition, a simple ditty is much more to the point.

Those who wish to be magickal herbalists must be able to recognize that all plants have a sacred spirit. Each species and variety has its own deva and each is divine. The number of herbes represented in this book make it one of the more complete volumes to date, but it is the smallest fraction of the knowledge which exists. Our work, my friends, is to continue collecting magickal lore and preserving it so that it can be used in a mature, grounded manner. In coming to recognize the spiritual nature of plant life, our view of the earth as the mother of these divine creatures begins to expand and, before you know it, the magickal herbalist understands the mystery: that all of life is sacred. Here at The Hermit's Grove we honor *every* plant and flower. We consider all trees divine and even treat the weeds with respect as we remove them from spaces reserved for the herbes and plants. We try to communicate with the devas and encourage them to recognize that they can all coexist if they but recognize each other's rights so that no one species has the right to obliterate another. We know that if our planet's atmosphere is destroyed that the blackberries and slugs will probably survive. Our gardening is meant to provide a sanctuary for as many species as possible. Part of this work is helping others learn of the divine nature of herbes. We hope that this book will help you learn that every herbal vegetable you eat has a sacred deva, that every meal (including vegetarian meals) involves the sacrifice of life and should be blessed.

My method has been to study folklore but not in the literal sense.

There is great wisdom in herbal folklore but the study of this lore requires taking the larger view, becoming aware of the patterns which emerge over many centuries. As the years have passed, I have learned to neither embrace folklore as the literal truth nor to reject it as superstition. I believe that folklore provides one of the keys to help us see how earlier peoples perceived the spiritual energy or deva of a particular plant. My only requirement is that I distinguish between authentic folklore and books created with new material which is purported to be old lore. The former I study, the latter I will reserve for a later incarnation. Authors whose work cannot be documented were not used as source material although many of their works are included in the list of additional resources provided near the end of this book.

You will be *meeting* many new herbes as you read this text. We hope this work will stimulate your interest in them and also your desire to become more conservation concerned, working toward their preservation. You will also learn fascinating magickal and religious uses of many herbes and herbal foods which you have already known from the sense of your palate and diet. Enjoy them. Learn to recognize the presence of divinity in all growing things. Come to love the plants' spirits or devas.

As Above, So Below:
Herbes and Herbs

My definition of herbes is very inclusive. Any plant which produces chlorophyll is likely to be considered an herbe, whether it is an annual or perennial, whether it is a fern or a mighty tree. So long as we, in our limited human wisdom, have been able to recognize that plant's medicinal or spiritual value, the word *herbe* applies. Some readers questioned my spelling of *herbe* in *The Master Book of Herbalism*. I neglected to explain the two spellings I work with. Much of my work as a Master Herbalist is in the treatment of the body. In this work I refer to *herbs,* as the word is commonly spelled and as it is found in common usage. However, when referring to their magickal uses, I use *herbes* with the variant spelling.

The two areas of work may seem very interrelated but there are significant differences. My remedial work (with herbs) is focused upon the physiological state of being. This includes the functions of the body, diseases, varying conditions of the body, and the treatment of symptoms when they occur. A holistic approach includes strengthening physiological systems in an anticipatory fashion, such as preparing tonics for flu season, for periods of stress, or in advance of an astrological transit which indicates the possibility of anatomical disruptions.

Early on in my studies I encountered the book by Dr. Franz Hartmann, *Occult Science in Medicine*, which shaped my path in ways no other book has done. Since that time, I have not attempted to separate my priesthood from my work as a Master Herbalist. I have spent twenty years studying herbes and collecting factual magickal history. My legacy, if there is to be one, is in showing people how to study folklore and the religious uses of herbes in many cultures and use that information to grasp the spiritual essence of a plant.

The magickal use of an herbe is for treating a patient's spiritual system. While much of the folklore (and the information within spell books) is designed for those who have immediate needs, the priest or priestess who seeks to learn the inner mysteries will discover that the lore (written in simple rhymes and superstitious beliefs) was for the uneducated, for those who could not read or write. They needed a simpler way of remembering the *energy* of a plant.

Herbes said to bring a lover into one's life have always been popular. But how do they really work? I believe that one can follow a formula and chant magick words with a candle while using the herbe and impose one's will upon the fabric of the Universe. Were I to do so, I would be imposing my will upon that of the Universe, allowing my ego to get in the way. But that is not my way. I would want for myself the spiritual assurance that I have been chosen by my beloved because of who I am, not because of a bay leaf.

I do have a theory, however. (Actually, I have many hundreds of them.) Now that we have barely begun to understand the effects of trace chemicals upon the brain, I believe that in the coming years many herbes will be found to have a subtle effect upon those sensitive, inner balances. Perhaps that Herbe of Love does not bring forth a lover but, rather, helps stimulate subtle internal changes which allow the practitioner to believe she is appealing or opens her to a possibility which was previously denied.

Certainly this is a feasible theory. I have continued to study the history of herbal lore in the belief that this is essential information to integrate into my ritual work and the healing of one's spirit. I see the role of a Master Herbalist as one who heals the body through the healing of the soul.

How to Use This Book:
the Compendium Format

This compendium is intended to help you better know the spiritual and magickal properties of herbes and provide you with guidelines in working with their energies. Today's publishing market includes an astounding number of books which include magickal information about herbes. The inconsistency and scattered quality of this lore renders much of it useless to the serious student. Our goal at The Hermit's Grove includes creating a core body of lore which is consistent. My personal contributions have benefited from twenty years as both Master Herbalist and Master Astrologer, and fifteen years as an educator in the fields of tarot, gem and mineral lore.

In the main body of this text, herbes are listed alphabetically by their *common name*. In many cases, the herbes have a number of names; we have listed these by the name we use at The Hermit's Grove. Following this name is the herbe's *Latin name*. There are, often times, more than one Latin name since more than one botanist has done work over the centuries. We have tried to use that name which will be most useful in the herbe's identification.

The next line or two lists the *planetary associations*. Research frequently uncovers two or more planets which various authors have assigned to an herbe. When the authors are reputable, we list all planetary associations. If there is a planetary correspondence we feel has the widest acceptance, one from the more reputable source, or one we prefer, it is marked with an asterisk. Just beneath the planetary correspondences are the *zodiacal associations* if there are any. There are far fewer zodiacal correspondences found throughout herbal history but, when possible, they have been included in the same manner. For additional material and an extensive listing of astrological correspondences, please refer to Part III.

Next are the *magickal classifications* which shows the ways an herbe has been used historically or might be used today. These classifications serve as a guide in helping you understand the different facets of energy an herbe possess. They are usually based upon the historical lore of an herbe and, less frequently, upon modern lore which has no basis. These are provided as a guideline and will be discussed in detail shortly.

When an herbe might be known by other names, those are included following the heading *also called* to help you more readily identify these plants. These names will always be listed without capitalization (unless a proper noun is part of the name) and are included in Part III for your convenience.

Associations with deities which indicate the herbe's ability to connect the practitioner with any specific deity are included in *invocatory* lists for reference. This information must have historical basis and implies that the herbe may be used to establish some level of communion with the archetype of the deity listed.

The *lore* provided for each herbe includes historical information, beliefs and uses associated with the herbe which help expand the understanding of the herbe. Please note that we have attempted to document as many references as possible without allowing the book to become overrun with them. In many cases the quotations or references do not do justice to the source. We urge you to turn to these sources and pursue your knowledge further than this book.

The *usage* section provides you with suggestions and information about the ways in which an herbe may be used. The section includes modern uses. The usage information is not to be treated as definitive but as a guideline for learning how to translate historical lore into modern usage. We see the usage section as a collection of seeds, hoping we will sow the seeds of myriad ideas for your magickal skills which will grow freely when mixed with your imagination.

With the additional lists and material provided in Part III, we have attempted to provide extensive cross-referencing to herbes in many different ways. Such a task is monumental and has kept the entire household at The Hermit's Grove busy beyond belief. Although we have done our best, there will be some lapses in which some word, herbe or reference does not appear in Part III or in some list. We trust that you will be understanding in this matter.

Notes About Resources

Mrs. M. Grieve is perhaps our best modern herbe historian. It is obvious from A Modern Herbal that she has referred to numerous sources, many of which are no longer readily available. Circumstances have not allowed me to seek out each of her sources. I trust that I will be granted many future incarnations so I may complete my studies.

In my opinion and that of many others, Robert Graves is a romantic revisionist. A great deal of his herbal mythology and magick is derived from The Golden Bough, much can be verified as accurate, but much cannot. Whether or not Graves was the creative force behind some of his material is irrelevant when one considers the tremendous influence The White Goddess has provided neopagan traditions. Graves' work has done much to shape modern thought. Some of Graves' references may be from his own creation rather than ages-old practices or beliefs. But, through Graves they have become wide-spread beliefs which merit inclusion in this compendium

I know it will be pointed out to me that certain popular authors have not been cited as sources. Where authors have derived their information from historical sources, the historical sources themselves are used. In many references by contemporary authors, customs and uses are suggested for herbes which we have been unable to document nor have they been supported historically through other source material. The better of these authors are included in the listing of additional references.

The text has numerous correspondences between herbes and tarot cards. Some of these were originally derived from a list given to me by a student some fifteen years ago. Some I did not initially agree with nor understand, but having taught courses in the interpretation of the symbols and archetypes represented by the cards for fifteen years, they make more sense and were kept intact. The source material has long since slipped through the cracks in my memory, but I believe it was from a list derived from the Golden Dawn. The original list has been substantially expanded based upon my work as both writer and educator of the tarot.

The Hermit's Grove
and Continuing Research

This compendium is not complete. Turn to the books and authors which are cited and take joy in your quest for herbal wisdom. Generations will pass before this research will near completion. You, as a reader, must do your part. We also urge you to please send us any other documented material. We collect lore and usage found in a variety of sources, ranging from newspaper articles to National Geographic television specials. We cannot accept material without the source being credited. We continue to update this information through the Grove's monthly newsletter, *The Hermit's Lantern*. Research and learning being what they are, I must state that I have grown more through the writing of this book than most students will be able to comprehend, and for that I will always be indebted to my publisher and to every reader.

With Love and Gratitude

This book could not have been completed without the devoted assistance of my partner, gerry Beyerl (gerry has chosen to spell his name with a lower case g as a reminder of his vows). Having devoted his life in service to the Mother as one of Her priests, he is a source of strength and inspiration and support for me. He helped me with the research, with many of the mundane hours of typing, and in untold other supportive ways. Without gerry, there would be no Hermit's Grove and I would not be living with the daily joy of our gardens. Special thanks go to Cliff Wagner who began assisting gerry and embraced countless hours helping me with proofreading and with sorting out the endless threads of trivia for cross-referencing. I also wish to express my thanks to Cris Bear, who is part of our Master Herbalist program, whose support and encouragement have helped considerably.

Appreciation is also expressed to the many herbal students I have served since 1976 when I began teaching my first herbalism course in Minneapolis. In retrospect, it stuns me to realize how little I knew then. Now I teach herbal medicine at Seattle Central Community College and Bellevue Community College, and in many ways, feel like I have just begun to grasp the knowledge we must hold firmly in order to do our work.

My beliefs are permeated with my priesthood. The Tradition of Lothloriën has grown and opened like the lotus. Its outer structure is The Rowan Tree Church which, as do all trees, has grown strong and thrives only because it has withstood the weather, endured pruning and even been transplanted with great success. To those of you who share in the intimate magick of Lothloriën, I give you my love.

PART I

The Magickal Classification of Herbes

When I began my training and research in herbal studies, one of my early tasks was to learn the ways remedial herbs were described by their function through a loose system of classification. To assist the practitioner in an understanding of herbal lore and herbal magick, we use a system of classifications developed during my research for *The Master Book of Herbalism* which has been greatly expanded since.

Aphrodisiacal Herbes

Herbes which have been used to stimulate sexual desire, lust or promote arousal are given the classification of aphrodisiacal. Some of these herbes are used through direct application to the sexual organs and may provide physiological results. Other herbes work upon the person's spiritual body, activating a chakra, stimulating mental images, or promoting a desire to seek union in the sensual arms of another.

These herbes serve as aphrodisiacs; their function is sexual stimulation. This should not be confused with the stimulation of love and/or romance. Aphrodisiacal Herbes should be used with care (even though they can be as common as the rose) for magickally increasing sexual tension within one's self when there is no outlet may lead to frustration and problematic behavior. Again using roses as an example, it is possible to work with roses in one's gardens, wear rose oil as a scent and even use rose petals as a strewing herbe without releasing the aphrodisiacal property of the herbe. Intent and focus are among the primary control mechanisms available to the practitioner in any spiritual work.

Aphrodisiacal Herbes are well suited for increasing the primal passion which may be unlocked during the Great Rite. During this ritually consecrated act of intercourse and consummation between two partners, the participants use disciplined mental images and visualization skills; they have developed adeptness in using invocatory energies to embody the polarities of the Universe.

Aphrodisiacal Herbes include the following: blessed thistle, cubeb, cumin, damiana, fern (male), ginko biloba, henna, holly (sea), kava kava, lemon, mandrake, marshmallow, matico, mistletoe, orchid, patchouli, rose, rose geranium, saffron, savory, sesame, Solomon's seal, southernwood, unicorn root (false), vervain.

Countermagick Herbes

Many herbes are said to serve a variety of functions which seem archaic in today's world. Some herbes are said to repel witches while another might turn back the evil eye. Today's practitioner is, hopefully, wiser in the mysteries of karma.

The practice of using manipulative magick to force other's lives to conform to one person's will was popular during the Middle Ages, but it is more likely that the majority of these superstitious practices arose out of fear and ignorance. Even today, in some cultures, one can find a person who will happily accept money in exchange for placing a *spell* upon another. The human ego can often be vengeful.

We hope that you will never need to use herbal magick (or any type of magick) to remove some type of negative energy imposed upon you by another magickal person. Even if someone does you wrong, our recommendation is that you wish them karma and leave such lessons in the hands of the Universe, for She is far more powerful.

Yet there can be many times in life when we find ourselves being affected by the energy created by another's emotions. One might receive a promotion and become the target of a coworker's resentment, envy and jealousy. How does one counter that destructive force? By using a Countermagick Herbe.

Herbes are considered countermagickal because of established beliefs or practices based upon their ability to both protect the practitioner against the negation and to render that energy harmless or, with some herbes, return it to its source.

Among the Countermagick Herbes are: agrimony, angelica, asafoetida, ash, avens, burnet (great), centaury, daffodil, dodder, fennel, fern (bracken), flax, fumitory, holly, hyssop, motherwort, pine, purslane, quince, rowan, rue, vervain.

Fertility Herbes

The fertility of one's fields was an urgent matter in earlier times when the success of one's crops meant survival. Abundance of grains and foods meant enough to be sold in the market, ensuring continued survival. Failure meant debts, possibly incurring indenture from which one could never escape.

The fertility of one's womb or of one's groin was also a matter of survival in earlier times. Families were able to maintain the farm or business only if there were enough children born to overcome the high mortality rate. In earlier times, children meant labor and labor was the way of life. Even today we find many women subjected to pity and scorn because they have not borne children.

Many Fertility Herbes have been associated with rituals of union and weddings, integrated into those rites to bring fruitfulness to the couple.

Herbes that were used in fertility charms or said to make one's stock reproduce or were believed to help women conceive children are all listed as Fertility Herbes. Many of these herbes have established lore associated with the fertility of a woman's womb, but each of us has many aspects in our lives which require that creative spark.

Fertility Herbes may be used to promote creativity in all aspects of our lives, such as bringing an idea into fruition. They are not limited to the fruitfulness of procreation.

These are Fertility Herbes: alder, anise seed, apple, ash, bamboo, barley, basil (sweet), bean (kidney), birch, cassia, catnip, chestnut, coconut, corn, fern (male), fig, ginko biloba, grapes, hawthorn, lavender, mandrake, marshmallow, mistletoe, oak, olive, orange, orchid, rice, Saint John's wort, stitchwort, vervain, wheat

Funereal Herbes

The herbes in this category have been associated with the death and burial customs of at least one culture. There are many herbes which are planted upon burial sites to bring blessings to the deceased and comfort to those left behind. There are herbes connected with funerals and rituals for the dead. There are herbes which have been used in connection with the death of a beloved.

All are included under the heading of Funereal Herbes.

Although the word *funereal* implies, by definition, those rites and services prior to burial or cremation, we have expanded this definition to include the entire process of death and dying and any rites of passage which a culture might weave about those natural processes.

Herbes used to embalm a body or which are placed with the corpse in a burial chamber are considered Funereal Herbes as are those which are included in this classification. These are also herbes which help one understand the importance of dying as a natural function of life and can teach us about the mysteries of death.

Funereal Herbes include the following: aconite, alder, aloe, amaranth, anise (star), asphodel, banana, basil (bush), basil (sweet), bluebells, camphor, castor, chervil, cinnamon, coca, coconut, dragon's blood, elder, elm, hemlock, holly, iris, laurel (mountain), marigold, marjoram (wild), marshmallow, myrrh, narcissus, nightshade (deadly), parsley, periwinkle, rose, rosemary, sandalwood, sycamore, tansy, thyme (wild), violets, willow.

Greene Herbes

Originally this category consisted of the obvious herbes, those where the green leaf was harvested and readily found in kitchen use, such as basil, dill and oregano. The classification of Greene Herbes has since expanded to include *any* herbe or spice used to flavor food which also has known magickal or spiritual properties. Does this mean that any food seasoned with Greene Herbes becomes magickal? No, the natural energy of these herbes is not put in motion without the cook's knowledge of magick. Each herbe is blessed, its deva invoked. The kitchen is transformed into a temple, an altar always ready. This domestic space is transformed into a ritual site, the chef working within a cast Circle.

Greene Herbes are the realm of the magickal chef; who is able to bring subtle blends of magick to a meal in ways which enhance those who partake of the food without allowing personal desires to interfere. The best uses of Greene Herbes are those which draw upon the herbal magick in order to promote warmth and sociability, which encourage a gentle healing of body and soul for all present.

There are Greene Herbes reputed to bring about types of change which should not be given magickal power without your guests' approval. The wise magickal chef does not play god nor does she attempt to work magick on her guests without their consent. Any magickal chef who releases the magick of Greene Herbes upon unwitting diners has targeted himself for sharp lessons from the Universe.

Most Wiccans believe that it is inappropriate to manipulate another's life without that person's consent. There are many ways in which a cook may bring magick to a meal. Even if you live with those who do not understand magick and your family is in need of some type of tonic for its budget, it is possible to use Greene Herbes believed to stimulate the flow of resources, and tell your kinfolk that you've made a special meal which will help them all prosper. It is essential to remember that an herbe does not make something happen so much as it stimulates change within a person which alters the course of that person's life.

Greene Herbes can be wonderful fun. Imagine inviting your magickal friends to a well-planned meal, with a salad which will help their insight and memory, a soup which will keep them safe and protected in the journeys of life and an entree which will promote friendship and conversation. Greene Herbes are, most generally, benevolent and gentle in their magick.

The following are Greene Herbes: anise seed, basil (bush), basil (sweet), bay laurel, bean (kidney), caraway, celery, chervil, cinnamon, cloves, coriander, corn, cranberry, cucumber, cumin, dill, endive, fennel, fenugreek, garlic, ginger, houseleek, potato, quince, rosemary, rue, saffron, savory, tarragon, thyme, turmeric, watercress, wheat.

Herbes of Consecration

Herbes of Consecration are those which can be used to bless or consecrate. They assist in changing the natural energy, elevating it to a purer state of being. These herbes have a history of use in ceremonies, such as those selected by Solomon or those used for the religious rites of a particular culture. Many of these herbes are also known for their ability to bring purification, although that quality is not inherent in every Herbe of Consecration. Herbes which have been used to consecrate any religious object or which have been used in some manner to provide sacred energy for religious purposes are considered Herbes of Consecration. Some Herbes of Consecration were placed in this category due to a history of use to seal or make permanent magickal energy. Herbes used in magick to bring about a transformation in a ritual tool, which assist in the blessing of a ritual item are also placed in this classification.

These. herbes assist in changing the energy of physical space (for they can be used to consecrate a temple or any sacred space) or the purpose of an object, removing it from the world of common, mundane usage and relegating it to the realm of the sacred. When consecrating an object, the herbe should be brought into direct contact. There are many ways this can be done. Some of the herbe may be added to water, creating an herbal bathing solution into which the ritual object is immersed. Dried herbes may be burned upon charcoal and the object passed through the smoke.

The very act of blessing often denotes applying words. While words, phrases or poems may be found in lore, the majority of those found in modern texts are modern incantations. The practitioner is encouraged to explore all options, to seek out ancient incantations, to use those offered by modern authors or to create original blessings.

Herbes of Consecration are known for their ability to bestow benevolent, empowering energy. They bring with them a positive energy, but it is more than positive. It is also an energy which brings change with it, for an item once consecrated is forever changed. The process of consecration should be approached in a serious manner. The claiming of an object from the mundane world, consecrating it for religious ritual should be recognized as a sacred act, one which will forever change the purpose of that object. A crystal goblet, consecrated for use as a ritual chalice, will never again be an ordinary drinking vessel. Empowered through ritual with Herbes of Consecration, it has been touched by the gods, kissed by the goddesses and should be given a secure future, its magick guaranteed protection long into the future.

Although a particular herbe may have a singular use, such as the consecration of a chalice, it is our belief that an herbe used to consecrate a sacred space may also be used in other acts of consecration. Herbes of Consecration may be used in a variety of creative ways either in the process of acquiring ritual tools and ritually initiating them into a new life of magickal use or to consecrate your circle or even a person.

These are Herbes of Consecration: acacia, aconite, almond, angelica, anise seed, anise (star), asafoetida, asphodel, balm of gilead, basil (sweet), broom, burnet (great), camphor, caraway, cedar, cherry, cinnamon, clover, dragon's blood, elfwort, flax, frankincense, fumitory, gum mastic, hellebore (black), hemlock, henbane, hyssop, ivy, lavender, lotus, marigold, marsh marigold, mistletoe, mugwort, mulberry, myrrh, nettles, nightshade (deadly), olive, pimpernel, rose, rue, sandalwood, sedge (sweet), Solomon's seal, tarragon, valerian, vervain, watercress.

Herbes of Immortality

An herbe given this classification can provide the practitioner an opening into the mysteries which extend far into the depths of the Universe. Herbes which have been used to keep one's spirit safe as it seeks rebirth and herbes which bring an understanding of the very nature of eternity are classified as Herbes of Immortality. Many of these herbes are said to provide the practitioner with longevity. However, more important than the preservation of one's physical body, these herbes bring an understanding of the true nature of one's spiritual self.

Through working with Herbes of Immortality one can come to perceive the essence of that which transcends death and is the nature of spiritual being which will again be incarnate upon the earth. Not all people believe in reincarnation, but most peoples have believed that there is a divine counterpart to the physiological self. Herbes of Immortality help you get to know that aspect of yourself.

Herbes of Immortality include the following: aconite, almond, amaranth, angelica, anise seed, apple, asclepias, asphodel, basil (sweet), cassia, chervil, chrysanthemum, coriander, cyprus, fern (bracken), foxglove, heather, hemlock, honeysuckle, ivy, life-everlasting, mistletoe, myrtle, pennyroyal, periwinkle, primrose, red clover, sage, sandalwood, sunflower, tansy, vervain, violets, willow.

Herbes of Love

There are many herbes believed to help us dream of a soul mate and help bring that person into our lives. In researching herbe lore we learn of herbes which will make someone fall in love with you against their will. But who could be content holding someone spiritually captive, knowing that they are not with you because they want you?

Herbes of Love are connected with the mysteries surrounding love and romance. Those which are believed to bring a lover into one's life are more likely to bring about changes within one's inner self, allowing us to be more lovable. Many of these herbes may seem harmless enough. However, using Herbes of Love in order to find romance and affection through another person is a process which surely begs the Universe to carry us through the fires of transformation, growing and becoming mature, shedding the security of our emotional baggage—no matter how self-de-feating—until we evolve into someone desirable.

We may work with these herbes to enhance a relationship which is already established. Many of these herbes are capable of re-minding us of the reasons we first fell in love and of revitalizing the sparks of love and romance in a relationship which has be-come mired in the daily routines of life.

The following are considered Herbes of Love: alder, almond, anemone (wood), anise seed, ash, balm, basil (bush), bay laurel, birch, butterbur, caraway, chestnut, cinnamon, coriander, crow-foot, cyclamen (ivy-leafed), damiana, fern (maidenhair), gorse (golden), hawthorn, hazel nut, hemp, heartsease, henna, house-leek, ivy, lavender, lovage, mandrake, marigold, marjoram (sweet), marjoram (wild), meadowsweet, mistletoe, myrtle, or-ange, orchid, patchouli, pepper (chili), periwinkle, rose, rose ge-ranium, scullcap, southernwood, thyme, thyme (wild), vervain, wormwood

Herbes of Protection

As I wrote in *The Master Book of Herbalism*, "these are the good guys in the herbe kingdom." With rare exception, Herbes of Pro-tection work not because their devas are effective warriors but through their natural energy which is good, strong and radiant. These herbes function as spiritual guardian energy. Used as bath-ing herbes or carried within an amulet, one may keep their energy around whenever needed.

Herbes of Protection offer a type of magick which can be worked for one's family or friends, which is benign and safe, nonmanipulative and does not need their specific permission. There are many times in life when we have an overwhelming desire to be of help for someone in need. Perhaps the person in crisis is not receptive to your growing magickal abilities but, at the least, you can burn incense at your altar set with an image or photo of the person or light a candle dressed with an oil made of protective herbes.

These herbes dispel negative energy through the generation of positive energy. They dispel darkness through the radiance of light. You may use these herbes under almost any circumstance.

Herbes of Protection include the following: aconite, agrimony, alder, alfalfa, alkanet, aloe, angelica, anise seed, anise (star), asafoetida, ash, avens, beech, betony (wood), birch, blackberry, borage, box, burnet (great), caraway, centaury, cinquefoil, clary, comfrey, coriander, cowslip, cumin, daffodil, daisies, dill, dogwood, elder, fennel, fern (royal), frankincense, fumitory, ginger, gorse (golden), gum mastic, hellebore (black), holly, horehound, houseleek, hyssop, iris, jasmine, juniper, loosestrife (purple), lotus, mandrake, marjoram (wild), milkweed, mints, mistletoe, motherwort, mugwort, mulberry, mullein, mustard, myrtle, nightshade (woody), oak, peaches, peony, periwinkle, pine, pimpernel, purslane, red clover, rosemary, rowan, rue, Saint John's wort, samphire, sesame, snapdragon, solomon's seal, sunflower, thyme, turmeric, valerian, vervain, watercress, willow, woodruff.

Herbes of Purification

There are herbes which are spiritually cleansing, which may be used to exorcise unwanted energies or to remove unknown energies from a newly-acquired possession. There are many herbes used to bring spiritual purification to the self, sometimes anointing a novice prior to initiation, or brought into one's bath to remove negative energies, or used to bless and purify a new living space. We have brought these herbes together in a new classification, Herbes of Purification.

Herbes of Purification include the following: angelica, asafoetida, basil (sweet), camphor, cinnamon, daffodil, elfwort, eucalyptus, frankincense, fumitory, gum mastic, hyssop, iris (yellow), juniper, lotus, mints, mullein, pellitory, periwinkle, pine, purslane, rosemary, rue, sage, Saint John's wort, tansy, valerian, vervain.

Magickal Herbes

This classification is the least defined. A Magickal Herbe is one which, well, has magick! These are the herbes ideally suited for candle magick, spell magick and household magick. They are ideal for amulets. They have been used to bring luck or to attract money, and for other uses outside the realm of religious rites. It is our belief that any Magickal Herbe may be used to enhance the power or magick of your working. These herbes may be used to strengthen the recipe already in use or may be used to empower your personal goals. But, primarily, a Magickal Herbe is used to bring about change.

What is *herbe magick* anyway? Herbe magick is the use of herbes to empower, alter or manifest an image. For magick is image and image is magick. Lighting incense in front of an image of a divinity is herbe magick. Burning a candle coated with oil of bay leaves as you chant a simple rhyme asking the Universe to bring money into your life is herbe magick. Using herbes to treat low self-esteem and empower self-image is a form of herbe magick. Leaving herbes in the form of grains and berries on a flat stone at the edge of the woods in memory of your ancestors, holding their images within your heart, is herbe magick.

When we wish to see an image of reality change, when we see an image of what the future might be and wish to work toward that goal, when we introduce the natural energy and spiritual power of herbes as we clear our minds of extraneous thought and hold the desired image clearly, we are working herbe magick. As a rule of thumb, Magickal Herbes may be considered neutral and available for your usage toward any positive goal.

The following are considered Magickal Herbes: agrimony, alfalfa, anise seed, arrow root, ash, balm, balm of gilead, balmony, basil (sweet), bay laurel, beech, benzoin, betony (wood), birch, blackberry, blessed thistle, borage, broom, bryony (white), buckthorn (sea), butterbur, calabar bean, calamint, caraway, catnip, catsfoot, cedar, celandine (greater) centaury, chamomile, cherry (winter), chervil, chestnut, chickweed, chicory, cinnamon, cinquefoil, clover, cloves, columbine, comfrey, coriander, cowslip, cumin, daffodil, daisies, damiana, dill, dragon's blood, elder, elfwort, elm, endive, eyebright, fennel, fenugreek, fern (bracken), fern (male), fern (moonwort), fern (royal), figwort (knotted), flax, gentian, ginger, ginko biloba, goosefoots, hazel nut, heather, hellebore (black), hemp, holly, hollyhock, hops, jack-in-the-pulpit, jasmine, jimsonweed, juniper, lachnanthes, lady's mantle, larkspur (field), lavender, lemon, lilac, lily, lily-of-the-valley, lime, magnolia, mandrake, marigold, marshwort, meadowsweet, melilot, mercury (dog's), milkweed, mints, moneywort, mugwort, myrrh, narcissus, nettles, nightshade (deadly), oak, oxalis, parsley, passion flower, pau d'arco, pellitory, pennyroyal, peony, pepper (chili), peppermint, periwinkle, plantain (common), pomegranate, potato, rose, rosemary, rowan, rue, samphire, sandalwood, savory, scullcap, senna, spikenard, stonecrop (orpine), storax, sunflower, tarragon, thistle, thistle (carline), thyme, thyme (wild), toadflax, trillium, tulip, turmeric, unicorn root, vervain, violets, watercress, willow, wisteria, wormwood, yarrow.

Religious Herbes

These are herbes which have been used in religious ceremony or which may be used in the practice of one's religion. Religious Herbes include those held sacred to a divinity, those which are associated with a religious holiday or sabbat. They are used as part of the observance of religious holidays or are integral to the religious beliefs (such as creation myths) of one or more religious traditions.

Religious Herbes are those considered sacred by at least one culture or religion. Many of these herbes were associated with the deities of a particular religion. Many were sacrificed as offerings to those deities or burned as incense. Some have been used to bathe icons of the divine, others used when initiating someone through a rite of passage. The use of herbes in religious rites is a universal activity, the sole exception being some of the more recently developed Christian sects which disdain anything other than the bible.

An herbe given the classification of Religious Herbe is one whose spiritual being has been recognized, an herbe which has been honored and which we believe continues to merit this special attention. We believe that herbes do not align themselves with any denomination, not even the Wiccan faith, and that an herbe recognized as having religious significance by one people may readily be used by any other so long as they work to maintain the nature of the spiritual identity of the herbe in a respectful manner.

31

The following are Religious Herbes: acacia, aconite, almond, aloe, amaranth, ammoniacum, anemone, anemone (wood), anise (star), apple, asafoetida, asclepias, ash, azadirachta, balm, bamboo, barberry, barley, basil (sweet), bay laurel, beech, benzoin, bilberry, birch, bistort, blackthorn, blessed thistle, bogbean, box, broom, broom (butcher's), buckwheat, cacao, camphor, carob, cassia, castor, catnip, cedar, celandine, chamomile, chaste tree, chervil, cinquefoil, cloves, coconut, coffee, corn, cornflower, costmary, cotton, cowslip, cranberry, cyprus, daisies, daisy (ox-eye), dandelion, dittany of Crete, dogwood, ephedra, fenugreek, fern (bracken), fig, fig (bo), fir, flax, frankincense, garlic, goosefoots, gorse (golden), gourds, grapes, haricot, hawthorn, heather, heliotrope, holly, hollyhock, honeysuckle, hops, horehound, hyacinth, iris, jack-in-the-pulpit, jasmine, juniper, kava kava, lady's mantle, larch, larkspur (field), lavender, life-everlasting, lily, lily-of-the-valley, lime, linden, lotus, maguey, mandrake, marsh marigold, meadowsweet, mercury (dog's), mescal, millet, mints, mistletoe, morning glory, mugwort, mulberry, mullein, mushrooms, myrrh, narcissus, nettles, nightshade (deadly), oak, olive, orange, palm, panic grass, pau d'arco, peaches, peony, pepper (chili), peppermint, peyote, pomegranate, poplar, poppy, potato, pumpkin, quince, red campion, rice, rosemary, safflower, saffron, sage, sago palm, sandalwood, sedge (papyrus), sedge (sweet), storax, sugar cane, sumbul, sunflower, sycamore, tansy, teak, thistle (milk), tobacco, uva ursi, vervain, walnuts, water lily, wheat, willow, woad, woodruff, wormwood, yarrow, yew, yucca.

Visionary Herbes

Herbes associated with the realm of spiritual vision are known as *visionary*. This is, however, far more than experiencing a vision. Being visionary extends an herbe into the realm of dreams or any practice which enables one to extend vision beyond one's physical eyes. These herbes include many used in the practice of divination and several which may be used to invoke an oracle. Visionary Herbes include those which enhance the quality of one's meditations. They assist in helping us extend our perception beyond the limitations of our physical eyes. It is through these herbes that we may be offered the gift of looking across the abyss or of having mystical dreams, of looking beyond the self in order to seek solutions and answers from the divine.

A number of the Visionary Herbes assist the transportation of the

32

practitioner through physiological effects, several of which may be narcotic and are included due to their sacramental role in the religious rites of indigenous peoples. We do not recommend the usage of controlled substances but recognize the importance of this work for some peoples.

Visionary Herbes include the following: aconite, alder, angelica, anise seed, apple, asafoetida, ash, basil (sweet), bay laurel, benzoin, buckthorn (sea), camphor, catnip, cedar, celery, centaury, cinnamon, cinquefoil, clary, clover, cloves, cornflower, cucumber, damiana, dittany of Crete, elm, eyebright, fern (bracken), foxglove, hazel nut, hemp, honeysuckle, hops, horehound, jimsonweed, kava kava, lavender, loosestrife (purple), mandrake, marigold, mescal, mugwort, peppermint, peyote, poke root, rampion, rowan, rue, sandalwood, thornapple, unicorn root, vervain, watercress, wormwood, yarrow.

A Guide to
the Usage of Magickal Herbes

There are many methods of extraction. In remedial work, extraction involves the use of water or oil-soluble solutions through which the natural minerals, metallic salts, vitamins, essential oils and other constituents are removed from the cellular matter (such as through a tea or through inhaling the molecules which have evaporated) so that we can ingest them into our body.

Magickal extraction provides us with a far greater variety of techniques for we may choose to extract the herbal constituents but we may wish to introduce the physical herbe to a selected environment in order to access its spiritual energy. Placing herbes in a vase, hanging them in a temple or wearing them are forms of extraction for the magickal practitioner. While the practice of magick focuses itself, by definition, upon an *image,* herbes may be added to any magickal procedure as a means of adding the power of that herbe or introducing the particular virtues of the herbe to the working.

Amulets

The words *amulet* and *talisman* are frequently used as if interchangeable. Many years ago, in order to distinguish between them, we adopted the following definitions. An amulet is a container which may be filled with herbes, stones or things to promote magick. A talisman may be a disk, pendant or solid item (even if two-dimensional) upon which may be depicted sigils or images. These definitions are used in this context only within The Hermit's Grove and The Rowan Tree Church. It is not suggested that other uses of these words are either wrong or inappropriate.

The making of an amulet could easily take up the space of a small book but I will attempt to distill a seven-hour workshop into a few paragraphs. An amulet is a tool created to help bring about changes within your life. An amulet is a small container which, when completed, has energy or power and is quite magickal. We believe that amulets may be among the oldest forms of herbal magick, when the village Wise One, sensing that a plant or stone had power within it, placed it in a pocket or container to carry it about.

A traditional amulet is one which has a purpose. All aspects of its design and creation are oriented toward the attainment of a goal. The amulet is assembled and constructed within the context of ritual, made very carefully and is considered every bit as powerful and sacred as any of your ritual tools. An amulet is given a specific blessing or consecration toward its purpose, just as a novice may be initiated and ever after be considered a priest or priestess.

One of the mysteries of an amulet is that it is a microcosm of the person for whom it is made, or of the situation which is the focus of its goal. It is like a small energy cell or battery, containing physical ingredients and focused energies providing a steady flow of energy. An amulet can be designed so that it will continually provide access to the infinite power of the Universe throughout its existence. To understand a traditional amulet, give thought to the concept of the Cauldron of Cerridwen, that infinite womb of creativity which is the core of the Universe. From another perspective, an amulet is somewhat like a miniature black hole, drawing energy from throughout the Universe and holding it within, focused, directed solely toward the *image* which encompasses all aspects of your goal.

Our custom is to begin with a circle cut of leather. It should be at least six or eight inches in diameter. This flat circle is symbolic of a pentacle, that flat, round ritual tool which represents earth, or manifestation within the physical world.

To the practitioner, leather represents a gift of the creatures of the earth, representing elements of sacrifice, touching the mysteries of life and death, and is the closest material we can find which corresponds to your physical body which is the temple of your soul. The use of leather should never be taken lightly—it is a very sacred and profound choice. Around the perimeter, a series of holes should be pierced using either a leather punch or, as we have often done, a simple paper punch. A cord (chosen so that the length, color and thread enhance your magickal desires) is then threaded through the holes creating a small drawstring bag.

Choose your herbes carefully. Any herbe, including those too dangerous to ingest, can be included. You may also select small gemstones, add a personal piece of jewelry or lock of hair, and even scribe sigils, images or words which will focus your will to bring this Magick into manifestation. We recommend assembling your ingredients over a period of time. When my leather is complete, I set up a small altar. I lay the leather upon my copper pentacle or upon my altar stone and upon it I set a hand-carved, round wooden container with a flat lid. On propitious days I add one herbe, replace the lid and set a votive candle upon the top. Sometimes I might cast a formal Circle and at other times I go about my activities, the light from the candle a constant reminder that there is magick brewing and an amulet in the works.

The final day should be one with natural power. Whether a full Moon or a birthday, your amulet will be more powerful if all aspects of the work have power. Within an intricate ritual, both formal yet playful, the leather is cleansed and all ingredients placed within it. All movement and sound within the ritual is designed to draw upon the natural forces and connect the amulet with their power. And then, with ritual poetry and song it is drawn closed with special candles used to drip wax upon the opening so it is sealed.

Once an amulet is sealed, it should never again be opened. It is not a medicine pouch. When your goal has been accomplished or the patterns of time have reached completion, the amulet must be returned to the Universe. My preference is to bury it as a gift to the Mother, but there have been times when one has been placed into a flaming cauldron until reduced to ash, the ash then strewn upon sacred soil. Amulets are a wonderful way to develop your magickal skill but they should be made rarely. The more lightly you treat the magickal use of herbes, the less likely they are to assist you with their magick. I have an amulet hanging in my truck. We have a household amulet and I can't imagine magickal life without a few of these sources of change.

Aspurging

When I read of the many herbes which Solomon, king and magician, is said to have chosen for his aspurger, I can only chuckle at the image of this unwieldy, thick bunch of herbes. The practice of aspurging a sacred space, or sprinkling sacred water about it, is found in nearly all religious and magickal traditions. Many herbes lend themselves to aspurging.

The obvious practice is to harvest, as one would with hyssops, either a healthy sprig or a bunch of the herbe while it is in its prime. This could be used fresh as an aspurger, dipped into a chalice or water container and shaken lightly as one walks about the Circle.

Some practitioners choose to harvest a bunch of herbes for use at a later date. These would be tightly bound and hung in a warm, dark place to dry. When thoroughly dried, a new binding would be tightly wound about the herbes. Dried herbes are notorious for slipping loose from their cords. It is possible to fashion a binding of leather should one wish to create a permanent aspurger, such as one made and kept in a sacred place until a singular ritual (such as an initiation or a ritual of death).

But there is another way in which an herbe may be used in aspurging. It can be infused into a wash and that liquid placed into the chalice or sacred vessel from which the holy waters are taken to cleanse one's ritual space. Hyssops, an herbe frequently used as an aspurger (as a tool) can transmit its spiritual energy to your circle by making hyssops water which is then used as sacred water for your ritual, even if aspurged with your fingers.

Balms

Herbalists have worked with balms for many generations. We know that the word *balm* was in use in the thirteenth century. Balms are relatively easy to make, although they can be messy if you are not careful.

The ingredients for making a balm are basically two: the herbe(s) selected and a fixative. The tools needed include a pot for steeping the mixture, a filtering system and controlled heat. There are no precise amounts of herbe or of fixative. You are encouraged to create your own recipes based upon personal preference, numerological ratios or any other approach. Select your herbes based upon your own creativity and magickal needs. You may explore different ways to combine an assortment of herbes, but always record your formulas for future reference!

A common fixative is a combination of vegetable shortening and beeswax (paraffin may also be used). The more wax added, the harder the finished product. If you need a starting point, try a quarter pound of vegetable shortening warmed gently until melted with several tablespoons of beeswax. This amount of fixative is capable of extracting the essential oils and constituents from as much as three quarters of a pound of herbes. There are other basic fixatives. Many recommend lard for, being an animal fat, it is more efficient at absorbing the natural oils from the solid structure than vegetable shortening. Lanolin, a solid oil washed from sheep wool is another option. Some practitioners expand the fixative formula to include cocoa butter, glycerine, agar agar or Irish moss to thicken the mixture before it is hardened with wax. The possibilities are many.

The first step is the easiest. Place the fixative(s) into your pot. The pot must be glazed, stainless steel or glass. Gently warm until completely melted. Do not raise the temperature any higher than is necessary. Lard, for example, should be kept at 98°F and no higher. Add the herbal mixture and stir thoroughly using a wooden spoon (a chopstick is a most practical stirring tool). Be certain the herbes are thoroughly immersed in the melted fat. To avoid damaging the delicate oils (which are volatile), I allow the mixture to cool, then raise the temperature again to 98°F. I keep it there for a short while then set it aside. This is done quite a number of times over a period of many hours.

The next step is to filter the solid matter from the liquid. I will usually take a regular kitchen strainer, although it is essential that it is of a good quality so there will be no metals entering the molecular structure of the herbal constituents. A strainer catches all of the larger particles, stems and pieces of herbe, but allows small particles to pass through. Be sure you use your fingers or a safe (glass, porcelain, silver or stainless) device to press on the mixture in the strainer to release every bit of liquid. The solids which have been removed are now garbage. (Due to the fat content they should not be put in your garden compost.) This filtration is only the first. Now I will use cotton. Although cheese-cloth is often recommended, two or three layers of cotton fabric will also work. I lay the fabric in the (clean) strainer and pour the warm liquid through it again. Before the process is complete, I squeeze the solids in the fabric to release as much of the liquid as possible. Both cloth and remaining solid matter should now be disposed of and we move on to the third step.

The third step seems the most difficult but allows for the most creativity. Into the warm liquid (adjust the heat to bring it back to the minimal temperature) add any thickeners or hardeners you choose and stir gently until they are thoroughly dispersed. Simple enough? If you feel uncertain about the proportions of wax or thickeners, start out with small batches so you can see the results of your first tries. It will be easy to see whether to increase or decrease these ingredients.

And last, pour the warm liquid into small containers, cover and let cool. Don't forget to label. With the passing of years, I would discover small, glass jars with wonderful mixtures but I could no longer remember which recipe it was or when it was made. Don't trust things to your memory. The more literate we herbalists have become, the more details our brains must manage, the more compassionate the Universe has been by giving us labels and computers and index cards.

A small container of balm will last a long time. Balm is used by lightly rubbing one's finger upon the surface of it. The smallest amount goes a long way. The balm may be massaged into one's temples or upon any chakra. Create a balm, wear it for ritual or for magick in *any* situation and enjoy.

Bathing Herbes

One of the more underrated forms of healing and magick is the ritual bath. For many of us a ritual bath is part of our preparation for lunar and sabbat rituals but, at other times, the bath becomes an expedient shower: something functional for the outer skin of the temple of the self. Considering the quick popularity of aromatherapy, it surprises me that few seem to make the connection of breathing in the molecular magick of the selected herbal remedy while soaking one's body in a luxurious ritual bath. In this sense, the bath itself has become the ritual, not relegated as a prelude to subsequent magick.

This method offers one of the simplest approaches to healing magick with herbes. There are few cautions and less dangers than most forms of herbal healing. In fact, I can think of only two: one is to avoid placing loose herbes in the bath. They tend to cling to the skin when you stand up and can easily clog the drain, requiring a call to a plumber. The other is to avoid any herbes which are toxic and poisonous (such as aconite) and which have a strong recommendation against internal use. A certain amount of the toxins may be absorbed into the skin and, subsequently, into the blood stream. Do not take risks. Apart from these two concerns, there is little to stop you from exploring this art of healing.

How do you avoid the plumber? Many texts, including *The Master Book of Herbalism,* recommend placing the herbes in a gauze bag or even a tea strainer. I've since turned to making a strong herbal infusion. It only takes about a cup of liquid and, when thoroughly strained, I add the liquid directly to the bath.

Bathing herbes are those commonly used in bathing, but an herbe need not be categorized as a bathing herbe to be worthy of use. There are myriad herbes which one turns to for internal use. Why not immerse one's self in their natural magick as well? Take time and do careful research when selecting your herbes. Know them well. Be able to identify their scent and, should you use more than one, to distinguish among them. If you are struggling to uplift your spirits, why not bathe with eyebright? Personally, there are few herbes I would avoid. Even with an herbe considered dangerous like aconite, a single, fresh flower floating upon the water's surface is well within my personal comfort and safety.

Using herbes in a ritual bath is one of the simplest forms of magick. All you need are your herbes and your tub filled with water. Take time to contemplate the element of water during your planning stages. What does it take to draw upon the energy of water? Consider how the water will bring you in contact with the herbe, not only as it caresses your skin but as you breathe in the warm aroma.

What transforms a bath into a ritual? There are many possibilities, so many that one's imagination can begin to spill over like a brook. Traditionally, one would add a sprinkle of sea salt to the bath water as well, not wanting to miss the cleansing of body and spirit which priests and priestesses have used since the Age of Aries. (In a pinch, table salt will do.) There are many ways to bring in the four elements, to ask of the Universe that you learn what is necessary to promote healing; there are infinite ritual forms one can create. Trust your imagination.

It is most important to avoid the temptation of turning a ritual bath into a long soak with a good book. Recreational reading is not bad but does not sustain the focus of your spirit. If you wish to read, focus upon a magickal text or your Book of Shadows. Meditation is another tool at your disposal, working with carefully planned and highly focused healing images.

At the bottom line, you may not attain miracles, but dramatic change is not outside the realm of reality. You are invoking the magick of the Universe and asking for change. Not only will you have access to the properties of the bathing herbes you have selected, but you will be working with the magick of transformation and of change as well. The amount of magick is directly related to your work and your mental focus. However, disciplined focus does not mean that your bath should be void of joy and pleasure. Using herbes for bathing combines magick with something wonderful for your body.

Decoration and Adornment

Sometimes the simplest ways of working with herbal magick can be the most elusive! Many brides know the flowers in their bouquets or those to be worn on their dress should be chosen with great care. And skilled gardeners know that the health of most species is dependant upon their willingness to *dead head* the plant or make certain that flowers are not allowed to remain on the plant past maturity. Many of us get so involved in magickal formulas and ritual processes that it is easy to forget how much magick can come into our lives by enjoying the flowering aspect of our herbes.

Here at The Hermit's Grove, we have a wonderful collection of vases and, when asked what we would like on our gift list, good vases are usually high on that list. Some herbes just do not provide the type of scent our fussy noses prefer but the herbes are exceptionally handsome and a source of magick nonetheless. Tansy may bring its magick to our ritual just as well by sitting in a vase upon our altar rather than offering its acrid smoke to the temple. No herbe, no matter how simple its flower, should be ignored.

Those who are handy with their fingers may weave herbes into wreaths to be worn for special rituals. Someone in your magickal group might make miniature corsages which blend a magickal formula so that each of you might wear one upon your ritual robe. If your group prefers working ritual in the nude, you might wear a band of herbes about your wrist or a wreath upon your head. When working with live herbes, cut them with love and respect, doing so in a manner which will enhance the future of the plant. Most species of perennials (and even annuals) thrive and are far healthier when cut before the flowers pass their prime. While some may make an ornate wreath or flowered ornament with florists' supplies, you can use a thread of a selected color and simply wind it around until your wreath or corsage stays together long enough for the ritual.

Never underestimate the power of having herbes and flowers to beautify your home. They bring beauty to far more than the eye, enhancing the overall magick and energy as well. It is not necessary that you be an artistic designer, merely to love what you are doing. A very simple process, it could be as easy as placing several sprigs of rosemary in a bud vase, set next to whatever it is that you're worried about forgetting the next day. Let the magick of remembrance permeate the immediate environment and work its magick upon you.

Elixirs

Technically, an elixir is, by definition, an herbal extraction combining both alcohol and water. Some methodologies consider an elixir to be 25 percent alcohol when the product is finished but there are no strict rules. Magickally, an elixir is considered very powerful. To medieval alchemists in their quest for the ever-elusive formula, the greatest elixir was like the Holy Grail: capable of granting immortality, of curing almost any diseases, yet always just beyond their fingertips.

In addition to our other herbal preparations, one we use literally on a daily basis is the elixir. Our basic method begins with a selection of herbes which will impart the virtues and changes we are seeking during the coming season. A batch of elixir sometimes lasts a month and sometimes longer, depending upon how long we wish to work with the same energies and the quantity we make.

We begin every day with a simple ritual in front of the altar in our Inner Temple, an altar used only by our family. This ritual includes lighting both candle and incense while affirming our vows to each other and to the Universe, asking for protection and asking the Universe to keep us in line, so to speak. We manifest that daily blessing and close the ritual by drinking small, antique glass chalices of herbal elixir.

The first step is to select the herbes. This can be a complex process and there are no instructions or guidelines I would offer.

Your creativity is essential. My most recent recipe includes 100 grams of herbes steeped for days in 1.5 liters of a gentle, pink Harvest Blush wine. After the wine has extracted all of the alcohol-soluble constituents, the mixture is filtered thoroughly. The alcohol extract is set aside and the filtered herbes are now exposed to hot water and steeped as one would for an infusion. Depending upon the volume of herbes, I might use from one-fourth to a full liter of boiling water. This is then filtered and the liquid filtered through increasingly fine sieves and paper toweling until it passes readily through a paper coffee filter. Both extractions poured together, the elixir is stored in a corked jug in the refrigerator with a small amount (about a half wineglass) decanted every morning for the altar.

The elixir we shared this very morning included birch bark, bayberry, lovage, kava kava, damiana, mistletoe and rowan berries. The previous recipe included birch bark, angelica, lovage, arnica, rowan and mistletoe berries and Solomon's seal. You can see how the present recipe evolved from the previous one and you can also tell that I love the flavor of birch bark!

There is another ritual time when I work with an elixir. Once each year, at the full Scorpio Moon (the first in those very rare years when there is a blue Scorpio Moon) within our tradition is a ritual which invokes an oracle. Over the past fifteen years Lothloriën has developed an oracle which is consulted annually to provide us with guidance and a sense of understanding for the coming year. Part of the working of this ritual, which is performed by a trained Elder, involves an elixir, one designed to assist the Elder in setting aside as much of the ego and the distractions of consciousness as possible. The last elixir of this nature included bay laurel, star anise, arnica, eyebright, gentian, mandrake, mistletoe berries, mugwort, rowan berries and unicorn root. Obviously, as the founder of The Rowan Tree Church, rowan berries are a recurrent theme in my herbal work for ritual and magick! You may have noted that some of the herbes I include are on the can-be-toxic list. When working with mistletoe berries or (true) mandrake, I include what I call token amounts. When working magickally, three or four mistletoe berries are more than adequate. They convey all of their natural magick to the elixir without being strong enough to induce any appreciable physiological reactions. When I was younger (and my body much more sturdy) I worked with far stronger mixtures of herbes, gradually acclimating my body to them over a period of weeks during which I adjusted my diet, decreasing various substances until eating only raw fruit and juices before entering a complete fast during which my only sustenance was the elixir.

Not everyone's body can tolerate alcohol. Those who must live alcohol-free might consider working solely with a water-extraction process combined with a commercial preparation or extraction of the herbe. Many of the herbal constituents which carry the actual essence and energy of the plant are, in fact, not water soluble. A water extract (e.g. tea or infusion) may be supplemented by a pure essential oil. If you avoid alcohol, please realize that tinctures and many extracts include alcohol so they are able to hold all of the essential constituents of the herbe.

Elixirs are now such an integral part of our lives that it is not possible to imagine not working with them on a daily basis. They are a major key in the cycle of each day and are a potent and wonderful form of herbal magick.

Feasting and Food Preparation

There are many ways to partake of herbes other than through ritual cakes and drink. Looking through all of the herbes which are readily used in cooking, it takes little imagination to see how the usual array of herbes and spices found in your kitchen offer you cooking magick at your fingertips. Many of the Greene Herbes make wonderful salad vinegars. Think of the magick available to your loved ones with bottles of herbal vinegar created not only to enhance their meals but to also bring blessings.

In addition there are many fruits and vegetables which are included in this book, for they, also, have been treated as sacred by peoples who live in harmony with the earth, seeking spiritual wisdom. When preparing potatoes, call upon Axo-mama. When eating fruits think of the fruit devas and of the ways in which these sacred foods were central to the religions of many peoples. By changing our awareness, our meals can become a joyful, sacred ritual, and the foods through which we nourish our bodies, whether during a feast, after a sabbat or as part of our daily sustenance, will in turn provide not only physical but spiritual fuel as well.

Fluid Condensers

This is a wonderful magickal technique introduced into the United States primarily through the writings of Stewart Farrar in the early 1970s with the publication of his book, *What Witches Do.* Mr. Farrar called it a "Universal Condenser." That technique has been used extensively within our tradition. Prior to their Second Degree Initiation, our students are required to create a fluid condenser, work with it and write a paper about the process.

Any combination of herbes within the classification of visionary are selected. The traditional choices are chamomile and eyebright, according to Farrar. One works with a fairly small amount of herbe, perhaps a quarter ounce. Farrar recommended that the two herbes are chosen to represent the *above* or macrocosm and the *below* or microcosm, a reflection of the Hermetic Principle often quoted "as above, so below," but which can also be thought of "as within, so without." One might as readily choose three herbes to represent the principle of manifestation embodied in the triple aspect or trinity or other constructs as well. There are no precise measurements nor rules in selecting your herbes.

Once chosen, place them into a pot, one which has no metal which will be in contact with the herbal mixture or liquid. Over your herbes is poured one pint of rapidly boiling water. The pot is quickly covered to set until approximately body temperature.

Traditionally, this mixture is filtered through four layers of purified linen. While we usually work with linen, other natural fibers create slightly different forms of energy and might be useful alternatives. We keep our eyes open when at garage sales for good linen napkins, now almost relics of the past, which can frequently be purchased for small change. Each layer of linen represents one of the four elements as is appropriately colored. We work with yellow for air, red for fire, blue for water and green for earth, but other traditions and cultures have many variations upon this.

In some variations twigs of a tree (sometimes willow but the choice is yours) are lit from your altar candles and plunged into the liquid prior to its being filtered. A Fluid Condenser may be daubed upon your chakras or put upon gauze or cotton and placed upon those centers of your body through which you seek visions and images. We recommend reading the appropriate passages in Farrar's book for more historical information.

Incense

By definition, incense refers to the substances which, when burned, release fragrance. The word *incense* also refers to the perfumed scent, itself, which is released from the burning of herbes and resins. Incense works its magick through stimulating our sense of smell, provoking emotional and spiritual responses to specific scents and, through sacred aromas, giving shape to our magickal images. At what point in human evolution did we begin to sacrifice herbes, burning them as an offering to our divinities, hoping to appease and please them?

We do not know how long ago our ancestors began using incense to enhance their communication with their divinities, but the use of incense is as old as any recorded religious or herbal history. How did this come to take place? Obviously, an awareness of herbes and plant substances as incense would have been a more recent development than the knowledge of fire as a tool. We suspect that one facet of this discovery arose out of learning that the wood of different trees offered different scents. It seems likely that the use of different dried plants offered another area of knowledge regarding the creation of scent. But the events through which this knowledge became associated with magick and religious mysteries are remembered only by the Universe. We cannot imagine a world without incense. As an indication of the popularity of incense, packages of commercial sticks and cones may be found for sale in most drug stores and supermarkets. The magickal herbalist will, however, wish to use incense made for a specific purpose and provide a ritual foundation for the manufacturing process.

The simplest form of incense is the loose variety. Loose incense consists of finely powdered herbes selected not only for their magickal and ritual properties but also to take advantage of the ways in which their scents stimulate our emotions and imaginations. The herbes are placed on round blocks of charcoal which will burn, causing the herbes to release their essential oils, scents and energy as they are transformed into smoke.

Is there a correct way to make loose incense? I cannot think of a single rule which must be followed, but I do have some recommendations. First, acquire a roll or package of charcoals. You will want a number of them to use during your exploration. Have some tool at hand which can take the extreme heat of a burning block of charcoal. You will need to be able to poke at the block, to scrape off all residue of the burned herbes so that the scent of the next herbe or mixture can be studied and sensed without interference.

It is extremely important to have a censer or container which can take a prolonged, focused heat. Many censers quickly become too hot to carry around a Circle. Even some with chains are poorly designed; the chains are made of a metal which conducts heat to your fingers quickly, with startling results. Never use glass and never use an ashtray. Although they might work once or twice, the odds are great that they will shatter, and flying glass is very dangerous. If you cannot find anything, you might try using a large clay saucer, made for a flower pot, filled with sand. No matter what you use, make certain you have a trivet or piece of cork designed to hold a very hot pan. The modern history of incense and charcoal is littered with the memory of burned fingers. Dropping a censer due to an unexpected burn is dangerous, but can readily be avoided.

Once the charcoal is lit and sitting in its safe container, you are ready to begin. Initially try working with just one herbe at a time. Resinous herbes such as amber, benzoin, copal, frankincense, dragon's blood or myrrh are often the most fun. Save them for last. Why? Because they're likely to gum-up your charcoal, leaving a lingering scent which interferes with your sense of smell. Take one herbe and drop a fairly small amount onto the charcoal. As you breathe in its scent, learn as much as you can about the herbe itself as well as your response to its aroma. Not all herbes will offer a scent considered pleasant, but they may offer a type of energy not available through a sweet-scented herbe. Leaves will often smell more like smoke than of essential oils.

Loose incense will often have a larger quantity of a base, such as powdered sandalwood or elderflowers. A good base functions as a fixative for many of the oils; it will have either little scent or a scent which is harmonious with the stronger aromas. The quantities of the individual herbes will vary depending upon the magick you are seeking and the aesthetic appreciation of your nose. It is also possible to mix an extracted oil into the loose mixture which is absorbed by the base and released when burned.

Speaking of essential oils, it is possible to burn the oils directly on charcoal as well. Although this is a sound way to extract the scent of the herbes, it generally is not as popular because the duration of aroma is relatively brief.

When we think of incense, we frequently think of solid incense, fashioned into cones or sticks. Solid incense is the most difficult to make but the easiest to use. Sticks and cones are made with the aromatic and Magickal Herbes you have chosen for their scent and spiritual properties. They must be powdered very fine, with no uneven pieces (such as bits of stem). You will want twice as much of your aromatic mixture as you do of your base. A good base is one which burns easily and has a scent which does not interfere with the scent of your aromatic mixture. The base is also thoroughly ground into a powder. One of the most popular bases is sandalwood. The base and the aromatics should be thoroughly mixed. To this mixture you will add an herbal substance which, when wet, forms a glue. Agar agar, tragacanth and gum arabic are often used. Some find that tragacanth dissolves better with a small amount of cold water.

Now that your dry ingredients are well mixed, it is time to add the liquid, a mixture of water and saltpeter (potassium nitrate). What you want to do is mix everything as well as you can. Using a small spatula helps although most of us use our fingers. You want the consistency of the moist mixture to be like soft clay. When you think it is ready, shape it into a cone and let it dry in the Sun, sitting upright on a wooden block, for two days.

What measurements will help you get started? A good basic recipe is 2 teaspoons of powdered aromatics, 1 teaspoon of powdered base, 1/4 teaspoon agar agar or gum arabic (or 1/8 teaspoon tragacanth which is stronger) moistened with 2 teaspoons of water in which is dissolved 1/8 teaspoon saltpeter (or less). Work with small batches so it doesn't begin to dry out before you have it formed into cones. Steven Smith, author of *Wylundt's Book of Incense*, offers a number of recipes in his book and is a good source for more detailed instruction.

Offerings

This usage includes food which is set out to honor one's ancestors or placed upon an altar as an offering for those deities which we wish to honor. If these herbal offerings are eaten by birds, squirrels and other creatures, we can be mindful that all which exists is part of the Divinity of the Universe. Thus our offerings are being eaten (indirectly) by the Holy Ones.

When I place herbal incense upon a block of burning charcoal, I think of this as an offering as well. In ancient times people offered the best of their harvest, the healthiest offspring of their herd, in the hope that the divinities would be pleased. Although there are some who believe that we no longer practice sacrifice, an herbalist is always mindful that we have taken life when harvesting herbes. Burning them as incense should be a profound and mindful religious act.

Perfumes and Oils

Oh, if only the extraction of essential oils from herbes were easy! There are a variety of ways to work with pure, essential oils. The easiest and, believe it or not, least expensive is to purchase them. A concentrated oil is very strong but offers us the purest and strongest actual scent of the herbe. The essential oils from many species require being diluted before wearing. At their full strength some may irritate the skin and a few can cause minor burns. To tone down the intensity of an oil we generally use sunflower oil for its magickal properties, consistency and lack of scent. Some prefer safflower oil as a base. Other herbes are not so strong and their oils can be worn full strength. Undiluted oil may be used as an incense or warmed in a fixture designed to hold oil above a lit candle so that the scent permeates the room.

If you wish to extract the essential oils of the herbes there are two options. One requires setting up a small laboratory in order to distill the oils. It is fairly expensive, requiring a constant source of gas heat and running water, and glass equipment such as a soxhlet extraction unit with condensers. Be prepared to spend as much as several thousand dollars. More information on procedures can be found in an excellent alchemy textbook by Manfred M. Junius, *The Practical Handbook of Plant Alchemy*.

For less intense concentrations, we can make our own oils through maceration. The oil you can obtain from this process is able to be far more magickal and appropriate for ritual than using a commercially extracted essential oil, but will not have as strong a scent. To make your own ritual oil, first select a base oil which will function as a fixative. Use two cups of oil (or less) per ounce of dried or fresh herbes. The proportion will vary depending on the herbe and whether the herbes are dry or fresh.

Experimentation will show you what works best. The principle involved in extraction with oil is to remember that the volatile and essential oils in herbes are frequently oil soluble but not water soluble. Extraction with oil will allow all of the fat-soluble constituents of the herbes to be absorbed by the fixative where they will remain when the mixture is filtered.

Place the oil and herbes in a sturdy pan, one which is not metal (unless a high quality stainless steel). If possible, place a heat shield between the flame and the base of the pan unless the pan is thick. You want to protect the herbes and oil even as you are warming them. It doesn't take much heat for the oil to scorch. Gently stir the herbes into the oil until they are fully immersed and there are no pockets of air. Very gently begin warming the contents of the pan. Stir carefully and frequently. Do not allow the oil to become hot—warm will do nicely. When not stirring your herbes and oil, keep the pan tightly covered. When the contents have been warmed, turn off the heat and let it set until the contents are room temperature. Then warm it again. This process should be repeated a number of times and can be timed with astrological schedules, with your convenience, with ritual work, or with any number of approaches which might enhance the magick. When filtered, you will want to store the oil in a tightly stoppered bottle.

The extraction of alcohol-based tinctures and perfumes can be accomplished without too much difficulty. The best product we've found on the market is called a Floralab Perfume Maker which is a reasonably priced product. This kit provides you with a very simple distillation apparatus and detailed instructions which allow you to extract the oils into fat, then dissolve them out of the fat into alcohol which is next evaporated out of the enfleurage and cooled through a coil, collecting in a small bottle. The instructions include simple formulas for making Eau de Cologne, after-shave, hand lotion or perfumed soap. The Floralab kit or Perfume Maker can be ordered form Mayer's Cider Mill, Inc., 699 Five Mile Line Road, Webster, New York 14580, (716) 671-1955.

The current popularity of aromatherapy shows how easily humans are affected by the scent of herbes. We can work with perfumes and oils and, as we breathe in their scents, be affected by their magick. We can also use the magick of scent to bring about change in our lives. Whether you choose to make your own or purchase essential oils is a personal matter but we believe all magickal herbalists will benefit from this aspect of herbal work.

Pillows

"Sleep on it" could be a motto stitched into a sampler which has been made into an herbal pillow. Although herbal pillows are often made as part of dream magick work or for protection during the night, the quick rise in popularity of aromatherapy should encourage the practitioner to use pillows stuffed with herbes for many types of magick as well.

What is an herbal pillow? First let me suggest that it is small. The dream pillows we make in our ritual workshop are sewn from two pieces of purple velvet, measuring approximately four inches to a side. They are filled with approximately one cup of dried herbes plus a few small gems, magickal stones, herbal oil and other types of magickal objects whose size will not interfere with the comfort or appearance of the pillow.

An herbal pillow made for ritual or magickal use should, in my opinion, always be sewn by hand. Anyone is capable of small, thoughtful stitches. Some are skilled and likely to create a lovely seam, even embroider designs upon the fabric. Some of us simply get the job done. It's not how *good* your needlework is, nor how it compares with another's. In this type of magick it is, truly, the thought that counts.

You can enhance the magick of your sewing by choosing a color of thread (using natural fibers) to correspond to the type of magick you wish to empower. There are many good books on color magick and associations. Our favorites are included in the reading list at the end of this book.

There are no rules in making an herbal pillow. You may add extracted, essential oils to the dried herbes for a stronger aroma. You may place other items in the pillow even as one might with an amulet. You need not even sleep on it. My oldest (and best-loved) dream pillow was made well over a decade ago and now provides a loving cushion for a small, quartz sphere which I keep on my bedside altar. Both are essential tools I use during my dreaming time.

Pillows can be made for any purpose or magickal goal. Given as a gift to a new Initiate, they might have the new priest or priestess's name or sigil lovingly stitched onto the top, each turn of the needle accompanied by a chant for good wishes. A dream pillow might contain herbes to bring changes into your life so you might be better able to provide the resources you need. Such a pillow may be placed near your head while you sleep, for more magick is worked while we sleep than most people can imagine. During sleep the physical activities of the body are slowed, one's consciousness is set aside and we move into the realms of the Dreaming where our spirit is free, carried by those emotions and desires which either help us soar or encumber us.

Ritual Cakes

No matter what the herbe or its flavor, it may be finely ground and added to your cake dough or batter. Some groups prefer cake, some share bread and some are cookie folk. No matter what your baking preferences, it is a simple matter to add some of your chosen herbes to the mixture before it goes into the oven. Even when working with herbes which might be dangerous in larger quantities, just the smallest pinch is all that's necessary for the power of that herbe to become manifest in your ritual cake.

I've often been asked to share my own ritual cake recipe, but there really isn't one. I put some butter or shortening in a bowl, add some sweetening, then flour and oatmeal and make adjustments until the texture is just right. Sometimes I begin with peanut butter and, once in a while, might even use an egg. The first recipe I encountered called for anise seed. I still frequently use anise for lunar cakes but am more likely to use an anise extract than try to mash the seeds. Because we of Lothloriën are more of the cookie-folk type, I flatten the dough into a glass pie plate and bake it at 350°F until it's done. It is possible to add herbal magick to your ritual cakes without a bitter herbe flavor becoming a distraction. Yet, there are times when the flavor of the herbe, even if not pleasing to your palate, is just what your ritual cakes are wanting for their magick.

Ritual Cup Mixtures

I was originally trained in a Wiccan tradition which used wine in the ritual cup or that chalice which, when united during the ritual with the athame, joined to represent the Great Rite or coming together of the polarities of the Universe. I continued using wine for many years, but as The Tradition of Lothloriën began to emerge (I did not set out to be the founder of a tradition by any means) our herbal nature continued to emerge. There were many times I made an herbal tea to use in the Great Rite chalice. For many years we moved back and forth between the water extracts and wine extracts and then settled into a water-extraction drink as Lothloriën came to work with a specific list of herbes so that at a Scorpio Moon we all, no matter our location, are united through the herbe basil.

At some point in time it occurred to me to combine the two methods, for I found myself missing that energy found through wine, an energy which is not present in water. Yet, when working with wine I felt I had been missing the herbal connection. Now for our lunar rituals, we steep a small amount of the herbe in wine for the fortnight leading to the ritual. I mention *small* amount as it takes far less herbe when steeping it for two weeks in wine than when making a tea just hours prior to your ritual. The evening of the ritual we filter the liquid and place the wine into our chalice. Alcohol-free members usually anoint themselves and feel every bit as connected as those who take a small sip from the ritual cup. Then, after cleaning the ritual tools and washing the chalices, the antique, glass-stopped bottle is refilled with wine and the herbe for the next ritual. During the next two weeks it is kept upon the altar in our herbal pantry and regularly swirled so that the extraction process is thorough.

After so many years it is no longer possible for me to think of the mysteries of creation embodied in the Great Rite or in the ritual cup without being touched by the magick of herbes.

Smoking Mixtures

There is much which can be said in favor of smoking herbes but there are words of caution required as well. Many herbes can safely be smoked. Many cannot. There are traditions which have adopted and adapted the sharing of a pipe to call upon elemental spirits and there are those who inhale the smoke from herbes as they seek transformation. Herbes which are dangerous or potentially toxic will usually cause a far more rapid and extreme physiological response. If you do choose to use this form of magick, do so with great care.

Strewing

We read of many old customs in which herbes were strewn about homes, public spaces and churches, yet many practitioners seem hesitant to use herbes in this manner today. In our tradition we have a beautiful custom which is used at Handfastings. We scatter flower petals from a basket when scribing the Circle. If our guests include friends and family who would not understand the use of a ritual knife, they are always deeply moved as the Circle is cast with the words, "Let your love be as the flowers to the breeze... Let it create an ever-growing Circle that spreads love and joy unto the Earth."

I would hesitate to scatter ground or powdered herbes upon carpeting, although dried flower petals are easily picked up with a vacuum. When possible, we work our rituals in our gardens in the Dancing Circle where scattering herbes is very good for the magick and very good for the grass and gardens as well.

Washes

Making a wash is very simple. It's like making several gallons of herbal tea but doesn't need to be nearly as concentrated as a tea or infusion. A wash may be used when cleaning your temple floor or when consecrating a ritual tool. You may immerse an object completely within a wash to permeate every bit of the surface with the herbal magick. A wash may be added to your bath (or hot tub) if well-filtered. The process may be as simple as floating a bay leaf in the bucket of water used to wash your storm windows each spring or as complex as you wish.

In conclusion

These processes are meant as guidelines. There are numerous ways in which you can bring your self, your loved ones, your pets in contact with herbal magick. There are many ways to touch an object with the spiritual energy of herbes, or to bring herbal magick into a situation. If you give yourself the freedom to be creative and imaginative, herbal magick will change your life.

PART II: THE HERBES

❦ Acacia ❦

Acacia Nilotica
Sun, Mars*
Religious Herbe ... Herbe of Consecration
Invocatory: Osiris
Also called: gum arabic

LORE

Acacia has a long history of use as a Religious Herbe. Lore tells us that the Ark of the Covenant was crafted of this wood. Some also believe the sacred Tabernacle of the ancient Hebrew tribes was made of acacia wood. Acacia is connected with some of the Hebrew atonement customs. Because of its religious associations, the mundane use of this herbe was proscribed.

Christian lore holds that acacia thorns were those used to fashion the crown of thorns placed upon Christ's head.

Robert Graves lists acacia as one of the nine materials of Nimrod's Tower and later writes that Jehovah selected the acacia from which to speak to Moses because that tree "constituted a definition of his godhead." Graves also writes in *The White Goddess: A historical grammar of poetic myth:*

> It was from its water-proof timber that the arks of the Sun-hero Osiris and his counterparts Noah and Armenian Xisuthros were built; also the Ark of the Covenant, the recorded measurements of which proved it sacred to the Sun. This is a host-tree of the mistletoe-like loranthus, Jehovah's oracular *burning bush* and the source of manna.

According to Graves, hedges of acacia were grown as a means of defining the spaces among the communities of the Essenes, separating the women's area from the men's. Graves believed that the acacia was grafted with a pomegranate and was the Tree of Life in the Garden of Eden. The Judeo-Christian god was very skilled at horticulture and botany.

USAGE

The wood of the acacia would be an excellent choice for a small chest or sacred box. Ideally, it would be handmade and used solely for containing your ritual tools. For those unable to obtain pieces of the wood large enough for box-making, the herbe may be used to consecrate the containers used for your sacred items. The dried gum may be burned as incense; the leaves or wood may be infused to create sacred water for aspurging. As an Herbe of Consecration, acacia may be used for blessing any sacred space, be it a temple, Circle or storage area for religious and magickal possessions.

Today acacia is known for its bonding properties and is a staple ingredient for those who make ritual incenses, more readily recognized by its common name of gum arabic.

❦ Aconite ❦

Aconitum Napellus
Saturn
Capricorn
Funereal Herbe ... Herbe of Consecration ... Herbe of
Immortality ... Herbe of Protection ... Religious Herbe ...
Visionary Herbe
Invocatory: Hecate, Medea
Also called: blue rocket, monkshood

LORE

Aconite is found written into the legends associated with Hecate. Mrs. Grieve reminds us of this association. Hecate, a Greek triple goddess of the Underworld, both protected and was worshipped at crossroads. Hecate is, even today, widely associated with witchcraft. Befitting a triple goddess, her familiar was Cerberus, a triple-headed dog which guarded the gates of Hades. As part of Hercules' passage, he fought with Cerberus. Aconite sprung from drops of saliva from Cerberus' foaming mouth which had dropped to the earth. It is said that the goddess Hecate later poisoned her father with this same aconite.

A dangerous herbe, herbal history holds that aconite was used to poison arrows. Grieve provides us with rich lore surrounding aconite, writing that the Greek name, *lycotonum*, is derived from this custom.

Grieve also relates aconite's association with the goddess Medea, sorceress and once a wife of Jason. Medea chose aconite in an unsuccessful attempt to stop a family argument. Now married to Aegeus, through her power as a seer Medea recognizes her husband's son, Theseus, by a former marriage. Theseus, her stepson, is a threat to her desire for her husband's throne. Medea's plan is to see her own son inherit the throne. She attempts to serve Theseus a poisoned cup. Unfortunately for Medea and Aegeus, Theseus learns of the plot and, just like a modern soap opera's plot, Medea escapes through the air with one son, and Aegeus is killed.

Linnæus is cited by Grieve as describing that property of aconite which is deadly to cattle and goats when eaten fresh yet, when dried, brings no harm to horses.

USAGE

Aconite is one of the herbes used in traditional twentieth century witchcraft to consecrate the athame or ritual knife. Its primary magickal use is in the consecration of magickal blades. An infusion may be made of the leaves or root, used both to banish all prior energy in the knife and to infuse it with the same protection and watchfulness Cerberus provided for Hecate. Either root or leaves and flowers may be burned upon a charcoal as incense to achieve the same end. Another option would be to gather the fresh, hood-shaped flowers and make a tincture of them which can be used upon occasion to refresh the power of one's athame.

Aconite may be used in a variety of forms. An infusion provides the practitioner with a magickal wash and may be used with any ritual tool or sacred space. This herbe has the power to bring protection and invoke a magickal watchfulness needed to guard the ritual against any negative energies. The mythologies surrounding aconite indicate that it would be a superior herbe to use in rituals designed to pierce the veil and allow the practitioner to look into the Underworld. The preparation and consecration of a cauldron might include bathing it in an aconite wash, anointing the cauldron with extracted aconite oil, or tossing aconite into its first fire as an offering to Hecate to guide the practitioner safely into the mysteries of death with the promise of a safe return.

Aconite may be used to invoke the presence of Hecate. To this end it may be burned as an offering or may, with great danger, be taken as an elixir of Hecate. Ingesting aconite is a very serious action and requires thorough research to avoid dangerous consequences. Mrs. Grieve accurately describes aconite as "one of the most formidable poisons which have yet been discovered." The mysteries of death and the realm of Hecate are not for the dabbler. Only the serious student, one who holds a deep and proper respect for this herbe, one who is willing to embrace all disciplines, should be permitted entry into this temple without finding the gates closed quickly behind, forever trapping the seeker in Hades. One of the herbes believed part of the legendary *flying ointment,* the symptoms of poisoning by aconite could lead the practitioner to experience sensations similar to flying. The varieties of aconite readily purchased to grow in one's garden are, typically, relatively benign. You are encouraged, however, to do careful research before growing or working with aconite.

The Master Book of Herbalism describes an unusual custom: "This herbe has been administered as a ritual cup when a person was dying (at the moment of death).... Following burial, this herbe would be planted on the grave." Aconite may be integrated into rituals of death and dying in a variety of ways ranging from tossing it into the fire, using it to aspurge the Circle, or through memorial plantings.

❦ Agrimony ❦

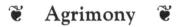

Agrimonia Eupatoria
Jupiter
Cancer
Countermagick Herbe ... Herbe of Protection ... Magickal Herbe
Also called: church steeples, sticklewort

LORE

Mrs. Grieve provides us with some history of agrimony. Included as an ingredient in a *spring drink* to provide cleansing and renewal, its name dates to the ancient Greeks, reflecting its remedial use in healing problems with one's eyes and to Mithridates Eupator, a king known as a skilled herbalist who died in 63 B.C.

Agrimony was once believed able to induce a deep, trance-like sleep through its magickal powers. In one of the many quotations Mrs. Grieve provides us in A *Modern Herbal*, we are given insight into the lore of the Middle Ages:

If it be leyd under mann's heed,
He shal sleepyn as he were deed;
He shal never drede ne wakyn
Till fro under his heed it be takyn.

USAGE

One of the most useful aspects of agrimony's magick is found through its ability to encourage sleep. Soothing to emotional discomfort, helping ease the thoughts and inner voices which seem to chatter throughout the night, agrimony is best used when sewn into a dream pillow. For this purpose it works well when mixed with mugwort.

Agrimony enjoys a reputation for enhancing magickal healing. It can be used either as a wash or an oil to increase the effectiveness of all forms of ritual healing, psychic healing, or any method of healing which employs energy at a distance. The extracted oil of agrimony is a fine choice for anointing one's hands prior to cleansing the aura of another. In the major arcana of the tarot, agrimony may be used to open the mysteries of the Wheel of Fortune card.

This attractive herbe may be used to create an effective barrier against all forms of negative and unwholesome energy. It should be incorporated into daily magick by any person who has genuine concerns regarding psychic attack or feels unable to transcend the negative influences of other people.

❦ Alder ❦

Alnus Glutinosa
Venus, Mars, Saturn
Cancer, Pisces
Fertility Herbe ... Funereal Herbe ... Herbe of Love ... Herbe of
Protection ... Visionary Herbe
Invocatory: Calypso, Embla, Minerva

LORE

Alder was a sacred tree and figures prominently in Celtic lore in the early centuries of the British Isles. In British myths as told in Robert Graves' *The White Goddess*, Gwydion is able to guess Bran's name which can be translated as crow or raven but may also be translated as alder. In Danish mythology, Bran appears as

Ellerkonge, later translated in Goethe's ballad as *the Erle King*.

Alder is the fourth letter, Fearn F in the Beth-Luis-Nion tree alphabet of which Graves writes, "the names of the letters in the modern Irish alphabet are also those of trees, and most of them correspond..." The alder is also the tree for the first month of spring. Graves associates the alder with Saturn and with Saturday.

Graves also writes that the alder is a "tree of resurrection" which was used at the entrance of the cave of Calypso, Atlas' daughter, on her Elysian island. The alder is associated with the goddess Minerva, Roman goddess of wisdom.

Responding to the fear of vampires which existed during the Middle Ages, a custom involving alder arose in some Slavic regions. To protect the souls of the departed, the dead would be disinterred and a stake fashioned of alder wood thrust through the deceased's heart. We suspect that the deva, or spirit, of alder was not pleased.

In Teutonic and Norse lore, the first woman, Embla is made from the wood of the alder as a partner to Aske. Odin breathes life into them.

USAGE

The bark of the alder may be used in most magickal workings to promote protection. Powdered bark or wood may be added to almost any incense mixtures. It is this protective aspect of alder which is associated with the energy of the planet Mars.

The association with Venus would include alder's natural green dye which the faerie folk are said to have used to dye their clothing. It is believed that the green helped them stay concealed in the woodlands. Alder also has the ability to enhance divinatory skills.

Alder may be included in rituals of death and dying as a means of providing protection for the beloved. When appropriate, an alder may be planted upon the grave site.

Under the entry for the herbe ash, usage is described which allows the practitioner to work with alder as a means of having access to the feminine archetype through the Great Rite. This work would fall under the correspondence of the planet Venus.

Alder has a strong association with the elements. It provides natural dyes. The red represents elemental fire; the green was associated with elemental water by the Celts; and the brown represents elemental earth. Alder usually is freshly in bloom during the Spring Equinox and is an herbe long associated with Eostara.

❧ Alfalfa ❧

Medicavo Sativa
Jupiter
Herbe of Protection ... Magickal Herbe

USAGE

Modern folklore includes the magickal use of alfalfa to help stimulate and increase the flow of resources and money coming into your life. Not only does this work magick to bring help but it also is believed to protect you against financial misfortune.

A small quantity of alfalfa should be harvested at an auspicious moment (such as when the Moon waxes full). Dried carefully in one's temple, the herbe should later be burned in one's cauldron which has been set in the center of a ritual circle. The ashes from this alfalfa are then placed into a ritually constructed and consecrated amulet.

❧ Alkanet ❧

Alkanna Tinctoria
Venus
Herbe of Protection

LORE

Grieve in *A Modern Herbal* cites Culpeper as the source for lore which ascribes a most unusual power to alkanet. It was believed so potent that "if any that hath newly eaten it do but spit into the mouth of a serpent, the serpent instantly dies."

USAGE

I do not know anyone who is willing to spit into a snake's mouth but the lore suggests that alkanet might be useful in protecting those who are foraging about in a snake's habitat. Rather than be used to harm a snake, the use of alkanet might help protect one against snakebite. We also recommend working with this herbe to treat fear of snakes.

❦ Almond ❦

Amygdalus Communis
Sun*, Mercury
Herbe of Consecration ... Herbe of Immortality ... Herbe of Love ... Religious Herbe
Invocatory: Artemis, Attis, Cybele, Hecate, Phyllis and Zeus

LORE

Grieve provides us with considerable lore regarding this graceful, flowering tree. In more temperate climates it comes into bloom in January, it signifies "the wakening up of Creation." For most readers this takes place closer to the Equinox. Grieve also writes that Aaron chose a slender branch of almond for his rod and that the nuts were used to decorate the golden candlestick kept with the Tabernacle. There are some indications that the almond may have been considered a Tree of Life by some of the older Hebrew cults.

This beautiful tree is associated with Phyllis, the Greek daughter of King Sithon of Thrace. She was to be married to Demophoön, son of Theseus and Phaedra. When Demophoön was late for the wedding, Phyllis was overwhelmed with grief, believed herself abandoned and committed suicide by hanging. The gods, being kindly, took pity upon the young lovers. Phyllis was transformed into an almond tree and Demophoön, properly remorseful, when shedding tears at the site, found the tree opening into bloom. Grieve, in *A Modern Herbal* gives almond the attribute of an "emblem of true love inextinguishable by death."

Attis is the Phrygian equivalent of Adonis. According to Graves, his mother Nana conceived him, as a virgin, by swallowing an almond. (In some versions this is a pomegranate seed.) In the

Phrygian myth, as cited by Sir James G. Frazer in *The Golden Bough: A Study in Magic and Religion*, the almond tree is seen as the "father of all things."

Plutarch, Greek philosopher of the first century, chronicles the attribute of almond as a preventative against drunkenness. According to Grieve, this lore was also mentioned by Gerard.

USAGE

Almond has long been used to invoke the energy of deities. It may be worn as a perfume, anointing oneself with the extracted oil. Incenses may be made by including the powdered bark or by adding the oil to any loose mixture. Almond bark or twigs may be placed into the fire as an offering or the flowers gathered to adorn the temple or sacred space.

Oil of almond may be used to anoint a magickal wand and the herbe itself may be used as a wash or incense in a ritual of consecration for empowering this tool. If one has access to a live almond tree, the wood would make an excellent wand. Such a magickal wand would be an ideal ritual tool to be used by ritual partners who share their love and magick in this life and, hopefully, in their lives to come. One may also work with the property of almond to consecrate ritual candlesticks.

An excellent herbe to incorporate in Handfastings and rituals of union, it adds a special magick to the bonding of the couple, workings its lore to keep love alive and strong. This would be the ideal situation for employing a wand of almond.

You might also use almond to provide magickal help for someone working to overcome alcohol dependency, employing it through any variety of magickal practices.

Almond may be associated with Candlemas, with the Spring Equinox and with Beltane or May Eve.

❧ Aloe ❧

Aloe Vera
Mars, Pluto
Funereal Herbe ... Herbe of Protection ... Religious Herbe
Invocatory: Venus

LORE

Aloe is sacred among many of the followers of Mohammed, particularly those living in Egypt. Mrs. Grieve describes one of their customs for us. Pilgrims who visit Mohammed's shrine hang the aloe above the doorway. In that culture it is also believed that the aloe provides protection to one's home and the practice has spread to other religions in Egypt as well. Grieve tells us that the Arabic name, *saber*, means patience and symbolizes the period of time spent between death and resurrection. The aloe is sometimes planted upon a burial site, believed to promote a peaceful existence until the deceased is reborn. The ability of the aloe to survive prolonged periods without water in arid regions must certainly enhance the belief in its ability to soothe one's soul.

Roman women believed that the plant was sacred to the goddess Venus, who bestowed love and beauty to those who gave her honor.

Among some tribes living along the Congo River in Africa, the juice of the aloe is ritually gathered and is integrated into their hunting rituals. The practical aspect is that, when the hunter's body is coated with the juice of the aloe, he can move among his prey without his scent giving him away. The aloe allows him to become more at one with his environment.

USAGE

Based upon lore and history, it would hold that growing an aloe would bring increased protection for your home. Should you live in a climate where it is possible, the custom of planting an aloe upon the grave of a beloved remains highly recommended.

Modern lore has suggested that the aloe increases one's likelihood of finding success in the world. The liquid may be used in a magickal balm or integrated into a daily, magickal tonic. Modern lore also purports that aloe may help those afflicted with feelings of loneliness.

❦ Amaranth ❦

Amaranthus Hypochondriacus
Saturn
Funereal Herbe ... Herbe of Immortality ... Religious Herbe
Invocatory: Artemis
Also called: love-lies-bleeding, velvet flower

LORE

Sacred to Artemis, Greek goddess of the Moon, it embodies her renowned ability at healing. Believed by the ancient Greeks to be a symbol of immortality, Grieve chronicles its use as a decorative symbol found with sacred images of the Greek pantheon and incorporated into their burial customs.

USAGE

Amaranth is an excellent herbe to use for the ritual cup. One may choose to seek the mysteries of immortality in order to move deeper into the Universe. Those who revere Artemis as the ideal of the Divine Feminine may find amaranth to be a wonderful and most useful herbe.

Although there is no established lore as a basis for this, we believe that amaranth will prove useful in helping those who suffer from hypochondria.

❦ Ammoniacum ❦

Dorema Ammoniacum
Jupiter
Religious Herbe
Invocatory: Jupiter

LORE

The ancient lore of this tree is cited by Grieve to date to an ancient temple dedicated to Jupiter Ammon, a site known for the collection of this resin.

USAGE

The dried resin may be used as incense in religious ceremony. It

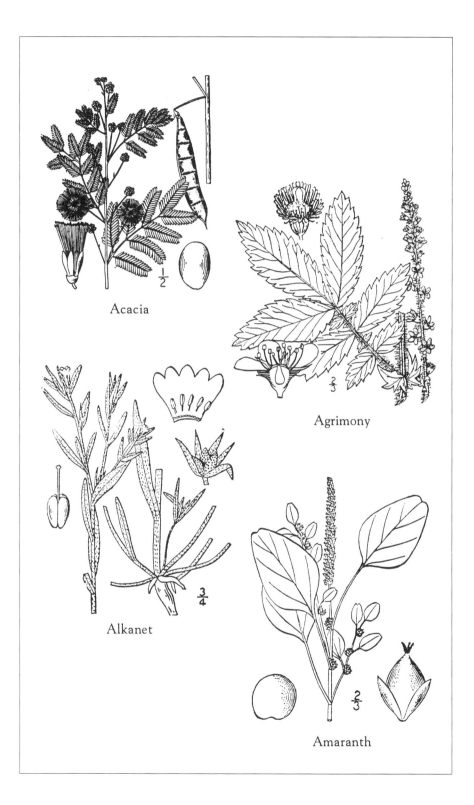

Acacia

Agrimony

Alkanet

Amaranth

should prove useful in bringing increased resources or invoking any of the benevolent aspects of Jupiter.

❦ Anemone ❦

Anemone Pulsatilla
Mercury
Religious Herbe
Invocatory: Adonis
Also called: pasque flower, wind flower, meadow anemone,
Easter flower

LORE

In Grieve we read that this herbe was named by Gerard, calling it the Pasque Flower due to the season when it bloomed, Pasque being another name for Easter. She also writes that the flower has been used to color Easter eggs. According to Frazer in *The Golden Bough*, the scarlet anemone was first created from the blood of Adonis after he was gored by a wild boar on Mount Lebanon, a mythical event which happens every year in the mythic cycles observed among the Phoenicians. As you will soon read, we often find this lore associated with the wood anemone.

USAGE

The association of this herbe with Easter lends its use to modern incorporation into Eostara, the celebration of the Spring Equinox.

❦ Anemone (Wood) ❦

Anemone Nemorosa
Mars
Herbe of Love ... Religious Herbe
Invocatory: Adonis, Anemos, Aphrodite, Eurus, Venus
Also called: crowfoot, wind flower

LORE

A tale of the origin of the anemone is found within Greek mythology. One story relates it to Adonis' death. Killed by a wild boar, the anemone sprang up from droplets of his blood which fell to the soil. Another version of the same myth is that Aphrodite, who deeply loved Adonis (who was only one of the many gods whom she loved), was so stricken by his death that she began weeping. When her tears fell to earth, the flower began to grow to immortalize her love for Adonis. Aphrodite is so associated with the Roman Venus that their myths are sometimes interchangeable. Mrs. Grieve, for example, attributes this myth to Venus.

There is much lore associated with the anemone. Among our favorite herbal legends is the anemone's association with faerie folk. Rural peoples once believed that the maturing flower of the wood anemone was an ideal nesting place for faeries.

Not all cultures believed the flower an emblem of love and beauty. Grieve tells us it is called the "Flower of Death" in China and that it represented ill health in Egypt. There are also areas of Europe in which the flower is associated with misfortune.

A *Modern Herbal* provides us with a magickal folk custom. "The Romans plucked the first Anemones as a charm against fever." The custom survived many centuries in different forms until relatively recent times, "it being considered a certain cure to gather an Anemone saying, 'I gather this against all diseases,' and to tie it round the invalid's neck."

The Greeks believed this herbe to be a gift from the wind god, Anemos. Grieve writes that "Anemos, the Wind, sends his namesakes the Anemones, in the earliest spring days as the heralds of his coming."

USAGE

Wood anemone may be used in a number of fascinating magickal ways, but any internal use should be considered restricted. It is moderately poisonous, unpleasant in flavor, and not recommended for internal consumption.

Associated with the wind deity Anemos, anemone can be used to invoke elemental air. The flowers could be used as an offering; powdered wood or bark could be used as incense; the herbe could be infused for the liquid or oil extracted and used to dress (or coat) candles one might burn in honor of the elementals of air.

During rituals of death and dying or for any rite of passing, the flowers may be tossed into a cauldron. Symbolically this may be seen as representing the passage of the beloved from incarnate being into that state of being which is pure energy.

The wood anemone is ideally suited for all forms of ritual healing. We know that it has been esteemed as an herbe with magickal healing properties since before the Age of Pisces and this energy remains available to us even as we move into yet another astrological age. Anemone can be used as an oil or incense, or even placed into a tub where the person in need of healing takes a ritual bath.

🍂 Angelica 🍂

Angelica Archangelica
Sun
Leo
Countermagick Herbe ... Herbe of Consecration ... Herbe of Immortality ... Herbe of Protection ... Herbe of Purification ... Visionary Herbe
Invocatory: Atlantis, the Archangel Michael

LORE

Grieve describes the remnants of an earlier pagan custom of Eastern Europe, in which people carry the flowering stalks of angelica into the village while, "chanting some ancient ditty in Lettish, so antiquated as to be unintelligible even to the singers themselves."

As seen by its name, angelica has been associated with the Archangel Michael. It comes into bloom near his feast day and has been connected to the Christian observance of the Annunciation.

Angelica is known for its protection against evil spells. Mrs. Grieve says it has been called "The Root of the Holy Ghost."

This majestic herbe is thought by some to have been grown in the gardens of the mythical Atlantis.

USAGE

The Master Book of Herbalism considers angelica "one of the most valuable Herbes of Protection." The magickal property of angelica works in two ways. One is through establishing protection, creating a barrier against energy which would be destructive or harmful. The other property is through filling the person with an abundance of good, radiant energy. Angelica has a pleasing flavor and may be used internally. It is also an excellent bathing herbe. The attributes of this relative of celery enhance one's aura, aid the person in maintaining a joyful outlook on life, and assist in allowing the internal, psychic self to be open and functional. Angelica may be used in ritual baths, self-blessings and in rituals of purification.

For the devotees of Atlantean myth, angelica may be integrated into meditations to help the practitioner have a sense of Atlantis, its lore and knowledge. Plato was the first to write of this legend and whether or not Atlantis ever existed in reality remains debated even today. The legends, however, have been believed by countless peoples over many centuries and there is great power within the myth. Angelica may be used to intuit other realities and the ancient civilizations of other times.

The belief in the protective and benevolent guardianship of angelic beings is a strong force in many religions. For these people, angelica is an essential herbe. For any person desirous of better reaching one's inner light, of finding inspiration and tapping into one's Highest Ideals, angelica will help you embrace and embody your own spiritual essence.

As a bringer of light, angelica may be used at Candlemas, the Feast of the Waxing Light, as the days grow brighter and our hope is rekindled. Angelica may be used with the Strength card through meditation.

❦ Anise Seed ❦

Pimpinella Anisum
Moon
Fertility Herbe ... Greene Herbe ... Herbe of Consecration ...
Herbe of Immortality ... Herbe of Love ... Herbe of Protection
... Magickal Herbe ... Visionary Herbe
Invocatory: Apollo, Hermes, Mercury
Also called: aniseed

LORE

Grieve posits that our modern spiced wedding cakes are derived from the mustacæ, a Roman cake served at the wedding feast; this cake contained anise and cumin. Anise has been highly valued as an herbe, and used by the Pharisees as a tithing.

USAGE

Anise seed is an ingredient in a number of modern recipes said to help a person find romance. The magickal properties of this herbe are more likely to deal with the inner personal issues surrounding a lack of fulfillment.

Commonly found in kitchens (which is why it is categorized as a Greene Herbe), it can easily be integrated into many recipes, providing a gentle, emotional bonus for one's guests. No, they won't fall passionately in love with each other, but anise may help them become more open to their own happiness and better enjoy one another's company.

Anise may be used in simple spells. It is known for its propensity to help bring happiness, and to protect those who suffer from frightening dreams. Its most useful property for the spiritual student is to bring protection while moving through the astral or taking a shamanic journey. The seed is often ground and added to cakes made for lunar rituals.

Help keep traditional customs alive. Include anise in Handfasting and wedding cakes. The scent is so wonderful, one might even toss it along with rice. Did you know that anise will grow from seed quite easily? It is a lovely plant, bringing its magickal scent and its blessings to the herbalist's garden.

There are several correspondences with anise, including the deities Apollo and Mercury. It has been connected with the Chariot card, and can be used in meditation to help one better understand this card of the major arcana. In *The Master Book of Herbalism* we read that one should store anise with a piece of amber, saying "anise is used to allow our physical awareness to be in communion with the spiritual immortal elements of our being."

A fun herbe to use in one's magick, anise makes a tasty elixir, adding a sense of sweet flavor to any herbal mixture, lending itself to almost any usage.

❦ Anise (Star) ❦

Illicium Verum
Moon, Uranus
Aquarius
Funereal Herbe ... Herbe of Consecration ... Herbe of
Protection ... Magickal Herbe ... Religious Herbe
Also called: Chinese anise, star anise

LORE

Grieve includes some essential lore in her text. According to her, the Japanese hold this herbe sacred. It is planted on temple grounds and burial sites, where it will bring sacred energies of protection and beneficence. The bark is collected from the tree, ground into powder and used as temple incense.

USAGE

It is always helpful to have solid lore upon which to base magickal usage. Powdered stars may be used as incense (or added to your existing mixture) either to invoke the deities of your choice or to assist in banishing all negative energies. As a Magickal Herbe, star anise is ideal for learning to live with the trust and joy of the Fool card of the major arcana.

Star anise is difficult to grow in most of the continental United States, but where possible it may be grown at burial sites. The herbe may also be included in the ritual cup used at rituals of death and dying. An infusion is an excellent drink for a person who is nearing the time for passing into the Otherworld.

Star anise has been included in herbal formulae for the consecration of ritual cups and chalices.

🍎 Apple 🍎

Pyrus Malus
Venus, Jupiter
Taurus
Fertility Herbe ... Herbe of Immortality ... Religious Herbe ...
Visionary Herbe
Invocatory: Abellia, Aphrodite, Diana, Freyam Froh, Gaea,
Hera, Idun, Odin, Pomona, Thiassi, Uttu, Venus

LORE

Few of our Mother's gifts are so celebrated in lore as the apple. Often associated with fertility goddesses, apple is, for many peoples, a Tree of Knowledge. Some consider the apple in that light when studying the original version of the myth of Eve and the Garden of Eden. The Sumerian goddess Uttu is offered an apple by the god Enki. By accepting his gift, she must also accept him and become his wife. The Celts call the god of the apple tree Abellia. Apples represented immortality. We find the apple associated with the great goddess Freya as well. Seen by many peoples as a symbol of fertility, Kara-Kirghiz women cure their childless state by rolling under a lone apple tree.

In Arthurian lore, a favorite mythology among neopagans, another name for the Isle of Avalon is "The Isle of Apple Trees." The apple has been found interwoven with unicorn mythology as well.

Graves describes the apple as a symbol of "poetic immortality." He lists the apple tree as the letter *Quert* and considers it one of the "seven noble sacred trees of the grove." He writes that ancient Irish law considered death appropriate for the cutting down of an apple tree. Graves also writes in *The White Goddess*:

> the Apple White Goddess is of happier omen than the
> Blackthorn White Goddess as introducing the summer...
> it is an axiom that the White Goddess is both lovely and
> cruel, ugly and kind.

In some legends Froh, a Norse fertility god who bestows fruitfulness (sometimes interchangeable with Odin), wins the giantess Gerda, daughter of Gymir, known for her beauty, by offering eleven golden apples. One of the stories told of Odin is that he was able to father a child with Rerir by sending her a magickal apple. Upon biting it, she gives birth.

The Teutonic Idun, goddess of eternal youth, beauty and patroness of spring, protects the golden apples. When the gods and goddesses become old, they are given these apples to eat and are magickally transformed into youths again. These apples contain eternal youth. Thiassi, the god of winter, steals the apples and hides them so that the gods and goddesses are kept in the Underworld, allowing winter to reign supreme and last year-round. Idun escapes, finds her magickal apples and feeds them to her friends. Spring can now return and they all live happily ever after. In another story Loki does his crafty best to obtain an apple in order to win favor with a powerful giant of questionable morals.

Golden apples are also well known in Greek mythology where they come from Gaea, goddess of the earth. Gaea gives golden apples as a gift to Hera when Hera is married to Zeus. These apples grow on a Tree of Life in the garden of the Hesperides at the far western realm of the known Greek world. The Hesperides are the daughters of Atlas and Hesperis.

Heracles, when seeking help for the troubles he has endured (killing his children, going mad) seeks wisdom from the Oracle at Delphi. He is advised to offer his cousin Eurystheus, the king of Mycenae, twelve years of service and must complete twelve tasks or labors as a type of community service. The eleventh labor was to find the famed golden apples. Heracles learns of their location through Nereus, the Old Man of the Sea. When it comes time to actually retrieve the apples, Heracles sends Atlas, who returns successful. Atlas wants to keep the apples, figuring he did all the work. The wily Heracles tricks him by seeming to agree but then asks Atlas if he could hold the heavens for just a moment. Poor Atlas! Somehow the wisdom inherent in the apples eluded him. With Atlas busy carrying the weight of the world, Heracles takes the apples to Eurystheus. Eurystheus in turn offers them to Athena, but she bids Heracles to return them to Gaea.

The golden apples are also connected with the cause of the Trojan War. Hera, Athena and Aphrodite become involved in a heated debate over who is the most beautiful, the winner of which would be given the golden apple. Paris is chosen to resolve this conflict. He considers carefully and gives Aphrodite the golden apple indicating that she is the fairest of them all. Aphrodite is very pleased and, expressing her pleasure, gives Paris the lovely Helen as a wife. Apparently the gods and goddesses make deals like this all the time. Paris and Helen elope to Troy where they are married. Somehow, Helen's husband Menelaus (she was already married at the time, you see) is displeased and declares war on the Trojans.

Apples continue, throughout history, to be a rich source of lore. Mrs. Grieve in *A Modern Herbal* describes the custom of "wassailing:"

> The once-popular custom of "wassailing the orchard-trees" on Christmas Eve, or the Eve of Epiphany, is not quite extinct even yet in a few remote places in Devonshire. The ceremony consisted of the farmer, with his family and labourers, going out into the orchard after supper, bearing with them a jug of cider and hot cakes. The latter were placed in the boughs of the oldest or best bearing trees in the orchard, while the cider was flung over the trees after the farmer had drunk their health in some such fashion as the following:
>> Here's to thee, old apple tree!
>> Whence thou may'st bud, and whence thou may'st
>> blow,
>> Hats full! Caps full!
>> Bushel—bushel-bags full!
>> And my pockets full too! Huzza!

The toast was repeated thrice, with the men and boys often firing off guns and pistols, and the women and children shouting loudly.

Roasted apples were usually placed in the pitcher of cider, and were thrown at the trees with the liquid. It is said to have been a relic of the heathen sacrifices to Pomona.

We also find in Grieve's fine book the following:

> The mixture of hot spiced ale, wine or cider, with apples and bits of toast floating in it was often called "lamb's wool," some say from its softness, but the word is really derived from the Irish *la mas nbhal* (the feast of the apple-gathering) (All Hallow's Eve), which being pronounced somewhat like "Lammas-ool," was corrupted into "lamb's wool." It was usual for each person who partook of the spicy beverage to take out an apple and eat it, wishing good luck to the company.

The goddess Diana was worshipped in Gaul as Diana Nemeton. From Robert Graves in *The White Goddess*, we learn this aspect of her was depicted with an apple bough. She was a goddess of the apple groves.

Frazer in *The Golden Bough* describes a wonderful custom involving a figure woven of straw:

> The straw figure, called "the great monard," and placed on the oldest apple-tree in spring, represents the spirit of the tree, who, dead in winter, revives when the apple-blossoms appear on the boughs. Thus the first person who plucks the first fruit from the tree...must be regarded as a representative of the tree spirit.

Frazer describes the custom of throwing a burning brand into the apple trees on the first Sunday of Lent to protect the villages from fires. Another custom is the planting of a new apple tree for a boy; the tree is seen as a "barometer" of the lad's future. Naturally, all hope the tree will be healthy and bear fruit.

USAGE

Apples may be incorporated into any ritual in which one desires to give honor to a god or goddess of fertility. The seeds may be planted in establishing a shrine of trees to Aphrodite or other fertility goddesses. Dried seeds and bark may be powdered to be used as incense. Apples may be eaten, the juice shared in the ritual cup, or incense offered when seeking knowledge through the Tree of Life, an act requesting wisdom from the deities. The apple may also be used as a symbol of security.

Apples are often associated with good luck. We see a trace of this belief in the custom of bobbing for apples. Even today the apple is sometimes used for good luck in the Hallow's Feast. Many enjoy cutting the apple in half horizontally, where the seed cavity produces a five-pointed star.

The apple is believed to improve one's spirits and elevate one's happiness. Apples are corresponded with Venus and with Friday, which is her day. Graves considers the apple as having a numerical value of five.

🦋 Arrow Root 🦋

Maranta Arundinaceæ
Jupiter
Magickal Herbe

USAGE

Arrow root has some popularity among modern practitioners. It is believed that this herbe may increase one's good fortune and make opportunity more visible on one's horizons.

🦋 Asafoetida 🦋

Ferula Fœtida
Pluto
Countermagick Herbe ... Herbe of Consecration ... Herbe of
Protection ... Herbe of Purification ... Religious Herbe ...
Visionary Herbe
Invocatory: Cernunnos, Pan, Priapus
Also called: devil's dung, food of the gods

LORE

The Master Book of Herbalism reported that some hold the belief that asafoetida came into being when the gods' semen came down from the heavens to meet the earth. Planted within the fertile soil, the asafoetida plant sprung forth.

USAGE

It is possible, according to Grieve, that asafoetida may affect activity within the brain. Whatever its physiological effects, it has a wide range of magickal uses. It is said that there is an affinity between a black diamond and asafoetida. Some believe that they should be stored together.

Asafoetida is used in a variety of rituals and ceremonies. It is recommended as an ingredient in incense. The resin is harvested from the plant by making a cut in the root, dried and powdered, readily lending itself to censing. *The Master Book of Herbalism* recommends it "for rituals of a somber, ceremonial nature. It is used to banish all negative energy, evil spirits and demons."

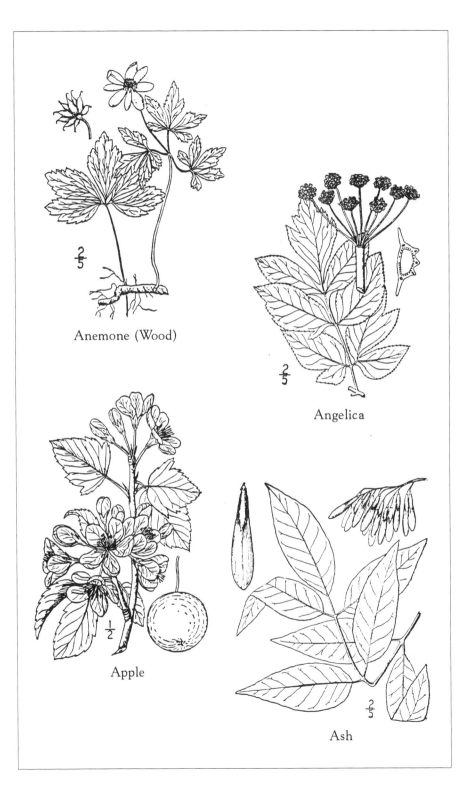

Anemone (Wood)

Angelica

Apple

Ash

The energy of this herbe is very focused and intense. It is associated with the Devil card of the major arcana. Used in meditations in conjunction with this graphic archetype, it helps one discover how the mundane attractions in our own lives have placed us in spiritual bondage. Once known, this herbe may also be used through rituals of self-purification or cleansing to help us break free of our own negative desires. Asafoetida is an excellent herbe for any student who has been accepted for training leading to initiation. As an incense, it works to increase the power of any ritual.

This herbe would be an excellent choice for those seeking entry into the mysteries of the Horned God. It is recommended for those who place Priapus upon their altars, for those who invoke the gods, particularly in their aspect as phallic, fertility deities.

❦ Asclepias ❦

Asclepiadaceæ sp.
Moon*, Mars, Jupiter, Saturn
Herbe of Immortality ... Religious Herbe
Invocatory: Bacchus, Indra, Soma

LORE

There is quite a bit of romantically embroidered mythology about the herbe asclepias. Holding a very sacred place within Hindu legends, this is the herbe from which the mythical soma is created. I'd like to present information from two sources. Grieve writes that:

> Soma, the Indian equivalent of Bacchus and one of the most important of the Vedic gods, is a personification of the Soma plant *Asclepias acida*, from which an intoxicating milky juice is squeezed. All the 114 hymns of the ninth book of the Rig Veda are in his praise. The preparation of the Soma juice was a very sacred ceremony and the worship of the god is very old. The true home of the plant was fabled to be in heaven, Soma being drunk by gods as well as men, and it is under its influence that Indra is related to have created the universe and fixed the earth and sky in their place. In post-Vedic literature, Soma is a regular name for the Moon, which is regarded as being drunk by the gods and so waning, till it is filled up again by the Sun. In both the Rig Veda and Zend

Avesta, Soma is the king of plants; in both, it is a
medicine which gives health, long life and removes
death.

Herbert Robinson and Knox Wilson in *Myths and Legends of All
Nations* concur with Mrs. Grieve and we also learn that:

As the sacred drink, soma was a necessary part of the
ritual of the Rig-veda. Soma was the second most important god of earth. He was said to give life, even endless
life, to the gods and to certain men.... He can hardly be
regarded as an anthropomorphic god, since the poets
who wrote of him were usually thinking of the plant and
its juice from which the intoxicating soma (or "mead" or
"drop") was made. Soma was naturally called the king of
plants and the lord of the wood. In time soma... came to
be mystically identified with the Moon.

❦ Ash ❦

Fraxinus Excelsior
Sun*, Uranus, Neptune
Countermagick Herbe ... Fertility Herbe ... Herbe of Love ...
Herbe of Protection ... Magickal Herbe ... Religious Herbe ...
Visionary Herbe
Invocatory: Gwydion, Odin, Poseidon

LORE

One of the famed magickal trees of Europe, the ash has figured in
lore and mythology since the Age of Aries. The presence of the
tree as a religious symbol central to a cultural cosmology is familiar throughout the world. The ash holds this honor among many
peoples. In the Norse creation myth, Odin divides day from night,
bringing creation into dualism. Following this, the gods and goddesses used the ash to create the Aske, the first man. The first
woman was next made from alder. In a sense, the ash is perceived
as a Tree of Life, as is the alder.

Other Norse beliefs about the ash center around the notorious
goddess Hel. She is the goddess of the dead, but in a most unpleasant manner. She represents the evils, fears and negative
beliefs about the unknown Underworld. Due to her vile nature,
the gods have exiled her to Niflheim, within the Underworld.
Where is this place? It is believed to lie beneath the roots of the

most sacred ash in the Nordic tradition, known as Yggdrasil.

In the sacred Edda, Odin and two of his fellow god-friends are strolling along the shore where they come upon a couple of tree trunks which had been washed up. These two are the ash and the alder from which the first humans were fashioned.

Robert Graves in *The White Goddess* posits that Gwydion myths are derived from the Norse Odin. Gwydion's horse was named for the ash. "Yggdrasill was the enchanted ash, sacred to Woden, whose roots and branches in Scandinavian mythology extended through the Universe." Gwydion was an "Ash-god" worshipped by early British tribes. The sacred ash of Gwydion had once been the site where the triple goddess provided advice and justice.

The Norse belief regarding the ash is comparable to a Greek myth cited by Hesiod which also maintains that the first human was made from the wood of an ash.

It is believed that the Celts used the ash for their spears which they used to defended their territory and fight their neighbors. Graves writes that the ash was used by the Druids for their ritual wands. The ash is the third letter, N or Nion, of the tree alphabet and sometimes corresponded with Wednesday. Although Graves places the ash with the planet Mercury, he is alone in that correspondence.

The Greeks held ash sacred to Poseidon as Graves writes. "The ash is the tree of sea-power, or of the power resident in water." Old English customs included using a carved branch of ash as protection against drowning.

USAGE

The lore of the ash is indeed varied. It is an excellent herbe to use in divination. Graves cites a finger-tip method of divination which includes the following stanza:

> Ash, middle finger,
> By power of divination
> Weatherwise, fool otherwise,
> Mete him out the winds.

This tree's usage ranges from removing spells and hexes to the removal of warts. Grieve describes the latter custom which Frazer says existed in Cheshire:

> The ash had the reputation of magically curing warts: each wart must be pricked with a new pin that had been thrust into the tree, the pins withdrawn from the wart and left in the tree, and the following charm repeated:
> Ashen tree, ashen tree,
> Pray buy these warts of me.

There was another superstition that if a live shrew mouse were buried in a hole bored in an ash trunk and then plugged up, a sprig of this shrew ash would cure the paralysis supposed to have been caused by a shrew creeping over the sick person's limbs.

Grieve describes yet another custom of magickal healing in which a sapling is split down the middle and a child passed through the opening. Frazer describes this in detail:

> Thomas Chillingworth, son of the owner of an adjoining farm, now about thirty-four, was, when an infant of a year old, passed through (an ash), now perfectly sound, which he preserves with so much care that he will not suffer a single branch to be touched, for it is believed the life of the patient depends on the life of the tree, and the moment that it is cut down, be the patient ever so distant, the rupture returns, and a mortification ensues, and terminates in death, as was the case in a man driving a waggon [sic] on the very road in question.

With such varied lore regarding magickal healing, the ash is recommended as an herbe for any magickal or psychic healing techniques. If working with the ash's association with elemental water it would seem more appropriate to correspond ash with the planet Neptune.

The leaf of the ash is reputed to help bring a traveler safely home. *The Master Book of Herbalism* recommends placing a leaf someplace within your automobile, motorcycle or vehicle for protection while on the road.

Ash has a well-established reputation as one of the finest choices of woods for wands or staves. A slender branch or sapling should be selected so that, once the bark has been peeled, none of the wood need be removed other than through a gentle sanding to provide the desired finish for your wand.

Ritual workings with the Great Rite can be developed using ash in combination with alder. The bringing together of these two can engender a very powerful energy. There are several options, one being the Yang partner working with ash and the Yin partner with alder. Another would be drying and powdering of wood or bark from each tree, which would be brought together upon a block of charcoal. Symbolic of divinity manifesting as the polarities which are brought together as the smoke rises, returning to the heavens, an experienced practitioner can use this to work very potent magick.

❦ Asphodel ❦

Asphodelus Ramosus
Jupiter*, Pluto
Funereal Herbe ... Herbe of Consecration ... Herbe of
Immortality
Invocatory: Bacchus, Dionysus
Also called: king's spear, royal staff

LORE

The correspondence with Pluto arises from asphodel's ancient association with death and dying. It was an herbe of choice for planting where the dead had been lain to rest and was said to grow profusely in the Elysian fields. Asphodel was held sacred to Bacchus and Dionysus (Dionysus is usually considered another aspect of Bacchus but is treated as a separate divinity by some).

USAGE

Asphodel remains an essential herbe in working magick for those who have passed into the Otherworld. It may be infused as a wash for the beloved's body, soothing the soul either during death or cleansing the corpse following the release of the spirit. This is one of the finest herbes to plant in sacred soil where the ashes of cremation are strewn, or upon a grave site. A bunch of the fresh herbe makes a superior aspurger during rituals of death and dying.

In addition, asphodel has associations with a ritual wand. Grieve says the name is derived from the Greek word for "sceptre" and contemporary usage employs asphodel in the consecration of a ritual wand or staff. It may be added to an incense mixture or infused as a wash for the initial magickal cleansing.

❧ Avens ❧

Geum Urbanum
Jupiter
Countermagick Herbe ... Herbe of Protection
Also called: clove root, colewort, herb bennet, way bennet,
wild rye

LORE

Again I am grateful to Mrs. Grieve for her outstanding preservation of extant herbe lore:

> It was called "The Blessed Herbe" (*herba benedicta*), of
> which a common name still extant—herbe Bennet—is
> a corruption, because in former times it was believed
> that it had the power to ward off evil spirits and venom-
> ous beasts. It was worn as an amulet. The *Ortus Sanita-
> tis*, printed in 1491, states: "Where the root is in the
> house, Satan can do nothing and flies from it, wherefore
> it is blessed before all other herbes, and if a man carries
> the root about him no venomous beast can harm him."

As a blessed herbe, avens acquired Christian associations. Many
herbes with trifoliate leaves, during the superstitious medieval
ages, came to be seen as symbolic of the Trinity and were once
commonly used as a metaphor for Christian beliefs.

Grieve cites the date of March 25 as the desired date for harvesting the root.

USAGE

Avens may be used in nearly any manner to bring protection to
self, kindred and home. As an amulet, the root of the herbe is
most desirable—a whole root being more potent than chopped
pieces or ground powder. The latter is eminently suitable for
incense. Avens may be integrated into any ritual designed to
promote blessings and good energy while keeping all negation
removed from one's surroundings.

❦ Azadirachta ❦

Melia Azadirachta
Jupiter
Religious Herbe
Also called: bead tree, holy tree, Indian lilac tree

LORE

A stunning, singular tree of lower Asia, its lavender-colored flowers produce hard nuts which are gathered for the making of prayer beads and rosaries.

❦ Balm ❦

Melissa Officinalis
Venus, Jupiter
Cancer
Herbe of Love ... Magickal Herbe ... Religious Herbe
Invocatory: Diana
Also called: balm melissa, lemon balm

LORE

The word *balm* is derived from the Latin, *balsamum*, indicating the presence of the oils which provide a pleasing scent. Grieve tells us that Paracelsus considered this among the most important of herbes, believing it capable of restoring life. She also cites the 1696 London Dispensary as listing balm as capable of preventing baldness and increasing one's mental faculties.

USAGE

For magickal purposes, balm is ideally suited for healing those who suffer from mental or nervous disorders. Balm is also very useful for those of sound mind who need to keep their mental processes in superior condition. A tea made of the leaves brings calm, which is appropriate for magickal students while studying and preparing for ritual work.

Modern usage finds balm associated with the pursuit of romance. It has been, upon occasion, used in love charms and spell magick designed to attract a partner.

Considered sacred to Diana, it is believed that it was once used in her temples. Balm may also be used as a bathing herbe toward a variety of goals. It may be used as part of the ritual process of invoking the Goddess; balm may be used when sharing a ritual bath with one's partner; or it may be used to find the fulfillment of one's personal desires. This usage of balm opens one to the divine love of the Goddess, but is also believed to add energy to one's being which makes you more appealing in the world of love and romance.

Balm is associated with the Chariot card.

❦ Balm of Gilead ❦

Commiphora Opobalsamum
Venus
Taurus
Herbe of Consecration ... Magickal Herbe
Also called: balsam tree

LORE

References to balm of Gilead are found in many places, ranging from the bible to Paracelsus, from Galen to Dioscorides. Grieve writes:

> Balm, Baulm or Bawm, contracted from Balsam, may be derived from the Hebrew *bot smin*, "chief of oils," or *bâsâm*, "balm," and *besem*, "a sweet smell".... It was taken from Arabia to Judea by the Queen of Sheba as a present to Solomon.

USAGE

The Master Book of Herbalism recommends balm of Gilead as one of the best sources of herbal oil for dressing candles to use in any form of magickal healing. The process of "dressing" uses a candle which has been bathed or cleansed of prior energy. The oil is applied beginning at the center and using one's fingers to work it evenly toward both ends.

🍎 Balmony 🍎

Chelone Glabra
Jupiter, Neptune
Magickal Herbe
Also called: hummingbird tree, snakehead, turtle bloom

LORE

We may associate this herbe with the turtle or tortoise. Grieve says the name Chelone is derived from the Greek word for tortoise, due to the flower's appearance.

USAGE

Balmony may be used to increase steadfastness, patience and perseverance. In reasonable quantity, it may be ingested as an elixir. This would be an excellent herbe for those whose totem animal is the turtle.

🍎 Bamboo 🍎

Bambusa Vulgaris
Moon, Mercury, Mars, Saturn
Gemini
Fertility Herbe ... Religious Herbe
Invocatory: Nuba

LORE

Bamboo is sacred to Buddhists. Many believe that Buddha once incarnated as a monkey king. During perilous times, he weaves a cord of bamboo and saves eighty thousand.

The Sudanese (particularly the Sara peoples) believe that bamboo was a gift from the sky god whom they call Nuba. In order for Su to descend to the newly created earth, Nuba extends a bamboo shoot down to the earth. Su comes down to the world of nature. They have agreed that when Su is ready to return, he will beat upon his sacred drum and Nuba will pull him back up into the sky. During his dangerous descent, Su forgets to pay attention and strikes his drum. Nuba quickly responds and the careless Su loses his grip as the bamboo is tugged quickly toward the heavens. Su falls to his death along with many seeds from the bamboo which scatter about and create the bamboo forests.

USAGE

Bamboo is an excellent wood for a magickal wand, representing all four elements. Growing up from the earth through water, it passes through the sky as it reaches toward the fire of the Sun.

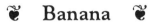

🜍 Banana 🜍

Musa Paradisiaca
Jupiter
Funereal Herbe

LORE

The banana is very important to the people of Madagascar. In *Larousse World Mythology* we learn of some of their beliefs regarding death. The first man and first woman, when they were being taught about the mysteries of death, had great difficulty accepting the harshness of death's reality. Their god gives them a choice, and offers them the right to choose between a death like that of the Moon or a death like that of the banana tree. They choose death like that of the Moon, for she is able to return again and again as one does through reincarnation. The other choice, that of the banana tree, is one of a permanent death but leaves behind numerous descendants.

USAGE

Bananas may be incorporated into a ritual diet as the only food (accompanied with herbal drink) when spending a period of days fasting in profound contemplation regarding the mysteries of death.

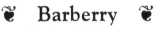

🜍 Barberry 🜍

Berberis Vulgaris
Mars
Religious Herbe

LORE

In some Italian cultures, this spiny herbe is known as Holy Thorn.

It is believe that it provided the crown of thorns worn by the Christ.

USAGE

Barberry makes an excellent herbe for Christian practitioners to incorporate into ritual work done during the season of Lent.

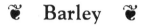 Barley

Hordeum Perlatum
Saturn
Fertility Herbe ... Religious Herbe
Invocatory: Cronus, Demeter, Rgl
Also called: pearl barley

LORE

Similar to the beliefs of several other northern European peoples, the Germans have a belief that dwarves are able to change their shape when not concealed by forests and woodlands. An old custom once existed which connected barley with the lore of dwarves. The last sheaf was believed to be a hiding place. Some years the hiding dwarf might be sacrificed with the scythe, other years the bundle of barley might be carried into the village in a ritualized parade.

Barley has been associated with the harvest and is held to be sacred to Demeter. According to Robert Graves in *The White Goddess* one of the old pagan gods of Russia, Rgl, is also associated with barley. An ancient Greek cult on the Peloponnisos peninsula used both barley and human sacrifice in their rituals in honor of Cronus and the Barley Mother. In Bavaria barley figured in an animistic practice. Frazer in *The Golden Bough* informs us that the last barley of the harvest is fashioned along with corn into a figure of a woman which represents the spirit of the harvest, but not without humor.

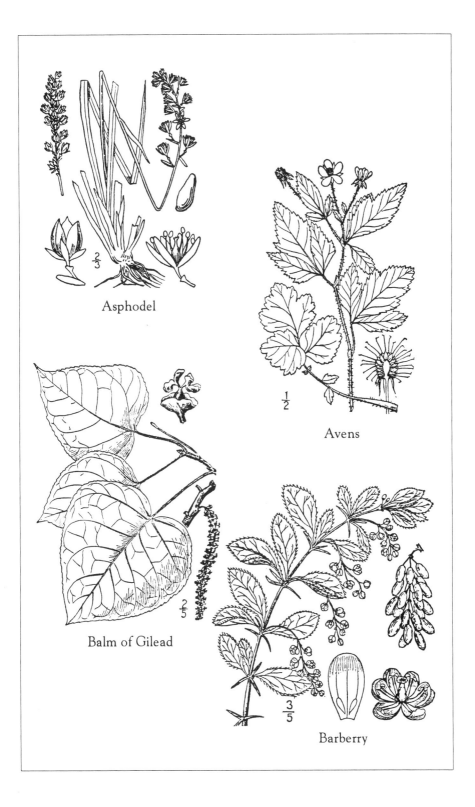

Asphodel

Avens

Balm of Gilead

Barberry

❧ Basil (Bush) ❧

Ocymum Minimum
Mars
Scorpio
Funereal Herbe ... Greene Herbe ... Herbe of Love
Also called: devil plant

LORE

Bush basil is associated with death in cultures as diverse as Iran and the Philippines and is often planted at grave sites. In Egypt the flowers are gathered and strewn upon the grave site.

Grieve writes about a very different perspective among the ancient Greeks who believed

> that it represented hate and misfortune. They painted poverty as a ragged woman with a basil at her side, and thought the plant would not grow unless railing and abuse were poured forth at the time of sowing. The Romans, in like manner, believed that the more it was abused, the better it would prosper.

Beliefs about basil can be passionate. At the other end of the emotional spectrum, we can consider the Moldavian custom Mrs. Grieve has recorded in her herbal. In this culture, a fresh cutting of basil is associated with betrothal. It is, similarly, associated with love and romance in some parts of rural Italy, where it is considered an emblem of love and romance. The inhabitants of Crete combined the beliefs both of romance and of misfortune. Grieve writes that they called it "love washed with tears."

A custom which once existed would be a modern blessing to many if it were resurrected: that of giving one's guests a small pot of basil.

USAGE

Bush basil is an outstanding herbe for rituals of death and dying. This pungent herbe may be added to the incense or infused to provide the holy water for aspurging. This variety of basil is used in correspondence with the Death card.

The romantic history of bush basil readily lends itself to modern

92

magick. The oil would be a fine ingredient in blended mixtures to enhance one's romance. The gift of a live basil would add magick to the endurance of one's relationship or a fine pesto sauce might be the featured item on the menu for a romantic evening. There is no finer herbe to use when incorporating ritual with your betrothal or engagement. Not only will it help a young man be strong of heart so that he can pursue his dreams, but bush basil can be used to bring blessings to the engagement ring as well.

❦ Basil (Sweet) ❦

Ocymum Basilium
Mars
Scorpio
Greene Herbe ... Fertility Herbe ... Funereal Herbe ... Herbe of Consecration ... Herbe of Immortality ... Herbe of Purification ... Magickal Herbe ... Religious Herbe ... Visionary Herbe
Invocatory: Krishna, Vishnu

LORE

Its old association with the basilisk explains sweet basil's contemporary correspondences with such creatures as salamanders and dragons. The basilisk was a mythological reptile which had two fatal weapons: its breath (could this be the source of the modern phrase "dragon breath?") or a look from its evil eyes. As a consequence of this association, the plant became associated with scorpions. Grieve writes that the "superstition went so far as to affirm that even smelling the plant might bring a scorpion into the brain."

It is believed that Solomon chose sweet basil when making his ritual aspurger to use in his temple. It should also be pointed out that a large number of herbes are believed to have been selected.

Sweet basil is a Religious Herbe associated both with Krishna and with Vishnu. Hindus grow this herbe to provide protection for the home and family and, as Grieve writes, a bit later, it is customary to send a good Hindu into the next life with a leaf of basil, ensuring a safe journey and access to Paradise.

USAGE

In *The Master Book of Herbalism* we find the following:

93

Basil should be added to the water used in scrubbing the floors, walls and in any cleaning of the home previous to the unpacking and getting settled. An often-used part of a house and home blessing is a planting ceremony. Basil is an herbe to plant, for it will bring protection and good fortune to those who live within.

Basil is widely associated with rituals of initiation. The sabbat frequently associated with basil is Candlemas, observed as a time of renewal. Sweet basil may be incorporated into these sabbat rituals. One of the best herbes for a candidate preparing for initiation, basil is useful for any ceremonial purification. It can be used as a bathing herbe, as one bathes the body in preparation before receiving a sacrament. It may be burned as an offering or worn as an adornment; sweet basil may be taken as drink or prepared with food.

We may use this type of basil to invoke salamanders, the elemental creatures of fire. The practitioner may dry and grind basil, spooning it upon burning charcoal as an incense. One may also use basil in the ritual cup, drinking a magickally prepared tea in order to meditate upon dragons or salamanders and to establish communion with these beings as astral entities.

Any person in need of courage should use basil. It brings strength and helps one move forward in a positive manner no matter how perilous the dangers. We can use basil to provide fortitude either when facing mundane dangers or when pursuing transformation in the visionary and psychic realms. Basil is known for its quality of protecting the seeker from fears one encounters when moving along a spiritual path and may be used to bring protection for our families as well.

❧ Bay Laurel ❧

Laurus Nobilis
Sun
Leo
Greene Herbe ... Herbe of Love ... Magickal Herbe ... Religious Herbe ... Visionary Herbe
Invocatory: Apollo, Daphne, Delphi, Fides

LORE

Bay was used by the Delphic priestesses, although extreme caution must be used by anyone who would emulate this profound practice. These priestesses were an intensely trained group, initiated following years of study and discipline. They underwent extensive dietary and spiritual preparation before they would chew the leaves during their rituals to enhance their mediumship and be capable of invoking the Oracle at Delphi.

Grieve posits the word *bachelor* as found in *bachelor degree* deriving from *bacca-laureus*. Bay has an ancient history as an herbe of choice for weaving wreaths and crowns which were worn in celebrations, honoring those who had achieved greatness both for society and as individuals through athletics and in scholarly pursuit. It is believed that wreaths of bay laurel were used to crown the winning athletes at the first Olympics.

Daphne, known for her virtue, was trying to escape vigorous pursuit by a passionate Apollo who was so entranced by her loveliness that he wanted her in no uncertain terms. Daphne, however, was not interested in his amorous ways. Daphne escapes his aggression by changing herself into a bay laurel tree—with a little help from her father, Peneus. When Apollo discovers that she is now a beautiful bay, he names the tree as sacred and lovingly picks leaves which he weaves into a wreath to wear upon his head in honor of his beloved Daphne. I'm not certain that she would have enjoyed having her leaves plucked. Sometimes male deities can be very chauvinistic.

In other Greek myths, bay is sacred to Apollo and to Zeus. The Romans dedicated bay laurel to Fides, a goddess who provided them with honor and fidelity through her intercession.

According to Albertus Magnus, bay is used in conjunction with marigold for a number of magickal purposes. (See Marigold.) Although it is the marigold of which he speaks, the bay is an essential element in the process.

In mythology we find the belief that Hermes invented fire by striking a pomegranate against a bay laurel.

USAGE

Bay is used to attract romance and love. There are a number of ways one can approach this process. The leaves of this herbe may be offered in a fire as a sacrifice to the gods. One may also extract the oil and use it to dress a candle which is then burned while meditating. The resulting energy is used to invoke those changes within one's self necessary to become more appealing to others.

A modern custom is to make or purchase a small box as a magickal gift for a friend. It should be decorated with magickal symbols and ritually consecrated. Three leaves from a live bay should be picked at the new Moon and placed within the box. As the Moon waxes, the friend should make a wish, writing the wish upon the leaves. At the full Moon the box, leaves and all, should be taken outside and burned in a cauldron beneath the Moon and the ashes buried. Patience is all that is needed before the wish comes true.

A potted bay is said to protect one's home during a thunderstorm, invoking the protection of Apollo. The otherwise brave Tiberius, emperor of Rome in the first century, was said to wear a wreath of bay laurel to conquer his fear of thunderstorms.

The solar aspect of this herbe may be explored in a number of ways. Apollo was known as a player of the lute and the herbe may be used in the consecration of musical instruments. The herbe or its oil may be used by a priest who is ritually invoking Apollo or any solar deity. Students of the tarot can use bay to better understand either the Sun card or the Strength card.

Branches of bay leaves may be woven into a crown and given as a gift at rituals of initiation. Bay is known as a symbol of esteem and glory, and of love and honor. In fact, magick can be extended to family members who are not so inclined. A wreath of bay leaves given as a household decoration or gift to a graduate, can be perceived as a lovely domestic gift but one also filled with hidden magick.

Not the safest of herbes to ingest, one can invoke an oracle by floating a leaf within a basin of water and scrying for one's divination. The priestesses of Delphi chewed bay leaves until the narcotic properties placed them into a trance. Such a practice is highly dangerous. There are many ways to work with bay which are safe and sane. One might put a leaf upon a blank piece of paper to stimulate poetic inspiration. It has long been believed that a bay laurel promotes divinatory powers or that its decline indicates the impending decline of its owner.

Bay is sometimes corresponded with Candlemas, when it is used to meditate upon the growing sunlight.

❦ Bean (Kidney) ❦

Phaceolus Vulgaris
Venus
Fertility Herbe ... Greene Herbe

LORE

Again expressing my gratitude to Grieve for her detailed recording of herbal customs and history, she recorded the belief found among the ancient Egyptians that the kidney bean was forbidden as food. In a similar approach to that of the Doctrine of Signatures, they believed it corresponded to the male testicle because of its shape. It was revered as sacred, representing virility and male potency.

Grieve also writes that

> in Italy at the present day, beans are distributed among the poor, on the anniversary of a death. The Jewish high priest is forbidden to eat beans on the Day of Atonement.

USAGE

Kidney beans may be used magickally to enhance male potency and increase male fertility. Although considered a vegetable, the kidney bean has properties which lead me to include it as an herbe as are many other plants. Like all Greene Herbes, they are very useful in kitchen magick and could be used by those working to understand men's mysteries.

❦ Beech ❦

Fagus Sylvatica
Mars, Saturn
Herbe of Protection ... Magickal Herbe ... Religious Herbe
Invocatory: Diana, Fagus, Itchita
Also called: bog, boke, faggio, fagos

LORE

Larousse is an important source when studying the myths surrounding this tall tree which can reach nearly 150 feet in height. Its botanical name is derived from the Celtic belief that a divine being named Fagus lives within the beech.

The Yakuts of Siberia believed in a triple goddess who is descended from the primary goddess, named Itchita, who lives within the beech. She can be invoked for protection, is a guardian of the devas and has an affinity for all the spirits of nature.

According to Frazer in *The Golden Bough*, Pliny described a beech grove on the Alban hills which was sacred to the goddess Diana. Beech was also once burned in the fires maintained during Lent as was the apple.

USAGE

Beech's leaves, bark or its powdered wood can be used within rituals to derive the protective quality for which this tree is famous.

For those who wish to make their gardens more receptive to devas, the wood may be dried, powdered and burned as incense as one walks along the garden paths. Beech's affinity with devas makes this an ideal herbe to use at Midsummer, should one desire to move into the realm of the faerie.

This is the ideal herbe for those seeking to improve their literary skills. It is recommended for those doing research, for writers and scholars, as Robert Graves writes in *The White Goddess*:

> "Beech" is a common synonym for "literature." The English word "book," for example, comes from a Gothic word meaning letters and...is etymologically connected with the word "beech"—the reason being that writing

tablets were made of beech.

We can imagine few herbes better suited for those working with a Book of Shadows. Placing the leaf of a beech in a carefully chosen place between the covers will increase inspiration. Those who are creating new ritual literature should consider the beech a patron herbe. The nuts can be dried and used on a small altar in order to give honor to the beech spirit. The ways in which one can use beech to invoke the literary muse are only bound by the limits of your imagination.

❦ Benzoin ❦

Styrax Benzoin
Mars
Religious Herbe ... Magickal Herbe ... Visionary Herbe
Invocatory: Aphrodite, Mut, Venus
Also called: styrax

LORE

Benzoin is considered sacred to Venus, Aphrodite and to Mut. It makes an excellent incense for use in their temples.

USAGE

This herbal resin is not naturally exuded from the styrax trees. The herbalist must make a small cut into the bark, deep enough to pierce the inner bark. This causes the tree to create the resin. It will then slowly seep out where it can be collected, dried and ground for ritual use.

Benzoin has become associated with two of the Wiccan sabbats. It is a superior incense for Candlemas and may also be used at the Autumn Equinox in order to help us understand the mysteries behind the turning of the seasons, when there is a balance between day and night. Benzoin can help the student understand the nature of transitions both in learning how to live with the Wheel of the Year and in gaining comprehension regarding the natural cycles of change.

Benzoin's best use may be found in its ability to provide focus, to enhance concentration and to assist the student when moving into the astral. Benzoin is desirable for those who seek to journey or to project their spirits into the astral. Magickally, benzoin is known for its ability to promote generosity; it can open a closed spirit which is suffering from selfishness. It may also be used to bring increased success to any magickal working or to attain magickal goals. Burned as incense during meditation, it increases the serenity of one's own energy and environment.

Students of the tarot may use this herbe to move beyond the mundane symbols of the Seven card of any of the four suits. Indeed, benzoin may be used to better understand any card of the cups suit.

❦ Betony (Wood) ❦
Betonica Officinalis
Venus, Jupiter*
Herbe of Protection ... Magickal Herbe
Also called: bishopswort

LORE

Betony has a long-established reputation as being very powerful in its ability to protect someone against dark forces and negative energy. It was once planted on sacred ground, particularly about churches and was sometimes planted in graveyards. It is believed to offer the power to protect against the darkest fears and the demons which arise out of one's own emotions and imagination.

USAGE

During the Middle Ages, betony had a somewhat superstitious reputation for its curative and healing power. This magickal property became near legendary and at least one myth developed in which, if the King Stag was wounded, betony would cure him. Betony remains an excellent herbe for magickal healing.

Modern usage of betony is primarily for its protective values. Those who wear an herbal amulet or medicine pouch should include betony among the dried herbes and magickal stones chosen for one's personal spiritual endeavors.

❦ Bilberry ❦

Vaccinium Myrtillus
Jupiter, Pluto
Religious Herbe
Also called: huckleberry, whortleberry

LORE

The Farrars' *Eight Sabbats for Witches* describe the bilberry as being deeply linked to the Celtic Harvest Festival, which today is commonly known as Lammas or Lughnasadh. In their text they write that "the King of Tara's diet had to include fish from the Boyne, venison from Luibnech, bilberries from Bri Leith near Ardagh, and other obligatory items."

USAGE

Bilberries may be incorporated into the Lammas Feast or used as part of the temple decoration.

❦ Birch ❦

Betula Alba
Sun, Venus*
Capricorn
Fertility Herbe ... Herbe of Love ... Herbe of Protection ...
Magickal Herbe ... Religious Herbe
Invocatory: Aino, Thor

LORE

Aino is a major goddess in the pagan culture of Finland. Wainamoinen, much older but a very powerful hero (one of the three heroes of Kalevala), desires her hand in marriage. He enters a contest with her brother, Youkahainen. During their fight, Aino escapes by swimming away to sit safely upon a large rock, removed from the storm created by the contest between the men. The storm becomes so intense that it shakes the rock and she tumbles into the sea. She is transformed into nature itself. Her flesh is transformed into the fish, her blood becomes the water, her hair gives birth to the seaweed and her ribs the willow. After her death, the animal world was so sorrowed that the cuckoos took refuge in a mountain forest of birch where their song of love and sorrow lasts throughout the ages. Because of this, the birch is sacred to the goddess Aino.

Graves writes of a custom in rural Britain in which a girl offers her desired partner a piece of birch as a sign that he may now begin wooing her. In Graves' system of finger divination, birch is used to "bring him news of love; Loud the heart knocks."

Birch is sacred to Thor. One is never to take the bark from this tree unless it has been kissed by Thor, stricken with his lightning. Once Thor has claimed the tree's spirit, then its bark is available for human use.

In the old lore of Siberia, it is believed that the birch is the axis upon which the Universe turns and is an intrinsic part of a shaman's journey. It may be considered a Tree of Life. Frazer writes in *The Golden Bough*:

> On the Thursday before Whitsunday the Russian villagers go out into the woods, sing songs, weave garlands, and cut down a young birch-tree, which they dress up in women's clothes, or adorn with many-coloured shreds and ribbons. After that comes a feast, at the end of which they take the dressed-up birch-tree, carry it home to their village with joyful dance and song, and set it up in one of the houses where it remains an honored guest....

Robert Graves presents a system in which the months are corresponded with the sacred trees of Europe. "Beth, the birch-tree; a tree of inception and the driving-out of evil spirits" corresponds to the time period when the Sun moves through Capricorn. Birch is the letter *B* in the tree alphabet. Graves corresponds the birch with the Sun and with Sunday. Frazer informs us that in Russia a bonfire of birch brings fertility with which to bless the flax harvest.

USAGE

Coleridge called birch the "Lady of the Woods" and modern pagans use this tree in order to give honor to the Goddess of the Woodlands. A circular grove of birch trees is among the most magickal of sites in the sacred woodlands.

The taking of bark from a living birch is forbidden in the folklore

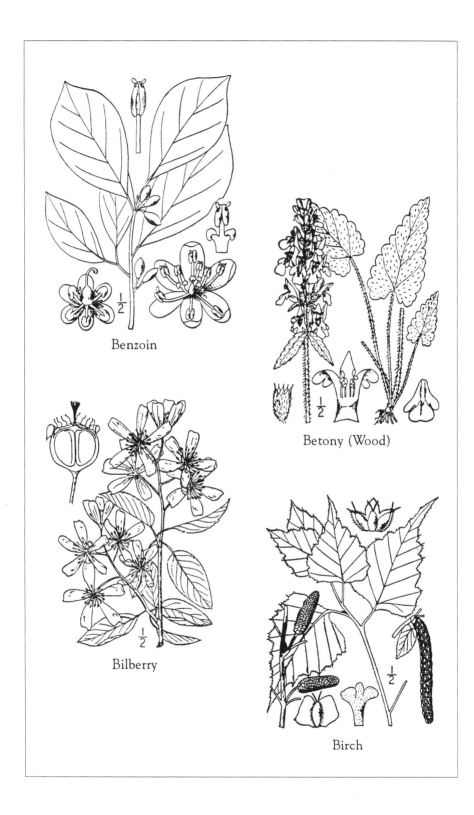

Benzoin

Betony (Wood)

Bilberry

Birch

of many cultures. It is said to anger the Lady of the Woods and to invite Thor's wrath. Collected wisely and within the natural law, you may gather a very potent magickal parchment. A small piece of parchment may be used to express your interest in another.

Birch may be used in any magickal way to provide protection or to banish negative energies. Thin birch branches were once used as switches to beat those who were mentally infirm in the belief that the evil spirits were being driven away, a cruelty which had nothing to do with this beautiful tree and everything to do with human ignorance. Robert Graves tells us "Birch rods are also used in rustic ritual for driving out the spirit of the old year."

Working with birch one may invoke the goddess Aino, whose blood gave birth to the waters of the world. Through her we might better understand elemental water.

❦ Bistort ❦

Polygonum Bistorta
Saturn
Religious Herbe
Also called: adderwort, snakeweed

LORE

Frequently used as a vegetable, one of bistort's common names reflects a custom found in northern areas of England. Grieve writes that "Easter-mangiant" indicates the custom of bistort being eaten at Easter.

USAGE

Based upon Grieve's information, it would follow that an association with Eostara, the Vernal Equinox, would be appropriate.

❦ Blackberry ❦

Rubus Fructicosus
Venus
Aries
Herbe of Protection ... Magickal Herbe
Also called: bramble, brameberry

LORE

We find within Grieve's Herbal old folklore which has survived well into the twentieth century:

> The leaves are said to be still in use in England as a remedy for burns and scalds; formerly their operation was helped by a spoken charm. Creeping under a Bramble-bush was itself a charm against rheumatism, boils, blackheads, etc. Blackberries were in olden days supposed to give protection against all "evil runes," if gathered at the right time of the Moon. The whole plant once had a popular reputation both as a medicine and as a charm for various disorders.

USAGE

Blackberry leaves may be used in magickal healing. It is also possible to dry the fruit and powder it, making a very pleasing infusion or tea for use in the ritual cup when working rituals for health and healing. Blackberry brambles may be gathered and woven into pentagrams or wreaths, hung in auspicious locations within the home to provide protection.

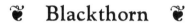

❦ Blackthorn ❦

Prunus Spinosa
Mars
Aries
Religious Herbe
Also called: sloe

LORE

Most modern practitioners will associate the blackthorn with its fruit. Most of us have heard of *sloe*, used in the flavoring of gin and some liqueurs.

Graves believes that the blackthorn was associated with black magick and used to place the forces of negation upon one's enemies. Graves is quite fixed upon the idea that this shrub represents strife and has negative values. On the other hand, the Farrars write in *Eight Sabbats for Witches* that:

> Blackthorn (sloe) is also a Goddess tree... but it belongs

to the Goddess in her dark, devouring aspect, as the bitterness of its autumn fruit would suggest. It used to be regarded as "the witches' tree"—in the malevolent sense—and unlucky.... Our women wear hawthorn in leaf and blackthorn in blossom, intertwined, in their celebrations for May Eve.

❧ Blessed Thistle ❧

Carduus Benedictus
Mars
Aries
Aphrodisiacal Herbe ... Magickal Herbe ... Religious Herbe
Invocatory: Pan

LORE

Blessed thistle may be used today in rituals to invoke the God principle, particularly embodied by Pan.

USAGE

An herbe which holds the ability to help a priest move into the more positive aspects of men's mysteries, blessed thistle is not known for its exceptional taste yet serves well in the ritual cup. It may be powdered and added to an incense mixture, or tossed into the fire as an offering. When working with sexual magick, blessed thistle assists in bringing the potent sexuality of Pan to manifestation within the priest. It may also be used in general when invoking any of the fertility gods.

This sacred member of the thistle family is sometimes associated with Yule, used to invoke the newly born Sun.

In the tarot, blessed thistle may be corresponded with the Emperor card, either to learn more about this major arcana or to bring those qualities into one's life. Blessed thistle is also used when studying the Page card of any suit within the minor arcana.

❧ Bluebells ❧

Scilla Nutans
Mars, Saturn, Uranus
Funereal Herbe
Also called: jacinth, wood bells

LORE

There is some confusion regarding a legend of Apollo, Hyacinthus and Zephrus. Hyacinthus is known as a very handsome (some might say beautiful) youth. Both Apollo and Zephrus are enamored of the boy, but Zephrus, a wind god, prefers Apollo and has just enough jealousy to lose his self-control. One day Apollo and Hyacinthus were playing at darts when a zephyr (a breeze under Zephrus' aegis) blows the dart off course. Apollo quickly tends to the dying lad who lays bleeding upon the grass. From Hyacinthus' blood arises the flower known today as the hyacinth. It is unknown whether this refers to what we think of as the actual hyacinth (*hyacinthus nonscriptus*) (which is not the domestic grape hyacinth found in our gardens) or to the bluebell (*scilla nutans*) which was known as *hyacinthus nonscriptus* before botanical clarification. Grieve records the myth for both flowers.

USAGE

Bluebells may be planted at grave sites and incorporated into rituals of death and dying. They may be used magickally in preparations to comfort those left behind and ease their sorrow. Bluebells make a wonderful memorial planting.

❧ Bogbean ❧

Menyanthes Trifoliata
Neptune
Religious Herbe
Invocatory: Puck
Also called: buckbean, marsh trefoil, water trefoil

LORE

In discussing the derivation of the name, Grieve suggests that an old English rhyme referring to "buckee" may indicate a connection between Puck and buckee, a nickname for bogbean.

USAGE

The use of bogbean to explore the myths of Robin Goodfellow and Puck is something which has merit, but is yet to be explored in modern times. Bogbean could be incorporated into ritual work to better understand the first aspect of the Horned God.

❦ Borage ❦

Borago Officinalis
Jupiter
Leo
Herbe of Protection ... Magickal Herbe

LORE

Some authors believe that the name borage is derived from either Celtic or Roman sources which implied its reputation as an herbe of good will or an herbe of courage and bravery (respectively). Borage has a long-standing reputation based upon its ability to improve one's outlook on life. It provides not only physical strength but also strength of character.

USAGE

Borage belongs in everyone's herbe closet. It is one of the best herbes to use when making a magickal tonic. The fresh flowers are beautiful when floated in one's bath, offering you a wondrous bathing herbe and a marvelous experience. The herbe itself may be taken as a tea or the root may be dried and powdered for use as an incense. Borage may be incorporated in a myriad of ways. No matter how difficult the times, borage is known for its ability to help raise one's spirits.

The Hierophant card is the major arcana card associated with borage. One may use the herbe in any magickal way to learn about the joyful responsibilities within this archetype.

❦ Box ❦

Buxus Sempervirens
Saturn
Herbe of Protection ... Religious Herbe

LORE

Box was once considered to be highly effective in the treatment of rabies.

USAGE

Box is a very valuable herbe for those who work with animal magick. Leaves of this herbe should be included in magickal workings to provide protection for one's pets and livestock, particularly those who roam freely out of doors.

The Farrars quote Doreen Valiente citing the custom of including box in Yule decorations.

❦ Broom ❦

Cytisus Scoparius
Mars
Herbe of Consecration ... Magickal Herbe ... Religious Herbe
Invocatory: Bloddeuwedd

LORE

Broom has a mixed reputation. Christian lore has, at times, considered it cursed, believing the seed pods made noise when Mary and Joseph passed nearby. In other cultures it is considered a symbol of good fortune. *The Master Book of Herbalism* suggests that this may be connected to the politics of the new (Christian) religion replacing customs and symbols of the old (pagan) religion.

USAGE

Broom is recommended for use when creating a sacred space. It makes an excellent ritual broom for sweeping any physical debris away as well as unwanted energy. The flowers are also considered symbols of good fortune and of plenty. The blooms may be picked, dried and added to magickal workings to increase your good fortune, but only if the plant is approached with humility and a fair exchange made with its deva before you begin your harvest. Small bunches may be gathered and dried with which to make an aspurger for your ritual circle.

This herbe is ideally suited for Handfastings, used to fashion the broom over which the newly joined couple will leap into their future.

When studying a Nine card of any suit of the minor arcana, broom may be used to better understand the nature of change life brings us as indicated within the symbols of these cards.

❦ Broom (Butcher's) ❦

Ruscus Aculeatus
Jupiter
Religious Herbe
Also called: Jew's myrtle, kneeholy, sweet broom

LORE

This variety of broom is used in Italy in the making of brooms, one of which would be among the best-suited ritual brooms for a Wiccan temple. The religious history of this herbe is indicated in its reference to the Hebrew peoples. Grieve records that it has been, at times, incorporated during the Feast of Tabernacles.

In the modern Irish alphabet the letter O or Onn is represented with broom, according to Graves. He also suggests that broom might be corresponded with the Sun, a correspondence not found elsewhere.

❦ Bryony (White) ❦

Bryonia Alba
Saturn
Magickal Herbe

LORE

Grieve researches the origins of the name in Greek, *bryo* meaning to shoot or to sprout forth. One of its common names in France is devil's turnip.

USAGE

This herbe would be superior for the deeper understanding of the spiritual path which exists within the Devil card. Appearing malevolent to many, one capable of moving within the inner mysteries will find profound spiritual understanding.

❦ Buckthorn (Sea) ❦

Hippophæ Rhamnoides
Saturn
Magickal Herbe ... Visionary Herbe

LORE

Believed to cure blindness in horses, its Latin name implies that it is able to bring light to an equine.

USAGE

Sea buckthorn may be used for animal magick, introduced to ritual workings in order to promote a special relationship between horse and rider. This herbe is capable of establishing a sense of communication which extends beyond sight.

❦ Buckwheat ❦

Polygonum Fagopyrum
Mercury, Pluto
Religious Herbe

LORE

Among some Hindu cultures, buckwheat is one of the few foods which may be eaten during certain religious holidays.

❦ Burnet (Great) ❦

Sanguisorba Officinalis
Sun
Countermagick Herbe ... Herbe of Consecration ...
Herbe of Protection

111

USAGE

Burnet is known for its ability to banish negative energy. It may be used in the consecration of ritual tools or may be used to treat depression and despondency. It is an excellent herbe for any type of magickal working.

🐾 Butterbur 🐾

Petasites Vulgaris
Sun
Herbe of Love ... Magickal Herbe
Also called: bog rhubarb, butterdock, umbrella plant

LORE

Grieve in *A Modern Herbal* has recorded for us a love custom:

> The seeds in some parts of the country have been used for love divination. The seeds of butterdock must be sowed by a young unmarried woman half an hour before sunrise on a Friday morning, in a lonesome place. She must strew the seeds gradually on the grass, saying these words:
> I sow, I sow!
> Then, my own dear,
> Come here, come here,
> And mow and mow!
> The seed being scattered, she will see her future husband mowing with a scythe at a short distance from her. She must not be frightened, for if she says, "Have mercy on me," he will immediately vanish! This method is said to be infallible, but it is looked upon as a bold, desperate, and presumptuous undertaking!

USAGE

Butterbur is used to raise one's spirits, increase a sense of hope and faith in life. For many centuries it was recommended infused in wine and makes a fine drink for the ritual cup.

❦ Cacao ❦

Theobroma Cacao
Uranus
Religious Herbe

USAGE

The first of its name, *Theobroma* by Linnæus, means "food of the gods." For some, chocolate may be used as a form of communion with the divinities.

❦ Calabar Bean ❦

Physostigma Venenosum
Saturn
Magickal Herbe

LORE

Some tribes of Africa use this herbe as a means of passing judgement over a person's guilt. Given to the accused to eat, the person either lives or dies which is seen as an indication of guilt or innocence.

USAGE

Dried beans may be employed in divination, used to determine the outcome of one facing judgement or in decision making. They should be used in the same manner as coins, straws or other objects. Under no circumstances should they be ingested.

❦ Calamint ❦

Calamintha Officinalis
Mercury
Magickal Herbe
Also called: basil thyme, mountain balm, mountain mint

USAGE

Calamint may be used as a tea or used as a bathing herbe. It is known for its ability to soothe one's sorrows, and help a person recover from emotional pain. This useful herbe can increase joy and restore a bright outlook on life.

❦ Camphor ❦

Cinnamomum Camphora
Moon
Funereal Herbe ... Herbe of Consecration ... Herbe of
Purification ... Religious Herbe ... Visionary Herbe

LORE

Camphor is employed in embalming and is also brought into burial rituals in some areas of East Asia. The wood of the tree is used when making masks for ritual theater performed in some Buddhist temples.

In *The Golden Bough* Frazer informs us that in Borneo the camphor tree is linked to beliefs about fidelity. By studying the way the knots grow in a tree, men determine whether their wives have been faithful. We consider this a questionable custom. It is not the property of camphor which lends itself to divination but the chauvinistic practice which has nothing to do with the camphor deva and everything to do with social manipulation.

USAGE

Known for its cleansing properties, camphor brings purification and removes all unwanted, dark energies. Leaving the natural energies cleansed and receptive, one's home or temple is able to readily absorb good, healing magick. Camphor is ideally suited for ritual cleansing prior to moving into a new home or for cleansing a temple before setting up one's altar and ritual tools. From the *Master Book of Herbalism* we find the following passage:

> When the home has been thoroughly cleansed, but before any possessions have been moved in, a thurible should be set in a central location and camphor burned upon a glowing block of charcoal. The smoke should be allowed to fill all the rooms of the residence, which is a sure way to exorcise old and unwanted energies.

Camphor also has divinatory properties. It may be burned upon charcoal with one's meditations in a quest for prophetic dreams. Some of the liquid may be added to water used in scrying. Camphor may be used as an incense in rituals of death and dying to

114

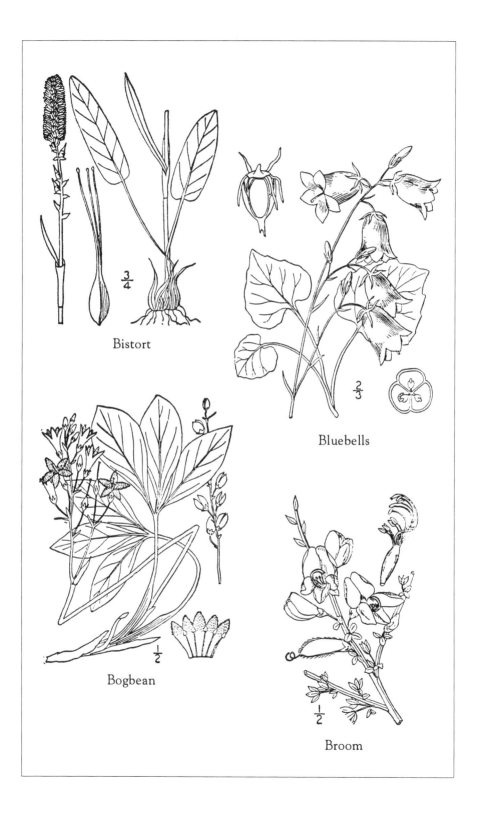

Bistort

$\frac{3}{4}$

Bluebells

$\frac{2}{3}$

Bogbean

$\frac{1}{2}$

Broom

$\frac{1}{2}$

help cleanse the spirit of the deceased of residual negative energy being carried into the next life.

Camphor is associated with two cards in the major arcana: the High Priestess card and the Chariot card and may be included in consecration rituals for any temple tools.

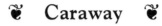 Caraway

Carum Carvi
Mercury
Greene Herbe ... Herbe of Consecration ... Herbe of Love ...
Herbe of Protection ... Magickal Herbe

LORE

Grieve has recorded for us two different aspects of folk customs involving caraway. In her entry, she writes that "caraway-seed cake was formerly a standing institution at the feasts given by farmers to their labourers at the end of the wheat-sowing" which should provide modern practitioners with insight into caraway's role in agricultural cycles and customs.

Even more fascinating is what Mrs. Grieve writes about caraway's retention property:

> A curious superstition was held in olden times about the caraway. It was deemed to confer the gift of retention, preventing the theft of any object which contained it, and holding the thief in custody within the invaded house. In like manner it was thought to keep lovers from proving fickle (forming an ingredient of love potions), and also to prevent fowls and pigeons from straying. It is an undoubted fact that tame pigeons, who are particularly fond of the seeds, will never stray if they are given a piece of baked caraway dough in their cote.

USAGE

Caraway has many uses beyond being included in recipes as a Greene Herbe. Baking is but one way to bring the virtue of longevity to a relationship and fidelity to the partners. It is as much fun to strew upon a couple as is rice, and should it later sprout from seed, a good addition to the local flora of the circle.

The quality of retention is an outstanding magickal property. Caraway may be used in any consecration of a ritual tool. It not only enhances the innate magick but will help that tool avoid straying from your home. In working to protect your possessions, avoid doing so out of a too-strong attachment to the mundane for this herbe will invoke the powers of the astral and could ask the gods to show you true wisdom.

Cakes or cookies made with caraway seed would be ideal for the ritual feast at either Lammas or the Autumn Equinox in celebration of the Harvest Festival.

❦ Carob ❦

Jascaranda Procera
Jupiter, Saturn
Religious Herbe
Also called: John's bread

LORE

Carob is found among the religious myths which describe how herbes came to be under human cultivation as gifts from their deities. Frequently, foods and herbes were stolen from a totem animal by a local hero. Among the Chiriguano tribe of South America, carob arrives through Aguara-Tunpa, a deity of foxes.

Sometimes called "John's bread" due to folk legends that this was the food Saint John the Baptist ate during his years in the wilderness.

USAGE

Carob may be used when making ritual cakes, for there is an aspect of divinity about its deva. It is an excellent herbe to use for anyone who has a fox as a totem animal or those working animal magick to protect foxes in their natural habitats.

❦ Cassia ❦

Cinnamomum Cassia
Mercury
Fertility Herbe ... Herbe of Immortality ... Religious Herbe
Invocatory: Heng-O

LORE

In Chinese mythology the lunar goddess Heng-O is associated with the cassia tree. Sacred to her is the rabbit which prepares the elixir of longevity and fertility. The hare, associated with the Moon, makes the elixir which Heng-O drinks in order to shape-shift into a toad, also considered a sacred lunar creature. In this lore, the cassia functions as a Tree of Life. It is called the "world tree" in some areas of the Himalayas and bestows knowledge of eternal life.

USAGE

Cassia imparts wisdom and gives us access to the mysteries of immortality. This relative of cinnamon brings a most agreeable scent to any temple mixtures, whether through incense or oil. It may be included in ritual cakes or in any other manner. It is well-suited for those who work with animals. Cassia may be used when working animal magick for rabbits or amphibians.

🐦 Castor 🐦

Ricinus Communis
Mars
Funereal Herbe ... Religious Herbe

LORE

The use of castor as a Religious Herbe predates the Christian era by many centuries. The Greek historian Herodotus documents its use among the Egyptians. Also known as *kiki*, according to Grieve it is "mentioned by Strabo as a production of Egypt, the oil from which is used for burning in lamps and for unguents." The seeds of the castor have frequently been found placed in tombs.

USAGE

There is not much modern usage of castor, although it is an herbe worthy of exploration. Modern tastes do not find the scent of the oil favorable and castor's importance in burial customs is not known.

❦ Catnip ❦

Nepeta Cataria
Venus
Libra
Fertility Herbe ... Magickal Herbe ... Religious Herbe ...
Visionary Herbe
Invocatory: Bast, Sekhet
Also called: catmint

USAGE

Although there is little documented magickal history, the magickal properties of catnip have brought it into contemporary prominence. It has some history as a charm to cure barrenness and may yet be used to bring fertility either to one's magick or to one's womb. Catnip is also corresponded with all four Nine cards in tarot's minor arcana. A tea of this herbe can enhance your ability to interpret these archetypes.

Catnip may be used when working with the Egyptian Bubastis, more commonly known as Bast. She is a daughter of Isis with human body and feline head and instinct. As does a cat, she loves the aspect of the Sun which is warm and loving. One might also use catnip to invoke Sekhmet, sister of Bubastis who is part human and part lion. This goddess works with the ferocious aspect of solar energy which can be both dangerous and fierce. Either of these divine feline goddesses would surely love this herbe. As one would guess, this favorite herbe of cats is corresponded with the Strength card in the tarot.

The Master Book of Herbalism cites a mixture of catnip with dragon's blood as an incense to be used to rid one's self of a behavioral problem or other bad habits.

There are many today who use catnip to enhance their skills at shape-shifting or journeying into the night in the guise of a cat. Catnip is an herbe which promotes a loving and healing energy for your feline familiars.

119

❦ Catsfoot ❦

Antennaria Dioica
Sun
Magickal Herbe

LORE

The folklore of England holds that this plant contains the power of a cat's nine lives and may help the practitioner live a very long life.

❦ Cedar ❦

Thuja Occidentalis
Mercury, Uranus
Virgo
Herbe of Consecration ... Magickal Herbe ... Religious Herbe ...
Visionary Herbe
Invocatory: Odin

LORE

The religious history of cedar may be contemplated when reading Grieve's study of the word *Thuja*, as "a latinized form of a Greek word meaning 'to fumigate,' or *thuo* (to sacrifice), for the fragrant wood was burned by the ancients with sacrifices."

Cedars are revered in many cultures. The oldest cedars in Lebanon are held to be very sacred and the cedar may be considered a Tree of Life.

Frazer describes a Hindu practice in which an oracle is invoked when the seer breathes in the smoke of burning cedar until she is overtaken with prophecy.

USAGE

Cedar is well known for its fragrance. It is often powdered and added to incense mixtures. An incense including cedar is considered ideal in the consecration of a magickal wand. Either a wand carved of cedar or a cedar-blend incense may be used to invoke Odin. This incense may also be used in Wiccanings and baby blessings. Cedar has an ancient history of being associated with the Summer Solstice. We may use it today when celebrating Midsummer.

Integrated into tarot correspondences, cedar may be used in the study of the Four cards of the minor arcana. Its magickal association with wands also lends it to usage with any card of the suit of wands or clubs. Cedar works within the major arcana when one seeks the mysteries which can be taught to us by the Magician card.

As a protected tree in magickal cultures, to harm a cedar is to invoke misfortune. The spirits of the cedar are believed to be both powerful and persistent.

Popular lore associates cedar with amethyst and sapphire. Cedar boxes, commonly found in gift stores, are appropriate for storing these gemstones. *The Master Book of Herbalism* states that "unicorns absolutely love to have little cedar boxes around in which to store their treasures." This entry goes on to say that "carrying a small piece of Cedar in one's billfold or wallet will attract money. It certainly will keep the moths away."

🍂 Celandine (Greater) 🍂

Chelidonium Majus
Sun, Mars
Leo
Magickal Herbe ... Religious Herbe

LORE

In medieval times it was believed that celandine could be used to help one be victorious over all enemies. Albertus Magnus wrote that this formula required the heart of a mole. Our gardens contain a beautiful celandine and are overrun with moles; despite their bothersome tunnels and mounds of dirt, moles are children of the Goddess as much as we are.

USAGE

Gerard believed that this plant was good for one's eyesight. It is used by some practitioners as an appropriate herbe to integrate in seasonal rituals to celebrate and represent the waxing of the Sun.

The solar victorious energy of this herbe remains useful today. Working with celandine is appropriate when seeking victory. It may be used in conjunction with the Sun card and may be used to increase one's self-confidence when facing adversaries. And no, you do not need to sacrifice any furry creatures—sacrifice only your fears.

❦ Celery ❦

Apium Graveolens
Mercury
Greene Herbe ... Visionary Herbe

USAGE

Pay attention when you use celery (especially the seed) in your cooking. It is believed that an infusion of the seed is good for one's mental abilities, increasing clarity and insight. Celery may be used to enhance one's divinatory skills. Modern use has occasionally found celery seed included in Candlemas rituals, during which it is sometimes ingested and sometimes strewn into the ritual fire.

❦ Centaury ❦

Erythræa Centaurium
Sun
Countermagick Herbe ... Herbe of Protection ... Magickal Herbe ... Visionary Herbe
Invocatory: Chiron

LORE

Centaury is associated with the legendary centaur Chiron. Chiron was the mentor of Jason, providing him with the training necessary for Jason's quest to obtain the golden fleece. Residing on Mount Pelion, Chiron is also noted for his role as father-figure for Aesculapius, later a famed physician in Greek mythology. Apollo rescued Aesculapius when he was but a boy after his father died and brought him to Chiron who would raise and educate the boy in the use of herbal remedies. Jason and Aesculapius were but two of a number of youths raised by Chiron. Of all centaurs, Chiron has the most wide-spread recognition and is later elevated to astral status within the constellation Sagittarius.

Centaury was a noted Magickal Herbe during the medieval era. It was used by witches who were said to mix it into their incenses, increasing their psychic powers and taking them into trance-like states. Mrs. Grieve's singular research provides us with the following reference from *Le Petit Albert*. It should be pointed out that *The Book of Secrets* contains an almost verbatim passage.

> The eleventh herbe is named of the Chaldees, Isiphon... of Englishmen, Centory...this herbe hath a marvellous virtue, for if it be joined with the blood of a female lapwing, or black plover, and put with oile in a lamp, all that compass it about shall believe themselves to be witches, so that one shall believe of another that his head is in heaven and his feete on earth; and if the aforesaid thynge be put in the fire when the starres shine it shall appeare yt the starres runne one agaynste another and fyghte. [English translation, 1619]

USAGE

Centaury may be added as a Magickal Herbe to most mixtures. It is one of those famed *witches' herbes* which adds power to the mixture. This is a useful herbe when working with meditation or visualization. Centaury is a patron herbe of herbalists.

This herbe may be used to repel anger and other hurtful energy. It is one of the more effective herbes for protecting the modern practitioner against unwanted energies.

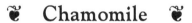

❧ Chamomile ❧

Anthemis Nobilis
Sun
Magickal Herbe ... Religious Herbe

LORE

Chamomile is a venerable herbe with a well-established reputation as a healer. It was believed that it brought health to one's gardens and promoted healing energies which were good for all plant species. Whereas centaury is a patron herbe of herbalists, chamomile is a patron herbe for the gardens.

USAGE

The strong association chamomile has with the Sun is an under-lying indication of its modern usage. Through incense or ritual drink it is used to assist a priest's call upon a Sun god (working with any of the solar deities). Some traditions have also used chamomile at Midsummer to give honor to the Father of Nature.

Useful in solar holidays, chamomile has been incorporated into Yule traditions. The options are endless, ranging from using it as a bathing herbe for the male chosen to represent the newly born Sun to powdering it and spooning it onto burning coals to cense the temple area and prepare it for a celebration of solar magick.

Chamomile, though not commonly recognized for its magick, car-ries the magick of success and may be included in most recipes.

❦ Chaste Tree ❦

Agnus Castus
Moon, Pluto
Religious Herbe
Invocatory: Ceres, Demeter

LORE

Grieve recorded the Greek belief that the chaste tree seeds repre-sented chastity and that the leaves were used ritually to invoke Ceres.

USAGE

Chaste tree is a most useful herbe for modern Goddess worship. The seeds may be used to invoke the maiden virginal aspect of the Goddess, and may also be used to move a priestess into the mysteries of the crone.

Historical association with Ceres, a Roman agricultural goddess, lends the herbe's use for religious fertility workings for the har-vest. In this association, chaste tree brings forth the under-standing of the Goddess as mother.

Often overlooked by modern practitioners, chaste tree has very strong associations with Goddess worship. The powdered seed or powdered dried berries would be an excellent incense for Drawing Down the Moon, the berries also making a superb ritual cup.

❦ Cherry ❦

Prunus Serotina
Venus
Herbe of Consecration

USAGE

Modern lore suggests that cherry bark be collected when one wishes to revitalize the magickal energy needed to complete an old project. Cherry blossoms or bark may be used as an incense to assist a novice in the pathworking when the time of initiation draws nigh.

❦ Cherry (Winter) ❦

Physalis Alkekengi
Mercury
Magickal Herbe
Also called: Chinese lanterns

USAGE

Eight berries from the winter cherry are taken to coincide with each of the lunar cycles, and are said to work with the Moon's quarters. Grieve cites this as a cure for gout using this practice. This lore suggests that winter cherry is a useful herbe for working a magickal healing.

❦ Chervil ❦

Anthriscus Cerefolium
Jupiter
Funereal Herbe ... Green Herbe ... Herbe of Immortality ...
Religious Herbe ... Magickal Herbe
Also called: anise chervil, British myrrh, sweet cicely, sweet fern

LORE

In *The Master Book of Herbalism* we find that "an elixir of the herbe, or its use as incense in a ritual will bring the user a greater sense of those parts of the self which will exist beyond life."

USAGE

Chervil is a superior herbe for placing one's self in touch with one's divine, immortal spirit. It may be used in almost any magickal working. In the tarot, chervil helps one learn about the Judgement card.

When working ritual to assist the beloved (one who has taken final leave of the incarnate body), it provides assistance in making contact and in helping the beloved reach those astral temples which were established during the incarnation as a gathering place for those of both worlds. Chervil is best used in rituals of death and dying performed after interment of either cremated remains or corpse.

❦ Chestnut ❦

Castanea Vesca
Jupiter
Fertility Herbe ... Herbe of Love ... Magickal Herbe
Also called: Jupiter's nut

USAGE

These hearty nuts are believed to enhance male sexuality. They are sometimes used to represent the male testes in ritual decoration and may be used to increase male potency.

Graves describes the chestnut as "bashful." This herbal tree might be of value for those who wish to overcome their shyness or for those with egos too demanding of attention.

❦ Chickweed ❦

Stellaria Media
Moon
Magickal Herbe

USAGE

This gentle herbe is useful when working with lunar magick. Many centuries have enhanced the belief that chickweed is an

Caraway

Castor

Catsfoot

ideal herbe for birds. Chickweed is a suitable patron herbe for those who work animal magick, particularly the healing of birds.

❦ Chicory ❦

Cichorium Intybus
Uranus
Magickal Herbe

USAGE

This herbe may be integrated into healing and magick in order to promote a more positive outlook on life and to improve one's sense of humor.

❦ Chrysanthemum ❦

Anacyclus Pyrethrum
Mercury, Uranus
Herbe of Immortality
Also called: anthemis, pellitory, pyrethrum

USAGE

Modern associations of the chrysanthemum make it a common flower seen when giving honor to those who have passed into the next world. It may be used in rituals of death and dying. In Japan, the chrysanthemum is honored on September 9. Since the time of Culpeper this herbe has been used to promote mental health.

❦ Cinnamon ❦

Cinnamomum Zeylanica
Sun, Uranus
Greene Herbe ... Herbe of Consecration ... Herbe of Love ...
Herbe of Purification ... Magickal Herbe ... Visionary Herbe

LORE

Cinnamon was used as an incense in the temples of ancient China.

USAGE

More than one modern love potion formula includes cinnamon along with other Herbes of Love. As a Magickal Herbe it can be added to any mixture for internal use or for incense, or it can be placed within an amulet to increase one's patterns of good fortune.

Cinnamon works magically with one's mind. It increases concentration and would be a well-chosen herbe for those who have trouble focusing. This bark may be used to learn about trust when decision making and is corresponded to the Lovers card. Cinnamon is sometimes associated with tourmaline and would be an ideal herbe for consecrating any ritual item set with that lovely gemstone. A container of cinnamon which is set aside for temple use would be empowered if a small piece of tourmaline is included.

Modern usage continues the custom of temple purification. The magick of this herbe is said to be peaceful, enabling the correct mind-set for ritual work. Cinnamon may be used to enhance one's skill with prophecy through channeling, working with an oracle or through divination.

❦ Cinquefoil ❦

Potentilla Reptans
Mercury, Jupiter
Virgo
Herbe of Protection ... Magickal Herbe ... Religious Herbe ...
Visionary Herbe
Also called: five-leaf grass, potentilla, synkefoyle

LORE

Cinquefoil is one of those herbes associated with vile mixtures of frequently noxious herbes and animal parts attributed to medieval witches. It was said to have been used in the legendary flying ointment and also in spells associated with the placing of hexes upon others.

This five-leafed herbe has positive associations and it is these which hold our attention. Cinquefoil is frequently found in spell magick associated with romance. It has also been used to promote an abundant harvest, particularly for those in fishing villages.

USAGE

The best cinquefoil is believed to be that which is gathered when the Moon waxes full as a Wednesday night becomes Thursday morning. A perfectly formed five-fingered leaf should be gathered, dried and pressed into one's diary. Such a leaf is considered solid magick to bring protection to a friend or loved traveler who is taking a journey.

Cinquefoil is associated with the maternal aspect of the Goddess as She permeates all of nature. As a Magickal Herbe it is used in divination (burned as incense) to dream of one's intended mate.

This herbe may be used as a patron herbe for those who love fishing and those who make their living from harvesting seafoods, helping to ensure a good catch.

Cinquefoil is believed to contain the energy which can be used in ritual to manifest one's ideas. It is a most useful herbe but should be used with care. Its religious properties are utilized through its association with both Beltane and Midsummer.

❦ Clary ❦

Salvia Sclarea
Moon
Herbe of Protection ... Visionary Herbe

USAGE

Clary is known for its ability to enhance vision, protecting not only one's physical eyesight but promoting increased skill while in meditation and visionary states. The seeds are the most useful part of the plant for this purpose and may be extracted as a wash to make a magickal lotion which may be used in the magickal healing of afflictions to a person's sight.

❦ Clover ❦

Trifolium Pratense
Mercury, Venus
Taurus
Herbe of Consecration ... Magickal Herbe ... Visionary Herbe
Also called: trefoil

USAGE

Although sometimes called red, it frequently ranges from a pink-ish red to the purple color we are more accustomed to seeing. One may offer a flower stalk when seeking a promise of fidelity from one's partner. If one agrees to monogamy, a white clover bloom may be given in exchange. Clover used when exchanging the promises made within a relationship is best gathered when the Moon is full.

In Ireland clover is associated with the Vernal Equinox and may be used to celebrate Eostara. In modern tarot magick, clover is used when studying the Five cards of the minor arcana. An excel-lent herbe with a strong association with elemental earth, clover is useful in the consecration of any ritual items made of copper and should be included when ritually consecrating a pentacle.

❦ Cloves ❦

Eugenia Caryophyllata
Uranus
Aquarius
Greene Herbe ... Magickal Herbe ... Religious Herbe ...
Visionary Herbe

LORE

From Frazer in *The Golden Bough* we learn that on certain islands of Indonesia in the Malay Archipelago the clove trees are consid-ered very sacred. When they come into bloom they are treated with the same care and respect given to pregnant women.

USAGE

This is a particularly delightful herbe to include in your kitchen magick. Although not green in color, its function as both a familiar kitchen herbe and a bringer of magick has it listed as a Greene Herbe. Cloves bring magick. You may find them included in love philtres, but they are more useful in bringing a sense of kinship to a social gathering.

Cloves may be used in ritual work. Adding them to an incense mixture furthers one's ability to be psychically sensitive. Those who desire astral sight should work with cloves. Although ground and mixed into one's personal incense mixture is the most common use, a tea of cloves may also be used. Cloves correspond with the Star card in the major arcana.

❦ Coca ❦

Erythroxylon Coca
Saturn, Uranus
Funereal Herbe

LORE

Some tribes of South America bury ritually prepared parcels of coca with the body of the beloved. They believe this will please the spirits and make entry into the next world easier.

USAGE

It is unfortunate that humans have abused the coca plant to the degree that any use of this herbe is strictly forbidden. One might, however, when being given a shot of novocaine during dental work think of that injection as somehow pleasing to the spirits so that you are kept free from pain.

❦ Coconut ❦

Cocos Nucifera
Moon
Fertility Herbe ... Funereal Herbe ... Religious Herbe
Invocatory: Lugeilan, Sri

LORE

Among the Melanesian Islands is a creation myth in which the first four men throw coconuts upon the ground. From these arise the first four women. There is very likely some correspondence with the four elements to be found among these four pairs of the first humans.

The peoples of the Caroline Islands believe that the coconut is sacred to their god Lugeilan and represents life. Lugeilan taught them all the ways in which this food and useful herbe could sustain life. Through the coconut they learn of both life and death. Frazer in *The Golden Bough* informs us of the following:

> In northern India the coco-nut [sic] is esteemed one of the most sacred fruits, and is called Sriphala, or the fruit of Sri, the goddess of prosperity. It is the symbol of fertility, and all through Upper India is kept in shrines and presented by the priests to women who desire to become mothers.

Many Hindu people place four coconuts into the coffin to bring the deceased good luck while the deceased is on the way to heaven. This is done before the coffin is cremated.

USAGE

A coconut shell may be hollowed and cleaned for use as a ritual container. If one wished to give honor to the creation magick of the Melanesian Islands, an offering of coconut milk could be offered at the four directions.

The coconut may also be integrated into rituals of death and dying. One method is to prepare a shell which can be carried among the family and friends collecting slips of paper for good wishes and expressions of love for the deceased.

❦ Coffee ❦
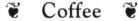

Coffea Arabica
Mercury, Uranus
Religious Herbe

LORE

Coffee has been a sacred drink within the pyramid cultures of the western hemisphere. The Aztec, Mayan and Incan peoples all revered the berries of this herbe. In Malaya the leaf is used, which is stronger than the berries.

133

If used as a ritual stimulant, the practitioner should abstain from drinking coffee on any other basis.

❦ Coltsfoot ❦

Tussilago Farfara
Venus

USAGE

The modern herbalist may consider coltsfoot as a patron herbe; during the French apothecaire, a likeness of flowering coltsfoot was painted on the sign to denote herbal medicines.

❦ Columbine ❦

Aquilegia Vulgaris
Venus
Libra
Magickal Herbe

LORE

This lovely, flowering herbe is associated with the eagle as a totem animal: its Latin name *aquila* means eagle.

USAGE

Columbine has long been one of our favorite herbes, adding a welcome to the plant devas in one's gardens. In the tarot, Columbine is associated with the Empress card.

Practitioners of animal magick, those working with the eagle as a totem animal and those wishing to invoke the protective spirit or divinity associated with the realm of birds may work with columbine.

❦ Comfrey ❦

Symphytum Officinale
Saturn
Capricorn
Herbe of Protection ... Magickal Herbe

USAGE

A leaf of comfrey is believed to provide safekeeping while travel-ing, bringing the traveler safely home from a journey. Comfrey is also a good herbe to include in any magickal healing.

❦ Coriander ❦

Coriandrum Sativum
Moon, Mars
Greene Herbe ... Herbe of Immortality ... Herbe of Love ...
Herbe of Protection ... Magickal Herbe

LORE

This herbe has associations with Saint Anthony whose interces-sion may grant healing. The use of coriander is very old; it was found among artifacts from ancient Egypt and those from the tribes of the Israelites.

USAGE

From *The Master Book of Herbalism* we learn that Coriander is believed to "protect the gardener and all who reside in the gar-dener's household. It may be gathered at the harvest season, and a bunch of it hung within the home as an Herbe of Protection, decorated with ribbon to bring peace and security to the house." As such, it is a patron herbe.

Magickally, the seeds of this herbe will bring peace within one's home and may be used ritually to promote peace among peoples who are unable to get along. It can be used within the ritual cup or the seeds can be ground and added to the incense. Coriander is also used to help one find romance and love and is an excellent herbe to add to an elixir shared when the Great Rite is celebrated. At rituals of union, it may be strewn in lieu of rice or added to the Handfasting cake.

135

This kitchen herbe has the ability to open one to the eternal nature of reality, helping one attune to the highest ideals of one's soul. One of its most sacred uses is to promote the astral nature of a union so that the couple may return together and continue their relationship in the next incarnation.

🍎 Corn 🍎

Zea Mays
Pluto
Fertility Herbe ... Greene Herbe ... Religious Herbe
Invocatory: Aitvarasm, Centeotl, Demeter, Deving Cerklicing, Fides, Hades, Laukosargas, Luatiku, Mithra, Saturn, Tammuz, Ukemochi, Veles, Zara-mama

LORE

This is truly one of the great Religious Herbes of all peoples, although "corn" was sometimes actually "barley" in ancient myths which may have created hybrid legends. The numbers of diverse peoples who recognize the existence of a feminine spirit within this essential grain create a long list. The Greeks believed corn sacred to the goddess Demeter, often showing her with ears of corn. Consistent with their belief that fruitfulness is found only when there is a balance between the fields and the deep world of spirit, corn is also associated with Hades. Roman culture also recognized the power of corn. Saturn is sometimes depicted carrying ears of this essential grain. European pagans worshipped the corn mother with customs that lasted well into modern times. Frazer in *The Golden Bough* describes the customs of many regions which utilize various aspects of fertility beliefs with the making of corn dollies. In many areas the corn mother later becomes a harvest goddess.

A bull was offered as a sacrifice to Mithra, a well-known deity who originated in what was Persia. An ear of corn attached to the bull's tail caused the offering to promote fertility among the harvests.

In the Slovak regions of Europe, the husks of the final ears of corn brought from the harvest are braided in honor of Veles, an agrarian goddess. This is done to ask her blessing for a fertile growing season in the coming year.

Baltic pagans believed that Laukosargas was the protector of the corn and guardian of the fields. This deity may have been more of a deva or nature deity than a major figure in their pantheon. Another agrarian spirit was Kurke, around whom ritualized practices developed. Kurke hid himself in the last ears of corn being gathered. Without the rituals offered to him, he would bring bad luck in the coming year.

A Prussian kitchen deity, Aitvarasm, who brings good luck is welcomed into one's home by leaving out some corn. A Latvian deity, Deving Cerklicing, was guardian of fields and corn. He was given offerings of beer.

The indigenous nature religion of Japan, Shintoism, has the belief that corn first grew from the body of the goddess Ukemochi. Corn is included in their harvest festivals along with prayers for abundance.

In the western hemisphere corn is equally sacred. Goddesses of corn or maize are found throughout the Americas. The Aztec goddess Centeotl is a patroness of agriculture and corn is under her domain. From Frazer in *The Golden Bough* we learn that the people of Peru recognize the spirits or divinities of the plants used for food, healing or other important functions in life. Their corn mother is known as Zara-mama. Peruvian mythology teaches that corn originated from the teeth of the first human child, born of the union of the first man and the first woman. The Aymara peoples of Bolivia connect the sly fox to their legends; the fox brought maize back from the sky. The legends of the Caingua teach that corn first grew upon the earth when their ancestral hero's body was dragged through the fields after his death (as he had requested). Maize sprung up from his sexual organs.

Corn was grown in many areas of North America and the Maize Mother is found in a number of different cultures. The Zuni peoples grew six varieties of corn, representing the four directions and above and below. From *Larousse World Mythology* we learn that the Keresan Pueblo peoples called the Maize Mother Lua-tiku. She was the mother of all and before she descended to the Underworld, she gave maze to the people, saying, "This is my heart, it will be your food, and the sap from it will be like milk from my breast."

Frazer writes of the Mandan and Minnataree women who celebrated the corn-medicine festival in the spring, giving honor to the Old Woman Who Never Dies, who maintains the life of the crops and brings migrating birds back as a sign of renewal. The wild goose heralded the success of the new growing season's corn crop.

In Central America the Huichol people, who derive much of their culture from the Aztec, believe that the cultivation of corn was taught by their ancestral hero, Majakuagy. The Quiche believed that maize was the one crop which elevated their race. There are numerous references to maize throughout *Larousse World Mythology* which provide us with a grand view of the sacredness of this plant.

From *The Golden Bough*, however, we discover that corn is not always associated with the realm of the Goddess. A tenth century author describes a long-existing festival which sees the Babylonian god Tammuz embodied in the corn.

USAGE

Corn is an appropriate herbe to be brought into the temple or carried through the fields to represent fertility, to invoke the Mother of Nature and ask for her blessings, or to work magickally for abundance. Corn is an integral aspect of so many religions and associated with a multitude of deities, primarily goddesses able to teach all mysteries of life, death and rebirth.

Those who work magickally with foxes might remember the legend in which the fox takes a divine role in bringing us corn.

Corn is grown in our garden in order to be integrated into the sabbat observed at the Autumn Equinox but assists us in turning the Wheel of the Year at Lammas as well.

❦ Cornflower ❦

Centaurea Cyanus
Venus, Saturn
Religious Herbe ... Visionary Herbe
Invocatory: Chiron, Flora
Also called: bluebottle, blue cap, bluet

138

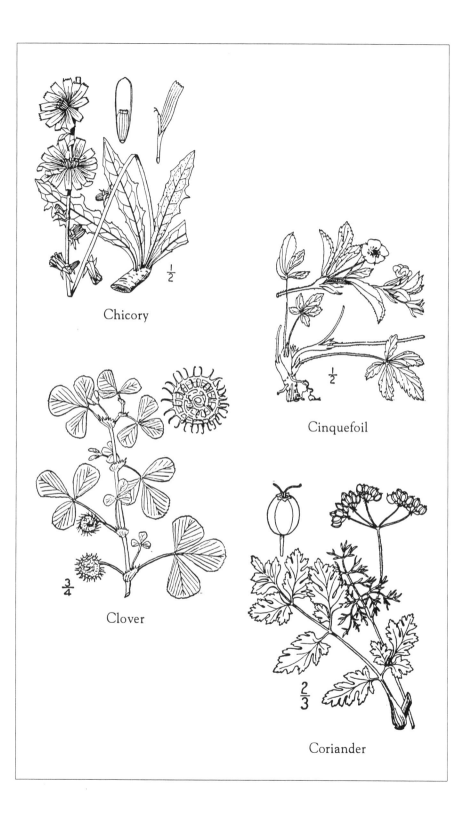

Chicory

Cinquefoil

Clover

Coriander

LORE

This beautifully flowering herbe is associated with both the goddess Flora and her annual celebration, Floralia, which is centered around Beltane, beginning in late April and running into May. Cornflower is also associated with the centaur Chiron and may be considered a patron herbe of herbalists.

USAGE

In *The Master Book of Herbalism* we are told that cornflowers may be

> filtered through three layers of blue linen and then ritually consecrated beneath the full Moon with a moonstone; it may be used to bathe the eyes, bringing an increased sense of clairvoyance, enabling one to see aspects of the creative forces of the Universe.

The beautiful, blue color of the petals lends their use to handmade ink, one which would be most pleasing for a Book of Shadows. These flowers may be used to decorate a temple or otherwise used to assist women in giving honor to the Mother of all Nature. The flowers may also be used in the ritual cup.

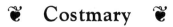

❦ Costmary ❦

Tanacetum Balsamita
Jupiter
Religious Herbe

LORE

A number of European cultures associate costmary with Mary, mother of Jesus. One of its older names was Herbe Sainte-Marie.

USAGE

It is possible that this lore reflects an earlier association of costmary with a goddess, and the practice was transformed as Christianity assimilated the earlier nature religion. We believe this herbe lends itself to rituals of Goddess worship.

❦ Cotton ❦

Gossypium Barrbadense
Sun, Pluto
Religious Herbe

LORE

The Munduruco tribe of South America believe that cotton is sacred to their creator who wove a rescue rope of cotton to save a friend of his. The friend had been chasing an armadillo and fell through a hole into the Underworld.

❦ Cowslip ❦

Primula Veris
Venus
Aries
Herbe of Protection ... Magickal Herbe ... Religious Herbe
Invocatory: Freya

LORE

This member of the primrose family is held sacred to Freya, the Norse goddess of love and was used in rituals giving honor to her. As with many herbes once associated with nature goddesses, following the Christian occupation cowslip became associated with Mary.

USAGE

The flowers can be decorative or the herbe can be infused into an elixir for any priestess desiring to invoke Freya, as this goddess represents the second aspect of the Goddess (that of mother). Cowslip may be similarly used in ritual work with any goddess associated with love. From *The Master Book of Herbalism* we discover the following:

> It is thought to bring a sense of direction to the practitioner, one which would take the spirit of the source of Freya's Goddess energy and bestow mysteries which would keep the practitioner in Freya's grace. Some believed that following the path of the mysteries to Freya would grant earth-plane treasures and abundance.

141

Cowslip is believed to increase one's attractiveness (this virtue referred to even by Shakespeare). It also brings an increase in one's romantic appeal and helps bring about internal changes which can stimulate the energy to attract that special partner.

Many rural people held this herbe as sacred. The flowers were gathered and hung in bunches over the doorway to bring protection.

Those who desire to grow a magickal garden would do well to have cowslips growing in one or more patches. Grieve cites lore which indicates its favor with the devas and the realm of the faerie:

> On the yellow disk are five red spots, one on each petal.
> In their gold coats spots you see,
> These be rubies fairy favours
> In those freckles lie their savours.

This is an excellent herbe for increasing one's skills at keeping a mental focus while sustaining concentration during any ritual work.

❦ Cranberry ❦

Viburnum Trilobum
Neptune
Greene Herbe ... Religious Herbe

LORE

The mythology of Finland contains a legend involving the cranberry with virgin birth. Marjatta, a maiden goddess, gives birth to a child conceived through her eating of a cranberry. She is sent away from her parents in disgrace because there is no father. Marjatta, homeless, gives birth to the baby in a stable. Wainamoinen, whose parents are the father of oceans and a goddess of air, adopts the baby as heir to his divine kingdom.

USAGE

Cranberries are well-suited for the Yule celebration. It is, possibly, their traditional use in the decorating of holiday trees which shares common bonds with the Finnish story.

❦ Crowfoot ❦

Ranunculus Acris
Mars
Herbe of Love

LORE

This buttercup relative is associated with Hymen, a Greek god who is a companion of Eros, the god of love. Hymen was known as the god of marriage and rituals of union. Hymen is also associated with the passage of the maiden into her new role as the mother.

USAGE

Crowfoot may be used in all rituals and ceremonies associated with Handfasting and marriage; with customs associated with asking for another's hand; in rituals which make commitments and vows sacred and binding. The ideal usage is when the blossoms are worn or used in other decorative ways.

❦ Cubeb ❦

Piper Cubeba
Mars
Aphrodisiacal Herbe

USAGE

Cubebs, according to *The Master Book of Herbalism*, have been "used as an aphrodisiac, ground and mixed with honey. Taking a regular dose of the mixture has been said to prolong erection, increase passion, and greatly increase the physical activity of lovemaking and sex. (They appear) to be used primarily for men."

There are a number of methods for using the cubeb to increase male potency. Customarily, these peppers may be macerated into oils which will be used as sacred lubricants during the Great Rite. Care must be exercised as excess amounts will cause uncomfortable irritation.

143

❦ Cucumber ❦

Cucumis Sativa
Moon
Greene Herbe ... Visionary Herbe
Invocatory: Uttu

LORE

Enki provided the goddess Uttu, of Sumerian myths, with cucumbers as part of his offering of marriage gifts. It is only after this final offering that she accepts him. Cucumbers are sacred to Uttu.

USAGE

Cucumbers have found modern use. Lunar by nature, they are cooling and soothing to one's soul and psyche. The peels have been used, sliced thin, lain across one's eyelids for meditation or to further one's ability to travel within the astral.

❦ Cumin ❦

Cuminum Cyminum
Mars
Taurus
Aphrodisiacal Herbe ... Greene Herbe ... Herbe of Protection ...
Magickal Herbe

LORE

Mrs. Grieve tells us that the Greeks saw this herbe as a symbol of greed, of one's self being out of balance through an excessive attraction to manifest reality. It is quite possible that there were political origins for this belief. We know that cumin was once so valuable that it was used as a means of payment.

USAGE

In correspondence with the Hierophant card, this herbe can be used to promote a healthy balance of one's interaction within both the spiritual and mundane worlds. It can be used magickally to provide protection for one's home and one's kindred. It has sometimes been employed in modern spells, calling for a small pinch of the ground seed to increase good fortune and prosperity.

144

Cumin is also found in some recipes designed to increase one's sexual appetite. There are some practitioners (usually men) who believe that a pinch of cumin should be part of one's daily diet in order to prolong virility.

❦ Cyclamen (Ivy-Leafed) ❦

Cyclamen Hederæfolium
Mars
Herbe of Love
Also called: sowbread

LORE

Research into older European spell magick shows this herbe was believed to have the ability to make someone fall passionately (and permanently) in love with the practitioner. This species of cyclamen was baked into small cakes and it was necessary for the practitioner to get her (his) intended to eat the cake.

USAGE

For those who are foolish enough to work herbal magick to bend another's will to romance, this is a useful herbe—but the price may well be dear.

Cyclamen is better used to reinforce the romance between consensual partners. It can be added to Handfasting or wedding cakes. It might also be baked into a different type of cake which might be used in the renewal of vows.

A couple which works ritual together and shares the Great Rite could use this herbe to further the astral nature of their work and increase the potential of their union carrying into the next incarnation.

❦ Cypress ❦

Cupressis sp.
Saturn, Neptune
Herbe of Immortality ... Religious Herbe
Invocatory: Apollo, Cyparissus, Hades

LORE

In one of the homosexual myths of Greece, Apollo becomes involved with Cyparissus. One afternoon near Midsummer, Cyparissus was hunting and playing in the woods, with his pet stag. Accidentally, he kills his stag with a spear. Apollo hears his lament which touches his heart deeply. Cyparissus longs for death to ease his sorrow and reunite him with his stag. Although Apollo wishes to honor his lover's request, he cannot bear to lose him forever. In a stroke of divine wisdom, Apollo changes him into the cypress. This tree is sometimes seen as a symbol of sadness, but is more often used as a symbol of resurrection and reincarnation.

The cypress is one of the trees considered sacred to Hades.

USAGE

Despite the sorrowful aspect of the Greek legend, there are many possibilities for the magickal use of this herbe. Sorrow is but a reaction to death among those who do not have divine knowledge of the mysteries.

In this legend, Cyparissus becomes the cypress only through Apollo's love for him. There is this aspect of the tree which lends itself to the expression of that romantic love between men, of a love so strong that one partner would endure separation to grant the wish of another, of a love capable of transcending death. This herbe may be considered a patron herbe

Cypress might also be used by those who wish to establish a bonding with their familiars which is capable of being carried into one's next reincarnation.

The association of Cyparissus with the stag should not be overlooked. There are many today who work with the magick of the legendary King Stag of the forest. Cypress bark, dried and powdered, would make a superior incense for this work. The bark could be collected and woven into a breechcloth to be worn when running as the stag. Those with imagination will easily find many joyful customs which will keep the magick of the cypress alive.

❦ Daffodil ❦

Narcissus Pseudo-Narciccus
Venus, Mars (yellow), Saturn
Countermagick Herbe ... Herbe of Protection ... Herbe of
Purification ... Magickal Herbe

LORE

Grieve refers to an ointment made in ancient times called Narcissimum, based upon the daffodil, but no other information on what it might be is available. We liked the name Narcissimum and wanted to share it with you.

Albertus Magnus suggests that the daffodil can be used to rid people of evil spirits and places this herbe under Saturn. He also writes that it can be used to keep evil devils from entering one's home.

USAGE

Little specific information can be found regarding the daffodil. In *The Master Book of Herbalism* we find this reference:

> For yellow daffodils, collect the root on Tuesday beneath the waxing Moon. The other colors are ruled by Venus, and may be gathered on a Friday, or beneath any full Moon. The root should be dried, finely ground, and this powder worked into magickal balms, ointments and unguents.

Coming into bloom at the spring in most climates, they are often used to decorate the temple. Holding with old beliefs, the daffodil can be used to repel negative energies from outside sources and would be useful in exorcising dark forces from within a person. According to the editors of *The Book of Secrets*, the madness which the daffodil cures is actually melancholy.

❦ Daisies ❦

Bellis Perennis
Venus
Cancer
Herbe of Protection ... Magickal Herbe ... Religious Herbe
Invocatory: Freya

LORE

Grieve's research led her to suggest in *A Modern Herbal* that there may be an association between daisies and a dryad (a woodland nymph) named Belidis.

USAGE

Modern practices include the growing of daisies as an herbe to further attract the devas. There are some gardeners of Magickal Herbes who believe daisies provide the means to communicate with the devas and the fairy folk. Dryads are often associated with elemental earth, and daisies may be used ritually to help one commune with this element.

Contemporary usage has linked the daisy to Freya, honoring her when brought into ritual primarily as floral decoration.

There is also magickal association with babies and newborn infants. The daisy may be incorporated into baby blessings and Wiccanings or used to bring protective magick into the baby's sleeping area.

❦ Daisy (Ox-Eye) ❦

Chrysanthemum Leucanthemum
Jupiter
Leo
Religious Herbe
Invocatory: Artemis, Jupiter, Thor, Zeus
Also called: dun daisy, field daisy, goldens, gowans, maudlinwort, Moon daisy

LORE

This variety of daisy has many associations with deities. Old

English custom associates it with the thunder gods; this association can be traced through the herbe's common name, dun daisy. It was also linked with Artemis, goddess of the Moon and perceived as containing feminine virtue. When pagan culture was replaced with Christian, it became linked to Mary Magdalene; this belief can be traced through its common name Maudelyn daisy.

USAGE

The ox-eye daisy may be grown in gardens to protect one's home against lightning. It may be used as a decorative bloom within the temple when rituals are performed to invoke the masculine deities of Zeus or Jupiter, or the gods of any culture associated with thunder.

This is a flower which is ideal for ritual working within women's groups, whether they choose to invoke Artemis or to work magickally with the flower to better understand the deeper mysteries. While there may seem to be a dichotomy between the masculine and feminine aspects of the ox-eye daisy, those who use it to understand women's mysteries find no discomfort with the cultural associations linking it with masculine energies.

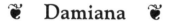

❦ Damiana ❦

Turnera Aphrodisiaca
Pluto
Aphrodisiacal Herbe ... Herbe of Love ... Magickal Herbe ...
Visionary Herbe

USAGE

Damiana enjoys a modern reputation as a sexual stimulant because it increases arousal. It is employed in a variety of ways, ranging from being a primary ingredient in smoking mixtures or being taken in some form of drink to being brought into direct contact with the sexual organs. It may be macerated in an oil to provide one of the best ritual lubricants. Some have used it to make an infusion with which to douche.

This herbe, found growing from the more temperate regions of South America to Texas is considered a magickal aphrodisiac. It is used ritually within the cup for the Great Rite, known for its ability to enhance pleasure and increase the intensity of sexual magick.

Solitary practitioners work with damiana to open their chakras and increase their psychic abilities in their quest for a heightened vision. It is believed that damiana should be stored with a quartz crystal in the container and that an herbal oil of damiana is among the best for preserving the energy being stored within quartz.

❦ Dandelion ❦

Taraxacum Officinale
Jupiter
Sagittarius
Religious Herbe
Invocatory: Hecate

LORE

Although known throughout ancient times, little magickal lore has survived. There appears to have been some association with Hecate.

USAGE

Modern use includes a custom which links the dandelion to the air spirits, or sylphs. It is thought that one might blow upon the seeds and, as they drift into the wind, they will carry your wishes to your lover. Dandelion may also be used to work with elemental air.

It is the root of the common dandelion which is able to descend deep into the Underworld and defies death. It would seem that the root might indeed work magickally to invoke Hecate. The root can be gathered fresh and sliced into pieces no more than a quarter of an inch thick. Pierce each in the center with a thick needle and string them upon a thick thread. These can be dried to wear as ritual beads when calling upon Hecate to give this goddess her due.

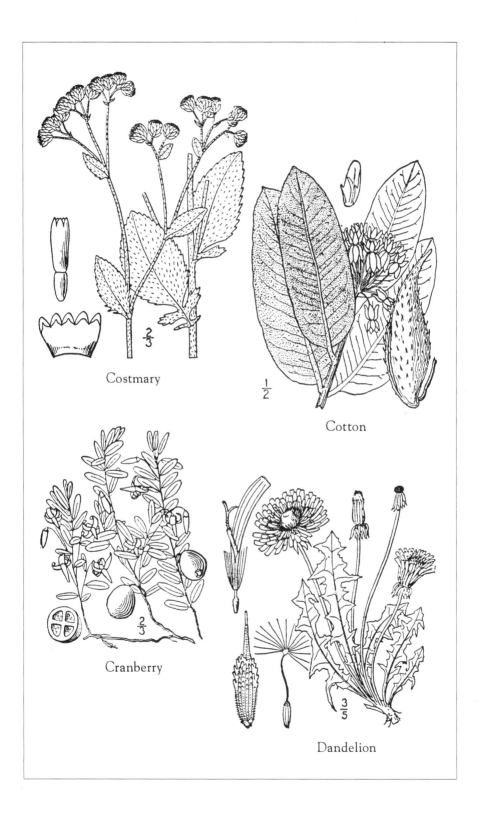

Costmary

Cotton

Cranberry

Dandelion

❦ Dill ❦

Peucedanum Graveolens
Mercury
Gemini
Greene Herbe ... Herbe of Protection ... Magickal Herbe

LORE

Commonly found in kitchens, dill may be used as a Greene Herbe so that one may bring magick to most dinner fare. Its spiritual use is documented well back into medieval times and is linked to beliefs of magick and witchcraft. It was considered good protection against black magick. Grieve in *A Modern Herbal* cites Drayton's *Nymphidia* with the following:

> Therewith her Vervain and her Dill,
> That hindereth Witches of their Will.

Obviously, these were not the good witches of today!

USAGE

Dill enjoys a long established reputation regarding its magick. Used as a Greene Herbe, one can bring good fortune and a healthy outlook to one's guests. Breaking and sharing dill bread imbued with subtle magick is a wonderful way to open a meal. Dill is very effective at keeping away dark forces and is well suited for the blessing of one's home.

Corresponded with the Temperance card of the major arcana, dill brings clarity of thought and helps one maintain inner strength in the ways of life. Dill is a good herbe for those who pursue magickal knowledge, for it keeps the mind clear between the realities of magick and superstition.

Dill is useful for those who desire strength of the mind and of the will. It provides a link between the two and promotes good energy which is useful in accomplishing one's desires.

❦ Dittany of Crete ❦

Dictamnus Alba
Venus
Religious Herbe ... Visionary Herbe
Invocatory: Hermes, Osiris, Persephone

USAGE

Although Culpeper discusses this herbe, I do not find it listed in Grieve's herbal. There are many modern magickal uses for this herbe which is popular among contemporary practitioners. It has some association with Hallow's Eve, when rituals are done throughout the world to seek communion with those who have passed into the Otherworld. Dittany may be added to the ritual cup. Dried dittany leaves can be burned as incense or burned in the Hallow's fire when seeking communication which brings wisdom from those who dwell beyond the veils.

Dittany is associated with the Underworld, and many have connected it with Persephone, Osiris and other deities who are able to transport one into that realm. Modern correspondences also place it with the Ten cards of all suits in the minor arcana.

❦ Dodder ❦

Cuscutua Europæa
Saturn
Countermagick Herbe
Also called: beggarweed, hellweed

USAGE

This parasitic plant, with its very curious appearance, has a history of use in helping overcome depression or sorrow. If someone is plagued with dark internal forces and is unable to let go of intensely negative thoughts, that person may believe their state of mind is the creation of black magick. Dodder can be very useful in these situations as dodder may be most effective in treating mental parasites within one's own mind.

❦ Dogwood ❦

Pyiscidia Erythrina
Moon, Pluto
Pisces
Herbe of Protection ... Religious Herbe
Invocatory: Consus

USAGE

Consus, an ancient Roman god, governed the ceremonies associated with the weighing of the crops and the Harvest Festival. Even today dogwood may be used in the Lammas or Autumn Equinox rituals. An agricultural deity, Consus' realm expanded and he was often invoked when any important meeting was being conducted. The use of dogwood is useful in any meeting when those attending need to maintain confidence regarding the topics of discussion or when all need to maintain an open mind during the proceedings.

Dogwood is useful in keeping not only meetings but one's writings private. It is a superior herbe for guarding one's Book of Shadows, diaries and journals. An oil of the dogwood flower is without peer in sealing letters and keeping their contents only for the intended's eyes.

As it blooms in spring, dogwood has been brought into spring rituals and celebrations. The flowers may be used to decorate, but the powdered flowers or dried bark can also be used in the temple incense.

❦ Dragon's Blood ❦

Dæmomorops Draco
Mars, Pluto
Gemini
Funereal Herbe ... Herbe of Consecration ... Magickal Herbe

LORE

Gathered from a very large tree by the Ganches tribe on islands off the northwest coast of Africa, dragon's blood is used in embalming, in much the same manner as was done by the Egyptians.

154

USAGE

Contemporary practitioners find this herbe corresponded with both the Lovers card and the Emperor card of tarot's major arcana.

Dragon's blood has stirred the imagination of many magickal herbalists. The powdered resin burns with a distinctive, highly pleasing aroma and the bright red color of the herbe itself lends the resin to many magickal workings. It is often used in homemade magickal inks. Such inks are useful for placing one's sigil upon a document, or for writing a vow upon a piece of paper or parchment when giving one's word to the Universe.

For those traditions in which a person's ritual tools and magickal possessions are set aside for a future incarnation, there is no better magickal ink for recording the secret sigils known only to the person's spirit. Dragon's blood may be included in the incense used during rituals of death and dying.

The Chinese variety of dragon's blood, *Dracœna terminalis*, is used in making a strong alcoholic beverage which may be used in promoting ecstatic states for those highly skilled with ritual.

❦ Elder ❦

Sambucus Nigra
Venus
Funereal Herbe ... Herbe of Protection ... Magickal Herbe
Invocatory: Hylde-Moer

LORE

Among those herbes with a rich history of lore, the elder stands as the equivalent of a high priestess. There is extensive material about this familiar shrub. Grieve's entry in *A Modern Herbal* runs to eight columns and is a valued source for many modern herbalists. We urge you to read her passages with care.

Among its best-known virtues, elder is believed to protect against all evils and dark magick. We find many cultures, separated by thousands of miles, consistent in their beliefs. Russian pagans believed elder was effective against evil. In southern Germany near the Black Forest elder was used magickally to heal. The pagans of Sicily knew elder and used it to protect their homes against theft. The northern pagans of Serbia gave elder at weddings to bless the new couple and give them good fortune.

For centuries, elder gathered for healing and magick has been harvested on Beltane Eve (the last day of April). Many believe the elder is more powerful the closer to midnight it is harvested. The more practical herbalist is likely to collect elder when the path is fully lit. Elder gathered on this date can increase the spirit of any magickal working. The lore regarding the harvesting of elder is well documented and affirms the wide-spread association with elder's protective spirit, a type of herbal goddess or dryad. In Denmark she was known as Hylde-Moer—the elder-tree mother.

Grieve cites Arnkiel in this quotation that is often found in herbal books:

> Our forefathers also held the Ellhorn holy, wherefore whoever heed to hew it down (or cut its branches) has first to make request, "Lady Ellhorn, give me some of thy wood, and I will give thee some of mine when it grows in the forest"—the which, with partly bended knees, bare head and folded arms was ordinarily done, as I myself have often seen and heard in my younger years.

Elder is associated with the eldritch, both through the history of its names and its association with magick. Grieve writes that its name is derived from the Anglo-Saxon word *æld*, in which times it was called eldrun. Æld means fire and indicates old customs in which hollowed stems were used to fan a coal into a fire. Even today elder may be associated with elemental fire.

Elder sticks are easily hollowed, giving them use as panpipes, a use recorded two thousand years ago by Pliny. Grieve also writes that Pliny documented their use in the manufacture of the sackbut, which she questions due to her belief that the sackbut is a stringed instrument. In truth, the sackbut was a wind instrument. So it appears that elder lends its magick to the manufacture of wind instruments.

The Christianization of pagan Europe changed some of the elder's lore for the dark side. The impossible belief that elder provided the wood for the Christ's execution (among other Christian figures) led to lore of its association with death and darkness. The folk practices generated by this errant belief, however, provided elder with increased safe space and respect. Superstitious country folk would not cut elder without proper prayers and for good reason. Grieve writes that Gypsies avoided using elder in their campfires.

Not all of elder's associations with death are born of Christian superstition. Grieve writes that "green elder branches were also buried in a grave to protect the dead from...evil spirits, and in some parts it was custom for the driver of the hearse to carry a whip made of elder wood." There are a number of folk beliefs which maintain elder offers protection against evil. Graves writes that it was often used in making cradles so that the babies would be kept safe.

If elder was collected without the proper respect, elder spirits were believed to follow the offender, plaguing the wrongdoer until the error had been rectified with the appropriate honor to Hylde-Moer. Graves lists elder with the letter R or Ruis, the thirteenth letter of the tree alphabet.

USAGE

Modern custom weaves elder's magick into the rites of Midsummer's Eve, a belief dating to the pagan customs of Denmark. An elder grove is considered an ideal location for moving into the realm of the faerie. But for those who desire to see the devas on this eve, elder flowers can be used in the ritual cup or in the incense. And fortunate are those who know the blessings of elder wine! This delectable drink may be enjoyed at Beltane.

Respect the writings of our elder herbalists. Gather your elder with great care. Of all herbes, none has such a link with its Mother. It is this natural magick which undoubtedly led to its impressive reputation.

One of the best protective herbes, it not only protects your home, but all that live within it. Elder has a history of providing safe-keeping for children as well as protecting pets and livestock. A grove or patch of elder should be treated as holy ground. If the growth is adequately established, it should be left open so one's stock can wander through it at will and be blessed. Rural folk are wont to grow elder, for its valued magick permeates all their land and protection is spread throughout.

Elder can protect your home in different ways. You can fashion the thin branches into crosses or pentagrams, hang dried bunches of berries, or make charms of the leaves. All of these can be hung above the doors and windows. Elder may be used in baby blessings but only if it has been gathered according to tradition! Elder ought to be included in any house or home blessing.

The connections elder has with the passing of one's body make it useful in rituals of death and dying. Some people make arrangements to have certain possessions (personal journals, one's measure, etc.) burned at the same time their body is cremated. There is no more sacred use for elder than to transport one into the Otherworld. However, long before one is ready to leave this incarnation, elder may be used in ritual and magickal healing.

Elder is associated with two cards of the major arcana. It works both with the Empress card and with the Moon card. Dried elder flowers are among our favorite fixative when making loose, dry incense. They hold herbal oils well and empower our rites.

🌿 Elfwort 🌿

Inula Helenium
Mercury, Uranus
Gemini
Herbe of Consecration ... Herbe of Purification ... Magickal Herbe
Also called: elecampagne, elf dock, wild sunflower

LORE

The "Helenium" in elfwort's Latin name is sometimes believed to be derived from the legendary Helen, who was carried off by Paris.

USAGE

Ranking as one of the favorite herbes in our pharmacopoeia, elfwort's strong association with the elven world is indicative of the type of magick which accompanies this herbe. The energy of this herbe can stimulate the inner child, but can also be capricious. There is a certain aspect of change for the sake of change which may not always suit essential stabilities in our lives. Elfwort can be used to work with the eldritch and the devas.

Few herbes have been found so strongly connected with the tarot. Elecampagne is associated with the Fool card of the tarot. This whimsical card brings one into closer contact with the inner child, helping us transcend our limitations and approach the unknown in life with trust. Elfwort is also corresponded with the Magician card, the symbolism of which represents the intellectual mastery essential in making one's magick work. In addition, we find elfwort listed with the Lovers card, for it can bring the practitioner the needed trust in the Universe essential in making the appropriate choice. When studying the minor arcana, elfwort is useful in learning the magick of all four Eight cards.

Only the root is generally available in the commercial market. Those who grow this stately herbe (which can attain heights greater than six feet) can also collect the flowers to dry and grind for incense. When burned, either the root or the bloom may be used to promote purification, cleansing the seeker who waits outside the Circle while awaiting initiation. Some have found this herbe useful in bringing magick to newborns with baby blessings. Others have found it a wondrous source of magick in the ritual cup.

❦ Elm ❦

Ulmus Capestris
Saturn
Capricorn
Funereal Herbe ... Magickal Herbe ... Visionary Herbe

LORE

In a few northern European cultural myths, it is believed possible that the sacred tree, from which human life emerged through the first man and the first woman, was an elm rather than an ash. Graves corresponds the elm in the modern Irish alphabet with the letter A or Ailm.

USAGE

Grieve wrote that it was once popular to use elm for the construction of coffins. Some believe this carries over from folk beliefs, implying that elm is an appropriate herbe to accompany the departed into the Otherworld during rituals of death and dying.

The dryad spirits of the elm are pleasant and cooperative with the magickal practitioner. Many believe that psychic communion, meditation and ritual workings, when embraced with an elm, are assisted in making contact with the faerie. *The Master Book of Herbalism* recommends establishing a personal relationship with a specific tree. The elm is a most suitable Tree of Life.

Elm leaves sometimes figure in spell magick and folk divination. Based upon this history, we can be assured that the leaf of this statuesque tree has useful magick.

❦ Endive ❦

Cichorium Endivia
Jupiter
Greene Herbe ... Magickal Herbe

USAGE

One may macerate the herbe in a fixative such as safflower to create an oil or work with a pure extraction of essential oil. In magickal working, the oil appears to be of primary use. However, endive has significant energy which can be released when it is used as a Greene Herbe, adding magick to meals.

Modern beliefs indicate that the magick of the endive assists the practitioner in opening the horizons of one's life. The magickal worker becomes more socially receptive to other people and more able to interact with strangers. Endive is recommended for those who are prone to feeling lonely, for whom a sense of inadequacy shades their eyes from recognizing opportunity. The oil can be worn, added to a bath or burned upon charcoal as an incense to build self-confidence and treat loneliness.

❦ Ephedra ❦

Ephedra Vulgaris
Mars
Religious Herbe

USAGE

Richard Miller in *The Magical and Ritual Use of Herbs* writes that ephedra is considered "the original source of life" among the

Chinese due to its stimulant properties and effect upon breathing. We recommend working with this herbe when studying the nature of elemental spirit, the fifth element, which can be absorbed from the Universe through disciplined breathing exercises such as those learned through yoga.

❦ Eucalyptus ❦

Eucalyptus Globulus
Moon, Pluto*
Herbe of Purification

USAGE

Eucalyptus is a very cleansing herbe. Both the leaves and the extracted oil are readily available, but those who live in southern climes are blessed by being able to gather the flowers to dry and use in their magick. Eucalyptus may be used to purify any space, whether preparing the temple or cleansing a home of unwanted energies.

❦ Eyebright ❦

Euphrasia Officinalis
Sun
Leo
Magickal Herbe ... Visionary Herbe
Invocatory: Euphrosyne

LORE

Zeus and his third wife had three daughters, known as the Three Graces. One of them, Euphrosyne, was known to have the bright-est outlook on life. She is a lesser deity to whom one can turn when life seems dark and a humorous outlook would be healing.

USAGE

The correspondence with the Tower card is not indicative of it being similar in energy, but is a reflection of its magick which represents eyebright's virtues. Working with this herbe can help one turn events akin to those of the Tower into opportunities for making wonderful changes. Eyebright helps us, magickally, to work with change internally, moving one's attitude from the dark and cloudy negative to a sunny, positive serenity.

Eyebright is an ideal herbe for making fluid condensers or infused solutions with which to bathe one's eyes, opening the chakras to increase inner sight. Eyebright is known for enhancing memory and aiding thought. Recommended as a magickal tonic, this herbe is useful for anyone making a concerted effort at studying occult sciences. Mrs. Grieve in *A Modern Herbal* provides us with insight into this history, with early fourteenth century references and a recipe from Culpeper:

> An excellent Water to Clear the Sight.
> Take of Fennel, Eyebright, Roses, white Celandine, Vervain and Rue, of each a handful, the liver of a goat chopt small, infuse them well in Eyebright water, then distil them in an alembic, and you shall have a water which will clear the sight beyond comparison.

Those having difficulty in transcending their sorrows should use this herbe to help them increase their gladness. Eyebright greatly assists in helping you count your blessings.

❦ Fennel ❦

Fœniculum Vulgare
Mercury
Countermagick Herbe ... Greene Herbe ... Herbe of Protection
... Magickal Herbe

LORE

Many herbalists over the past two thousand years have written of fennel's property of preserving and strengthening sight. Fennel was also considered effective in protecting one against black magick.

Greek legends about the development of fire as a tool include this relative of the celery family. From *Larousse World Mythology* we learn that Prometheus

> went up to Olympus and stole some sparks from the "Wheel of the Sun;" then he brought them back to earth, hidden inside a giant fennel (a pithy stalk sometimes used as a kind of tinder).

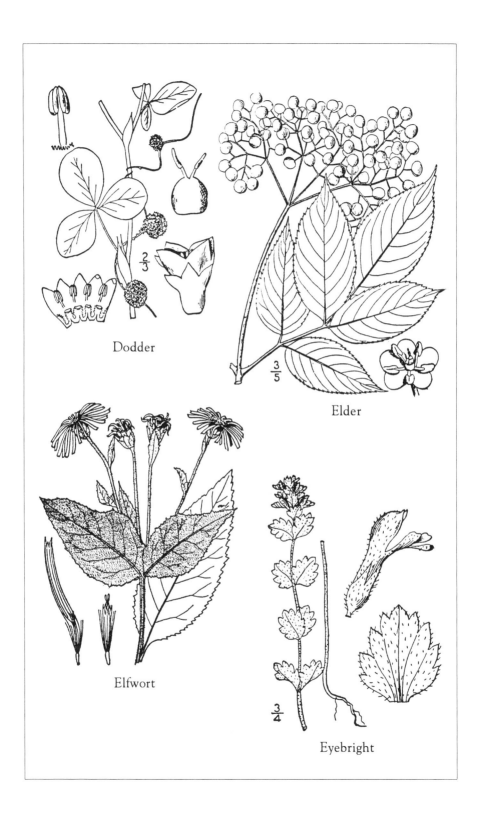

Dodder

$\frac{2}{3}$

Elder

$\frac{3}{5}$

Elfwort

Eyebright

$\frac{3}{4}$

USAGE

Fennel is purported to increase the length of one's incarnation. It also provides us with help when facing danger, making us strong of heart and capable of facing dire times. We may work with fennel to protect us against negative energy from external sources.

As fennel is popular in cooking, the modern practitioner can provide protection and well-being for dinner guests. Fennel is best gathered at Midsummer's Eve and then hung as a protective charm in one's home. Modern lore holds that this is another of the herbes Solomon used to aspurge his temple. Fennel is an excellent herbe to use in ritual working dealing with elemental fire.

❦ Fenugreek ❦

Trigonella Fœnum-Græcum
Mercury
Greene Herbe ... Magickal Herbe ... Religious Herbe
Invocatory: Apollo

USAGE

Contemporary association (possibly through the Golden Dawn) has placed this herbe within Apollo's care; making it useful for those who wish to invoke this most popular of solar deities. As a Greene Herbe, it might be used in a meal to bring a sunny disposition to those gathered about your table.

Some practitioners use this herbe at Lammas, the beginning of the harvest season, to be ceremonially connected with the waning Sun. Within the tarot, fenugreek corresponds with the Magician card and may be used to gain access to his insight or to better develop the powers of mind which the Magician represents.

❦ Fern (Bracken) ❦

Pteris Aquilina
Sun*, Mercury, Saturn
Countermagick Herbe ... Herbe of Immortality ... Magickal
Herbe ... Religious Herbe ... Visionary Herbe
Also called: brake fern, female fern

LORE

Old lore from the British Isles associates this herbe with the gods
both of the Christians and of those who worshipped in the woodlands before the arrival of Christianity. The belief in the power of
fern seed may have risen simply from the amazing appearance of
the fern spores, but the belief in their magick has a long and
established history.

Many writers attribute ferns with the power of allowing one to
move unseen through the world. This quality is specific to the
bracken fern according to the lore provided by Grieve. She quotes
Shakespeare in *Henry IV*, "We have the receipt of Fern seed—we
walk invisible." The spore of the fern should be gathered on
Midsummer's Eve.

Frazer writes that in an area of northwestern France, when fern
seed is gathered on Midsummer's Eve, it is believed to radiate
light, appearing to be like flaming gold. Some believed it could be
used to divine hidden wealth or buried treasure from within the
earth. This belief is also found in parts of Russia, Switzerland and
in the Italian Alps. In the Tyrolean Alps and also in Bohemia fern
seed is believed to keep your savings from dwindling. In Austria
the most valued fern seed is gathered on Christmas night. As
Frazer writes in *The Golden Bough*:

> Hence, when we consider that two great days for gath-
> ering the fabulous seed are Midsummer Eve and Christ-
> mas—that is, the two solstices,...we are led to regard
> the fiery aspect of the fern-seed as primary, and its
> golden aspect as secondary and derivative. Fern-seed, in
> fact, would seem to be an emanation of the Sun's fire at
> the two turning-points of its course, the summer and
> winter solstices. This view is confirmed by a German
> story in which a hunter is said to have procured fern-
> seed by shooting at the Sun on Midsummer Day at

165

noon; three drops of blood fell down, which he caught in a white cloth, and these blood-drops were the fern-seed. Here the blood is clearly the blood of the Sun, from which the fern-seed is thus directly derived.

Graves also writes of the ferns ability to render one magickally invisible and Mrs. Grieve in *A Modern Herbal* quotes Ben Jonson:

I had no medicine, Sir, to walk invisible
No fern seed in my pocket.

Bless Mrs. Grieve. Additional folklore recorded in her book includes the belief that fern preserves one's youthfulness and keeps death from one's door. At one time beds of bracken fern were burned to bring rain, a custom she wrote continued during her lifetime.

USAGE

Whether or not you can work with the spore of bracken to make yourself truly invisible is questionable. Modern practitioners, however, could make excellent use of the spore, carrying it in an amulet or magickal pouch in order to increase privacy and provide protection against others discovering the practitioner's personal business.

There are those who believe that using bracken fern in your Midsummer rites will enable you to enter the visionary realm of the faerie.

In *The Master Book of Herbalism* we wrote:

the spore is also useful in seeing one's future. Within a properly prepared ritual circle, cast the spore upon a basin of water, and watch your image as it begins to shift and pass through the potential of the future.

The belief that fern seed can have a positive and expansive effect upon one's financial situation is worth remembering in today's economics. Bracken fern corresponds with the Hanged Man card.

❧ Fern (Maidenhair) ❧

Adiantum Capillus-Veneris
Mercury
Virgo
Herbe of Love
Invocatory: Venus

LORE

This delicate fern is sometimes referred to as the "Hair of Venus."

USAGE

The attributes of Venus may be invoked through working with the maidenhair. Elixirs and potions based upon this fern are said to increase one's physical attractiveness and enhance the qualities of the Goddess within. Although an Herbe of Love, the maidenhair does not bring about the love of another so much as enable one to recognize and love the divine within.

Although it may seem an unlikely association, the maidenhair fern works the energy of the Hermit card, growing in untrod places and preferring to radiate its magick in out-of-the-way woodlands.

❧ Fern (Male) ❧

Dryopteris Felix-Mas
Mars, Pluto
Aphrodisiacal Herbe ... Fertility Herbe ... Magickal Herbe

LORE

In folk magick, the root of the male fern is sometimes called the "Hand of the Gods" or the "Lucky Hand." It is considered a powerful talisman associated with great power, and is capable of wielding either good or evil.

USAGE

There is strong male energy associated with this herbe. Working as a Magickal Herbe, it is considered a superior aphrodisiac for men. When using the herbe to stimulate and invoke the potent energy of any of the fertility gods, it is recommended to gathered the root on Midsummer's Eve.

Dried male fern root is burned until ash; this ash is added to sensual oil mixtures which will anoint the sexual organs and be used as lubricants during the Great Rite. If one wishes to gather the root whole for use as a powerful talisman, folklore recommends drying it over a fire. However, the far slower traditional drying would be preferable.

The root of this fern is gathered and dried, burned within a ritually prepared Circle (preferably outdoors beneath a full Moon) and used to enhance potency. For maximum strength, male fern should be harvested at Midsummer's Eve—or as close to that night as possible. This fern may be used to represent the polarity of the female fern (bracken fern), with each partner using the respective fern prior to the Great Rite.

🍎 Fern (Moonwort) 🍎

Botrychium Lunaria
Moon
Magickal Herbe
Also called: moonwort

LORE

Grieve writes in *A Modern Herbal* that this herbe was held in high regard for its magickal properties. "The Ancients regarded it as a plant of magical power, if gathered by moonlight, and it was employed by witches...in their incantations." She also refers to its use in alchemy as an herbe containing exceptional power.

Grieve goes on to cite Culpeper "Moonwort (they absurdly say) will open locks and unshoe such horses as tread upon it; but some country people call it *unshoe the horse*."

USAGE

It would seem that the dried fronds of moonwort belong in everyone's herbe closet. In addition to their magickal qualities, Culpeper's reference would indicate that we could work with moonwort to gain access or entry when we desire to open the portals of the Universe when seeking greater knowledge of the deeper mysteries or wish to gain access to the wisdom of earlier civilizations. Moonwort might be ideal as a patron herbe of locksmiths.

❦ Fern (Royal) ❦

Osmunda Regalis
Jupiter
Herbe of Protection ... Magickal Herbe
Also called: water fern

LORE

The royal fern has been associated with the god Thor, although this bit of mythic history is not conclusive and we cannot recommend it as being useful in invoking that deity.

USAGE

Royal ferns are used to protect one's possessions against loss and to assist in their return should they actually be lost or stolen. This fern is believed to provide protection to the traveler. Its power of protection is quite strong, keeping one's family safe during times of war and strife.

❦ Fig ❦

Ficus Carica
Mars, Jupiter*
Fertility Herbe ... Religious Herbe
Invocatory: Bacchus, Saturn

LORE

References to the fig date back well into the Age of Aries. The fig was a symbol of peace and fruitfulness to the Hebrew tribes. The Moslem belief is that the fig was a fruit of heaven, and an aspect of divine manifestation remaining elevated just above that of the animal. Figs were an important element of the diet among the soldiers of Sparta, providing them with sustenance and bolstering their courage.

Figs were sacred to the Romans and are significant in several of their myths as we learn in *Myths and Legends of All Nations*. "The Romans invented a line of Roman rulers who were supposed to have reigned in the times long ago passed. The first of the legendary kings was Romulus, twin brother of Remus, offspring of Mars and Rhea Silvia. The brothers were cast adrift in a basket as infants...but were found by wolves who suckled them and raised them. When they grew up they organized a warlike band of shepherds and founded a city which came to be known as Rome.

It was believed that the mother wolf which nursed these legendary twins rested under a fig tree. Figs were held in esteem, considered important gifts and were significant in some festivals. One festival described by a number of authors is the Nones Caprotines, or the "nones of the wild fig." Nones (meaning nine) indicates that this celebration is held nine days before the ides. This could be a raucous festival with an abundance of pagan merriment, reclaiming the wild heritage of Romulus and Remus on what was believed the anniversary of their deaths. The fig was also considered sacred to Bacchus, furthering its association with revelry.

Grieve in *A Modern Herbal* writes that "the inhabitants of Cyrene crowned themselves with wreaths of figs when sacrificing to Saturn, holding him to be the discoverer of the fruit."

From *The Golden Bough* we discover the fig is considered a Tree of Life among the original natives living around the Arafura Sea both in northern Australia and on nearby islands. These people see the Sun as the male divinity which fertilizes the female divine earth. He is represented by an oil lamp kept on an altar beneath the fig.

USAGE

Figs should find their way into many of our celebrations. Their Spartan heritage makes them useful for practitioners who have careers as modern warriors, such as attorneys, negotiators and entrepreneurs. Those who enjoy the bacchanalia could serve them, yet those who seek peace in the world could work with the fig from a different heritage.

Some of the deepest mysteries are those in the realm of Saturn. Figs can be placed upon an altar as an offering. One could partake of a fig, slowly (as slowly as the lessons of Saturn cut through the heavens) savoring its taste, taking in Saturn's wisdom as one is nourished. Figs would be useful for those working with the wolf as a totem animal. The fig should be revered as a Tree of Life. We may partake of many of the fig's virtues, including courage, fruitfulness and wisdom.

❦ Fig (Bo) ❦

Ficus Religiosa
Jupiter
Religious Herbe
Invocatory: Mithra

LORE

Buddhists believe that the Bodhi, the tree of wisdom under which Gautama Buddha reached enlightenment was the bo, a type of fig. The oldest living bo predates Christ. The fruit of this species of fig is believed to contain wisdom and bits of bark and leaf are carried by students working toward enlightenment.

USAGE

If one had access to a bo, the fruit would be among the most sacred of foods, one to be reserved for solemn religious rites.

❦ Figwort (Knotted) ❦

Scrophularia Nodosa
Saturn
Magickal Herbe

LORE

The leaves of this herbe were sacred in Wales, called *Deilen Ddu*. Gerard believed that a leaf worn about one's neck brought good health.

USAGE

Figwort can be incorporated into amulets for good health and related aspects of good fortune. The herbe lends itself to the making of magickal balms.

❦ Fir ❦

Abies Larix
Mars, Pluto
Religious Herbe
Invocatory: Artemis

LORE

The fir was the sacred tree of the Keresan Pueblo peoples. They believed it was created by the Maize Mother, their primary goddess. It was by ascending this tree that humans rose from the lowest world and reached toward the spirit. One of the firs, the silver fir, represents the vowel A or Ailm in the old Irish tree alphabet.

USAGE

The fir should be considered sacred, deserving of recognition as is any tree considered so closely linked with divine manifestation. It is a Tree of Life and can give you access to great wisdom.

According to Graves in *The White Goddess*, a fir branch with a cone at its tip, representing a phallic wand, was wrapped with ivy and used to honor the goddess Artemis.

❦ Flax ❦

Linum Usitatissimum
Mercury, Saturn, Uranus
Countermagick Herbe ... Herbe of Consecration ... Magickal
Herbe ... Religious Herbe
Invocatory: Hulda
Also called: linseed

LORE

Hulda, a northern European goddess and elf queen, was believed to be the deity who taught humans how to spin flax into thread. This blue-flowering herbe was sacred to her. Although not found in many cultures, there are some who recognize a flax mother.

In central Germany, according to Frazer in *The Golden Bough*, flax is believed to have the magickal power to "remove giddiness." It was believed that you should frolic skyclad three times around the flax. Just the thought of this custom gives one much to think about, for it would seem to me that dancing naked in my gardens would be anything but grounding!

Grieve describes a custom of Bohemia which sends children in their seventh year to the flax fields to dance and play. This is done to bring them Hulda's blessings and, as they mature, will ensure beauty and protection. According to a Prussian custom described in *The Golden Bough*, the tallest village maiden took food into the field for the god Waizganthos. She not only prays to him but stands upon a stool so that, when mature, the flax will have grown to reach the same height.

In many parts of Europe, old pagan fertility rites performed during the spring became part of the Lenten activities leading to Easter. Many of these involved fires. In Switzerland, a burning wheel was rolled down the hill. Dancers would leap as high as possible which was believed to encourage the flax to grow equally tall. In western Bavaria, bonfires for the same purpose are lit at Midsummer.

The cultivation and use of flax was known in ancient Egypt. Flax seeds have been found by archaeologists excavating tombs. Its significance as a valued herbe is found throughout the Old Testament. Flax and barley were destroyed by the plague of hail in Exodus. We also read that the Pharaoh rewards Joseph, skilled in dream divination, with a fine linen robe. Other references show that spun flax (linen) was used as fabric in temples, for ritual garments and some believe it was the fabric of the Christ's shroud.

USAGE

Costumers, dressmakers, tailors and any who have skill with needle and thread would be blessed with the gift of a vase of flax flowers, for it would serve them as a patron herbe. Flax provides us with one of the most sacred fabrics with which to make altar cloths and ritual robes.

The oil of the flax seed is known as linseed oil. This oil is used to consecrate magickal items and crystals, particularly those used for divination. The items should be lovingly anointed when the Moon is full. A beautiful herbe for one's gardens, the lovely blue flowers are much loved by the devas.

Flax is one of the few herbes with a history of providing what has come to be known as grounding. Flax has a well-established history of use for banishing negative energies. It is sometimes used in baby blessings. For magickal purposes, the flowers should be gathered when first dry from the morning dew. They may be powdered for incense or kept whole and strewn around one's home during a house blessing. Linseed provides an appropriate oil for maintaining a wooden altar, religious furniture or other wood items which should regularly have oil rubbed into them.

Flax has strong connections with both Eostara and Midsummer. Through its association with Hulda, flax can connect you with elves and the eldritch.

🍂 Foxglove 🍂

Digitalis Purpurea
Venus, Pluto*
Scorpio
Herbe of Immortality ... Visionary Herbe
Also called: fairy caps, fairy's glove, fairy thimbles, folks' glove, witches' gloves

LORE

A quick look at the other names for foxglove indicate a rich associations with the faerie, with the little people and the herbe devas as they have been perceived by diverse cultures.

USAGE

To quote *The Master Book of Herbalism*:

> Foxglove is an herbe of the Underworld, and has been used by those with intense initiatory training to commune with those who live there. This is a dangerous practice for the untrained, for foxglove is also capricious, and the unwise or foolhardy could easily find the communion with the Underworld permanent and too vivid.

The juice of this herbe can be ritually collected (choose your time according to the Moon). In ritual it can be later used to mark the very center of your Circle, where you shall sit and wait to see the realm of the faerie. Perhaps the best use of this charming herbe is

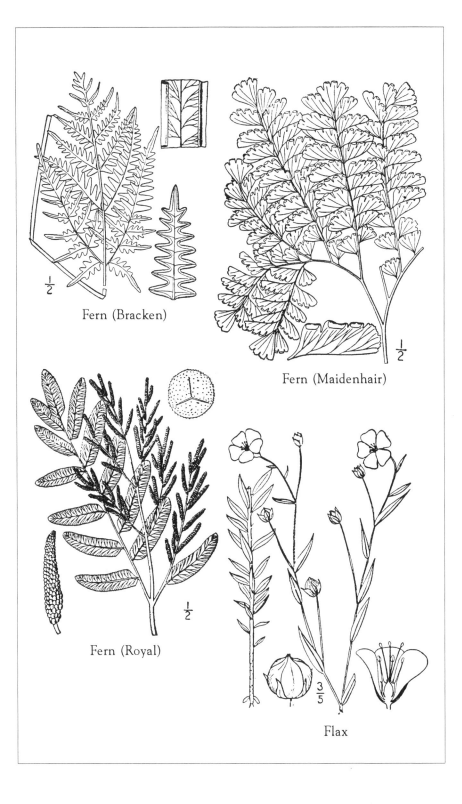

½

Fern (Bracken)

½

Fern (Maidenhair)

Fern (Royal)

½

³⁄₅

Flax

for growing in one's garden as a specimen, where there is no danger from its potency, but where it will attract all manner of delightful plant devas to bring true magick to your gardens.

🐾 Frankincense 🐾

Boswellia Thurifera
Sun
Herbe of Consecration ... Herbe of Protection ... Herbe of
Purification ... Religious Herbe
Invocatory: Adonis, Apollo, Baal, Demeter, Ra
Also called: olibanum

LORE

With strong associations with the Sun, frankincense has been used to give honor to solar deities. It was a powerful and valued herbe of the ancients. Its use during the times of the Old Testa-ment is well documented by ancient Hebrew. Frankincense has also been associated with Apollo and Adonis. The Romans ex-panded their use of this incense beyond that of the temple, giving it significance at political occasions as well. In addition, it was used within the Chaldean priesthood and burned by the Babylo-nians to invoke Baal, their solar deity.

It remains an important herbe throughout those countries along the eastern end of the Mediterranean. In Egypt it is heated and blackened. The sticky, black substance is used cosmetically. From *A Modern Herbal* we learn the following:

> According to Herodotus, Frankincense to the amount of 1000 talents weight was offered every year, during the feast of Bel, on the great altar of his temple in Babylon. The religious use of incense was as common in ancient Persia as in Babylon and Assyria. Herodotus states that the Arabs brought every year to Darius as tribute 1000 talents of Frankincense, and the modern Parsis of west-ern India still preserve the ritual of incense.

Interestingly, frankincense has also been linked with Demeter and several lunar goddesses, believed capable of bringing forth the soul and compassion of the feminine nature of the Universe.

Frankincense has been highly esteemed in the western Judeo-Christian religions, used in many of their ceremonies. It remains a primary ingredient for ceremonial mixtures within the Roman Catholic Church, carrying on an ages-old tradition. We can read about its history in *A Modern Herbal*:

> The ceremonial incense of the Jews was compounded of four "sweet scents," of which pure frankincense was one, pounded together in equal proportion. It is frequently mentioned in the Pentateuch. Pure frankincense formed part of the meet offering and was also presented with the shew-bread every Sabbath day. With other spices, it was stored in a great chamber of the House of God at Jerusalem.

USAGE

Frankincense is used for ritual primarily as an incense. It is one of the best herbes for an offering or sacrifice due to the nature of its harvest. A special knife is used to make a cut into the bark of the tree. When the sap oozes out, it dries into tear-shaped beads which are gathered and processed for the market. It has been used at many of the solar festivals, and is particularly used at Beltane, Lammas and Yule.

This resin may be burned or infused in a light tea, making ideal fare for studying the Sixes of the minor arcana. Frankincense shares an affinity with topaz. Either will enhance the power of the other. This resin is suited for the consecration of wands and of other ritual items associated with self-will, self-control and the disciplines of one's ego. It is of particular use for those with Leo planets, although some slip into an illusory state of mind and perceive it enhancing the ego, rather than placing one in humble admiration of all which is divine.

The history and the combination of feminine and masculine energies lend frankincense a singular place among Magickal Herbes. It represents the divinity's ability to move into manifestation.

Frankincense is often associated with ritual workings to bring success. However, this use of frankincense will only be of benefit when the practitioner is balanced both in the spiritual and in the mundane daily life.

Of value in ritual, it assists the conscious mind in maintaining focus and generates a sense of reverence and respect for the larger world of spirit and the stunning beauty of the manifest Universe.

Frankincense has a cleansing quality within one's astral self, bringing purification to one's spiritual being but also providing protection for those who walk in the world of spirit when taking their astral journeys.

❧ Fumitory ❧

Fumaria Officinalis
Saturn
Countermagick Herbe ... Herbe of Consecration ... Herbe of
Protection ... Herbe of Purification

LORE

Recognized by herbalists since the dawning of the Age of Pisces for its ability to purify and cleanse, fumitory also has curious associations with the Underworld. It was believed to have been created out of the gases rising from the bowels of the earth and has a history of use in exorcisms.

USAGE

An excellent herbe to use on Hallow's Eve, fumitory is among the better incenses for dispelling all negative energies. It may be used to cense a temple but is also useful as a wash, infused in water for the consecration of ritual tools. Fumitory lends itself to rituals of purification, such as the preparation of a new residence before moving in and unpacking.

An interesting use for fumitory is as an incense prior to the Great Rite, where it is used to remove natural tendencies and attractions toward the sensual, thus allowing for better mental discipline and increased spiritual focus.

❧ Garlic ❧

Allium Sativum
Mars
Greene Herbe ... Religious Herbe
Invocatory: Hecate

LORE

Garlic cloves were once placed upon cairns, small piles of stones heaped at the intersections of paths and roads, in order to give honor to Hecate. Garlic appears to have been associated with the Underworld by more than one culture. Moslem lore holds that garlic and onion rose from the spots where Satan's feet first touched the earth.

Again, we are indebted to Mrs. Grieve who cites that Pliny recorded that garlic was treated by the Egyptians as divine, and was included in oath-taking. She also cites Homer's belief that Ulysses used garlic when he and his men escaped from Circe's anger.

USAGE

The modern use of garlic is often centered around its association with Hecate. There are many who give her honor during the new Moon and during the times when the Moon is waning. It may be included in ritual breads eaten in her honor. There are also some who set a clove out upon a cairn, continuing customs of ages long since passed.

❦ Gentian ❦

Gentiana sp.
Mercury, Mars
Virgo
Magickal Herbe

USAGE

Culpeper wrote that gentian may be used when helping someone who has suffered from matters of the heart and needs emotional strength.

❦ Ginger ❦

Zingiber Officinale
Moon*, Mars
Greene Herbe ... Herbe of Protection ... Magickal Herbe

USAGE

Ginger has a history which associates it with one's health. Although it may be grown in your garden to indicate the state of your health as a type of botanical barometer, a more effective use of ginger is to place pieces of the dried root in an amulet or medicine bag in order to magickally promote good health. Ginger may be used in any variety of magickal ways to bring protection to your physical being. Those who grow ginger may seek a root which has grown into some semblance of human form. Although it is difficult to dry without becoming misshapen, success in this endeavor creates a very powerful magickal token.

Ginger has been found within modern Wicca in recipes of herbal mixtures used in the consecration of athames. It both strengthens and provides excellent energy for the workings of this ritual blade.

Within the Tarot, ginger is associated with the High Priestess card. It may be infused in a tea or used as an incense to set before the card. Someone with a sweet tooth might bake ginger into a snap as a sweet cookie to eat when meditating upon the Priestess card.

❦ Ginkgo Biloba ❦

Salisburia Adiantifolia
Mars
Aphrodisiacal Herbe ... Fertility Herbe ... Magickal Herbe

LORE

Ginkgo nuts are consumed at weddings and feasts and are sometimes substituted for lotus seeds. There is a fair amount of the mystic surrounding this tree. The wood is sometimes carved into amulets and charms which are believed capable of curing all sorts of illnesses.

USAGE

Ginkgo is very useful in ritual healing. It has a history of this use in China, where it is revered in folklore. Many consider the ginkgo sacred and a Tree of Life.

The age of this species gives the spirit of a living specimen the type of energy which I can only describe as being an elder among tree spirits. There is a depth to the tree's energy which, when explored, can provide a gateway to ancient wisdom.

The nuts, when dried, may be used to represent male fertility.

Although they have been used as an aphrodisiac, they are useful in all creative work and may be included in a Handfasting feast.

❧ Goosefoots ❧

Chenopodium Bonus Henricus
Jupiter
Magickal Herbe ... Religious Herbe
Also called: English mercury, mercury goosefoot

LORE

According to the lore we find in *A Modern Herbal*, this naturally growing herbe has strong associations with the world of devas. Mrs. Grieve cites Grimm as a reference for the lore indicating Goosefoots as an herbe of elves.

USAGE

Goosefoots would be a useful herbe for those seeking entry into the realm of the faerie. But one ought to be careful, for there is a trickery about the natural magick of this herbe.

❧ Gorse (Golden) ❧

Ulex Europæus
Mercury
Herbe of Love ... Herbe of Protection ... Religious Herbe
Invocatory: Jupiter
Also called: broom, furze

LORE

In *The White Goddess*, Graves writes about gorse by its older name of furze. He places it with Onn, the vowel O in the old Irish alphabet.

> The second tree is the furze, which with its golden flowers and prickles typifies the young Sun at the Spring Equinox; the time when furze fires are lighted on the hills.

Graves associates gorse with the hand's finger associated with the god Jupiter. He suggests it should be offered as a sacrifice to Jupiter to bring protection to shepherds.

USAGE

Golden gorse has a long history associated with romance and weddings which has extended into modern times. Gorse is sometimes included in the bride's bouquet to help keep romance alive in the marriage—it is a lovely herbe for Handfastings. It can be used to further the romance in a relationship, but only when this magick is consensual. Grieve in *A Modern Herbal* quotes an old saying:

> When gorse is out of bloom,
> Kissing is out of season.

Gorse has long been believed to protect against dark magick, evil spells and the like.

The customs cited by Graves which associated it with the Spring Equinox lend gorse to usage as an Eostara herbe. This herbe could be used as a patron herbe by anyone who is a caretaker of animals.

🍃 Gourds 🍃

Cucurbitaceae sp.
Moon
Religious Herbe

LORE

Peruvian myths believe that the first gourd came from the flesh of the first child born upon the earth. There are other myths in South America which tell that the planet and goddess which we know as Venus, once hid in a gourd.

USAGE

The lore of this herbe lends its use as a chalice or other vessel used in ritual. It can be dried, cut, fashioned and decorated into a container. One may also dry it and decorate it as a rattle.

❧ Grapes ❧

Vitis Vinifera
Jupiter
Fertility Herbe ... Religious Herbe
Invocatory: Bacchus, Dionysus, Iznagi, Svantevit

LORE

We find references to grapes in numerous cultures, some as ancient as thirteen hundred years before the birth of Christ. The ability of grapes to ferment and lead to the wonders of wine have given them sacred status almost worldwide.

Japanese Shinto myths relate the story of Iznagi. Known as the "Male who invites," Iznagi is coupled with his sister Izanami, the "Female who invites." They cross the Floating Bridge of Heaven and descend down to the earth where they are to be married. Together they are very procreative. Their union produces the sea, even the god of fire. But reality sets in and Izanami dies. Iznagi is filled with sorrow and must see her. He descends into the Underworld wearing a ritual headdress, only to find her body decomposing. Her spirit is quite upset at her husband and lover finding her so ugly and she calls forth demons from this dark world. In his flight, Iznagi removes his headdress and throws it at the demons. It turns into succulent grapes and, when the demons stop to eat them, he escapes. Later, peaches figure into his flight.

Probably the best known mythologies associated with grapes and wine are those of Dionysus. The Greek Dionysus was a late comer to Olympia but one who became very popular, undoubtedly due to the type of celebrations which gave him honor. Dionysus was fathered by Zeus, which proved troublesome. Zeus' wife was not at all pleased by this. Dionysus' mother, Semele, caused Hera great jealousy. When a dispute between Hera and Zeus led to Semele's death by one of Zeus' thunderbolts, the yet unborn Dionysus was rescued by Zeus, taken by his father and hidden within Zeus' thigh until time for his birth. Being twice born became part of his legend. For a time Zeus tried to protect Dionysus by dressing him as a girl and having him cared for by Amanthus and Ino. Hera was not to be tricked and drove the foster parents mad, destroying their lives. Zeus again rescued Dionysus and the child was raised by the nymphs of Mount Nysa. When

Dionysus was growing up around the mount, he led a charmed life, meeting various deities and traveling to many lands. Through his journeys he acquires the women known as Bacchantes as his followers, along with the satyrs and the god Priapus. Dionysus is known for his great love of wine and of the vine.

Dionysus enjoyed a great following among the Romans as well, but they knew him as Bacchus.

On the southern shores of the Baltic, the Strong Lord or the god Svantevit was worshipped. With strong phallic overtones, wine was the focal point of the annual ritual which predicted the harvest. A sacred basin of wine was set in the temple. No one could enter, not even those of the college of priests. The designated priest who entered the temple to measure the wine was not allowed even to breathe the air. If the priest found that the level of wine had dropped, a bad harvest was predicted. If the bowl was still full, the crops would be bounteous. Wine was then offered in sacrifice to the god.

USAGE

Wine has many ritual uses. It is used for the ritual cup by many peoples. It is ideally suited for extracting herbal constituents. A cup of wine set aside in the morning is well suited to infuse the herbes that one has chosen for that night's ritual. We are among the many who use pure grape juice as an alternative to alcohol.

Grapes represent fruition, fertility and success. They may be used to adorn the temple or may be included as part of the feast.

❦ Gum Mastic ❦

Pistacia Lentiscus
Mars
Herbe of Consecration ... Herbe of Protection ...
Herbe of Purification

USAGE

The resin of this Mediterranean shrub is widely used today. It lends itself readily as an incense and is ideally suited for the cleansing of divinatory tools. Indeed, it is considered superior for preparing any ritual tool for use.

If one is unduly influenced by another's negative energy or magick, standing over a thurible of gum mastic brings excellent protection. Gum mastic is used to purify and cleanse a ritual space. It is well suited for temple incense.

❦ Haricot ❦

Phaseolus Vulgare
Moon, Jupiter
Religious Herbe
Invocatory: Ukemochi

LORE

The beans of the haricot are considered sacred to the Shinto. Lore tells that the beans arose from the blood of the goddess Ukemochi who provided food (particularly boiled rice) and benevolence for people. Despite this, she was murdered. The story of Ukemochi is part of the creation lore which leads to the explanation of the Sun and Moon being separate in the sky.

Among the Fali tribe in areas of northern Africa, the haricot is considered one of the twelve sacred foods.

USAGE

These honored beans would be most useful in rituals which celebrate the fertility of the harvest and the fruition of Mother Earth. Employed in the foods of the ritual feast, they would assist in connecting you with the Goddess as mother.

❦ Hawthorn ❦

Cratægus Oxyacantha
Mars
Fertility Herbe ... Herbe of Love ... Religious Herbe
Invocatory: Bloddeuwedd, Cardea, Flora
Also called: haws, mayblossom, thorn

LORE

From the time it blooms in May until the ripening of its small, red fruit, the hawthorn is a singular tree, adding grace and beauty to any garden. We have several surrounding the main ritual site in our gardens and recommend the hawthorn to anyone living in a compatible climate. It is considered sacred among many people in the British Isles and is frequently the herbe referred to when called "thorn" (although some think that reference might apply to the blackthorn). It is believed that the hawthorn is protected by a goddess and one should never harm the tree nor harvest it; the one exception, according to the Farrars, being at May Eve. Blod-deuwedd, the May Queen, is said to be a daughter of the hawthorn according to Robert Graves in *The White Goddess*.

Graves writes that the goddess Cardea, mistress of Janus, protected infants through the hawthorn which was sacred to her. The letter H in the tree alphabet is Uath, or the hawthorn, which is the sixth letter. As he does with some others, Graves considers this tree unlucky although many with more experience would think otherwise. The historical uses recorded by Graves are very interesting:

> The ascetic use of the thorn, which corresponds with the cult of the goddess Cardea must, however, be distinguished from its later orgiastic use which corresponds with the cult of the goddess Flora, and which accounts for the English mediaeval habit of riding out on May Morning to pluck flowering hawthorn boughs and dance around the maypole. Hawthorn blossom has, for many men, a strong scent of female sexuality; which is why the Turks use a flowering branch as an erotic symbol.

The hawthorn is held sacred in some Christian traditions as well, being one of many herbes believed to be the source for the Christ's crown of thorns.

USAGE

Because of the proscription against harvesting or cutting into the hawthorn, any use of it should be with care. It has a strong magick but should only be used wisely in a ritual context, in a way that works with the traditions of time, giving honor to the turning of the seasons and giving honor to Mother Earth and Her customs. When working within the context of this tree's lore, it provides a most desirable wand, but one must work with its deva. The hawthorn is closely associated with Beltane.

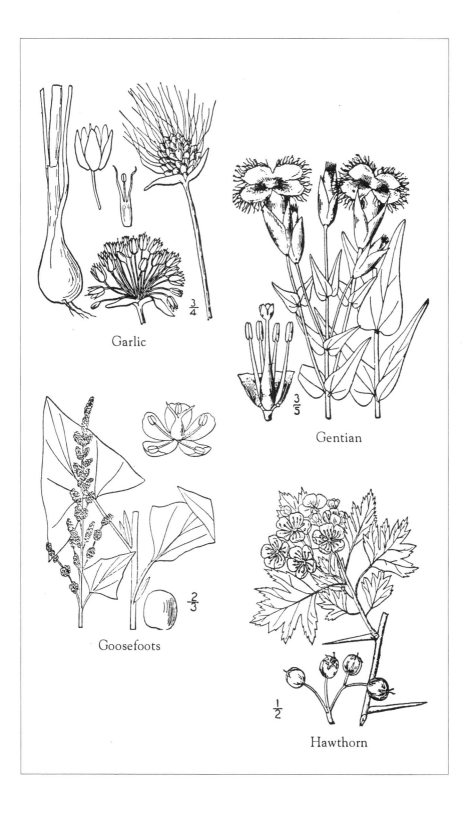

Garlic

$\frac{3}{4}$

Gentian

$\frac{3}{5}$

Goosefoots

$\frac{2}{3}$

Hawthorn

$\frac{1}{2}$

❦ Hazel Nut ❦

Corylus Avellana
Mercury
Herbe of Love ... Magickal Herbe ... Visionary Herbe

LORE

The hazel has sometimes been associated with poetic inspiration. Hazel is Coll, the ninth tree or the letter C in the tree alphabet. Graves writes in *The White Goddess* that "the nut in Celtic legend is always an emblem of concentrated wisdom."

Also according to Graves, a forked hazel branch was once a useful divining tool, used for dowsing. He describes a custom in which hazel may be given as a token that romance may proceed.

The hazel corresponds with the planet Mercury and is sometimes considered the herbe of Wednesday.

USAGE

A magickal tree such as the hazel stirs one's imagination through the myriad ways one can touch the inner muse. The nuts, sitting near one's desk, can be a source of nutrition not only for the body but for the soul. The oil can be used in making a balm for one's temples or used in dressing a candle to light when creating images with words.

❦ Heartsease ❦

Viola Tricolor
Saturn
Herbe of Love
Also called: call me to you, wild pansy

USAGE

The wild pansy has been known as a love charm, as we can even find in Shakespeare's *Midsummer Night's Dream*. Grieve lists numerous common names which indicate the widespread use of this herbe as a means of bringing romance into one's life.

❧ Heather ❧

Calluna Vulgaris
Venus
Taurus
Herbe of Immortality ... Magickal Herbe ... Religious Herbe
Invocatory: Isis, Osiris, Venus

LORE

Heather is Ur, the third vowel *U* in the Irish alphabet. Graves believed it sacred to Venus and to Isis. He also believes that heather is "the midsummer tree, red and passionate, and is associated with mountains and bees." Perhaps one of Graves' more interesting comments is that heather was "a suitable tree for the initiation of Scottish witches."

Heather is considered sacred to the Egyptian god Osiris. In some legends, Osiris is enclosed in a heather tree. Associated with the Empress card, heather is believed to bring one in touch with one's divinity and to increase physical beauty.

USAGE

> Partaking of it as a daily tonic, or wearing an amulet of the wood will bring a long physical life and will enable one to perceive the truly immortal soul and remain in touch with the ever lasting elements of the Universe. A valuable herbe for those who pursue initiatory paths, as they work to unfold the inner self.

The preceding is from the *Master Book of Herbalism*. You may work with heather as a bathing herbe, but herbal extracts of heather may be included in one's toiletries as well. However, any work with heather needs to be done with moderate caution. Employing heather to achieve one's desires works within the web of the Universe, within which nothing is received for nothing.

The Farrars associate heather with Midsummer's Eve, used both to decorate the temple and as an aspurger. More information can be found in their work *Eight Sabbats for Witches*. Some traditions also associate heather with Lammas, gathering it to place in urns to decorate the ritual site. Many also bring this herbe of the heaths into their Circles at Candlemas; frequently, this would be heather that was gathered at the previous harvest and carefully dried.

❦ Heliotrope ❦

Heliotropium Peruviana
Sun
Leo
Religious Herbe
Invocatory: Helios

LORE

The heliotrope is sacred to the Greek god of the Sun, Helios.
When a young nymph falls madly in love with him and cannot
turn away her eyes, she forsakes all food and wastes away until she
dies. Helios takes pity upon her and transforms her into the
heliotrope. Even today the heliotrope "watches" the Sun throughout the day.

USAGE

The heliotrope may be used in any ritual of Drawing Down the
Sun or in any magickal work in which one wishes to strengthen
solar aspects of the self. The heliotrope is sacred to all solar
deities.

❦ Hellebore (Black) ❦

Helleborus Niger
Saturn
Herbe of Consecration ... Herbe of Protection ... Magickal
Herbe
Also called: Christmas rose

LORE

Parkinson records a belief that hellebore can cure an animal
which has been poisoned. Mrs. Grieve in *A Modern Herbal* also
records further associations with animals:

> Once, people blessed their cattle with this plant to keep
> them from evil spells, and for this purpose, it was dug up
> with certain mystic rites. In an old French romance, the
> sorcerer, to make himself invisible when passing through
> the enemy's camp, scatters powdered hellebore in the
> air, as he goes.

190

The following is from Burton's *Anatomy of Melancholy*:

> Borage and hellebore fill two scenes,
> Sovereign plants to purge the veins
> Of melancholy, and cheer the heart
> Of those black fumes which make it smart.

USAGE

Black Hellebore is used to provide one with an aura or mantle of invisibility. Those who have need of the ability to move through a public area without being seen, those wishing to blend into a crowd, those who need to escape detection would do well to avail themselves of this herbe. This is not an herbe one may safely ingest. The best approaches for usage would be placing some of the herbe (pieces of the root, dried berries) in an amulet or magickal pouch. One might also place the dried leaves upon charcoal, then pass one's body thoroughly through the smoke (without inhaling).

Modern usage includes black hellebore when blessing farm animals and household pets. When harvested for the purpose of protection of one's stock, it should be gathered live, with clear images and visualizations held in one's mind. It is of essential value when one works with a familiar.

❦ Hellebore (False) ❦

Adonis Autumnalis
Saturn
Scorpio

LORE

This poisonous herbe has long been known. According to *A Modern Herbal* by Mrs. Grieve, "Its Latin name, *Adonis autumnalis*, is derived from the ill-fated Adonis, from whose blood it sprang, according to the Greek legends."

Graves writes that hellebore was once used by the ancient Irish pagans mixed with other herbes to poison their arrows when defending their land.

🐾 Hemlock 🐾

Conium Maculatum
Saturn
Funereal Herbe ... Herbe of Consecration ... Herbe of
Immortality
Invocatory: Hecate

LORE

Lore holds that Solomon used hemlock when consecrating his ritual knife. It should be noted that a good number of herbes share this lore. It is considered sacred to Hecate.

The juice of the hemlock has, in past times, been used to carry out death sentences. Not only did Socrates die, condemned to drink this herbe, but many were executed with the juice. Poisoning from hemlock causes extreme dizziness.

USAGE

Hemlock should be used carefully. It offers a very powerful type of magick, one which is capable of moving the energy out beyond the abyss. It may be used with one's athame but should never be taken internally.

🐾 Hemp 🐾

Cannabis Sativa
Saturn, Neptune
Pisces
Herbe of Love ... Magickal Herbe ... Visionary Herbe

LORE

Although hemp has been used as a medicinal and recreational drug within many cultures, surprisingly, this herbe has not entered the mythos of very many belief systems.

From Frazer in *The Golden Bough* we learn that Midsummer in Bavaria was the time when bonfires were used to encourage the hemp crop to be bountiful.

USAGE

In researching spell magick found in the mid-twentieth century (particularly the 1970s), we found hemp seeds were sometimes used in love spells. *The Master Book of Herbalism* cites "one in which a young woman sows the seeds in a large circle around a church on Midsummer's Eve. Any maiden capable of doing this without notice, surely deserves her beloved."

Hemp is seductive in many ways. It is unfortunate that many practitioners are seduced by the pleasant effects of this herbe. The majority of magickal and religious uses which would otherwise be available is diluted by false beliefs. The ability of this herbe to promote entry into the astral is as illusory as are the sensations promoted by its resins. Despite the numbers of those who believe hemp enhances their ability to meditate or work within the astral, serious spiritual practitioners would only use it internally on rare occasions and then only after following intensive fasting, seclusion and preparation under the auspices of trained guides. If hemp is to be treated as a sacrament, then one ought to be willing to live the appropriate lifestyle, partaking of the herbe on very infrequent occasions and only when properly prepared and, at all other times abstaining completely from the herbe. If you choose to use it as a recreational substance outside the law, then we urge you as strongly as we can to avoid using it spiritually or connecting that energy with any others in ritual, unless you have their consent. Avoiding the latter requires six or seven days' abstention prior to sitting in Circle with others.

The only safe use of this herbe we can recommend is using the extracted juice (alcohol may be added to create a tincture) to anoint one's divinatory tools prior to moving into a state of mediumship. This does *not* imply that one's internal physical body should be anointed. It will not make you psychic!

❦ Henbane ❦

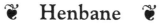

Hyoscyamus Niger
Saturn
Herbe of Consecration

LORE

One of the traditional herbes of historic, medieval witchcraft,

193

henbane figures in literary references as an herbe added to oint-ments and brews. The ability of henbane to induce delirium cre-ated substantial beliefs that this herbe was diabolic and filled with dark magickal powers.

As the dead roamed the banks of the Styx they were said to wear henbane. One of the most interesting aspects of henbane's lore is found in Grieve's Herbal:

> the most striking feature of the plant is the curious seed-vessel, a very detailed description of which is given in the works of Flavius Josephus, as it was upon this capsule that one of the ornaments of the Jewish high priests' head-dress was modelled.

USAGE

Henbane does not find much use in modern practice. Used with wisdom, it could be an important herbe in the consecration of ceremonial vessels. Albertus Magnus recorded henbane being used to attract hares. It would be an excellent herbe for those who raise rabbits.

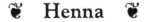

❦ Henna ❦

Lawsonia Alba
Jupiter
Aphrodisiac Herbe ... Herbe of Love

LORE

Henna is well known along the eastern Mediterranean. In Egypt it is used to adorn the body, coloring both hair and fingernails. In some Arabian cultures, henna was made into a lubricant with olive oil, and massaged into the phallus with the rising and setting of the Sun in order to promote virility.

USAGE

Henna may be used today for its sensual values. The color which will be imparted to the sexual areas of the body has great magickal value, serving as ritual adornment. Such markings can have pow-erful ritual significance. Henna's color is not permanent, although it does not instantly disappear with soap and water. Henna is recommended for use in the Great Rite at the most important ritual occasions.

❦ Holly ❦

Ilex Aquifolium
Mars, Saturn
Countermagick Herbe ... Funereal Herbe ... Herbe of
Protection ... Magickal Herbe ... Religious Herbe

LORE

Holly belongs to the small collection of herbes which have such strong historical lore that they have become part of our western heritage.

Holly has become bound to the observance of Yule, Christmas and holidays associated with the Winter Solstice. In *A Modern Herbal*, Grieve informs us that this custom dates to the Druids, "who decorated their huts with evergreens during winter as an abode for the sylvan spirits." We know that holly was given as a desired gift during the Roman festival of Saturnalia.

Holly is a very important herbe in the folklore of the magickal British Isles. In the Irish tree alphabet, the holly is *T* or Tinne, the eighth tree. In fact, Grieve describes it as the "most important" of those evergreen plants brought into holiday celebrations and folklore. In contemporary neopagan customs, holly which has been used to decorate the temple at Yule is kept sacred until the fires are lit at Candlemas and then it is burned in the cauldron. Many traditions work with a Holly King, a variation of the Green Man or male fertility figure. The Holly King (if he can endure wearing the sharp points of the leaves) is crowned with these hard, green leaves. The Farrars in *Eight Sabbats for Witches*, provide us with exceptional information:

> An extraordinary persistent version of the Holly King/Oak King theme at the Winter Solstice is the ritual hunting and killing of the wren—a folklore tradition found as far apart in time and space as ancient Greece and Rome and today's British Isles. The wren, "little king" of the Waning Year, is killed by his Waxing Year counterpart, the robin redbreast, who finds him hiding in an ivy bush (or sometimes in Ireland in a holly bush, as befits the Holly King). The robin's tree is the birch, which follows the Winter Solstice in the Celtic tree-cal-

endar. In the acted-out ritual, men hunted and killed the wren with birchrods.

The holly is a most important herb in Irish lore. In *The White Goddess* Graves cites the *Romance of Gawain and the Green Knight* in which "the Green Knight is an immortal giant whose club is a holly-bush."

The prominence of holly within religious beliefs dominates many European cultures. It is possible that its very name is a variation of *holy tree* which some people call it, believing that it first grew from the blood of the Christ and later came to be identified with Jesus. Despite the pagan origins of holly's lore, holly remains woven throughout herbal history. From Mrs. M. Grieve's *A Modern Herbal*, we learn more of the origins of holly's modern use in Christmas celebrations.

> [It is believed to be] derived from a custom observed by the Romans of sending boughs, accompanied by other gifts, to their friends during the festival of the Saturnalia, a custom the early Christians adopted. In confirmation of this opinion, a subsequent edict of the Church of Bracara has been quoted, forbidding Christians to decorate their houses at Christmas with green boughs at the same time as the pagans, the Saturnalia commencing about a week before Christmas. The origin has also been traced to the Druids, who decorated their huts with evergreens during winter as an abode for the sylvan spirits. In old church calendars we find Christmas Eve marked *templa exornantur* (churches are decked), and the custom is as deeply rooted in modern times as in either pagan or early Christian days.

The beliefs surrounding holly are far older than the time of Christ. Older beliefs, as recounted in Grieve's *A Modern Herbal*, written by the great historian, Pliny, state that "if planted near a house or farm, (holly) repelled poison, and defended it from lightning and witchcraft, that the flowers cause water to freeze, and that the wood, if thrown at any animal, even without touching it, had the property of compelling the animal to return and lie down by it." An herbe of Mars, holly is sometimes associated with Tuesday.

USAGE

Holly is an ideal herbe to fashion into a wreath with which to celebrate the welcome of a new priest or priestess into the com-

196

munity. Despite the wonderful illustrations which romanticize the wearing of holly, it is not well-suited for human flesh. The thorns of the leaves are extremely sharp whether the leaves are fresh or withered. Holly can be included in decorative fashion, carefully added to other herbes for a wreath or even placed into vases which are set about the temple. Some have carefully taken holly leaves and used them to decorate a ritual robe and many have adopted holly as a design.

There is much more to holly than its leaves. It can grow into a good-sized tree. Graves wrote that the wood was once used for chariot axles by ancient European pagans. It can be cultivated into a straight shaft suitable for a magickal staff.

The wood of a mature holly is well-suited magickally for the handle of a ritual knife. It contains a magick which can both attract and repel; it is powerful when defense is needed and its strength can protect the Circle and cherish the gentleness within.

The beliefs recorded by Pliny are an indication of the power of this herbe. While holly's ability to freeze water or control animals are in the realm of the fantastic, there is a very strong energy about this herbe which transcends our tangible reality. Perhaps it is for this reason holly is sometimes associated with death and dying. It is an herbe which can be added to the fire in rituals of death and dying.

Those who move into the mysteries of the crone might press a leaf and add it to their Books of Shadows.

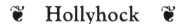

❦ Hollyhock ❦

Althæa Rosea
Venus
Libra
Magickal Herbe ... Religious Herbe

USAGE

A dried pod, filled with bursting seed, is sometimes taken as a token of a filled purse. Some practitioners work with ripe seed pods to increase success in the material world, to increase the flow of money or to acquire new possessions.

These old-fashioned flowers are known for their ability to attract devas and help provide shelter for the little people. When grown near a home, they help the success of the family flourish.

Hollyhock finds modern ritual usage with the beginning of the harvest season, ritually celebrated at Lammas, as described in *The Master Book of Herbalism*:

> One long stalk of hollyhock may be carried by the children, at the beginning of the ritual procession to the fields.

❦ Holly (Sea) ❦

Eryngium Maritimum
Moon
Aphrodisiac Herbe

USAGE

The dried root is used in a variety of ways to enhance sexual magick, ranging from preparations taken orally to external applications. The use of sea holly as a source of strength was established by the eastern Mediterranean cultures.

❦ Honeysuckle ❦

Lonicera Caprifolium
Mercury, Mars
Cancer
Herbe of Immortality ... Religious Herbe ... Visionary Herbe

USAGE

Honeysuckle is used to enhance one's spiritual sight. The best application of this herbe is obtained through using the extracted oil. Honeysuckle can increase one's understanding of the images and impressions collected in the astral.

Associated with the Magician card, honeysuckle is used in rituals designed to connect one with the mysteries of the Cauldron of Cerridwen.

Representing rebirth and the survival of life through the long winter's death, honeysuckle decorates the Eostara temple, repre-

Heartsease

Heather

$\frac{3}{4}$

$\frac{2}{3}$

Heliotrope

$\frac{2}{3}$

Hemlock

senting the renewal of spring. It may also be used at the other side of the Wheel of the Year at autumn. When used in sabbat rituals the dried, powdered bark may be used as incense.

❦ Hops ❦

Humulus Lupulus
Mars, Pluto
Scorpio
Magickal Herbe ... Religious Herbe ... Visionary Herbe

USAGE

The best use of hops is as an ingredient in dream pillows. Hops can be mixed with most other herbes associated with dream magick. It is believed that hops increases the restfulness and serenity of your dreaming time.

Hops may be brought into rituals which honor the gods and goddesses who brought the gifts of ale and beer to humankind.

❦ Horehound ❦

Marrubium Vulgare
Mercury
Gemini
Herbe of Protection ... Religious Herbe ... Visionary Herbe
Invocatory: Horus, Isis, Osiris

LORE

Linked with both the Magician card and the Wheel of Fortune card in the tarot, horehound is sacred to the god Horus. It was called the "Seed of Horus" by ancient Egyptian priests. Horehound was used by the Hebrews during Passover as a bitter herbe.

USAGE

Horehound is an excellent herbe to use in blessing one's home. A moderate amount may be added to the ritual cup. One can also make a horehound-flavored candy, used to impart blessings to the first guests.

It is possible to explore the religious aspects derived from its use as one of the bitter herbes of Passover. As a beverage, there are a number of reasons horehound might be brought into your rituals. During the invocation of a deity or of a religious attitude, the priest or priestess must learn to relax and move with the flavor rather than allowing the body to work against it. Horehound is a most useful ritual herbe and should be explored.

As a general herbe to use when working ritual forms, horehound increases your concentration and focus. It increases the mental skills needed to keep distractions at bay and the ability to integrate one's mind and body into the realm of the spiritual. Horehound can give you the freedom to weave your creativity into your magick.

Small bunches of the flowering stems may be gathered when the bloom is ripe. These should be bound with a ribbon and hung in one's home to keep it free from negative energies.

As an oil, horehound may be used in spiritual and psychic healing or any type of healing or restorative work involving magick and energy. Some believe that horehound corresponds with Hod on the Tree of Life.

❦ Horseradish ❦

Cochlearia Armoracia
Mars
Scorpio

LORE

Some lore suggests that horseradish may be another of the bitter herbes of Passover.

❦ Houseleek ❦

Sempervivum Tectorum
Jupiter
Sagittarius
Greene Herbe ... Herbe of Love ... Herbe of Protection
Invocatory: Jupiter, Thor
Also called: ayegreen, donnersbart, Jupiter's beard

LORE

Mrs. Grieve in *A Modern Herbal* provides us with considerable information about the houseleek, lore which would encourage any practitioner to grow this herbe at home.

> It was supposed to guard what it grows upon against fire and lightning, and we read that Charlemagne ordered it to be planted upon the roof of every house, probably with this view... Welsh peasants believe it protects their houses from storms, and ensures the prosperity of their inmates. Superstitious country-folk in Wiltshire are often found to have a strong objection to the removal of a plant of Houseleek from their roof, or even to the plucking of the flowers by a stranger, believing it will bring death to the dwellers; it was formerly believed to be an efficient guard against sorcery as well as against lightning.

Albertus Magnus suggests that, when combined with periwinkle, a potion can be made which will cause two people to fall in love.

USAGE

Lore indicates that growing houseleek is the most efficient way to access its magick. We believe that one may also benefit from using the leek in cooking, although this is desirable only when they are grown around (or upon!) one's home. Commercial leeks do not seem to provide ready access to the natural energy.

Albertus Magnus also maintains that the juice of the houseleek mixed with nettles can attract fish. When the mixture is rubbed on one's hand and the hand dipped into water, fish are attracted. Perhaps this might be a winning combination. We would recommend working with the houseleek as a patron herbe for those who enjoy fishing.

❦ Hyacinth ❦

Hyacinthus sp.
Mars, Saturn
Religious Herbe
Invocatory: Apollo, Hyacinthus

LORE

There are many variations on the ancient stories of this lovely flower. Let me cite *Larousse World Mythology* for one version which links Hyacinth with Apollo.

> Apollo loved young boys, in accordance with a time-honored custom among the Dorian people. His adventures with Hyacinthus...did not end happily. (Hyacinthus) was a young Lacedaemonian prince of great beauty and Apollo fell in love with him. One day when they were both throwing the discus in the gymnasium, either the wind caught the projectile or else it hit a rock and rebounded to strike Hyacinthus on the head and kill him. Apollo was distraught; to make his friend immortal he transformed his body into a flower, the hyacinth, and its petals were said to be marked with the initial of Hyacinthus' name.

The version related by Grieve in *A Modern Herbal* includes the rivalry between Apollo and the wind god, Zephyrus.

> Tradition associates the flower with the Hyacinth of the Ancients, the flower of grief and mourning, so Linnæus first called it Hyacinthus. Hyacinthus was a charming and handsome Spartan youth, loved by both Apollo and Zephyrus. Hyacinthus preferred the Sun God to the God of the West, who sought to be revenged. One day, when Apollo was playing quoits with the youth, a quoit that he threw was blown by Zephyrus out of its proper course and struck and killed Hyacinthus. Apollo, stricken with grief, raised from his blood a purple flower on which the letters *ai, ai*, were traced, so that the cry of woe might for evermore have existence on the earth.

USAGE

The Justice card is associated with the hyacinth. Hyacinth, as with all herbes, can be used to correspond with the cards in a number of ways: the oil may be placed upon one's body or burned as an incense, flowers can be placed around the cards or the herbe can be taken as an elixir.

The hyacinth is a patron herbe for gay men. The legends provide them with an affirmation of their masculinity and brings them the special protection of Apollo.

❦ Hyssop ❦

Hyssopus Officinalis
Jupiter
Cancer, Sagittarius
Countermagick Herbe ... Herbe of Consecration ... Herbe of
Protection ... Herbe of Purification

LORE

Hyssop is a name of Greek origin. The Hyssops of Dioscorides was named from *azob* (a holy herb), because it was used for cleaning sacred places. Grieve in *A Modern Herbal* tells us it is alluded to in the scriptures: "Purge me with Hyssop, and I shall be clean." Hyssop is one of many herbes which Solomon is said to have gathered and made into his aspurger for ritual work. Some believe that small bunches of hyssop were used by the Hebrew people to paint their portals with blood, protecting their children until Moses could lead them safely away. Hyssop corresponds with the Chariot card and may also be used with any of the four King cards.

Robert Graves in *The White Goddess* wrote that the ancient (pagan) Hebrews considered hyssop an herbe of the Winter Solstice.

USAGE

One of the best herbes for cleansing and purification, hyssop should be gathered, bound into small bunches and dried. These bunches may be used to protect one's temple or home by hanging them at the windows, doors and any other portals.

Hyssop is believed to keep away all negative energies. Some cultures also believe that hyssop will protect your property against burglars and trespassers. To accomplish this, gather a bunch of hyssop, bind it with a cord and hang it to dry. Small bunches may be hung at all windows and doors. The ideal time for gathering hyssop is at the Cancer new Moon. It should be dried for at least a fortnight until the following full Moon.

Hyssop is a most useful herbe. The extracted oil may be used for all forms of spiritual healing, particularly work such as Therapeutic Touch. As well as imparting healing to the patient, it protects the healer.

This holy herbe may be used to consecrate any magickal tools or heirlooms which are made of tin. It has an affinity for amethyst and for lapis lazuli. Either of these stones (not both) could be stored in your hyssop jar. The herbal oil can be used for cleansing either of these stones when set in jewelry.

There is probably no herbe better suited for the physical cleansing and washing of one's temple, ritual tools or even ritual robes. The easiest method is adding some liquid extract to your cleaning water. Hyssop also makes a superior bathing herbe, bringing puri-fication to the spiritual, emotional and physical selves.

It would be good to utilize the value of hyssop at Yule or Midwinter.

 Iris

Iridaceæ sp.
Moon, Mercury
Funereal Herbe ... Herbe of Protection ... Religious Herbe
Invocatory: Hera, Hermes, Iris, Juno

LORE

This is one of our favorite flowers and it is popular in many gardens. Yet the lovely iris is also an herbe of substantial lore. In *Myths and Legends of All Nations* we discover that the iris is named after "the beautiful goddess of the rainbow." A virgin goddess, she is "a female messenger of the gods...the counterpart of Hermes." The goddess Iris is sometimes depicted standing near Hera. She has sometimes been considered the mother of Eros.

In *A Modern Herbal* Grieve writes:

> from ancient times the stately iris stood as a symbol of power and majesty; it was dedicated to Juno and was the origin of the sceptre, the Egyptians placing it on the brow of the sphinx and on the sceptre of their kings, the three leaves of its blossoms typifying faith, wisdom and valour.

USAGE

The deity Iris guides souls between the worlds, conducting them to the Otherworld. As such this herbe may be used in rituals of death and dying to bring peace to the beloved. Associated with the rainbow, it represents a belief in a happy reincarnation. Other attributes of the rainbow carry over to this flower as well, such as hope. It is a symbol of the eternal quality of the soul or spirit. The iris' strong association with goddesses has led to the custom of planting beds of this flower upon graves of women or as memorials in their honor.

The iris may be used to decorate one's temple. For a few weeks out of every year it provides us with a stately stalk of blooms to place in vases within our temples. The flowers or the root (and oil extracted therefrom) may be used to invoke any of the deities associated with the iris. Symbolizing faith, wisdom, and valor, herbal preparations of the iris can be used to consecrate a ritual wand.

Magickally, the orris is most desirable. This variety of iris (*Rhizoma Iridis*) is believed to enhance romance, help one attain companionship and love. The oil may be worn or the powdered root burned as incense to work internal changes and promote the qualities of personality which lead to having a loving, intimate relationship.

The root may be sliced and dried, with pieces added to amulets. The iris is known for its ability to bring protection in both worlds: that of the spirit and that of the flesh.

Iris is associated with the Temperance card. The orris may be used to study the mysteries of the High Priestess card. Any of the iris may be brought into rituals associated with the Spring Equinox, helping one work with Mother Nature and further one's work with the new growth of spring.

The promise of the iris lends itself to rituals designed for baby blessings. Some choose to plant a small bed of iris in the baby's honor. If this is not practical (not all babies are born during the ideal planting season of autumn), plant them the autumn following the baby's birth and have your baby present at the planting.

❦ Iris (Yellow) ❦

Iris Pseudacorus
Moon
Herbe of Purification
Also called: daggers, Jacob's sword, yellow flag, yellow iris

LORE

We can learn about the iris from Mrs. Grieve in *A Modern Herbal*.

> [This iris is] called the *Flower de Luce*, or *Fleur de Lys*, being the origin of the heraldic emblem of the Kings of France. The legend is that early in the sixth century, the Frankish King Clovis, faced with defeat in battle, was induced to pray for victory to the god of his Christian wife, Clothilde. He conquered and became a Christian and thereupon replaced the three toads on his banner by three Irises, the Iris being the Virgin's flower. Six hundred years later, it was adopted by Louis VII of France as his heraldic bearings in his Crusade against the Saracens, and it is said that it then became known as *Fleur de Louis*, corrupted into *Fleur de Luce* and then into *Fleur de Lys* or *Lis*, though another theory for the name is that it was not named *Fleur de Lys* from Louis, but from the river Lys, on the borders of Flanders, where it was peculiarly abundant...
>
> The Romans called the plant *consecratix*, from its being used in purifications, and Pliny mentions certain ceremonies used in digging up the plant.

 Ivy

Hedera Helix
Saturn
Herbe of Consecration ... Herbe of Immortality ... Herbe of
Love
Invocatory: Atys, Bacchus, Cybele, Dionysus, Osiris

LORE

Ivy has twined itself solidly into our herbal history and lore. It was highly respected by the ancients, in particular by the Greeks, who wove it into crowns worn to celebrate victory. Its tenacity and ability to survive most climates possibly led to its reputation as an herbe symbolic of fidelity and valor. In *A Modern Herbal* we learn more about this aspect of ivy.

> Its leaves formed the poet's crown, as well as the wreath of Bacchus, to whom the plant was dedicated, probably because of the practice of binding the brow with Ivy leaves to prevent intoxication, a quality formerly attributed to the plant. We are told by old writers that the

effects of intoxication by wine are removed if a handful of ivy leaves are bruised and gently boiled in wine and drunk.... The Greek priests presented a wreath of Ivy to newly married persons, and the ivy has throughout the ages been regarded as the emblem of fidelity. The custom of decorating houses and churches with ivy at Christmas was forbidden by one of the early councils of the Church, on account of its pagan associations, but the custom still remains.

A delightful reference is this from Grieve's *A Modern Herbal*:

In former days, English taverns bore over their doors the sign of an Ivy bush, to indicate the excellence of the liquor supplied within: hence the saying "Good wine needs no bush."

Ivy is associated with the likes of Dionysus and Bacchus. These lusty gods bring to my mind Disney images where they are wreathed with mirth and ivy, but ancient myths connect their affinity with this herbe in other ways as well. Dionysus once escaped pirates by magickally filling their boat with ivy. Ivy was consumed during the Bacchanalian festivals. Frazer in *The Golden Bough* tells us this led to "inspired fury."

There is another aspect of ivy found among Greek paganism. A minor deity, Atys, was worshipped by a cult of priests who castrated themselves. Atys was a shepherd known for his sensual beauty. The legend of Atys (sometimes spelled Attis), as told in *Myths and Legends of All Nations*, is that he was tormented by his desire for Cybele until he could bear it no longer and "unmanned himself." Priests of Atys went through extensive ritual preparations for their initiation which included fasting, purification, and being bathed in the fresh blood of a bull. Castration was also included in some of their rites. These priests were readily recognized by the patterns of ivy leaves tattooed upon their flesh. Although not widespread, there are priests and priestesses today who practice celibacy for whom ivy might provide additional strength.

Stewart Farrar writes in *Eight Sabbats for Witches* about another myth, one found in the legends of Robin Hood:

In the popular superstition Robin himself escaped up the chimney in the form of a robin and, when Yule ended, went out as Belin against his rival Bran, or Saturn...Bran hid from pursuit in the ivy-bush disguised as a Gold Crest Wren; but Robin always caught and hanged him.

We find ivy in the old Irish alphabet as the letter G or Gort. In Egypt it was considered a sacred herbe of Osiris. As Graves writes in *The White Goddess*, ivy has long been associated with the Saturnalia, "ivy being the nest of the Gold Crest Wren" the bird belonging to the god Saturn.

USAGE

Ivy may be woven into wreaths and included in floral arrangements when one is decorating for the union of a couple, acknowledging desired success for the marriage. Ivy might also represent victory or the virtues of this herbe may be used to enhance celebrations.

Capable of invoking gods known for their joy of revelry and of late-night partying, ivy is said to prevent drunkenness. I suspect this would only be the case were the vine used to bind the hands of one prone to excess.

Ivy is associated with the suit of Pentacles, as well as this ritual tool. When consecrating individual cards and portions of your deck, there are a variety of interesting ways one might use ivy. A piece of vine could be used to bind the silk wrapping the suit of Pentacles, or the woody stem chopped and ground to use as incense when studying this suit.

Wreathes of ivy may be worn for Beltane Eve. Ivy may be woven into the structure of the temple, as well. A number of years ago, when I was presenting a performance of ritual theater in a large meadow, the stage was a circle of Greek-style columns, all held upright by a stunning growth of vines connecting the tops. There was great magick felt among the people and the setting helped transform the actors into Pan and the Lady.

"Deck the halls with boughs of ivy" is more than a line from a Yuletide carol. Ivy's association with many of the sabbats is worthy of attention. Not only is ivy used at Yule and Beltane, Farrar refers to Doreen Valiente's description of using ivy at Candlemas, a time when the ivy placed decoratively about one's temple is given to the Candlemas fire.

❧ Jack-in-the-Pulpit ❧

Arum sp.
Jupiter, Neptune
Magickal Herbe ... Religious Herbe
Also called: arum, cuckoo-pint, friar's cowl, starchwort,
wake robin

LORE

Folklore holds that bears use this spring herbe to help them
restore their energy after the long winter's hibernation.

USAGE

Growing a patch of arums helps encourage the devas to choose
your garden as a place to frolic. The root, when collected whole
and dried, is used as an amulet to promote male fertility. This
provides us with an interesting aspect of herbal polarities, for the
jack-in-the-pulpit with its phallic jack nestled in the pulpit rises
in our woodlands in the spring, just as the Mother of Nature is
restoring Herself after the long winter.

Drawing upon the lore, jack-in-the-pulpit would be an outstanding patron herbe for those working with the bear as a totem
animal.

❧ Jasmine ❧

Jasminum Officinale
Jupiter
Cancer
Herbe of Protection ... Magickal Herbe ... Religious Herbe
Invocatory: Diana, Vishnu

LORE

Jasmine is associated with the feminine, maternal aspect of the
Divine Universe, sometimes corresponded with the feminine
number nine. Jasmine was held as a sacred herbe of Diana of
Ephesus, or Quan Yin and even associated with Mary, the mother
of Jesus. Jasmine is also used with the High Priestess card.

Grieve, in *A Modern Herbal*, describes a custom by which "the

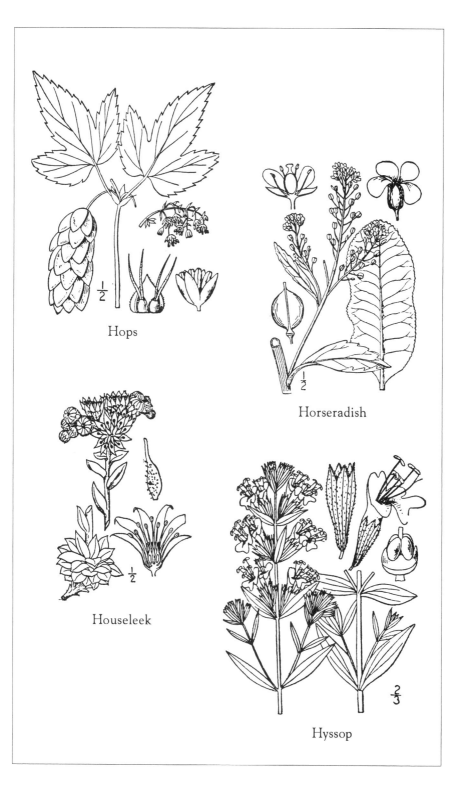

Hops

Horseradish

Houseleek

Hyssop

Hindus string the flowers together as neck garlands for honored guests. The flowers of one of the double varieties are held sacred to Vishnu and are used as votive offerings in Hindu religious ceremonies" and in Borneo the "women...roll up jasmine blossoms in their well-oiled hair at night.

USAGE

The oil extracted from jasmine is considered one of the best for dressing a candle; burning a candle with this oil gives psychic protection and brings health to one's aura.

Jasmine is associated with quartz crystals by some modern practitioners. The magickal potency of the jasmine in your herbe closet can be maintained by placing a small point of quartz in the bottom of the container. Jasmine works both with the High Priestess card and the four Nine cards of tarot.

Known for its ability to promote mental creativity, jasmine helps promote new, innovative ideas. It is also used in Eostara celebrations. It may be included in the ritual drink or used as an incense, or its flowers be worn by the high priestess. Jasmine should be considered an herbe of choice for Dianic women.

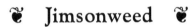

❦ Jimsonweed ❦

Datura Stamonium
Jupiter
Sagittarius
Magickal Herbe ... Visionary Herbe

LORE

In some of the shamanic cultures of northern Mexico and in some of the religions which pay homage to the Universe with peyote, jimsonweed is held in poor esteem, believed to be an herbe which is used by negative practitioners. Established lore does not recommend this herbe for use.

❦ Jujube ❦

Zizyphus Vulgaris
Pluto

The jujube is believed by some as the source of the crown of thorns for Christ (remembering that more plants share this lore than the crown could ever have contained!). The Birhor tribe of India includes the jujube in its myths. How the jujube's leaves got their shape is described in a story of the search for Rama.

❦ Juniper ❦

Juniperus Communis
Mars, Saturn
Aries
Herbe of Protection ... Herbe of Purification ... Magickal Herbe ... Religious Herbe

LORE

A tribal belief in South America relates the story of the Moon god, a young man, who visits his sister, the Sun goddess. Because he only arrives during the night, she takes him as her lover. Wanting to find out who he really is, she rubs the juice of the juniper upon his face. Unable to wash it off, his identity is discovered and he flees into the sky. This tale is used to explain the face of the Moon.

According to Frazer in *The Golden Bough*, central Europeans once used juniper as an incense to purify their homes of all negative energies in preparation for Beltane.

USAGE

The resin of the juniper can be gathered, dried and powdered, making an excellent (if pungent) incense. The berries of this evergreen are also very useful. They may be dried and placed into amulets, or ground and added to incense mixtures or even infused as a tea. The needles may be used fresh or dried, placed upon burning charcoal as incense. The incense may be used to protect and cleanse one's home or temple.

Juniper is also used to keep one healthy and to assist those who need healing. Juniper is believed to keep disease at bay and to help keep one safe from injury. This is accomplished by both banishing dark energies and by attracting good and positive healthy energy.

❦ Kamala ❦

Mallotus Philippinensis
Mars

USAGE

Kamala is used among the Hindu to dye silk. The result is a fabric which radiates a vibrant flame color. Kamala may be used by modern practitioners as a dye for ritual robes and clothing.

❦ Kava Kava ❦

Piper Methysticum
Venus, Pluto
Aphrodisiac Herbe ... Religious Herbe ... Visionary Herbe

LORE

Miller, in *The Magical & Ritual Use of Herbs*, provides us with the following belief from the Samoan people:

> The annual Sun sacrifice of a girl of great beauty, Ui, was offered. The Sun was so pleased he took her for his wife. After a period, consent was given for her to return to her people to give birth to their Child. Ui was sent flying through the sky and miscarried. The fetus, however, floated upon the water and was cared for by a hermit crab. The child, Tagaloa Ui, when he grew up, taught mortals how to make Kava as well as Reverence for the ceremony.

USAGE

Kava kava has grown in popularity, and has many uses for the modern practitioner. Its action upon the sexual organs and nerves within them is well documented in this century. This property has led to kava kava's use in the Great Rite and in sexual magick. The following comes from *The Master Book of Herbalism*:

> [Kava kava is] used as a sacramental drink, first fermented into a potent beverage, and taken before important rituals. It then induces visions and altered states of perception. The root is also made into a potion and this also is used.
> Due to the physical action of the herbe upon the

214

sexual organs, they are stimulated and yet the sensation is dulled, making kava kava one of the most effective of aphrodisiacs. It is most used in ritual today, when sex is being explored as a sacred tool of the gods.

In the early 1980s we worked with a Hawaiian student who related that this herbe is used by the Huna when working within the astral.

When celebrating the Great Rite, kava kava can be part of the ritual cup or might be macerated in the oils which are used as lubricants. It may be steeped in very hot water, the mixture then *thoroughly* filtered through paper (such as a coffee filter). The resulting liquid may be used as a douche prior to the Great Rite.

❧ Lachnanthes ❧

Lachnanthes Tinctoria
Saturn
Magickal Herbe
Also called: gyrotheca, paint root, red root

USAGE

Mrs. Grieve cites Millspaugh, who reports that the Seminole believe lachnanthes empowered one's speaking ability, providing a way with words and the ability to bring forth wondrous speech. Useful for bards and for those who use their voice as a magickal tool, this root should be used with extreme caution.

❧ Lady's Mantle ❧

Alchemilla Vulgaris
Venus, Mars
Magickal Herbe ... Religious Herbe
Also called: bear's foot, stellaria

LORE

During the Middle Ages when extensive folklore and magick was assimilated into European Christian lore, lady's mantle, previously sacred to several earth goddesses, became associated with Mary, the mother of Jesus. From Grieve in *A Modern Herbal* we learn the following:

The generic name *Alchemilla* is derived from the Arabic word, *Alkemelych* (alchemy), and was bestowed on it, according to some old writers, because of the wonder-working powers of the plant. Others held that the alchemical virtues lay in the subtle influence the foliage imparted to the dewdrops that lay in its furrowed leaves and in the little cup formed by its joined stipules, these dewdrops constituting part of many mystic potions.

When working with the tarot, lady's mantle is the appropriate herbe when studying the four Aces.

USAGE

Lady's mantle belongs in everyone's garden and herbe closet. It has a recognized ability to increase the power of any magickal working. It not only makes the magick more effective, but it also provides focus toward the successful manifestation of the intent of the working. Lady's mantle can be used to work with Mother Earth.

The reputation of this herbe among ancient alchemists is preserved in its Latin name. Lady's mantle was said to contain the ability to transmute the formulae of an alchemist. Alchemilla is a patron herbe of alchemists.

Although lore indicates that great magick can be worked with the morning dew, there are other ways in which this herbe may provide service in one's temple. The pollen may be collected from the flowers, the roots dried and powdered or, although not as potent, the dried leaves may be powdered. One may think of lady's mantle as having the ability to add a metaphorical exclamation mark to one's magickal intent.

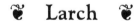

❦ Larch ❦

Pinus Larix
Jupiter
Religious Herbe

LORE

Studying the references to larch found in *Larousse World Mythology*, one finds a fascinating view of the Siberian cosmology. It is not that dissimilar from the cosmologies of other major religions, such as those of Tibet, Egypt or the Celts.

> The universe, as described by the Siberian peoples, may be compared to a large and almost symmetrical egg divided vertically. On the far horizon the jaws of heaven clash with those of earth, thus producing winds. There are three registers altogether: upper, middle and lower "earths." Between the world above and the world below, which is often a mere reflection of the former and, like it, is composed of an equal number of layers or floors, the earth proper seems to be a thin surface.... The axis of the universe, [the] larch...connects the three separate registers and goes through the earth at its centre or "navel" and through the sky at the point of the pole star.... Its branches span the different spheres, and its roots go down into the nether world. The ancient earth goddess dwells in the tree itself or by its roots, and the souls of unborn children inhabit its branches like frail birds, while the Sun and Moon take their seats near the top.

USAGE

The resin of the larch (which some tribes believe is sacred food for giants) may be dried and used as incense. The needles of this pine may be dried and powdered or the wood can be turned into sawdust. Larch is an excellent herbe when seeking to understand the underlying meaning of any religion for it is a respected Tree of Life. It would lend itself to students of Kaballah, runes, Hermetics or any system or religious cosmology which is compatible with the above-mentioned metaphorical structure.

❦ Larkspur (Field) ❦

Delphinium Consolida
Mars
Magickal Herbe ... Religious Herbe

LORE

We find references to larkspur passed down with Midsummer celebrations. Farrar writes in *Eight Sabbats for Witches*:

> another custom widespread throughout Europe was to strengthen the eyes by looking at the [ritual] fire through bunches of larkspur or other flowers held in the hand.

USAGE

Larkspur may be used in ritual healing, particularly when the eyes are involved. Those wishing to improve the quality of their sight, not only the physical but their ability to perceive the world around them, would be wise to work with this herbe. A well-filtered wash could be used to bathe the eyes.

Larkspur (or even the delphinium found in our gardens) makes a lovely decoration for the Midsummer temple. We suspect, but cannot verify, that the name is derived from Delphi.

❦ Laurel (Mountain) ❦

Kalmia Latifolia
Mars, Saturn
Funereal Herbe

LORE

Modern lore records some Native peoples of eastern North America who have used strong extractions of the juice found in the leaves as a means of causing the death of their bodies in order to release the spirit and move into the Otherworld.

USAGE

We do not recommend the use of this plant due to its narcotic and potentially lethal properties.

❦ Lavender ❦

Lavendula Vera
Mercury
Virgo
Fertility Herbe ... Herbe of Consecration ... Herbe of Love ...
Magickal Herbe ... Religious Herbe ... Visionary Herbe
Invocatory: Hecate, Saturn

LORE

How would one describe this well-known herbe's color? Its very name could be the only accurate description of these pale, purplish flower stalks. Lavender is a staple of the magickal herbalist.

Among the lore is the belief that lavender is associated with snakes. In the second volume of Grieve's A Modern Herbal we find this reference:

> Dr. Fernie, in Herbal Simples: "By the Greeks the name Nardus is given to Lavender, from Naarda, a city of Syria near the Euphrates, and many persons call the plant 'Nard.' Saint Mark mentions this as Spikenard, a thing of great value.... It was formerly believed that the asp, a dangerous kind of viper, made Lavender its habitual place of abode, so that the plant had to be approached with great caution."

We know that lavender has been an herbe treated both with respect and as a sacred herbe since ancient times. Customs date to pre-Christian times in which lavender is brought into Midsummer rites. It is one of the many herbes said to have been selected by the legendary King Solomon, son of David who lived some three thousand years ago, to aspurge his temple.

Lavender was very popular in the Middle Ages. The lore at this time is impressive, even if inconsistent. Used by some to promote lust and romance, others believed it kept them from the temptations of the flesh.

USAGE

Modern usage includes lavender's being burned in birthing rooms, the scent of its smoke filling the room, keeping it pure, and welcoming the new life into the world. Established customs indicate that lavender may have the properties of a Fertility Herbe. It has been woven into small wreaths to crown newly married couples, and is often used in Handfasting rituals today. There are other ways it can be brought into a rituals of union: it can be part of the elixir in the ritual cup shared by the newly joined couple, adding permanence to their vows; the blossoms can be added to the bridal bouquet; ritual bathing prior to the nuptials might make use of lavender soap; a wise cook might grind the flowers into a fine powder to be mixed into the cake's batter. It is suspected that lavender's use in Handfastings and marriages comes from a belief that it promoted fertility in women.

Lavender was thrown into fires on Saint John's Day. Today lavender is often included in Midsummer incense, but it can be used at any time of the year. Lavender is known for its ability to increase one's clarity when viewing the world and to assist the evolution of one's spirit through life. This well-known herbe is used magickally to assist bringing any work into manifestation. The herbe has an associated with the god Saturn, which enhances the potential for permanence of its magickal workings.

Despite lavender's mercurial nature, it is believed capable of invoking deities such as Hecate and Saturn. And yet this powerful herbe is known to bring calmness and serenity to one's inner self. It is used in a remedial fashion to alleviate stress and may be used magickally for the same purpose. If working with ritual or magick to promote healing from a depression, lavender is a superior choice.

As mentioned in the lore, there is some association with snakes. Whether this is an aspect of lavender's ability to increase one's wisdom (the snake has been associated with knowledge since early biblical times) or of folklore (snakes may find comfort resting beneath the bush), this information may be of value to many practitioners. There are a significant number of deities associated with snakes and lavender might be used in a ritual to any of them. Lavender would also serve as a patron herbe for those who work with or keep snakes.

Lavender is sometimes used to increase one's ability to manifest money or to attract desired possessions; however, if the motive for the magickal working is desire rather than genuine need, the magick could work in reverse.

Associated with the Hermit card, lavender is also used in the blessing of one's home. A bunch of lavender bound together is well used in the aspurging of one's home, temple or ritual circle.

❦ Lemon ❦

Citrus Limonum
Venus, Neptune
Aphrodisiac Herbe ... Magickal Herbe

LORE

Among the lesser deities of the Buddhist pantheon we find Jambhala, a very rotund god. In one hand he holds a mangosteen, a thick-skinned, juicy fruit and in the other hand he holds a lemon.

USAGE

Some contemporary books containing herbal mixtures to bring romance into one's life include dried, powdered lemon rind. Those living in southern climes should pick a lemon beneath the full Moon. If the lemon cannot be found growing in your area, you might make a journey to the market as part of your full-Moon work.

Peel the rind and place it to dry. When it is completely dry (which could take weeks), grind it into a powder. This fine lemon powder may be added to a potion or the natural oil could be extracted for use in the making of a lubricant to use when working the Great Rite or any sexual work to achieve magickal goals. Do not use too strong a mixture and be sure it is filtered well. Another technique is to cut a small, heart-shaped piece from the rind to dry and carry as a magickal token in a pouch, pocket or purse. It is believed that this will help attract a partner. A fun bit of modern lemon lore is that the cutting of the rind from a lemon without breaking it, so it comes away in a single piece, will help attract a new love within a lunar cycle. We can adapt this folklore by cutting the rind in a continuous, single spiral, drying it, then grating the rind finely to add to the incense mixture for the Great Rite.

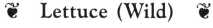

❦ Lettuce (Wild) ❦

Lactuca Virosa
Moon

LORE

Grieve's entry for wild lettuce tells us that Emperor Augustus paid great homage to this herbe. Augustus lived during the time of the birth of Jesus. A near-fatal illness fell upon the emperor. He was treated with wild lettuce and, in an expression of gratitude and thanks to this herbe, had a statue erected in its honor.

❦ Life-Everlasting ❦

Antennaria Margaritaceum
Sun
Herbe of Immortality ... Religious Herbe

LORE

From *The Master Book of Herbalism* we learn that if life-everlasting is grown in one's garden, it will help carry the soul of the gardener far into the spiritual realms upon death.

USAGE

Life-everlasting has long been loved by gardeners and is one of their patron herbes. The flowers are so well preserved when dried that the herbe seems almost mystical to even the nonbelievers. Modern practitioners are able to use the herbe to call upon undines (for communion with the spirit of elemental water) or gnomes (which represent the energy of elemental earth). Fresh blossoms may be floated upon the water's surface while dried blooms may be offered as a sacrifice, placed in one's ritual fire.

❦ Lilac ❦

Syringa Vulgaris
Moon, Venus
Magickal Herbe

LORE

In some Baltic lands, there is the belief in a sprite known as Pusait. His favorite place to wait around was beneath the lilac. Known as a friend of dwarves and earth spirits, he would send the dwarves forth to village homes to bring him bread, beer and cooked foods. Offerings would sometimes be put out for him. Sometimes, if food was missing from the kitchen, it was believed that it had been carried away by the dwarves at Pusait's bidding.

USAGE

Modern herbal magick does not have any established customs regarding the lilac, despite the popularity of its scent. Lore indicates that lilacs in one's garden encourage the devas to take up

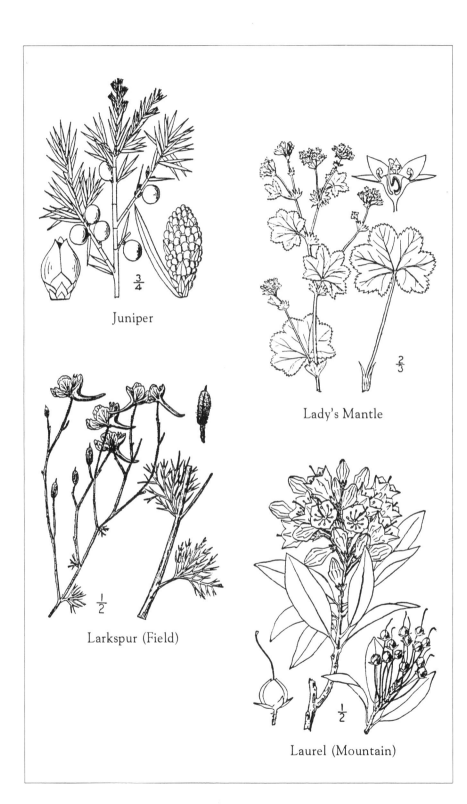

Juniper

Lady's Mantle

Larkspur (Field)

Laurel (Mountain)

residence within their environs.

❧ Lily ❧

Lilium sp.
Moon
Magickal Herbe ... Religious Herbe

LORE

The cultivation of lilies dates back to very ancient cultures. Many of the Mediterranean religions associated lilies with goddesses. Some believe the first lily came from the tears of Eve, shed when banished from the Garden of Eden. Some Christian lore associates the white lily with Mary, mother of Jesus. She is sometimes de-picted carrying them in her arms. The white lily is also considered a symbol of purity.

From *Myths and Legends of All Nations* we learn the story of the purple lily. Ajax, after Achilles' death, lost a battle with Odysseus for Achilles' armor. He was so distraught by this that he killed a herd of innocent sheep. When he realized what he had done, he felt his honor could never be recovered and, despondent, killed himself. "From his blood, according to legend, grew the purple lily bearing on its petals the first two letters of his name."

We find medieval lore from *The Book of Secrets of Albertus Magnus* regarding this beautiful plant:

> Take thou wilt gather this herb, the Sun being in the sign of the Lion, and wilt mix it with the juice of the Laurel, or Bay tree, and afterward thou shalt put that juice under the dung of cattle a certain time, it shall be turned into worms, of the which, if powder be made, and be put about the neck of any man, or in his clothes, he shall never sleep, nor shall not be able to sleep until it be put away.

USAGE

There are many ways to use this popular flower. The white lily is widely associated with Eostara, Christian Easter, and renewal and rebirth. The lily has strong associations with fertility goddesses.

❦ Lily-of-the-Valley ❦

Convallaria Magalis
Mercury
Magickal Herbe ... Religious Herbe
Invocatory: Apollo
Also called: Jacob's ladder, male lily, May lily

LORE

Who can resist this simple flower? Its charming bell-shaped flower stalk, "like a pearl of fairy bells, each bell with the edges turned back with six small scallops" writes Grieve. The lily-of-the-valley's charming appearance belies the potency of its medicinal value. It is often depicted in illustrated books of fairy tales and stories for children.

Grieve in *A Modern Herbal* describes folklore of Sussex, England, in a wooded area called Saint Leonard's forest, where lily-of-the-valley grows thickly. Local legend tells that, in fiercely battling a great dragon, Saint Leonard was wounded several times. Wherever his blood fell to the forest floor, this herbe sprung up and grows to this day. She goes on to write that "legend says that the fragrance of the lily-of-the-valley draws the nightingale from hedge and bush, and leads him to choose his mate in the recesses of the glade."

Grieve also writes that Apuleius, an herbalist living four centuries after the birth of Christ, relates the belief that the herbe was discovered by Apollo.

USAGE

The lily-of-the-valley seems to be a highly favored herbe of the devas. One of the most useful ground covers for deeply shaded areas, there is a magick about using an herbe of such medicinal value, one associated with the fairy folk found beneath trees which can be planted to fill out-of-the-way places in one's garden.

The flower may be gathered, dried and powdered as a magickal additive to any incense or mixture. Some prefer doing the same with the rhizome or with the fruit (the flower produces a berry which turns red as it ripens). Under no circumstances should lily-of-the-valley be consumed or taken internally for magickal

225

purposes.

We might make use of the association with Apollo. Lily-of-the-valley would be most useful in herbal alchemy and would be among an alchemist's patron herbes. The lore connecting lily-of-the-valley with a Sun god combined with the preference for the flower of growing in the shade and the astrological association of Mercury, that deity who moves between the light and the dark all provide a paradigm for an invaluable magick.

❦ Lime ❦

Citrus Acida
Jupiter
Magickal Herbe ... Religious Herbe

LORE

Larousse World Mythology records the Latvian customs involving the lime. Extremely animistic, these people had a large pantheon of minor deities. The Latvian people "had to make sure of the good will of all these little gods by means of offerings left on stones partially hidden in the earth. These rites were observed under oak-trees for men (and) lime-trees for women."

USAGE

It would follow that the lime might be given a significant role in the workings of women's groups. Although most readers might not have a lime growing in their back yard or neighborhood, women everywhere would be able to purchase a lime at the market.

❦ Linden ❦

Tiliaceae sp.
Saturn
Sagittarius
Religious Herbe
Invocatory: Zeus

LORE

Poor Sagittarius! Half man and half horse, his father was Cronus, a very powerful deity who fathered Saturn and sired numerous offspring. After Cronus successfully seduced Philyra, they were caught in the act. Cronus, not always of the highest morals, changed himself into a horse and galloped off. Upon Sagittarius' birth, Philyra was so ashamed at her baby's appearance that she turned herself into a linden. Philyra is the mother of Chiron.

In another story, the linden is associated with Zeus. In his travels upon the earth, Zeus was given hospitality by an elderly couple after being turned away by many human travelers. When Zeus turned his anger upon the countryside, causing a great flood, he protected the elderly couple by taking them to a hill, giving them a temple and making them priest and priestess in his honor. Their final wish was that they would not be separated at the time of their death and Zeus changed them into an oak and a linden.

USAGE

The lore associating the linden with Sagittarius makes linden an excellent herbe for working with animals, especially horses. There are many possible ways to explore magick with this patron herbe of equestrians. This herbe can provide protection for one's steed and might even help in winning races or contests. We are aware of no modern usage, but recommend exploring linden as beneficial for animals.

The linden may also be used to invoke the blessings of Zeus. It may be grown in his honor and the wood may be gathered and burned as an offering. Powdered linden may be included in incense mixtures.

❦ Loosestrife (Purple) ❦

Lythrum Salicaria
Mars
Herbe of Protection ... Visionary Herbe

LORE

The common name, *loosestrife*, dates back to an old belief that any species of the loosestrife family held the power to calm and soothe animals and creatures. In other words, the herbe could set loose any strife.

USAGE

Purple loosestrife is considered one of the finest herbes for preserving eyesight, soothing sore eyes and the like. This herbe may also be used in fluid condensers; these are herbal preparations used to gently bathe one's eyelids, providing sight into the astral. Purple loosestrife is ideally suited for any magickal preparation intended to extend visionary sight.

Although any of the loosestrife family might be used to promote peace, the purple is among the best. Purple loosestrife has grown rampant since set loose in the wilds; this aggressive behavior by such a lovely herbe is due to human error.

Loosestrife can be carried in one's pocket to any meetings or encounters which have the potential for argument and emotional disagreement. It was once believed that loosestrife could stop two animals from fighting by simply tossing the herbe into the midst of the battle. If it were only that easy to calm human animals, perhaps the fast-spreading herbe could be sown throughout the world! There are many ways to bring purple loosestrife into animal magick.

❧ Lotus ❧

Nymphæa Lotus
Neptune
Herbe of Consecration ... Herbe of Protection ... Herbe of
Purification ... Religious Herbe
Invocatory: Brahma, Hermes, Horus, Isis, Lakshmi, Mithra,
Osiris, Sri, Vishnu

LORE

There is more than one lotus in the world of myths. In Homer's *Odyssey*, the lotus tree bore the fruit which fed the lotus eaters, keeping them in a state of reverie.

But the lotus we refer to in this compendium is found within the water lily family. This flower is depicted in the religious symbolism of several cultures and can be found dating back to the worship of Mithra. With its long stem connecting the stunning flower with the roots deep beneath the water, the lotus has been recognized as sacred to deities which move between the worlds.

We find the flower revered among the Hindu peoples. The primary deity, Brahma, has four heads and four hands. Brahma was born in a lotus and this flower is central to his being. Brahma's hands hold the sacred books of the laws, but he must move deeper than the written pages to seek the meanings of purpose. The following is from *Larousse World Mythology*:

> "Who am I," he asks, "who sits upon this lotus-flower? Whence comes this lotus which grows in isolation on the waters? Perhaps there is something beneath it which holds it up?"
>
> So he climbs into the lotus stem, but abandons his exploration when he finds nothing, and he enters into meditation. Vishnu then appears to him, blesses him and advises him to surrender to fervent austerity. Only the heat he therein engenders enables him to proceed to the work of creation.

The next god of the Hindu trinity is Vishnu. The consort of Vishnu is known as Lakshmi or Sri. She is believed to have been born from the frothy foam floating upon the sea (as was Aphrodite). She is often shown holding a lotus. When this age of the world comes to an end, it will be flooded as we learn in *Myths and Legends of All Nations*:

> The waters of the world will cover everything and on the topmost point of the stalk, high above the water, Brahma will appear to again carry out his periodic task of creating the earth anew.

The Hindu history of the lotus carried this flower into Buddhist beliefs as well. Buddha uses a lotus to explain the mysteries. Of the Buddhas associated with the four directions, Amitabha, of the west, holds a lotus. Many of the deities are described in lotus imagery.

In Tibetan Buddhism Padma Sambhava, the Lotus-Born, is believed to have been a guru who was an incarnation of the Buddha. In Tibet there is also found the goddess Kunda who, in her many arms, holds a veritable arsenal of weapons (including a sword and a thunderbolt) in addition to a golden lotus. We could write about these references for several paragraphs. We urge herbalists studying the lotus to turn to Buddhist texts.

Found throughout Egyptian mythology, the family trinity of Memphis was completed by the god Nefertum who is usually shown wearing a lotus upon his head. The creation myths of this Egyptian culture saw the Sun come into creation above a lotus which emerged from the ocean. As found in many cultures, legends were written of two brothers who fought. Seth once tore out Horus' eyes. Seth, usually considered of questionable ethics, planted them on a mountain to bring light to the earth. The bulbs grew into lotuses.

The lotus also grows in Japan and is found throughout Japanese Buddhism. When a twelfth century movement to restore Buddhism was founded by Nichiren, an activist monk, the sacred writings known as the Lotus of the Good Law became an object of worship. Within the Japanese pantheon, many deities and a number of great Japanese teachers or Boddhisatvas are shown seated upon lotuses. The color may vary but the spiritual significance is universal.

The Chinese goddess of the North Star, Tou Mu rules over her kingdom of the heavens from a lotus throne.

USAGE

The pod is one of the most striking seed pods found among the realm of flowers. It may be used for burning incense (generally small cones or joss sticks). When conducting a ritual of death and dying to guide a soul to the Otherworld, the pod of the lotus provides an ideal thurible. The unusual shape of the pod lends its use as a ritual container to sit upon one's altar. With imagination, one might use it for salt or other uses.

The oil of the lotus is singular for ritual work. It is among the finest for dressing candles. Lotus oil will add an aura of protection to any candle both consecrating it and bringing protection to all that fall within the candle's light. The ability of the lotus to cleanse and purify is transferred through the light emanating from the flame.

The lotus may be used when studying the Hanged Man card. Working with the herbe may help you understand how to emulate the character in the card, using withdrawal from activity as the medium for manifesting dreams.

What a marvel is the seed of a lotus. Shaped like a marble, the seed can be treated as an item of power. For many years I have kept a seed within my box of home-ground incense. It holds the energy and particular magick I blend with herbes and preserves it so that the power is not diminished when a new mixture is added.

Associated with both amber and aquamarine, it is believed to enhance the energy of either gemstone. This may be accomplished through the oil, by storing the stones in the wells of a seed pod or by storing a seed in the same container as the gem. We regret the limitations of our knowledge of Asian deities but encourage you to explore the potential of using the lotus in its proper context.

Lovage

Levisticum Officinale
Sun
Taurus
Herbe of Love

USAGE

Despite the absence of written lore, lovage is a much-used herbe among modern practitioners. We have found a custom of Bohemia in which young maidens wear lovage in a small muslin bag hung from a cord about the neck. This is done to attract the perfect boy during the dating years. Lovage is associated with romance and love and may be used as a bathing herbe. Not only does it provide a delicate scent, but it is said to increase one's appeal, thus helping to bring romance into one's life. From *The Master Book of Herbalism* we learn:

> not only will it bring you love, but regular bathing with this herbe will enhance your beauty, physically, and will also allow the inner radiance to shine forth more brightly.

The romantic aspects of lovage may be most useful for a couple preparing for the Great Rite. Adding some of the herbe to the water and bathing together is one method; another would be to massage lovage oil into each other's body.

Lovage is an excellent herbe to use when studying either the Hierophant card or the World card of the tarot. It may be powdered for use as an incense or sipped as a tea.

❦ Magnolia ❦

Magnolia Virginiana
Jupiter
Magickal Herbe

USAGE

Although there is no verified lore found in the history of magnolia available to us, it was found corresponded with the major arcana. There is an affinity between the magnolia and the Wheel of Fortune card. This is one of those references which may have arisen at the turn of the last century. One may work with the extracted oil or even place a magnolia bloom in a bowl of water when meditating upon this card.

❦ Maguey ❦

Agave Furcraea
Mars
Religious Herbe

LORE

In the Aztec creation myth, the process of bringing the Sun into being was not easy. With the world created, life was unable to exist due to the lack of sunshine. The gods assembled to discuss this deep concern. Nanahuatzin, until that time an insignificant deity, offered to intervene and made a great sacrifice. In addition to reeds, he offered the thorns of a maguey as a blood offering, after they were stained with his own blood. In some versions he is also believed to have then offered his life, casting himself into a great fire.

USAGE

This lore provides us with insight into the religious customs and beliefs of the western hemisphere. Blood offerings were more prevalent than archaeologists and historians once believed. In our (European) western magick, blood is not often acknowledged as a source of power. Blood makes modern people uncomfortable. The common modern custom of using one's own blood in the conse-cration of a ritual knife is but one of the few blood offerings used within contemporary witchcraft, although menstrual blood is a source of power widely recognized within women's mysteries.

Should one choose to work with blood harvested by blood-letting, there may be no more honorable herbe to use as a ritual implement than the maguey's thorn.

🐛 Mandrake 🐛

Atropa Mandragora
Mercury, Uranus, Pluto
Aphrodisiacal Herbe ... Fertility Herbe ... Herbe of Love ...
Herbe of Protection ... Magickal Herbe ... Religious Herbe ...
Visionary Herbe
Invocatory: Circe, Diana, Saturn

LORE

There are few herbes as steeped with magickal lore as is the mandragora. (Be aware that some vendors will sell American Mandrake which is known as Mayapple. This plant is *Podophyllum Peltatum* and not related.) Grieve provides us with such extensive information that it is difficult to avoid quoting everything she has in her Herbal. References to mandrake are found in many sources; it is often associated with the most intense practices of magick. Perhaps this is why some Arabian cultures refer to this herbe as Satan's apple. Mandrake is often linked with death, witchcraft and evil. An herbe historically considered evil is almost always an herbe with more power than the common person can comprehend. Those things beyond human understanding (like storms) were usually feared. The following two quotes are from Grieve's *A Modern Herbal*:

> Among the old Anglo-Saxon herbals both Mandrake and periwinkle are endowed with mysterious powers against demoniacal possession. At the end of a description of the Mandrake in the Herbarium of Apuleius there is this prescription:
> For witlessness, that is devil sickness or demoniacal possession, take from the body of this said wort mandrake by the weight of three pennies, administer to drink in warm water as he may find most convenient— soon he will be healed.
> Bartholomew gives the old Mandrake legend in full, though he adds: "It is so feynd of churles others of

233

wytches." He also refers to its use as an anæsthetic. Bartholomew gives two other beliefs about the mandrake which are not found in any other English Herbal—namely, that while uprooting it the digger must beware of contrary winds, and that he must go on digging for it until sunset.

Josephus says that the mandrake—which he calls Baaras—has but one virtue, that of expelling demons from sick persons, as the demons cannot bear either its smell or its presence. He even relates that it was certain death to touch this plant, except under certain circumstances which he details.

Bartholomew's passage may provide insight into a belief often found in modern herblore. I suspect this is one of the origins of the twentieth century superstition of standing downwind when harvesting Magickal Herbes. The belief that mandrakes should be gathered using ritual can be found in many sources. Emboden in *Narcotic Plants* quotes Theophrastus, the father of botany, with:

One must make three circles around the mandragora with a sword while looking to the west. Another person must dance about the plant in circles reciting as much as he knows of love.

It is a common belief in the folklore of many areas that mandrake has strong associations with the human body. A mature root, carefully removed from the soil, can sometimes resemble a human body, although this usually requires a highly active imagination. With the combination of the natural power of the herb, the seeming madness induced by excessive dosage and the growing lore, it is no wonder the mandrake figured strongly in folk and spell magick. Mrs. Grieve provides us with the following in *A Modern Herbal*:

The roots of mandrake were supposed to bear a resemblance to the human form, on account of their habit of forking into two and shooting on each side. In the old Herbals, we find them frequently figured as a male with a long beard, and a female with a very bushy head of hair. Many weird superstitions collected round the mandrake root. As an amulet, it was once placed on mantelpieces to avert misfortune and to bring prosperity and happiness to the house. Bryony roots were often cut into fancy shapes and passed off as Mandrake, being even trained to grow in moulds till they assumed the desired

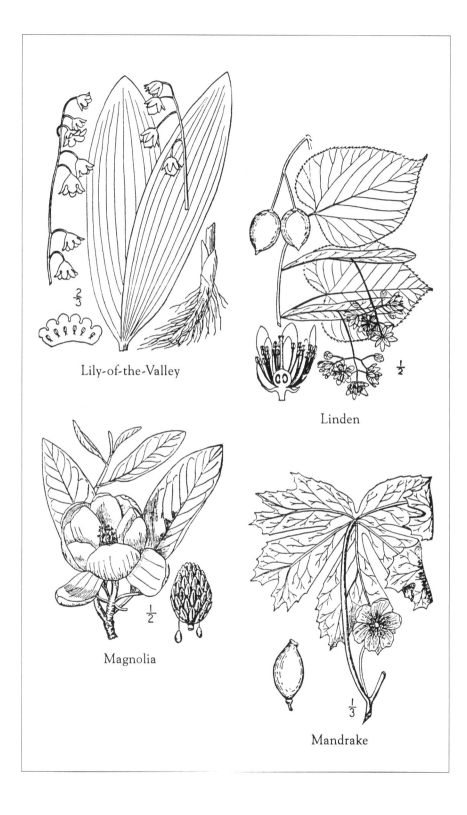

Lily-of-the-Valley

Linden

Magnolia

Mandrake

forms. In Henry VIII's time quaint little images made from bryony roots, cut into the figure of a man, with grains of millet inserted into the face as eyes, fetched high prices. They were known as puppettes or mammettes, and were accredited with magical powers. Italian ladies were known to pay as much as thirty golden ducats for similar artificial mandrakes.

Some of the most horrid of tales surround this herbe. Its associations with death and with evil led to the belief that it could grow from the blood and sperm of murderers and it was likely to be found growing beneath a gallows. Recognized as a Magickal Herbe back when the Old Testament was being recorded, the mandrake is an essential herbe for the magickal herbalist.

Mandrake had a long history of use as an anæsthetic during ancient surgery. Mrs. Grieve believes that Juliet's potion which was to put her to sleep with the appearance of death would have included mandrake. Mrs. Grieve thinks that the wine of Circe, known as Circæon, was made of mandrake.

USAGE

How does one use an herbe so potently fabled? For those who seek to learn more of the crone, it can be used in ceremonies giving honor to those deities presiding over the realm of the dead. It may also be used in rituals giving honor to Circe, the enchantress, revered as a deity within some modern covens.

As one would expect, any herbe so linked with death is also considered an herbe capable of increasing one's sexual power. There are spells in which the root is used to manipulate and take control over the object of one's lust and desire. (Who would want an unwilling partner?) Perhaps the best and most useful romantic aspect of this potent herbe is the custom of using it to seal the commitment between partners. A few grains of dried root might be added to an elixir or integrated into the signing of a license or contract between the partners.

In mixtures to be taken internally, never add enough to induce any physiological change, merely a token amount which is more than adequate to work the magick of the mandrake. Magick is no fun when your body is being violently purged by the herbe!

There are many ways to work with potentially dangerous herbes (when ingested) within the bounds of safety. Mandrake might be used to cense the space where the Great Rite will be celebrated or placed beneath one's bed. If one has the imagination to crave increase in sexual magick, we would hope one has the imagination to creatively use mandrake.

Sometimes used in rituals of exorcism, mandrake may be added to an amulet or herbal bag worn for magick. Interestingly, this practice has sometimes been done to maintain purity and chastity and is sometimes done to attract a sexual partner.

Mandrake has great power as a Visionary Herbe. It empowers one's visions, providing the impetus to bring them into manifestation. Perhaps this is why mandrake is sometimes feared? If it is taken internally, with caution, it will make the practitioner more psychically aware and capable of clairvoyance and other psychic skills. Working with mandrake when exploring one's dreams invites the Universe to stir Her fingers, shifting the tides within the astral. An excellent time to work with this herbe is at the full Moon as we learn from *The Master Book of Herbalism*:

> Take a piece of mandrake root and place it in a container of water. A chalice or special vase would be appropriate. This should be set in "moonlight" each night until the Moon is full. In practise this means to set it out from twilight to just before dawn, keeping it away from sunlight. This, when done, is known as Moon Water.

Linked with the World card and with the Fool card, mandrake will intensify the magick of any situation. When used with the tarot, it shows the bond between the Fool as he steps out into the unknown, beginning his exploration of the world. That journey and its potential rewards are depicted in the symbolism of the World card. When meditating upon this intricate process which can lead one through all of the major arcana, one might work with Moon water.

❦ Mangosteen ❦

Garcinia Mangostana
Jupiter

LORE

From *Larousse World Mythology* we learn Jambhala, a minor Buddhist character "is outrageously corpulent and brandishes a lemon and a mangosteen."

❦ Manioc ❦

Manioca Cassava
Jupiter

LORE

> A particularly famous...myth was found on the coast of Peru in the sixteenth century. In the beginning the man and woman created by Pachacamac had nothing to eat. The man died of hunger. One day the woman, who was gathering wild fruit, accused the Sun of letting her pine away. The Sun made her fertile. The god Pachacamac killed the child that was born from her womb and cut it to pieces. He planted the teeth, which were transformed into ears of maize, the bones, which became manioc roots, and the flesh, which produced gourds and other vegetables.

That was from *Larousse World Mythology*. In another myth of the same Bacairi culture, manioc was part of a mythological food chain. Originally manioc belonged to a fish. Then a stag came along and took it from the fish. Finally the manioc was stolen by one of a pair of twins who figured in their creation myths.

Manioc plays a part in a story we will share later in this text arising from the myths of Madagascar and telling of the divine origins of rice.

❦ Marigold ❦

Calendula Officinalis
Sun
Leo
Funereal Herbe ... Herbe of Consecration ... Herbe of Love ...
Magickal Herbe ... Visionary Herbe
Also called: pot marigold

LORE

Grieve in *A Modern Herbal* cites Macer, saying that one can heal diseases of the eyes and head and cleanse negative energy merely by gazing upon the marigold and she provides us with a quotation preserving some essential lore, which appears to be derived from Macer's *Herbal*:

> It must be taken only when the Moon is in the sign of the Virgin and not when Jupiter is in the ascendant, for then the herb loses its virtue. And the gatherer, who must be out of deadly sin, must say three Pater Nosters and three Aves. It will give the wearer a vision of anyone who has robbed him.

Marigolds are strongly linked with the customs associated with honoring the dead in modern Mexico, customs that date back centuries. The marigold is also associated with love divination, as you will find in the following entry for marjoram.

The marigold was also noted by Albertus Magnus in the first English edition of his *Book of Secrets* printed around 1550. He considers the virtue or marigold to be "marvelous:"

> For if it be gathered, the Sun being in the sign Leo, in August, and be wrapped in the leaf of a Laurel, or Bay tree, and a Wolf's tooth be added thereto, no man shall be able to have a word to speak against the bearer thereof, but words of peace. And if any thing be stolen, if the bearer of the things before named lay them under his head in the night, he shall see the thief, and all his conditions, and moreover, if the aforesaid herb be put in any church where women be which have broken matrimony on their part, they shall never be able to go forth of the church, except it be put away. And this last point hath been proved, and is very true.

In Frazer's *The Golden Bough* we are told about an Eastern European belief where a woman should carefully collect the soil where her desired mate has stepped. The print of the man's foot was considered an essential part of the spell. This soil was potted with a marigold and the health of the flower was considered an indicator of the health of their relationship. We would think a perennial a far better plant for this than an annual! Who wants their relationship to die off at the first frost?

USAGE

The history of the marigold's use with aiding sight and providing visions to reclaim property indicate that the dried petals may be used alone or mixed with a dry incense to consecrate tools of divination, and the petals may also be macerated in sunflower oil to make an oil of consecration. Indeed, marigold petals may be gathered and dried and strewn around one's Circle to provide the magick of consecration and sight with a decidedly protective flavor.

Sometimes associated with the Virgin Mary, this common herbal link usually indicates a previous association with a nature goddess. Marigold flowers are well suited for today's altars.

There are few flowers better for rituals of death and dying than marigolds. The dried petals may be added to incense, petals may be strewn in the path of a casket or urn and the marigold may be planted at the grave site. When giving honor to the beloved who has passed over, using marigold will add a special, loving magick.

The magickal properties have a history which suggests the marigold would be suited for those who have lost property to theft. *The Book of Secrets* indicates that marigolds can be used to help one see the thief in one's mind and be able to identify the location of the stolen property.

Those who are the subject of gossip or slander might try the old medieval technique or a modern combination of carrying marigold petals with a bay leaf. We recommend doing your work without the wolf's tooth which was once required!

❦ Marjoram (Sweet) ❦

Origanum Marjorana
Mercury, Mars
Aries
Herbe of Love
Invocatory: Venus

LORE

Sweet marjoram has been associated with the goddess Venus. This lore is believed to date back to Roman times.

From the book *Popular Rhymes and Superstitions*, Mrs. Grieve, in *A Modern Herbal*, quotes the author Halliwell with the following:

> On Saint Luke's Day, says Mother Bunch, take marigold

flowers, a sprig of marjoram, thyme, and a little worm-wood; dry them before a fire, rub them to powder, then sift it through a fine piece of lawn, and simmer it over a slow fire, adding a small quantity of virgin honey and vinegar. Anoint yourself with this when you go to bed, saying the following lines three times, and you will dream of your future partner "that is to be":

> St. Luke, St. Luke, be kind to me,
> In dreams let me my true love see.

If a girl desires to obtain this information, let her seek for a green peascod in which there are full 9 peas, and write on a piece of paper—

> Come in, my dear,
> And do not fear;

which paper she must enclose in the peascod, and lay it under the door. The first person who comes into the room will be her husband.

USAGE

Marjoram may be used to give honor to the goddess Venus. It may be used to bring blessings to a newly wed couple if wild marjoram is not available.

❦ Marjoram (Wild) ❦

Origanum Vulgare
Mercury
Aries
Funereal Herbe ... Herbe of Love ... Herbe of Protection
Invocatory: Jove, Jupiter, Thor

LORE

Wild marjoram shares aspects of romantic lore with its sweet cousin. When Greek and Roman cultures were at their prime, marjoram was gathered and woven into braids which crowned newly wed couples.

It was a Greek custom to plant wild marjoram upon a grave. This was believed to bring peace and happiness to the soul as it moved into the afterlife.

Grieve also writes in *A Modern Herbal* that "it is said that Marjo-ram and Wild Thyme, laid by milk in a dairy, will prevent it being turned by thunder."

USAGE

Wild marjoram may be used in Handfastings and marriages. The ancient custom may be kept vital even today, weaving marjoram into circlets of herbes and flowers for the couple to wear. When in bloom, it may be added to the bouquet. It is also recommended as a bathing herbe, particularly for the woman, as part of her ritual preparation at the beginning the joining day.

The custom of growing wild marjoram continues to have value. It may be planted upon the grave, but a patch of marjoram in one's garden may be grown both to keep the memory of the departed beloved alive and to encourage all to extend blessings and good wishes for a joyful reincarnation.

The custom recorded by Grieve is believed to be connected with an association of this herbe with Thor or Jove. The protection given milk during a thunderstorm would have been obtained through the intercession of the god of lightning. Wild marjoram may be used in rituals to invoke this god by either of his names.

🍂 Marshmallow 🍂

Althea Officinalis
Venus
Aphrodisiacal Herbe ... Fertility Herbe ... Funereal Herbe

LORE

With the marshmallow we see again that dichotomy between love and death. The ancient Greeks planted the flower upon the graves of loved ones. This cousin of the hollyhock (itself a mal-low) has a greater magickal history than its modern use in herbal medicine suggests.

Graves writes about the marshmallow and its relationship to the goddess Althea, a fertility deity of the gardens who comes to a tragic end upon learning that her brothers had died at the hands of her son. Sadly, she hangs herself. Graves in *The White Goddess* does not write of this myth, but instead:

> The marshmallow—in Welsh hocys bendigaid the holy
> mallow—was Althea's flower, and she loved Dionysus

the Vine-god. She became the mother by him of Deianera...who played the part of Bloddeuwedd to Hercules.

USAGE

Keeping the customs of ancient pagans, the marshmallow may be grown upon hallowed ground, particularly those places where loved ones have been buried or where their ashes have been strewn in Sacred Circles.

The marshmallow is also associated with sexual potency. It is considered, by some, an aphrodisiac and has been used to help impotency as is recorded in *The Master Book of Herbalism*:

> The seed of the herbe may be gathered beneath a full Moon, and made into an oil which is used upon the genitals. An amulet may be made of either leaf or root, and its energy kept near the genitals for the same purpose.

High in vegetable gum, the root may be used to prepare a lubricant, well suited for use in the Great Rite. Marshmallow might be a wise choice if one partner has been anxious or if the goal of the Sacred Union is conception. Marshmallow combines well with other herbes and may be used as a fixative in making sacred lubricants.

❦ Marsh Marigold ❦

Caltha Palustris
Sun, Uranus
Herbe of Consecration ... Religious Herbe
Also called: cowslip

LORE

The generic name of the herbe, *caltha*, is, according to Mrs. Grieve, derived from the Greek *calathos* which refers to a cup or goblet. There are definitely feminine associations with this flower.

Although related to a buttercup, this herbe was commonly called a marigold because of its connection with the Virgin Mary.

Grieve also writes in *A Modern Herbal*:

It was also used on May Day festivals, being strewn before cottage doors and made into garlands.

Frazer in *The Golden Bough* writes in more detail about these customs:

> At the towns of Saffron Walden and Debden in Essex on the first of May little girls go about in parties from door to door singing a song...and carrying garlands; a doll dressed in white is usually placed in the middle of each garland.... The garlands are generally in the form of hoops intersecting each other at right angles...wreathed with rowan and marsh marigold, and bearing suspended within it two balls, is...carried on May Day.... The balls, which are sometimes covered with gold and silver paper, are said to have originally represented the Sun and Moon.

USAGE

The use of marsh marigold in connection with Beltane and May Day celebrations is well documented. The Farrars quote Frazer's *The Golden Bough*, and we would like to believe this indicates the custom was still practiced in the latter half of the twentieth century:

> It appears that a hoop wreathed with rowan and marsh marigold, and bearing suspended between it two balls, is still carried on May Day by villagers in some parts of Ireland.

This bright, yellow flower offers us access to wonderful historical customs, should we use it to celebrate our May Day rites. Its association with Mary most likely conceals a strong association with nature goddesses. Its solar energy is that of a radiant, growing Mother Earth, feminine and strong.

With this verified history and lore, could any herbe be so appropriate for the consecration of one's ritual chalices or a goblet from which a couple would sip an herbal elixir before beginning the Great Rite?

❦ Marshwort ❦

Helosciadium Nodiflorum
Neptune
Pisces
Magickal Herbe

USAGE

According to *The Master Book of Herbalism* Marshwort may be:

> used in the magickal healing of animals. Place both
> leaves and flowers at the four directions beneath either
> altar or altar stone. The animal is kept in the center of
> the Circle and the ritual of healing is performed. An
> amulet may also be made, and secured within the build-
> ing or near the sleeping place of the animal to keep it in
> good health.

Marshwort is one of the more outstanding herbes to use when
working animal magick, either in the ritual healing of animals in
one's care or, if acceptable to the creatures, injured or sick animals found in the wild. Marshwort is a patron herbe of veterinari-
ans.

❦ Matico ❦

Piper Angustifolium
Mars
Aphrodisiacal Herbe
Also called: moho-moho, yerba soldado

USAGE

Like its cousin kava kava, this shrub is considered an important
aphrodisiac. Popular in some areas of South America, particularly
Peru, matico is readily available as a sexual enhancer, due to its
usefulness in a variety of remedial treatments. Matico may be
used to enhance the magick of the Great Rite.

❧ Meadowsweet ❧

Spiræa Ulmaria
Mercury, Jupiter, Saturn
Gemini
Herbe of Love ... Magickal Herbe ... Religious Herbe
Invocatory: Bloddeuwedd, Danu
Also called: bridewort, Lady of the Meadow, Queen of the
Meadow, spirea

LORE

There are many indications that our ancestors associated this herbe with the Goddess. According to Graves in *The White Goddess*, the goddess Bloddeuwedd, wife of the god Llew, is created from meadowsweet and six other trees and flowering herbes. Meadowsweet is also sacred to the goddess Danu in her aspect as Ana. Later it was considered sacred to the Virgin Mary, a transition that often occurred to herbes sacred to Mother Nature, allowing their lore to survive.

When reading Mrs. Grieve's *A Modern Herbal*, we find that Culpeper "states that for acquiring the 'merry heart' (which Gerard mentions) 'some use the flowers and some the leaves.' " Even today we can use meadowsweet to improve our disposition.

USAGE

The lovely meadowsweet belongs in the closet of any woman working with the mysteries of the Goddess in her aspect as maiden. As a favorite of brides, meadowsweet, included in a bouquet, not only invokes the blessings of our Mother, but also brings extra joy and blessings to the new bride.

While single, a woman desiring to find her true love might use an oil extracted from the flowers. Breathing the scent of this oil nightly is believed to make her more attractive and to help her cross paths with her soul mate. This magick is considered best on Beltane Eve.

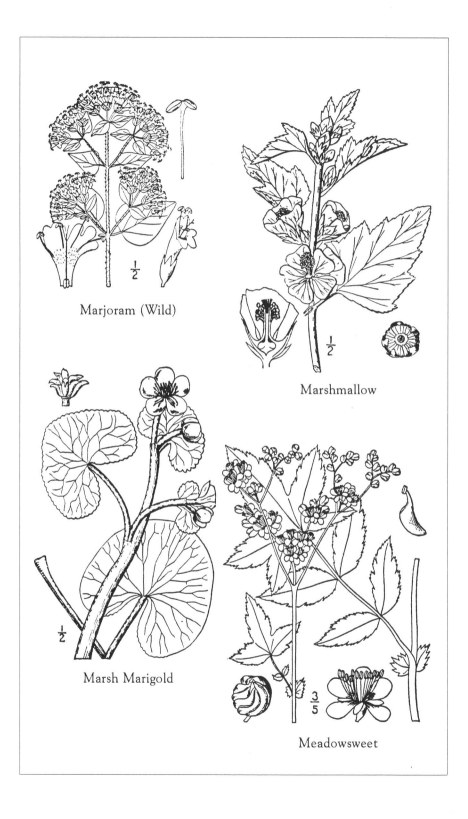

Marjoram (Wild)

Marshmallow

Marsh Marigold

Meadowsweet

❧ Melilot ❧

Melilotus Officinalis
Mercury
Magickal Herbe
Also called: king's clover, sweet clover

LORE

What is this herbe with such a curious name? None other than one of the sweet clovers. Well over 300 years ago the melilot was known for its ability to raise one's spirits and it may be so used today.

USAGE

Modern practitioners may find several usages for this clover. It continues to be a useful herbe for improving one's outlook, promoting a more positive attitude. It is most helpful in providing one with strength during a Saturn transit or in easing one out of a heavy, negative state of emotions. .

Once used to keep furs scented and protect them from moths, dried melilot is an excellent herbe to lay with one's ritual robes and altar cloths.

❧ Mercury (Dog's) ❧

Mercurialis Perennis
Saturn
Magickal Herbe ... Religious Herbe
Invocatory: Hermes, Mercury

LORE

From *A Modern Herbal* we learn dog's mercury "derives its name from the legend that its medicinal virtues were revealed by the god Mercury. The Greeks called it Mercury's grass."

USAGE

Dog's mercury has great potential as a Magickal Herbe. Despite its ability to work with the deity Mercury, it is corresponded with the planet Saturn. As Grieve writes:

248

we find it spoken of in the old herbals as possessing wonderful powers, but it has been abandoned as a dangerous remedy for internal use.

It must be kept in mind that this herbe is poisonous, capable of killing even a large sheep and has been known to kill humans.

The herbe grows both male and female. It is best used as an offering, planted in one's garden, or burned as an incense when asking for guidance from Mercury, the guide of those who move from one world to the next. Few herbes are so known for their connection with this god.

🐣 Mescal 🐣

Anhalonium Lewini
Neptune
Religious Herbe ... Visionary Herbe
Also called: pellote, peyote

USAGE

Mescal has a long history as a Visionary Herbe and a Religious Herbe. It must be used with extreme care. It is capable of provoking visions of various dimensions of time, of other-life experiences, and of one's spiritual potential. As an herbe of Neptune, great care must be maintained after the experience to keep reality and visions separate. This is a most serious herbe for the practitioner, and must never be taken lightly. Spirits are said to be associated with mescal who can plague those who use the buttons for pleasure rather than for serious religious experience, and they will bring confusion and illusion to the abuser.

This variety of peyote and other varieties are sacred to many western peoples. (There are several varieties of cacti buds all commonly called peyote.) The Kiowa, Chichimec and other North American tribes as well as the Aztec and other peoples of more southern climes all consider this herbe a direct link with the Universe. Many people believe this herbe is deserving of religious respect and consider it belongs only to those trained by descendants of this land.

❦ Milkweed ❦

Apocynum Androsæmifolium
Jupiter
Herbe of Protection ... Magickal Herbe

USAGE

Well known for attracting monarch butterflies, a patch of milk-weed provides essential sustenance as these royal butterflies migrate thousands of miles. Modern usage, because of this affinity, sees milkweed as a patron herbe for these stunning insects. Its presence is believed to encourage nature spirits and the presence of devas within your garden.

The juice may be extracted and used to bless babies or a tall stalk can be laid in the arms of a child at a Wiccaning.

Used in almost any manner, milkweed enhances one's creative energy and imagination, bringing out the child within. Some believe that the milkweed should be used at Autumn Eve in order to enter the realm of the faerie and be able to see nature spirits.

The variety of milkweed found in India and nearby parts of Asia is an important herbe for religious and magickal use. This Asian variety is listed under Asclepias in this compendium.

❦ Millet ❦

Panicum Miliaceum
Jupiter
Religious Herbe
Invocatory: Ukemochi

LORE

As with many herbal foods, myths were developed around millet which told of the divine origins of this essential grain. Let's examine one from *Larousse World Mythology* in detail:

> In Japanese mythology the legend regarding millet involves either Susanowo, an impetuous god of storms or Tsukiyomi, a Moon god (there are similar versions of the myth with either deity). As the legend unfolds, this god must descend to the earth and offer himself into the

service of Ukemochi, goddess of foods.

When the god reaches her palace, the goddess welcomes him by turning her head towards the earth and vomiting boiled rice; then she turns towards the sea, into which she spills all sorts of fish, and finally she raises her face to the mountains and sends in that direction different varieties of game. All these products are presented to the divine messenger as if it were a great banquet. But he is angered by this offering from the goddess's mouth and draws his sword and kills her. On his return to heaven he recounts these events to the Sun-goddess who displays extreme irritation at the thoughtless action of her messenger. In the account in which the Moon-god appears, she shows her disapproval by refusing to meet him again face to face. The result is that Sun and Moon remain apart, the day being assigned to the one, and the night to the other. But the story does not end there. The goddess sends another messenger to the dead food-goddess. He discovers that her inanimate body has given birth to several things: an ox and horse have emerged from her head; from her forehead has come forth millet-grass; silkworms from her eyebrows; rice from her stomach; corn and haricot beans from the lower parts of her body. The messenger takes these products and shows them to the Sun-goddess, who extracts their seeds and gives them to another deity to sow...

A very interesting appearance of millet in another Shinto myth is with a curious minor divinity, a dwarf named Sukun-bikona who rides upon waves in a tiny boat. The dwarf joins with the deity Okuninushi to help construct the physical world. Next, they create the means by which humans can conquer illness and escape the harsh sorrows of life. When this is done, the dwarf runs up an ear of millet, the stalk bending beneath his weight. As it straightens up, he is propelled off into the Otherworld. There is a sense of the trickster about Sukun-bikona.

From *The Golden Bough*, we learn that the Ainu (Caucasoid people native to Japan) see millet as growing in both male and female genders. When both grains are combined they bear a resemblance to the Great Rite and they are called "the divine husband and wife cereal" or *Umerek haru kamai*.

In Bambara cosmology, according to *Larousse World Mythology*, reality is perceived in a division of seven stages. There are "seven skies, seven earths, seven waters and seven stages in the growth of millet."

A folk belief of the Guarani tribe of South America was recorded by Frazer in *The Golden Bough*. A woman was believed likely to conceive "twins if she ate a double grain of millet."

USAGE

Millet is an appropriate herbe for harvest celebrations. Those who are fortunate might have garden plantings of several different grains which they can utilize when the Turning of the Wheel brings harvest celebrations.

Mints

Mentha sp.
Venus
Herbe of Protection ... Herbe of Purification ... Magickal Herbe ... Religious Herbe
Invocatory: Hades, Mintha

LORE

Mints play an important role in our lives. Although we may prefer spearmint, peppermint or others of the mint family, we can find lore which applies to mints in general due to the very nature of mint. If you leave the different varieties alone in your garden, they will crossbreed until you have a generic garden mint.

Described as one of the herbes used by Solomon when aspurging his temple, mints are believed sacred to the goddess Mintha. How did she become a goddess?

Hades was the god of the Underworld. Not the most popular place of deities to visit, Hades was feeling lonely and, most likely, sexually unsatisfied. Anxious to help his brother, Zeus offered Persephone as a bride. Persephone was the daughter Zeus had fathered with Demeter. Incidentally, Demeter was also Zeus' sister which means.... Anyway, Hades and Persephone did not quite live happily ever after. Hades was not the most faithful husband and the lovely Mintha caught his eye. To protect her marriage against Hades' rampant hormones, Persephone turned the beautiful nymph Mintha into the mint plant.

USAGE

Generally, the scent of a mint brings a sense of pleasure, denoting success and bringing an aura of protection. Perhaps, without realizing it, this may the reason mint seems to be the most common herbal flavoring found in toothpaste, medicines, candies, and numerous other commercial concoctions. Mint was woven into the laurels that the ancient Romans used to crown themselves and their heroes at great feasts and celebrations. Mint may be given not only to celebrate success but also to invoke success.

Mints are excellent herbes for blessing one's home. It can be bundled with other herbes, dipped into blessed water, and used to aspurge away all previous energy and bring purification.

❦ Mistletoe ❦

Viscum Album
Sun, Jupiter
Aphrodisiacal Herbe ... Fertility Herbe ... Herbe of
Consecration ... Herbe of Immortality ... Herbe of Love ...
Herbe of Protection ... Religious Herbe
Invocatory: Balder, Odin

LORE

Of all the many herbes reputed to have wondrous and magickal powers, few stir the imagination or are so widely used as mistletoe. The seed of the berry is sown by birds which have carried the seeds to branches and forks of trees. Attempts to grow it in soil do not work. The favored host of the mistletoe is the mighty oak and this relationship has led to wonderful lore and mythology in herbal history. Despite some modern authors that indicate otherwise, even Graves in *The White Goddess* maintains that mistletoe did not figure in Irish paganism, but it was a very sacred herbe within the Gallic Druids of Britain.

The majority of our most ancient lore about the Druids is based on the writings of Pliny, who lived in the first century of the Common Era. In the *Larousse World Mythology* we find the following from Pliny's *Natural History*:

> Druids have their sanctuaries in oak woods and they
> perform no sacred rite without oak leaves. They believe

that the presence of mistletoe on a tree is indicative of the presence of the god. They gather it with great ceremony. After sacrificing two white bulls, a white-robed priest climbs the tree and cuts the mistletoe with a gold sickle, and it is then caught in a white cloth.

Larousse goes on to say:

the cult of this plant has left its trace in our own customs. A number of people, either sincerely or jokingly, think it brings good luck. This tradition is particularly alive on the English side of the channel.

To this lore, Mrs. Grieve in A Modern Herbal adds:

The mistletoe was always cut at a particular age of the Moon, at the beginning of the year, and it was only sought for when the Druids declared they had visions directing them to seek it. When a great length of time elapsed without this happening, or if the Mistletoe chanced to fall to the ground, it was considered as an omen that some misfortune would befall the nation. The Druids held that the Mistletoe protected its possessor from all evil, and that the oaks on which it was seen growing were to be respected because of the wonderful cures which the priests were able to effect with it. They sent round their attendant youth with branches of the mistletoe to announce the entrance of the new year. It is probable that the custom of including it in the decoration of our homes at Christmas, giving it a special place of honor, is a survival of this old custom.

A most interesting note to our modern beliefs comes from Graves in The White Goddess when, in referring to Frazer's Golden Bough, says that "Frazer does not clearly explain that the cutting of the mistletoe from the oak by the Druids typified the emasculation of the old king by his successor—the mistletoe being a prime phallic emblem."

The Druids were not alone in their religious beliefs regarding mistletoe. A wonderful Germanic legend is related in Larousse World Mythology; an abbreviated version follows:

Balder, the second son of Odin and Frigg, is handsome, radiant and known for his good heart and temperament. He represents purity which is also a source of vulnerability for him. Wanting to protect his innocence and radiance, the gods take promises from all the elements and creatures that they will never harm Balder. Once done, it is decided to test these promises. Sticks and stones are thrown at the young god but he is not touched. Now comes the villain. Loki, god of mischief and destruction, just can't deal with something which cannot be destroyed. Loki dresses up as an old woman and goes to visit Balder's mother, Frigg. In passing, Frigg mentions that the mistletoe, being too young at the time, had not given its promise. This is all that Loki needs. He goes off, takes a twig of mistletoe and, arriving where the gods were gaming and testing all creatures, throws it at Balder. The dart strikes the golden god who falls dead, ending an age of purity and innocence which lasts until the rebirth of all creation. As Mrs. Grieve writes in *A Modern Herbal*:

> He was restored to life at the request of the other gods and goddesses, and mistletoe was afterwards given into the keeping of the goddess of Love, and it was ordained that everyone who passed under it should receive a kiss, to show that the branch had become an emblem of love, and not of hate.

Despite its being a parasite, mistletoe has developed a complex mystique. In some parts of Europe, according to *The Golden Bough* it was the law that mistletoe "may not be cut in the ordinary way but must be shot or knocked down with stones from the tree on which it is growing." The following also comes from Frazer's *The Golden Bough*:

> In the Swiss canton of Aargau all parasitic plants are esteemed in a certain sense holy by the country folk, but most particularly the mistletoe growing on an oak. They ascribe great powers to it, but shrink from cutting it off in the usual manner. Instead of that they procure it in the following manner. When the Sun is in Sagittarius and the Moon is on the wane, on the first, third, or fourth day before the new Moon, one ought to shoot down with an arrow the mistletoe of an oak and to catch it with the left hand as it falls. Such mistletoe is a remedy for every ailment of children.

The belief that mistletoe brought protection against fire was found both in Italy and in Sweden. In Sweden small bunches are hung about the home, believed particularly effective against fire brought about by lightning. Mistletoe is considered more powerful if gathered on Midsummer's Eve.

There are many folk beliefs about this herbe, including its ability to keep nightmares away and to bring protection against all evils. As Frazer puts it:

> Mistletoe acts as a master-key as well as a lightning conductor; for it is said to open all locks.

USAGE

The potency of mistletoe is legendary. The white berries grow in pairs, their appearance linked by sympathetic magick to male testicles. Over the ages they have come to represent one of the most powerful sources of fertility known in herbal magick. Most fitting for a herbe which grows in the most sacred of trees, both tree and parasite protected by Odin. As with many Fertility Herbes, mistletoe may be integrated into the Great Rite or rituals of union to ensure conception.

Mistletoe is associated with rebirth. When fresh, the whiteness of the berries may be a reflection of Balder. But Balder dies, vulnerable, and the age of purity comes to a close. Yet Balder's death is closely linked to the belief in rebirth and reincarnation. Mistletoe, found growing upon the tree green in the midst of a leafless winter's drab hues, represented the life-force and life itself. As time passed, mistletoe, with all its symbolism, came to be used at Yule to celebrate the birth of the god of light, a custom which has survived the rise and fall of religions.

The association with rebirth and life are undoubtedly very similar to the magick of fertility which permeates this herbe's history. Mistletoe may be used to promote the fertility of creation, whether toward conception of child or artistic endeavor. Many work with mistletoe in the same manner as an aphrodisiac, cautiously adding a few dried berries to an elixir in order to increase one's sexual and magickal potency.

Mistletoe is not an herbe which can be ingested safely. A few dried or fresh berries may be considered, but personal research needs be undertaken before working with this herbe in any internal manner.

Used in the celebration of Yule, there are many customs to explore. It is not uncommon in Britain to save the Yule mistletoe until Candlemas, when it is burned in the fire, completing the transition from the winter solstice. Others give mistletoe berries to their guests, gathered and dried from the previous year, which (during the Yule Rites) are tossed into the flaming cauldron.

The association of the mistletoe with the sacred knives of the Druids gives us pause. Some believe that the wood of the mistletoe (which would require a most venerable plant for a stalk of any thickness) makes the most powerful of wands, and others believe it may be used to fashion the handle for a ritual knife.

The protective energy of mistletoe may be brought to one's home. Hanging a small bunch bound with a red cord appears to bring winter blessings and kisses, and the mistletoe can be renewed (assuming you have access to the fresh herb) to coincide with the holidays. Mistletoe can also be added to a household amulet. When used for protection, this herbe reminds us that it invokes the god Balder, so pure that nothing evil or dark can exist in his presence.

At a practical level, Albertus Magnus held that mistletoe would help one open things which were locked. It might be considered a patron herbe for locksmiths.

❦ Moneywort ❦

Lysimachia Nummularia
Jupiter
Magickal Herbe

LORE

Old folk beliefs tell that this herbe has the power of healing, and is recognized as such by snakes and creatures who live in gardens.

USAGE

The use of moneywort to seek benevolence from the Universe is not widespread but one worth remembering. The bloom should be picked at its prime and set to float in a ritual basin of water. Used to focus one's visualization for increased resources, the practitioner is also asking the Universe for lessons in transcending temptation.

Moneywort may also be used in animal magick, particularly with snakes and amphibians.

❦ Morning Glory ❦

Convovulus sp.
Saturn
Religious Herbe
Also called: bindweed

LORE

Aztec priests used the seeds of the morning glory in a mixture with the ashes of certain poisonous insects, other live insects and native tobacco. This mixture was made into an ointment and rubbed upon human sacrifices, allowing them to better face their death. Known as *tlitlitzin*, "the sacrament was used to create a more receptive atmosphere to the ceremony." According to *The Magical & Ritual Use of Herbs* by Richard Miller, it is used by Mayatecs today to help them when journeying for information.

❦ Motherwort ❦

Leonurus Cardiaca
Venus
Leo
Countermagick Herbe ... Herbe of Protection

LORE

Motherwort is found in an herbal by Macer, as cited in *A Modern Herbal* as "one of the herbs which were considered all-powerful against 'wykked sperytis.'"

USAGE

Motherwort is a strengthening herbe; it gives a person a sense of purpose and joy in the completion of work. It brings an attitude that all will succeed, and allows for the growth of inner trust, knowing that all will work toward a good and positive conclusion.

Most useful in magickal tonics: drinking motherwort on a daily basis bolsters one's ego and allows the inner light to radiate outward for all to see. Few herbes are so good for building confidence.

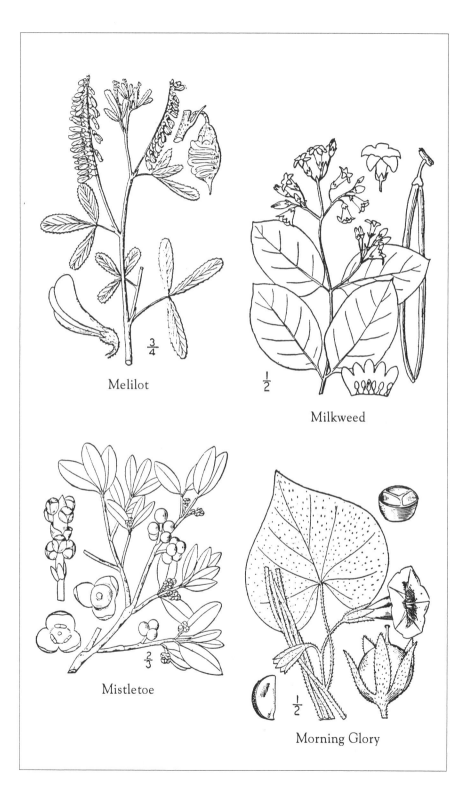

Melilot

$\frac{3}{4}$

Milkweed

$\frac{1}{2}$

Mistletoe

$\frac{2}{3}$

Morning Glory

$\frac{1}{2}$

❦ Mugwort ❦

Artemisia Vulgaris
Venus, Neptune
Herbe of Consecration ... Herbe of Protection ... Magickal
Herbe ... Religious Herbe ... Visionary Herbe
Invocatory: Diana

LORE

In *A Modern Herbal* we find the following:

> In the Middle Ages, the plant was known as Cingulum
> Sancti Johannis as it was believed that Saint John the
> Baptist wore a girdle of mugwort in the wilderness.
> There were many superstitions connected with it: it was
> believed to preserve the wayfarer from fatigue, sun-
> stroke, wild beasts and evil spirits generally. A crown
> made from its sprays was worn on Saint John's Eve to
> gain security from evil possession. In Holland and Ger-
> many one of its names is St. John's plant because of the
> belief that, if gathered on St. John's Eve, it will protect
> against diseases and misfortunes.

USAGE

Mugwort is, today, a very popular Magickal Herbe and its usage
has greatly expanded in this century. It figures prominent among
many women's covens where its use has moved beyond the remedial into the mystical. Many use it to express adoration of the
goddess Diana.

Mugwort has many associations. Its essential oil has become a
traditional herbal for the consecration and anointing of a crystal
ball. This use carries over to the preparation of any tool of divination. Mugwort is associated with quartz crystal and silver, and
with pearls and moonstone. When pursuing the deeper mysteries
of the major arcana, mugwort is the herbe for the Moon card. And
when turning the wheel at Midsummer, mugwort has many uses.
As a bathing herbe prior to the shortest night, mugwort offers
many blessings. Bunches of dried mugwort from the previous
year's harvest may be tossed into the Midsummer fire. And mugwort may be an herbe for the ritual cup, shared during the ceremony or feast.

Perhaps the most widespread use of mugwort today is to enhance dreams. When on a quest for a visionary dream, dried mugwort provides the stuffing for a dream pillow. The pillow is sewn from two squares of deep purple velvet to form a pillow not larger than the palm of your hand. Sleeping with this pillow beneath your head (beneath your bed pillow), or just keeping it in or near your bed, is believed to assist you in moving into the realm of the mystical and divining the future in your dreams.

The protective energies of mugwort keep one safe against all dark forces. Among women's mysteries, mugwort touches upon the mother: it is a special herbe, able to protect one's children. When cleaning the children's rooms, mugwort water might be aspurged. The herbe might also be burned upon a coal, the incense bringing protection. Mugwort brings your loved ones safely home from their journeys: it may be added to amulets and medicine pouches.

When your home is battered by a raging storm or when your life feels threatened by impending dangers, it is believed that dried mugwort should be tossed into the hearth fire (burned in a cauldron will also do) to keep you safe.

Mugwort is a fine herbe to use on a regular basis. Working like a tonic for one's soul, it helps us remain aware of our spiritual direction.

❧ Mulberry ❧

Morus Nigra
Mercury
Gemini
Herbe of Consecration ... Herbe of Protection ... Religious Herbe
Invocatory: Athena, Minerva

LORE

The common mulberry was revered by the ancients. "As the wisest of its fellows, the tree was dedicated by the Ancients to Minerva." Minerva was the goddess of wisdom in the Roman pantheon. In Greece she was known as Athena. The fruit of the mulberry is considered sacred to the triple goddess.

From *Myths and Legends of All Nations*, we learn an ancient story every bit as passionate as that of *Romeo and Juliet*:

> Pyramus and Thisbe were a youth and a maiden who lived in ancient Babylon. They loved each other, but their parents forbade them to marry. Their only means of communication was through the chink of a wall. Here every day they met, Pyramis on one side, Thisbe on the other, and spoke words of love until night fell.
>
> Unable to endure their separation any longer, they resolved to meet one night and run away. At the appointed time Thisbe appeared at the meeting place. Suddenly a lioness, with blood dripping from her jaws, appeared. Frightened, Thisbe fled, but in doing so she dropped her cloak. The lioness snatched it and tore it to shreds with her fangs, then ran off into the woods.

Well, you can pretty much guess the rest. Pyramis finds the robe. Feeling overwhelmed with guilt and loss, he takes his blade and commits suicide. As the blood from his ruptured hearts spurts forth, the nearby mulberry is covered with blood and the berries are forever reddened. But there's more to this gruesome story. Thisbe returns to find Pyramus not quite dead. She kisses him. His eyes open. He dies. She kills herself and the mulberry was recorded in another legend.

In Chinese mythology we find the belief that there are ten Suns which take their turns traversing the sky, riding in a horse-drawn carriage driven by their mother. Every morning she takes them to the lake by the po tree, which is a giant, hollow mulberry. As they climb out of the lake they ascend the tree. Only one Sun moves into the topmost branches and then into the sky.

USAGE

Mulberry may be used as an herbe to increase one's understanding of life. The fruit, ripened and dried, may be used to infuse a tea to drink as a daily tonic, increasing one's access to wisdom and ability to think clearly. Minerva was originally celebrated during a five-day observance, Quinquatrus, in March.

For students of any discipline or for those creating a Book of Shadows, leaves of the mulberry should be dried and pressed, then placed within the pages. Fresh berries may be set out as an offering and the dried leaves used for bathing.

Mulberry is believed to offer protection for children and babies.

When used for magickal protection, it should be picked just before the Sun sets in the west (would he set in any other direction?) and spend that night sitting upon your altar with a candle burning until morning's first light. Then it may be dried or prepared as one would any leaf or berry.

🌱 Mullein 🌱

Verbascum Thapsus
Saturn
Herbe of Protection ... Herbe of Purification ... Religious Herbe
Invocatory: Circe, Odysseus, Ulysses
Also called: candlewick plant

LORE

> The down on the leaves and stem makes excellent tinder when quite dry, readily igniting on the slightest spark, and was, before the introduction of cotton, used for lamp wicks, hence another of the old names, 'Candlewick plant.' An old superstition existed that witches in their incantations used lamps and candles provided with wicks of this sort.

Grieve in *A Modern Herbal* goes on to write:

> both in Europe and Asia the power of driving away evil spirits was ascribed to the mullein. In India it has the reputation among the natives that the St. John's Wort once had here, being considered a sure safeguard against evil spirits and magic. and from the ancient classics we learn that it was this plant which Ulysses took to protect himself against the wiles of Circe.

According to Frazer in *The Golden Bough,* an old, pagan custom which long survived in western France involved passing mullein through the Midsummer's Eve bonfire. The mullein would protect the herds and the ashes from the fire were considered most magickal.

USAGE

Few herbes have such a strong association with the elemental fire. There are many folk names ("torches" is but one) for mullein which demonstrate this connection. Mullein may be used to invoke the elemental energy of fire and bring literal fire into the ritual. Dried leaves may be soaked in oil. Some ingenious (and dramatic) practitioners dip them into a liquid mixture of saltpeter and water, then hang them to dry. When tossed into a fire, they blaze brightly! This may be done in the ritual cauldron, bonfire or one's fireplace.

The entire flower stalk may be harvested and dried. You may choose to pick them when the flowers are at their prime, their yellow a reflection of the Sun. You can also harvest them as part of the autumn harvest when the mullein's work is done: the stalks naturally drying and turning brown, the flowers spent, the seeds sown naturally by the plant itself. The head of the stalk is then soaked in a tallow mixture so it may be carried, burning as a torch. Such torches would be ideal for lighting the dark and fearful night of Hallow's Eve. When you walk between two rows of mullein torches lining the path to the Hallow's Circle, you *know* you are ready to commune with the dead!

Mystery schools and monasteries often grew mullein as protection, although *growing* mullein is like *owning* a cat! Seeding itself naturally, this biennial does not always take to transplanting. Seedlings must be allowed to grow to adequate strength. The ideal weather for transplanting is damp and no warmer than cool. Mullein grows best when left on its own. Each year holds surprises. You never know where a mullein will spring up.

Modern usage includes an affinity between this herbe and women. A number of Dianic groups have introduced mullein into their herbal work, finding it a source of comfort and strength.

❦ Mushrooms ❦

Basidiomycetes Cl.
Mercury
Aries
Religious Herbe

LORE

Graves writes in *The White Goddess* that "a secret Dionysiac mushroom cult was borrowed from the native Pelasgians by the Achaeans of Argos. Dionysus's centaurs, satyrs and maenads, it seems, ritually ate" one variety of mushroom. He also reports that followers of the "Eleusinian, Orphic and other mysteries," Portuguese witches, and others use various hallucinatory mushrooms in the seeking of "universal illumination, as I can attest to from my own experience of it."

Miller in *The Magical & Ritual Use of Herbs* cites R. Gordon Wasson who describes mushroom worship dating back several centuries before Christ with some images in stone dating to 1000 B.C. in Guatemala.

USAGE

There are a great many varieties of mushrooms. As Webster describes it, a mushroom is the fruiting body of a fungus. Without going near a discussion of psilocybin and the ritual visionary uses of those varieties, mushrooms in general have often been associated with Pan and other fertility gods, undoubtedly due to their phallic appearance. When rituals are done to invoke the god's joyful lust, *safe* mushrooms might be included as part of the feast.

❦ Mustard ❦

Brassica sp.
Mars
Herbe of Protection
Invocatory: Aesculapius
Also called: flixweed

LORE

Ancient herbalists believed mustard was discovered by Aesculapius, who was trained by the centaur Chiron, famed surgeon of the gods. In one myth, it was Aesculapius, son of Apollo who is sometimes seen as the god of medicine, who was destined to diagnose Persephone as having eaten enough of the pomegranate seed that she must live in both worlds. In this version of the myth, Demeter is furious at her daughter's fate and unfairly takes out her anger by transforming Aesculapius into an owl.

USAGE

Mustard has a well-established reputation for being an exceptional herbe in providing good health. Common mustard was once renowned as a cure for laryngitis. It may now be used in bringing magickal protection to the voices of those who speak or sing in public. For use as an Herbe of Protection, the root or the flowers should be gathered and dried, then placed in an amulet which is to be worn. An oil may also be extracted from the flowers which could be used to anoint the throat.

Flixweed (a variety of mustard) is noted by Mrs. Grieve in *A Modern Herbal* as having been called *Sophia Chirugorum* or The Wisdom of Surgeons. This variety of mustard makes an excellent patron herbe for all who are in the medical profession or who seek skill within the arts of healing. One way of gaining the benevolence of this herbe is by cultivating it in one's garden and taking time with the plant as it grows. There is wisdom available to the practitioner in this manner.

❦ Myrrh ❦

Commiphora Myrrha
Sun, Moon
Funereal Herbe ... Herbe of Consecration ... Magickal Herbe ...
Religious Herbe
Invocatory: Adonis, Aphrodite, Cybele, Demeter, Hecate, Juno,
Rhea, Saturn

LORE

Adonis, whose historical origins lie in Semitic myths, was said to have been born of a myrrh tree. From *Larousse World Mythology* we learn the Greek version:

> The king of Syria, Theias, had a daughter called Myrrha or Smyrna, who was cursed by Aphrodite and forced to commit incest with her father; with the complicity of her nurse she succeeded in deceiving him for eleven nights, but on the twelfth Theias discovered who she was and prepared to kill her. Myrrha fled, and the gods, taking pity on her, turned her into a tree, the myrrh-tree. Ten months later the bark peeled off and an infant emerged and was given the name of Adonis.

The myths surrounding myrrh include its being cast into the fire out of which the legendary phoenix is reborn. The myrrh has long been considered sacred to Aphrodite.

USAGE

The dried resin of the myrrh tree is collected and, most frequently, burned as an incense. The scent of myrrh is well loved and was used in the religious ceremonies of the ancients in many cultures. It was so revered that it was written into the myths surrounding the birth of the Christ child.

In burial ceremonies of ancient Egypt, it was used as incense and included in the herbal mixtures used for embalming the body. Myrrh remains an essential herbe in today's rituals of death and dying. We should also consider myrrh as capable of providing access to the mysteries of death and rebirth.

Myrrh helps one understand the nature of being spiritually aware. It not only assists in expanding your wisdom, but provides a gentle comfort from the Universe as one moves further into the mysteries. One must always remember that the mysteries do not lead to happiness: there are as many mysteries of sorrow and of death as there are of joy and of birth.

There are few herbes so useful in working through personal sorrows and tragedies. Myrrh is of unequaled value for those recovering from sexual abuse, whether incestuous or not. Myrrh brings comfort to those who have lost a loved one, whose troubled hearts need the healing strength of understanding the mystery of death. Myrrh will help ease the troubled soul in its grieving. The simplest method of seeking sacred relief is by working with a candle which has been anointed with an oil of myrrh. In this way one might bring ease to many who would otherwise shun herbal magick.

Most useful in ritual work, myrrh helps one perceive the way patterns of energy move throughout the Circle. The mind is more able to see the overlaying patterns created by the ritual choreography and discern the nuances of the magick's texture and power. A practitioner who uses myrrh in ritual will have a heightened awareness of the energy flow within both worlds. In addition to being used in the ritual incense, myrrh water may be used in aspurging the Circle and the oil is one of the best for dressing one's temple candles.

Associated with many deities, a wash may be made (a myrrh tea) which is superior for consecrating pearls. Although not always recommended for sacred use, a pearl's magick is enhanced and an aura of protection added when consecrated with myrrh. In the minor arcana, myrrh helps one understand both the Queen cards and the Three cards of all four suits. In the major arcana, myrrh is corresponded with the Wheel of Fortune card.

Although not widely used in this manner, myrrh has come into use at two sabbats among a number of practitioners. At Candlemas, in addition to its use as an incense, myrrh may be used in the ritual cup. Drinking myrrh opens one to the gestation of waxing energy which will continue to grow until it bursts forth at spring. In this form, one draws more upon the solar energy of Adonis than of the more common association with Jupiter. At the Autumn Equinox myrrh is sometimes used when working with elemental fire, drawing upon its lore and association with the phoenix.

🍎 Myrtle 🍎

Myrtus Communis
Mercury
Virgo
Herbe of Immortality ... Herbe of Love ... Herbe of Protection
Invocatory: Aphrodite, Bona Dea, Hathor, Venus

LORE

Myrtle has some sorry associations with domestic violence. Bona Dea, invoked to bring goodness to women, was said to have been beaten with a myrtle branch by her lover Faunus. In one version he is her husband, in another her father. Myrtle was, as a consequence, banned from Bona Dea's temples.

Ancient myths link myrtle with the most intimate of women's mysteries. The myrtle is sacred to the goddess Aphrodite. Considered by some to be a tree associated with death, it was beneath the myrtle, according to Graves in *The White Goddess*, that Aphrodite sits with Adonis and teaches him of the mysteries of immortality.

USAGE

Believed to work its magick in both worlds, myrtle is associated with life and death. When brought into a Union (Handfastings, weddings or any exchange of vows), myrtle is believed to give extra power to the couple's love and to bring protection against any misplaced anger that could turn into violence.

We recommend that those who are working to remove violence from their lives work with this herbe. Myrtle can be used to ward off violence. It does not bring the comfort of myrrh, being a more forceful type of magick. It may be used in ritual work to inhibit the violent partner through planting the seeds of awareness. This is, however, a slow process and we urge any victim of domestic violence to seek help at once.

Grown near the Temple of Venus on Aventine Hill (in Rome), myrtle is today linked both with Venus and also with Aphrodite. Its association with love is also found through its connection with Hathor, Egyptian goddess of mirth and romance.

Some believe that the Hebrew tribes used myrtle to shade their sacred Tabernacle. That aspect of protection can be worked with myrtle today, bringing protection to any of one's sacred spaces.

❦ Narcissus ❦

Narcissus sp.
Neptune
Funereal Herbe ... Magickal Herbe ... Religious Herbe
Invocatory: Hades, Isis, Pluto

LORE

The natural order, Amaryllidaceæ, contains the daffodil (sometimes called lent lily), narcissus, pseudo-narcissus, paper white, jonquil and other close cousins which share the name narcissus. All the varieties of this order will be treated as a group when discussing narcissus' lore. According to Mrs. Grieve in *A Modern Herbal*:

> The botanical name of the genus, Narcissus, is considered to be derived, not...from the name of the classical youth who met with his death through vainly trying to embrace his image reflected in a clear stream, but from the Greek work narkao (to be numb), on account of the narcotic properties which the plant possesses. Pliny describes it as *Narce narcissum dictum, non a fabuloso puero*, "named narcissus from Narce, not from the fabulous boy."

The theory presented by Frazer in *The Golden Bough* regarding the Narcissus myth is quite interesting. He writes about the belief that looking at your reflection was a taboo. Many cultures believed that seeing your reflection would lead to death. "We can now understand why it was a maxim both in India and ancient Greece not to look at one's reflection in water.... They feared that the water-spirits would drag the person's reflection or soul under water, leaving him soulless to perish."

USAGE

The bulbs contain very strong chemicals. Some varieties are poisonous, some narcotic, and none should ever be taken internally. Working with the funereal aspects of this herbe are easily accomplished through planting the bulbs. The association with death dates back to the Greeks, undoubtedly enhanced by the occasional death by poisoning which is known to have occurred. In the same entry, Mrs. Grieve cites Herrick as calling the daffodil a "portent of death." A beautiful custom which is still observed today is to plant daffodils in memory of a loved one.

From Frazer's *The Golden Bough* we learn narcissus was called the "Chaplet of the infernal Gods" by Socrates. Modern practitioners find various types of the narcissus family associated with Hades and Pluto. It may be placed in vases when conducting ceremonies to honor these deities or to seek their intercession when a loved one is entering the Otherworld.

Narcissus are associated with the Hermit card of the tarot. An extracted oil may be burned upon a block of charcoal. The dried flowers may be ground into powder and added to loose incense or fashioned into joss sticks. There has been some association with the goddess Isis in her first aspect as maiden. A patch of bulbs may be set at a sacred site, along a path or in front of a shrine to Isis.

The dried flowers may be most useful in herbal magick. Storing a peridot in the container is believed to help sustain the natural power of the herbe. Narcissus may also be used to enhance the energy of this gem. Due to the nature of the bulb, we recommend working only with the flowers.

Modern usage is varied. When researching *The Master Book of Herbalism* fifteen years ago, I discovered the following:

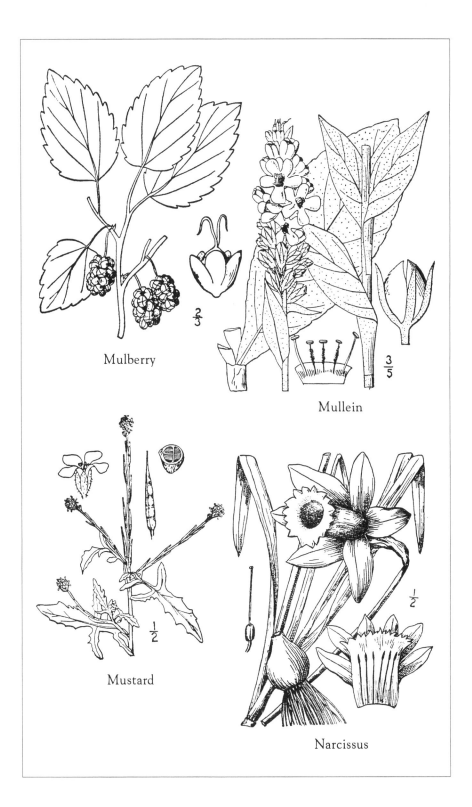

Mulberry

$\frac{2}{3}$

Mullein

$\frac{3}{5}$

Mustard

$\frac{1}{2}$

Narcissus

$\frac{1}{2}$

The sexual lore of narcissus sets it apart from nearly all other herbes. It is said to contain the magick of parthenogenesis, and as such may be used to create inspiration and creativity. The narcotic constituents of the herbe function as an anaphrodisiac, quieting desire, and allowing one to turn to less physical sources of inspiration.

Whether or not the narcissus is named for the god may be debated. In other sources such as *Myths and Legends of All Nations*, the myth is clear. Narcissus (the young deity), "happened to see his own image reflected in a clear pool and became so enamored of it that he could not leave it. He pined away, and was converted into the flower which bears his name."

Narcissus may be used to help one deal with an ego which is turned too much to the self. We have much to learn from this flower which arises from the dreary death of winter, its sunny disposition uplifting any heart. Yet it is quick to fade, returning by summer to the Underworld to prepare and labor for the many months of work before it will again hold our attention.

❦ Nettles ❦

Urtica Dioica
Mars
Herbe of Consecration ... Magickal Herbe ... Religious Herbe
Also called: stinging nettles

LORE

In times past, according to *A Modern Herbal*, it was believed that nettles were of such healing power that "a fever could be dispelled by plucking a nettle up by the roots, reciting thereby the names of the sick man and also the names of his parents."

In no less a magickal story than that of *The Princess and the Eleven Swans*, by Hans Christian Anderson, we find nettles were the herbes chosen to have their fibers woven into little coats. In *The Book of Secrets of Albertus Magnus* we find the following:

> He that holdeth this herb in his hand with an herb called...Yarrow...is sure from all fear and fantasy, or vision. And if it be put with the juice of Houseleek, and the bearer's hand be anointed with it, and the residue be put in water; if he enter in the water where fishes be,

they will gather together to his hands.

USAGE

One of the traditional rites of consecration for an athame calls for nettles to be added to the herbal wash into which the heated blade is plunged.

Nettles have been used to provide green dye. They are sometimes associated with the coming of spring, both in folk practices and in some Christian cultures. In some parts of Russia, it is the custom to use nettles as one of the dyes to stain eggs on Maundy Thursday in preparation for Easter morning.

Nettles, an often neglected Magickal Herbe, are associated with the ability to dispel darkness. Taken as a magickal tea, they are not only good for the body but also good for the spirit. The old lore regarding combining nettles with yarrow to help one take heart against deep fears makes this mixture an excellent magickal remedy. Nettles may work their magick when fishing.

❦ Nightshade (Deadly) ❦

Atropa Belladonna
Saturn
Funereal Herbe ... Herbe of Consecration ... Magickal Herbe ...
Religious Herbe
Invocatory: Atropos, Bellona, Circe
Also called: belladonna, devil's herb, naughty man's cherries

LORE

As are many plants which can be dangerous or even fatal to humans, belladonna has much lore attached to it. During the Dark Ages and the Burning Times, this plant became associated with the devil as we see in this quote from Grieve's *A Modern Herbal*:

> Who goes about trimming and tending it in his leisure, and can only be diverted from its care on one night in the year, that is on Walpurgis, when he is preparing for the witches' sabbath.

Walpurgis Night is derived from the feast day of Saint Walpurgis, an English saint from the eighth century. Today Walpurgis Night refs to the Beltane Eve or the night before May Day which became associated with evil views of witchcraft during the times of persecution.

In addition to the common association of deadly nightshade with the most intense of magickal energies, Mrs. Grieve includes a far different aspect of this herbe's lore, reporting that some believe it to be named for Bellona, the sister of the Roman god of war, Mars.

It has been said that Bellona's priests drank the juice of the herbe in her honor. Known for her great passion and ability to plunge into battle with torch in one hand and a long whip in the other, a cult formed around her of which we can read in *Myths and Legends of All Nations*:

> ...degenerate priests, the Bellonarii, dressed in black [who] honored her at sacrifices by screaming, shouting, and wounding themselves in the arms and legs. Bellona's temple, built by Appius Claudius Caecus outside the city walls, was used for meetings of the Senate when it was negotiating with ambassadors from foreign countries, and to receive Roman generals returning from a victory.

USAGE

The association with Saturn is easily seen when we look at the word *Atropa*, in the generic name for deadly nightshade. Named for one of the Greek Fates, Atropos was most Saturnine in her behavior, holding her magickal blade with which she cut the threads of life when a person moved into the realm of death. Today belladonna may be used in rituals for the dead. Added to the chalice of water which will aspurge the Circle, it may be used to help the spirit let go of its longing for the life just ended, helping the beloved to move forward into union with the Universe toward rebirth. This herbe is corresponded, for obvious reasons, with the Death card as it can be used to help cut the old away, allowing you to enter a new stage in life.

Burning some belladonna (do *not* inhale the smoke) as an offering to Bellona would be appropriate when preparing to do battle, such as when one must work through negotiations, enter a courtroom, or otherwise engage in competition which is not a sport.

Deadly nightshade may be used to invoke Circe (known as The Enchantress) and is considered the appropriate herbe when consecrating ritual items which contain the metal lead. There is an affinity with onyx as well. Belladonna and onyx share similar legends and similar energies. To keep your deadly nightshade empowered for ritual, store an onyx in the container. Belladonna may be used to consecrate any jewelry made with onyx.

Although lore suggests harvesting at Beltane Eve, practical gardening suggests that, climate allowing, you harvest at Hallow's Eve. The reality is that the berries should be gathered when they are ripe.

❦ Nightshade (Woody) ❦

Solanum Dulcamara
Mercury, Uranus
Herbe of Protection
Also called: bittersweet, scarlet berry

LORE

As its cousin belladonna (deadly nightshade) became associated with black magick, the more common nightshade, bittersweet (which is harmless), became associated with the balancing energy. In agrarian cultures it was used as a protective herbe for one's livestock.

USAGE

The benevolent properties of woody nightshade remain known today. Collected and hung in bunches, it protects one's home and those who dwell within it (whether human or animal) from negative energies and misfortune. For its magick to work, however, no one else must ever know where it has been placed.

❦ Oak ❦

Quercus sp.
Jupiter
Sagittarius
Fertility Herbe ... Herbe of Protection ... Magickal Herbe ...
Religious Herbe
Invocatory: Athena, Blodeuwedd, Donar, Hercules, Hermes,
Jupiter, Odin, Perkunas, Perun, Rhea, Robur, Shu, Thor,
Thunar, Zeus

LORE

The oak is honored throughout the world. It was considered one of the most sacred trees among the Greeks, Romans and the Druids. Indeed, Frazer writes that "the worship of the oak tree or of the oak god appears to have been shared by all the branches of the Aryan stock in Europe." In *The Golden Bough*, Frazer goes on to describe a holy place in Greece, Dodona, where an oak was the site of an oracle of Zeus. When the Aryan peoples spread throughout Europe and Asia, they took their beliefs with them to many distant places. It was considered the Tree of Life among one of the peoples of Siberia who believed the Universe turned on an axis of oak.

The oak is deeply planted into the history of the British Isles. For many years it was a symbol used to represent England. Mrs. Grieve writes in *A Modern Herbal* that "King Arthur's Round Table was made from a single slice of oak, cut from an enormous bole, and is still shown at Winchester." Druid legend holds that groves of oak were very sacred, treated as holy places and used as ritual sites.

There is a link between the Celtic god Robur, who is associated with trees. Robur was worshipped among the Pyrenees. The Celts of that region had a number of tree deities in their pantheon. The Celts and Druids worshiped in oak groves. The Celts of Gaul, a fierce warrior tribe, took their reverence for the oak with them when they conquered other lands. The following comes from Frazer's *The Golden Bough*:

> In the heart of Asia Minor the Galatian senate met in a place which bore the pure Celtic name of Drynemetum, "the sacred oak grove..." Indeed the very name of Druids is believed by good authorities to mean no more than "oak men."

Grieve also cites a custom which demonstrates the prevalence of old pagan ways even in twentieth century Christianity. In this practice, the clergyman and his flock visit oaks at the boundaries of the parish where they read from their holy books and ask for blessings. Mrs. Grieve tells us about a fairly specific custom which occurs on May 29 in which people take home branches and wear acorns to bring good fortune. In other parts of Europe people are known to take small statues of Mary, mother of Jesus, and place them in oaks while praying for protection against lightning. The oak becomes a receptacle for magick in many parts of the world. In some parts of Russia, boar tusks are set into the tree, also remnants of pre-Christian practices.

The oak was considered sacred to Zeus. Indeed, the very rustling of the breeze among the leaves of an oak was believed to indicate that Zeus was beginning to speak. The sacred marriage of Zeus and Hera was seen as the union of the oak god and oak goddess. There are many deities linked with the oak, including the Greek goddess Rhea, wife of Cronos; Jupiter (the Roman Zeus); Odin; and Bloddeuwedd.

The Italian's oak god was Jupiter. Jupiter's association places the oak in modern correspondence with Thursday.

Oak figures prominently in the Greek stories of Jason and the Argonauts. The prow of his ship, the Argo, is made of sacred oak from the Temple at Dodona which was dedicated to Zeus and where an oracle resided. This wood had been provided by the goddess Athena and was, in its own way, an oracle able to speak and provide prophecy at crucial times in Jason's journey. It was said that the golden fleece, itself, was kept safe hanging from a sacred oak.

In Egypt the equivalent of Hercules would be known as the god Shu, who considers the oak and acorns sacred to him because it attracts the lightning and also provides shelter for his creatures.

In the mythology of Finland there is a wonderful legend which explains the origins of the Milky Way. An oak grew so large that the light of the Sun, the Moon and the stars was unable to reach the people. Clouds were caught by the branches and life was increasingly in peril. A creature emerged from the Underworld with a golden hatchet and chopped the tree until it fell, clearing the sky and spreading acorns to form the Milky Way. Some stories say this wondrous tree, known as *iso tammi* (the great oak), was planted by three maidens.

Lithuanians held the oak sacred to Perkunas, their thunder god, and an uproar resulted when Christian missionaries cut down their trees. Germanic tribal leaders held their councils beneath an oak, well into the thirteenth century. The oak was a sacred tree among old Germanic tribes and was "dedicated to the god of thunder, Donar or Thunar, the equivalent of the Norse Thor." According to Frazer in *The Golden Bough*, the Slavic pagans worshipped the oak as the tree of Perun, their god of thunder. "It is said that at Novgorod there used to stand an image of Perun" where a perpetual fire was kept burning.

There are many associations between the oak and the mistletoe. It is said that one should not harvest any oak from a tree within which grows mistletoe. The spirits of these trees lend themselves to ritual work within their shade and shelter but the trees, themselves, should be left alone. It was believed that the mistletoe was a symbol from the heavens that a deity resided within the tree. The oak is found even in Hebrew legends which often hold that Abraham was visited by an angel of god while at a sacred oak.

As a site for ritual work, oaks have been preferred in many cultures. The pagans of Lithuania sought out sacred oaks which grew near water for their ceremonies. Worship was closely tied to the oak throughout the Balkans with many of the oak gods closely resembling Zeus or Thor. Offerings are left on sacred stones set beneath oaks in Latvia. The oak's affinity for attracting lighting was not unnoticed by the ancients. Oaks were sites for ritual work throughout many parts of Russia well into the fourteenth century. A Baltic god called Rueivit had seven faces, all carved of sacred oak.

Graves writes that oak was the wood used for carving erotic, phallic statues of Hermes. The oak is found in the Irish alphabet as Duir or *D* which is the seventh tree. This sacred tree has many magickal associations. Some believe the Oak King was sacrificed on Midsummer Day and the fires of this sabbat were often fueled with oak. Graves, in *The White Goddess*, writes that the fires that were kept burning in honor of the goddess Vesta were of oak.

The oak is prominent in many of the original sabbat customs associated with fire. Frazer writes in *The Golden Bough* that "it may have appeared to the ancient Aryan that the Sun was periodically recruited from the fire which resided in the sacred oak." Through this association, the oak was intrinsically linked with Midsummer and, particularly through its association to mistletoe, with Yule. Frazer also believes that the ancient pagans of Wales may have provided the belief that the oak blooms at Midsummer Eve.

USAGE

The bark of the most sacred oak in your life may be gathered at propitious times and dried, then ground and used as an incense to invoke or honor any of the deities associated with the oak. The oak's association with Vesta and fire festivals lends itself to working with this herbal tree in conjunction with elemental fire.

In folklore, a charm is made of oak by finding two equal lengths of twig or of a small branch and binding them together in a cross which represents keeping one's self in balance within the manifest world of the four elements.

The oak has long been a symbol of fertility. Whether it is the profusion of acorns or their ability to bring forth life, the oak has represented a potent force to the ancestors of many cultures. Those who have gardens beneath an oak readily attest to the fertility of all those acorns. When I gardened in Minneapolis, each spring meant a time for digging many hundreds of baby oak trees out of my herb beds. Certainly as a Fertility Herbe the squirrels had tapped the oak's bounty. The oak also represents the virtues of endurance and of triumph. These can be instilled in one's life by working magick with the bark, the leaves or the nuts. In addition to fertility, the oak may also represent phallic virility.

Acorns are easily used as symbols of fertility. They can be strung as beads, set about a temple for decoration or, for the ambitious, dried and ground into flour for some of the best ritual cakes to be found. Long used in magickal practices to promote conception, acorns are best used today to promote creativity, sharing in the celebration of life's continuity which survives death at winter and sprouts anew at spring. Acorns may be adapted into amulets and tokens. Acorns and oak leaves are highly appropriate for the Hallow's Eve celebration.

Modern lore keeps the oak one of our sacred trees. Many believe that the Yule log should be of oak. When it is but ashes, those are strewn throughout one's land to bring good fortune and wealth in the coming year. In many traditions an Oak King is crowned by placing a wreath of oak leaves upon a priest's head. In *The White Goddess*, Robert Graves writes of kindling a fire by using a dowel and drilling into an oak plank. The ritual fire for Midsummer should include oak.

Today many believe there is no wand as sacred as one made of oak. We decorate our altars with leaves, some as early as Lammas and most at Hallow's. Acorns are worn for decoration, beaded for fertility necklaces and charms. Some are known to collect an acorn and empower it throughout the winter then plant it before the snow melts so that the new tree will be one of magick and power.

The modern practitioner will carefully collect leaves and acorns but may also harvest bark from branches. The bark may be dried and powdered and used to unite one with the gods and goddesses of many peoples. Oak is used to bring protection against the ferocity of the elements and the dangers of life, and we use oak to ask for divine assistance in having our needs met. Those who are wise will always love the oak.

❦ Olive ❦

Olea Europæa
Sun
Fertility Herbe ... Herbe of Consecration ... Religious Herbe
Invocatory: Athena, Concordia, Fides, Poseidon, Zeus

LORE

The olive has been intrinsically linked with religious observance throughout the western world. Grieve writes that Moses exempted the men who worked in the olive groves from military service. Perhaps the most notable association of the olive is with the goddess of war and of wisdom, Athena, she who was worshipped at the Parthenon. Even the gods and goddesses are caught by politics and Athena falls into disagreement with Poseidon. Their argument arose because each claimed to be the patron deity of Greece. A council of divinities was called and it was decided that whomever gave the best gift would hold the honor. Poseidon used his trident to bring forth a spring of finely salted water. But Athena came forward and planted an olive tree and was easily the victor.

In Greek legends, Heracles probably has the most adventure. Born in Thebes to Zeus and Alcmene, Heracles represented masculine ideals. In the well-known trial with the Nemean Lion, Heracles is victor through using a club made of olive wood. The

Dionysus and a few mortals as well. It is sometimes said that the red rose gained its color from spilled blood after Aphrodite caught her foot on a thorn when with Adonis. In some legends it is the anemone. In Rome the rose was associated with Venus, Cupid and Bacchus. To the Romans according to A *Modern Herbal*, "the Rose was a sign of pleasure, the companion of mirth and wine, but it was also used at their funerals." Sappho, legendary lesbian poet of ancient Greece called the rose the "Queen of Flowers." From *Rodale's Illustrated Encyclopedia of Herbs* we learn that Cleopatra had her floors covered with rose petals in order to seduce Mark Antony because she believed that the rose promoted love and passion.

Despite the sensual pleasures associated with the rose, it has also been used to represent secrecy. It was suspended from the ceiling at meetings which were held in the strictest of confidence and placed by the confessional in Roman Catholic churches.

USAGE

Roses represent all aspects of the Goddess: the ability to love and nurture, and to see beauty in all things. Roses may be used in rituals to honor the Goddess or used by a priestess when Drawing Down the Moon. The rose represents the love the Goddess has for Her children and is a patron herbe of lesbians.

The rose is associated with emeralds. If one is consecrating jewelry set with an emerald or empowering a stone for magickal work, the emerald should be dressed with rose oil. The rose is also associated with the Seven of Cups card.

There is much energy associated with this flower. It represented the quality of joy to the Romans and can be used to create joy today.

A flower so popular that it has come to be associated with Handfastings and rituals of union, roses fill vases, are worn by the participants and guests, and are oftentimes strewn to bring divine blessings to the couple's love.

Some bring roses into their sabbat rites, recommending white for Autumn Equinox and yellow for Eostara, while Midsummer calls for red, but we can use any color for Beltane!

313

❦ Rose Geranium ❦

Pelargonium sp.
Venus
Libra
Aphrodisiacal Herbe ... Herbe of Love

USAGE

In my earliest days as an herbalist I recall encountering rose geranium leaves as an important ingredient in recipes to be used when making love philters. When I first breathed their scent I was quite charmed and I grow them in my garden to this day. The extracted oil is worn to enhance one's sensual appeal and may be integrated into the Great Rite. Rose geranium may be used for romantic pleasures in the same way one might use patchouli (but they should not be combined).

❦ Rosemary ❦

Rosmarinus Officinalis
Sun
Funereal Herbe ... Greene Herbe ... Herbe of Protection ...
Herbe of Purification ... Magickal Herbe ... Religious Herbe
Also called: compass plant

LORE

> The ancients were well acquainted with the shrub, which had a reputation for strengthening the memory. On this account it became the emblem of fidelity for lovers.

This comes from A *Modern Herbal*.

Rosemary has a long history of use in all manner of religious rites ranging from weddings to funerals and has often been used for decoration at Yule and Christmas as we learn from A *Modern Herbal*.

> At weddings, it was entwined in the wreath worn by the bride, being first dipped into scented water. A rosemary branch, richly gilded and tied with silken ribands of all colours, was also presented to wedding guests, as a symbol of love and loyalty. Together with an orange stuck

with cloves it was given as a New Year's gift—allusions to this custom are to be found in Ben Jonson's plays.

USAGE

Even today rosemary is used to increase one's ability to remember things. We find numerous quotations in literature which cite rosemary's ability to empower memory. When combined with its history of usage for important occasions, this herbe is ideal when someone wants to mark a celebration deserving of being remembered. Not only will rosemary make the occasion more sacred, but it will keep the memories alive in everyone's mind. We recommend keeping alive the custom of giving small bunches of rosemary to the guests at a Handfasting or ritual of union.

This evergreen perennial has been considered a symbol of wisdom and love, of loyalty, fidelity and remembrance. Rosemary is such a useful herbe that we may make use of its magick in almost every imaginable way: from placing sprigs of rosemary in with flower arrangements to wearing the essential oil as perfume, from bathing in it prior to a ceremony to using it when baking or cooking. We should always remember to use rosemary.

A wonderful quotation comes from *The Treasure of Botany* in *A Modern Herbal*:

> There is a vulgar belief in Gloucestershire and other counties, that rosemary will not grow well unless where the mistress is "master"; and so touchy are some of the lords of creation upon this point, that we have more than once had reason to suspect them of privately injuring a growing rosemary in order to destroy this evidence of their want of authority.

We can only recommend this herbe as an important one for women who carry positions of responsibility, who are striving for success in the corporate world or who wish to increase their control over their own lives. Spanish Christians of an earlier time believed rosemary provided protection and courage for the Virgin Mary. In modern times rosemary may be used to provide protection when interviewing for a job, perhaps helping the prospective employer remember you when making that important decision.

Grieve writes that rosemary was used in ancient times as incense. Once used to purify places of illness and distress, rosemary makes an excellent incense for all ritual work. Even today we may use rosemary to protect us against dark forces or to bring purification. Rosemary is one of the many herbes said to have been used by Solomon when aspurging his temple.

Rosemary may be used as incense at rituals of death and dying. It may be cast upon the coffin when it is slowly lowered into the burial place. Thus will we all remember with love and fondness the one who is passing into another life, and thus will we also remember that we inhabit mortal bodies as we walk this earth. When Mrs. Grieve wrote her herbal this custom was still practiced in Wales.

There is an interesting deva with this plant. In Sicily it was believed that faerie folk inhabited rosemary and they were able to shape-shift and appear as small snakes.

❦ Rowan ❦

Sorbus sp.
Moon
Countermagick Herbe ... Herbe of Protection ... Magickal
Herbe ... Visionary Herbe
Also called: quickbeam

LORE

How can I not consider this one of my favorites, having used this tree as the symbol for the Church I founded? For us, the rowan is a Tree of Life, from which we gain wisdom. The berries of the rowan have been called the "Food of the gods," according to Graves in *The White Goddess*.

One of the magickal trees of ancient Britain, the rowan is the letter L or Luis in the tree alphabet. Also from *The White Goddess* we learn that in ancient Greece, the rowan was designated as sacred and could only be eaten when giving respect and honor to one's ancestors.

The belief in the protective qualities of the herbal tree is well established. From protection against lightning to protection against negative energies, the rowan is sure to keep us from bad times so long as we respect its guardian spirit which is a sacred tree mother. A popular charm was made by taking two small branches of the same length and binding them into an equal-armed cross with red cord.

The rowan, also known as European mountain ash, has been used to protect cattle. Familiar throughout Scotland, it is said that once there were nearly no homes without the tree growing nearby.

USAGE

Graves says that this tree is connected with the White Goddess and the *Master Book of Herbalism* says that we may use the rowan to "ritually... invoke the Goddess and ask Her for help, direction and bounty. The leaves are commonly used, but the berries may be gathered, dried and ground to add to the incense." The rowan represents the Divine Mother manifest upon the earth.

The magickal properties of the rowan are many as shown by Graves in *The White Goddess*:

> The berries of the magical rowan in the Irish romance of Fraoth, guarded by a dragon, had the sustaining virtue of nine meals; they also healed the wounded and added a year to a man's life."

The berries or the wood may be used to invite familiars, astral guides and teachers from the world of spirit, or to invoke elemental creatures. Conversely, the rowan may also be used to banish those things we do not wish in our lives. When used in ritual, particularly the berries as part of the feast (they make a lovely jelly), we may find that the creative process has been set in motion. A ritual wand may be made of rowan. Such a tool is believed to be a source of wisdom and knowledge. Graves in *The White Goddess* writes that "the oracular use of the rowan explains the unexpected presence of great rowan thickets in Rügen and the other Baltic amber-islands." Is there an affinity between the rowan and amber? We would like to think so but this is based upon conjecture.

Although the rowan may be used in house blessings in any form, our favorite method of use is to plant a young tree so that the home has its own rowan.

❦ Rue ❦

Ruta Graveolens
Sun, Mars
Leo
Countermagick Herbe ... Greene Herbe ... Herbe of
Consecration ... Herbe of Protection ... Herbe of Purification ...
Magickal Herbe ... Visionary Herbe
Invocatory: Mars

LORE

What a handsome herbe is the rue. We have planted two small
hedges of it in our gardens. Rue has been esteemed for its
magickal properties since ancient times, and during the Middle
Ages it was valued as a Countermagick Herbe, used to reverse
manipulative spells. This belief is much older than we might
think. "The Greeks regarded it as an antimagical herb," writes
Mrs. Grieve in *A Modern Herbal*.

USAGE

Rue is much used in home blessings and in herbal magick to bring
both protection and good fortune to one's home and family.

Rue has a strong, sunny disposition. It was once grown around
temples in Rome which had been dedicated to the god Mars.
Today it is used to banish negative energy or to exorcise a new
object which will later be consecrated for ritual use.

Associated with the Strength card, rue is recommended for consecrating sacred items made of iron. Rue is believed to have an
affinity for rubies. A small ruby should be stored with your ritual
rue. For those who work within the astral or who journey often,
rue is a good herbe to carry with you. It will bring protection and
keep you safe from any external influence.

❦ Rye ❦

Secale Cereale
Pluto

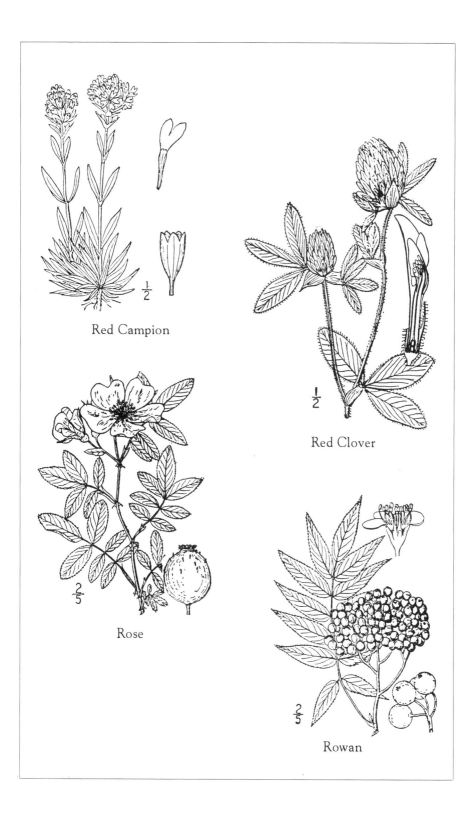

Red Campion

Red Clover

Rose

Rowan

LORE

The belief in a Rye-Mother is found in a number of areas of the Old World. It is the feminine spirit of the grain which nourishes her children.

❧ Safflower ❧

Carthamus Tinctorius
Sun, Saturn
Religious Herbe

USAGE

Among the constituents of safflower are yellow and red natural substances which are used to provide color. The red is the most desirable and, when mixed with the finest of talcs, it is used to create the cosmetic known as rouge. These substances may be used today for ritual face decorating. Safflower oil has become readily available in modern times and is highly desirable as a base oil when creating herbal oils.

❧ Saffron ❧

Crocus Sativa
Sun
Leo
Aphrodisiacal Herbe ... Greene Herbe ... Religious Herbe

LORE

Saffron comes from a type of crocus and its lore is closely connected with its sacred color. Saffron-colored robes are not only found in Asian monasteries but also in some American airports. The wearing of saffron-dyed robes is not a modern custom at all. As we learn from Grieve in *A Modern Herbal*, even "Homer sings 'the Saffron morn'; gods and goddesses, heroes and nymphs and vestals, are clothed in robes of Saffron hue." Used as a dye for cloth since ancient times, it was used to dye the shoes of Persian kings. Reference to saffron is found in the *Song of Solomon*. Highly prized, saffron was also valued for its scent. As Grieve writes in the same entry: "the scent was valued as much as the dye; saffron water was sprinkled on theater benches, the floors of banquet halls were strewn with crocus leaves, and cushions were stuffed with it."

USAGE

Some of the modern usage of saffron dates to Pliny, who believed that it would keep one from intoxication during the great feasts. It has also been believed that saffron functions as an aphrodisiac, its power considered almost intoxicating. While this may seem in contradiction with saffron's history as a coloring for religious robes, it provides us with insight into the innate magick of this herbe.

Those wishing to use a rare and precious incense might place amounts of saffron on the burning charcoal as an offering or to bless a most important occasion.

 Sage

Salvia Officinalis
Venus, Jupiter
Leo
Herbe of Immortality ... Herbe of Purification ... Religious Herbe
Invocatory: Cadmus, Consus, Jupiter, Zeus

LORE

It should be pointed out that the sage growing wild in North America is not the *Salvia* of the western herbal pharmacopoeia. Native sages are *Artemisias*, but when used for spiritual purposes the two are treated by most people as relatively interchangeable. *Salvia* is used by many peoples to fumigate or cense a sacred space, bringing purification and cleansing.

The Roman god Consus was a harvest deity whose realm included sowing and reaping. At a later time Consus was invoked at councils, his presence believed essential when important decisions were being made. Sage is an appropriate herbe for bringing the energy of wisdom and sagacity into a meeting.

According to Mrs. Grieve in *A Modern Herbal*, there is an old tradition which recommends planting rue among the sage to protect its health. This belief may be derived from the ancient Arabian belief that sage was an Herbe of Immortality. It was believed that the health of your sage plants reflected the health of your business affairs. Another folk belief was that sage grew best when the woman was the person in charge of the gardens and the household.

USAGE

From *The Master Book of Herbalism* we learn that sage offers the herbal virtues of strength, mental health and wisdom, and it banishes all evil. There are many beliefs regarding sage's ability to keep one's mind strong and clear. Years ago I found a verse in several sources which, sadly, I forgot to note. I have oftentimes in the past twenty years had a cup of sage tea to rid my mind of negative thought patterns while chanting, "Sage make green the winter rain. Charm the demon from my brain."

As a healing tonic, sage is more than remedial for it can be used to promote health throughout one's physical, spiritual, emotional and mental being. Sage may be used to purify one's self, removing negative energy and providing a healthy attitude toward life. It helps one deal with grieving and loss, both through healing and by helping one see beyond the immediate loss. Old folklore recommends eating fresh sage leaves nine mornings in a row, timed with either a new or full Moon.

Some legends maintain that sage's healing powers were first discovered by Cadmus, brother of Europa, whose mythological life was filled with adventure. Sage is also considered sacred to Zeus and to Jupiter. It is an excellent herbe to use when consecrating a thurible and is associated with the Temperance card. In some traditions sage is the herbe for the Autumn Equinox and/or for Hallow's Eve. I have also read of those who like to work with sage at Yule, to help them and their kindred remain bright when the days are at their shortest.

Albertus Magnus in his *Book of Secrets* relates a very odd belief: a magickal formula including sage and a cremated snake will allow one to conjure up thunderstorms and rainbows.

The belief cited by Mrs. Grieve leads us to recommend the use of sage by women who desire to hold their own in the world of business or who are working to manage a household. It would also seem to be an herbe most useful for single mothers.

322

❦ Sago Palm ❦

Metroxylon sp.
Venus
Religious Herbe

LORE

In the creation myths of the Melanesian Islands, much of manifest reality is created by Qat who is a creator spirit (but not treated as a god). On the Banks Islands it is believed that the first man was sculpted of clay and the first woman made of braided sago palm.

❦ Saint John's Wort ❦

Hypericum Perforatum
Sun
Leo
Fertility Herbe ... Herbe of Protection ... Herbe of Purification
Also called: hypericum, Saint Joan's wort

LORE

How strong is Saint John's wort? From *A Modern Herbal* we discover:

> its name *Hypericum* is derived from the Greek and means 'over an apparition,' a reference to the belief that the herb was so obnoxious to evil spirits that a whiff of it would cause them to fly.

USAGE

Today a connection is often found between Saint John's wort and Midsummer and, by proxy, with the element of fire. Saint John's Day is June 26, which once may have had more to do with Midsummer than it does now. Saint John's Day is celebrated on June 24 when many observe John the Baptist's birth. I will not attempt to sort out the threads of the Christian-pagan synthesis for this herbe.

Believed effective in protecting a home against lightning, fires and severe storms, one of the common customs was to burn the herbe in the fireplace. If you do not have a fireplace, you could

323

toss it into a cauldron and let the pungent smoke permeate all of the rooms. We have not done this, although hypericum grows profusely in our climate and we have it growing all about the gardens. Many believe that the herbe is more powerful when gathered at Midsummer. Saint John's wort will also protect you against all types of negative forces. Modern usage associates the herbe with elemental fire and with the elemental creatures of fire, often called salamanders. The herbe may be tossed into the fire when studying the spiritual nature of this primary element.

A custom reported by the Farrars in *Eight Sabbats for Witches* reminds us of so many folk spells using herbes.

> One Midsummer tradition may be of interest to any
> woman who is anxious to conceive... She should walk
> through (a vegetable garden) naked on Midsummer Eve
> and also pluck some Saint John's Wort, if there is any.

Extremely curious behavior—another requires dancing around a church in *your* neighborhood at midnight—what would your neighbors think! Many of these customs are deviant enough from one's usual patterns that all sorts of possibilities may be set free.

❦ Samphire ❦

Crithmum Maritimuum
Neptune
Herbe of Protection ... Magickal Herbe
Also called: sea fennel

LORE

Samphire is a patron herbe of fishers. The name is a derivation of "Saint Pierre" (or Saint Peter, a well-known fisher) which later appeared as "sampier."

USAGE

All who enjoy fishing could use an herbe just for them. Some may use it to encourage a good catch and others might use it to protect them while fishing from a boat. Samphire, a patron herbe of fishers, is usually found growing along the rocky shores and readily survives salt water.

❦ Sandalwood ❦

Santalum Album
Jupiter
Funereal Herbe ... Herbe of Consecration ... Herbe of
Immortality ... Magickal Herbe ... Religious Herbe ... Visionary
Herbe
Invocatory: Venus

LORE

In some parts of Asia, sandalwood is used both in embalming the physical body and in assisting the spiritual body into its next life. The wood is sometimes considered sacred and used in the construction of temples.

The great spiritual teacher Mahavira, one of the Jain *tirthamkaras* or great sages, according to *Larousse World Mythology* is said to have been showered with great gifts at his birth, including "gold and silver, pearls, diamonds, nectar and sandalwood." Followers of the Jain Lord Bahubali worship at a huge (over sixty feet tall) statue of the nude spiritual teacher. Every twelve years a festival is celebrated (determined astrologically) at which the statue is bathed, then anointed with the juice of sugar cane, milk and then sandalwood.

USAGE

Sandalwood has stirred both imaginations and spiritual aspirations for many centuries. In modern times sandalwood is associated with the goddess Venus and also with the Empress card.

A most sacred herbe in Jainism, sandalwood is widely used today as a Religious Herbe. It is commonly used to assist with meditation, trance work and all forms of divination as it calms the mind and helps one become spiritually focused. It is also most valuable in rituals of death and dying.

Many gems have become associated with sandalwood, including diamonds, emeralds, pearls and turquoise. Sandalwood is recommended for use when consecrating altar cloths and is said to be associated with Hod on the Tree of Life.

Magickally, this herbe may be used to increase opportunities and assist in achieving success in life.

🍎 Sassy Bark 🍎

Erythrophleum Guineense
Saturn

LORE

"In West Africa the drug is used as an ordeal poison in trials for witchcraft and sorcery," according to *A Modern Herbal*.

🍎 Savory 🍎

Satureia Hortensis
Mercury
Aphrodisiacal Herbe ... Greene Herbe ... Magickal Herbe
Invocatory: Pan

USAGE

This herbe has been associated with satyrs since ancient Roman times (note its Latin name). It may be used to invoke the spirit of Pan in his playful, fun-loving persona. Used in preparing a meal, it will help people feel lighthearted and promote laughter and joy.

It was long believed that summer savory would increase one's sexual drive. How to bring it in balance? Use winter savory (*Satureia Montana*).

🍎 Scabious (Devil's Bit) 🍎

Scabiosa Succisa
Jupiter

LORE

According to *A Modern Herbal* a "legend referred to by Gerard tells how the devil found it in Paradise, but envying the good it might do to the human race, bit away a part of the root to destroy the plant, in spite of which it still flourishes, but with a stumped root."

❦ Scullcap ❦

Scutellaria Galericulata
Saturn, Pluto
Herbe of Love ... Magickal Herbe

LORE

It is very difficult for this herbe to shake the mistaken lore that
its name is derived from being shaped like a human skull. It is
frequently spelled incorrectly, even done so when I first wrote *The
Master Book of Herbalism*! We have learned and now agree with
Grieve in *A Modern Herbal*, who maintains that the "generic
name is from the Latin *scutella* (a little dish), from the lid of the
calyx." We have also seen references which relate the shape to a
scull or a shell-shaped boat.

USAGE

Scullcap is used to bind oaths and consecrate vows and commitments. It may be used in Handfastings, where both parties wish to
make their vows to each other binding (and the breaking of them
of dire magickal consequence) or in rituals of initiation.

❦ Sedge (Papyrus) ❦

Calamus Papurus
Mercury
Religious Herbe

USAGE

Often used not only for manufacturing paper but also for adorn-
ing statues of deities, this variety of sedge may be used as a
Religious Herbe to show the connection between the earth and
the Divine. Paper made of sedge papyrus would make a very
sacred Book of Shadows.

❦ Sedge (Sweet) ❦

Acorus Calamus
Mercury
Herbe of Consecration ... Religious Herbe
Also called: calamus

LORE

According to *A Modern Herbal*, "the floors of Norwich Cathedral until quite recently were always strewn with calamus at great festivals." The history of calamus as a Religious Herbe is very old. From *The Magickal & Ritual Use of Herbs* we learn that some believe Moses, in order to please Jehovah and make himself presentable, mixed sedge with other herbes with which he anointed his body.

USAGE

In the same entry where Miller makes reference to Moses, he also writes that "in larger amounts it can be used as a mind-altering sacrament for the initiation of a boy into a Warrior." We are not familiar with the results of using sweet sedge in large quantities and are hesitant to suggest this without further research.

As a Religious Herbe, sweet sedge can be used to bless any space. It may be used as a strewing herbe, but may also be added to incense or used in a variety of ways. *Calamus Draco* (also known as *Dæmonorops Draco*) is one variety of calamus which herbalists know more familiarly as Dragon's Blood.

❦ Senna ❦

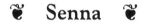

Cassia Acutifolia
Mercury
Magickal Herbe

USAGE

An herbe which enhances tact and diplomacy, this is an herbe for bards and for those who represent others as agents or envoys. Ideal for managers, senna may be used as a bathing herbe or with a few leaves tucked safely into one's briefcase. Senna encourages cooperation and decisions made with compassion.

❦ Sesame ❦

Sesamum sp.
Moon
Aphrodisiacal Herbe ... Herbe of Protection

USAGE

The oil derived from the seed is used to preserve the health and vitality of the sexual organs. The oil provides an excellent base when making herbal lubricants to promote sexual joys and enables one to work with herbes which release sexual magick; it is easily integrated into the Great Rite.

❦ Snapdragon ❦

Antirrhinum Magus
Mars
Scorpio
Herbe of Protection

LORE

"It was valued in olden times like the Toadflax as a preservative against witchcraft," according to *A Modern Herbal*.

USAGE

The popularity of snapdragons lends them to easy usage. They can provide a loving protection for one's family and friends when given in bouquets or integrated into a small corsage. Growing them in your garden brings protection for your home and those within it. Despite the bigotry once promoted against magickal people, as an Herbe of Protection, the many-hued snapdragon will actually help preserve the good witches in your life!

❦ Solomon's Seal ❦

Plygonatum Multiflorum
Saturn
Gemini
Aphrodisiacal Herbe ... Herbe of Consecration ...
Herbe of Protection
Also called: lady's seals, Saint Mary's seal

USAGE

This may be a situation in which the name contributed to the lore of the plant. Grieve in *A Modern Herbal* writes that the roots, when sliced, "somewhat resemble" letters of the Hebrew alphabet which led to the connection with Solomon, who "set his seal upon them in testimony of its value to man." The lore surrounding the magickal properties of Solomon's seal have greatly expanded in the twentieth century and the herbe is now much used in magickal workings. From *The Master Book of Herbalism* we learn that the root "is used in ceremonial magick to bind magickal works, and to make sacred oaths and promises, and to keep them ever binding. The flowers and roots have been used in aphrodisiacs, and sometimes the herbe is found in recipes of love potions."

Solomon's seal is an excellent herbe to use when consecrating a ritual room or space for the first time. As an Herbe of Consecration it ranks among the best and may be used in preparing any ritual item for sacred use.

Less well known is the use of this herbe in a mixture with Aphrodisiacal Herbes. When it is included, its function is to amplify the commitment between the partners and to make binding the connection created when their astral bodies merge during the ecstatic union of the Great Rite. It should be noted that this masculine herbe is also known by feminine names among many peoples.

❦ Southernwood ❦

Artemisia Abrotanum
Mercury
Aphrodisiacal Herbe ... Herbe of Love
Also called: boy's love, lad's love

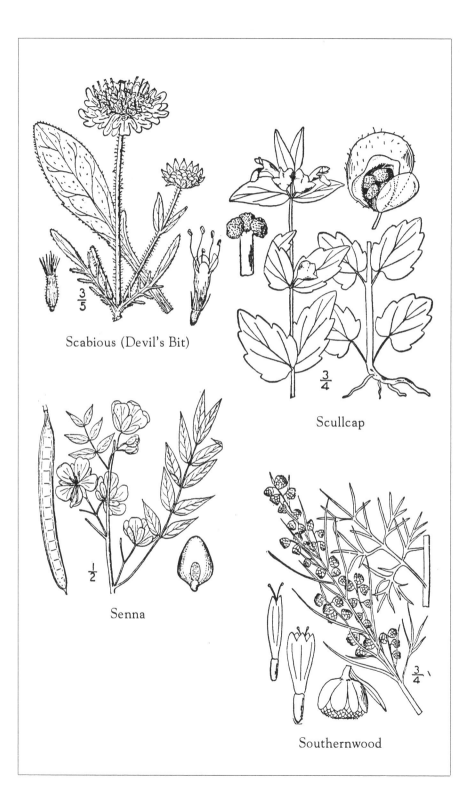

Scabious (Devil's Bit)

$\frac{3}{5}$

Scullcap

$\frac{3}{4}$

Senna

$\frac{1}{2}$

Southernwood

$\frac{3}{4}$

This is a southern variety of wormwood which is associated with attractiveness and sexual appeal. It has been used by men to increase their virility. Young men placed southernwood in bouquets of flowers to encourage young women to feel love and lust for them.

USAGE

Southernwood may be used to represent a promise to be faithful to one's intended lover. One usage of this herbe would be in the ritual baths in preparation for a Handfasting or ritual of union. Men who wish to increase their magickal testosterone might try working with southernwood.

The history of this herbe suggests that it is ideal for use in a rite of passage for a boy, assisting in bringing him into manhood.

❦ Spikenard ❦

Inula Conyza
Mars, Uranus
Aquarius
Magickal Herbe
Also called: cinnamon root, great fleabane, horse heal

USAGE

This is a wonderful herbe for students, whether those of spiritual disciplines or those preparing themselves for a profession. Spikenard will help clear your mind so that you can focus on what you are studying and obtain greater retention. Spikenard has sometimes been associated with Hod on the Tree of Life.

Magickally spikenard is also useful when training a horse; it helps establish an improved sense of communication between animal and human.

❦ Stitchwort ❦

Gramen Leucanthemum
Moon
Fertility Herbe

LORE

During the time of Dioscorides it was believed that potions of stitchwort, a relative of chickweed, would help a woman bear sons.

USAGE

Stitchwort may be used to encourage fertility. Women who are having difficulty conceiving and wish to use their spiritual skills to accomplish this end might make use of this herbe.

🐦 Stonecrop (Orpine) 🐦

Sedum Telephium
Moon
Magickal Herbe

LORE

A Modern Herbal informs us that "the specific name, *Sedum Telephium*, is derived from Telephus, the son of Hercules, who is said to have discovered its virtues."

USAGE

The orpine variety of stonecrop is used to increase one's strength, both physical prowess and/or strength of character. It is a singular herbe for athletes.

🐦 Storax 🐦

Liquidambar Orientalis
Sun
Magickal Herbe ... Religious Herbe
Invocatory: Hermes, Loki, Mercury, Thoth

USAGE

Storax promotes change and is corresponded with the Eight cards of the minor arcana. It has been considered a sacred herbe of the various aspects of the divine energy depicted within these cards and may be used in their invocation.

❦ Strawberry ❦

Fragaria Vesca
Venus

USAGE

Grieve in *A Modern Herbal* quotes an old recipe which requires strawberry leaves to be gathered on Lammas Eve. This association with Lammas Eve suggests that there is a connection with this sabbat that could be employed to benefit us all.

❦ Sugar Cane ❦

Saccharum Officinarum
Jupiter
Religious Herbe

LORE

Larousse World Mythology informs us that the native peoples of "Saa in the Solomon Islands believe that their ancestors sprang spontaneously from sugar-cane when, one day, two buds burst open and a man and a woman emerged."

USAGE

With the prevalence of sugar in modern civilization's diet, the devas of the sugar cane must have been very pleased that this sacred food permeates our culture, even if that culture is unaware that sugar cane represents a creation myth. Sugar cane can be used when exploring the mysteries of creation in all their aspects.

❦ Sumbul ❦

Ferula Sumbul
Saturn
Religious Herbe
Also called: musk root

LORE

Mrs. Grieve mentions that the root was used as an incense in the religious ceremonies of Persia and India.

❦ Sunflower ❦

Helianthus Annus
Sun
Herbe of Immortality ... Herbe of Protection ... Magickal Herbe
... Religious Herbe
Invocatory: Apollo, Demeter

LORE

There is something which catches one's imagination upon seeing these tall, solar flowers rising stately above our heads. If you have never seen a field of sunflowers, you have missed a wondrous experience. Grieve writes in *A Modern Herbal*:

> In Peru, this flower was much reverenced by the Aztecs, and in their temples of the Sun, the priestesses were crowned with sunflowers and carried them in their hands. The early Spanish conquerors found in these temples numerous representations of the sunflower wrought in pure gold.

Among one of the native peoples of British Columbia the deva of the sunflower was deeply revered. Frazer writes in *The Golden Bough*:

> [Thompson Indians] cook and eat the sunflower root... but they used to regard it as a mysterious being, and observed a number of taboos in connection with it; for example, women who were engaged in digging or cooking the root must practice continence, and no man might come near the oven where the women were baking the root. When young people ate the first berries, roots, or other products of the season, they addressed a prayer to the Sunflower-Root as follows: "I inform thee that I intend to eat thee. Mayest thou always help me to ascend, so that I may always be able to reach the tops of mountains, and I may never be clumsy! I ask this from thee, Sunflower-Root. Thou are the greatest of all in mystery." To omit this prayer would make the eater lazy and cause him to sleep long in the morning.

USAGE

Sunflower oil is one of our favorites to use as a fixative when using an oil extraction method for making ritual oils. This adds to the natural magick of the sunflower, the virtues of which include the ability to increase the sense of happiness in one's life.

The solar energy of this herbe is readily apparent. The petals may be gathered and used as a bathing herbe. The creative practitioner can find numerous ways of using the sunflower, ranging from using the seeds as a snack to baking cakes of sunflower.

Often associated with the solar festivals, we find that this herbe has been linked to many of the Sun gods, Apollo in particular. In many cultures the sunflower has become associated with harvest deities and is sometimes linked with Demeter. Sunflowers also have a strong connection with Lammas.

For those who are dealing with depression or sorrow, using sunflower will help fill the loneliness and emptiness with light. Sunflower brings protection against negative energy. Sunflower may be used as a bathing herbe, to attract joy. An oil of this herbe can be used to consecrate ritual robes. In addition, the sunflower may be used to improve dexterity and alleviate clumsiness. We recommend communication with the sunflower deva to ask for this protection.

❦ Sycamore ❦

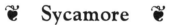

Ficus Sycomorus
Venus
Funereal Herbe ... Religious Herbe
Invocatory: Hathor

LORE

Hathor, Egyptian goddess of the dead, is sometimes called the "Lady of the Sycamores."

USAGE

The powdered bark of the sycamore may be used in incense mixtures for rituals of death and dying. The base of a sycamore would be a lovely setting for the burying of one's ashes. This tree may be used as a guardian spirit for the beloved.

❦ Tansy ❦

Tanacetum Vulgare
Venus
Funereal Herbe ... Herbe of Immortality ... Herbe of
Purification ... Religious Herbe
Invocatory: Ganymede

LORE

Tansy has a long history of association with women's mysteries and with goddess worship. At some unremembered point in time this belief was carried over from one religion to another and it became associated with Mary, mother of Jesus.

Mrs. Grieve in *A Modern Herbal* says that the Latin name is derived "from the Greek *Athanaton* (immortal) either, says Dodoens, because it lasts so long in flower, or, as Ambrosius thought, because it is capital for preserving dead bodies from corruption. It was said to have been given to Ganymede to make him immortal." Ganymede was a Trojan prince who was captured by Zeus and taken to Olympus where he became a cup bearer for the gods.

Among the many customs of the Old Ones which survived through being adopted by the new churches, the Christian clergy were known to play handball during the Easter celebrations to win the trophy of a tansy cake. Tansy became associated with Easter, representing the eternal quality of spiritual life as embodied by their Christ. Known as tansies, these cakes were eaten on Easter day. As well, tansy is one of the bitter herbes included in Passover.

USAGE

Tansy is useful as an Herbe of Immortality, particularly with regard to the Divine Feminine principle of the Universe. This is an excellent herbe to bring to rituals of death and dying. A bunch of tansy may be used to aspurge either the Circle during the rite or the physical remains of the deceased.

Its association with rebirth is strong. Although unlikely to be in bloom at Eostara, the new, green growth is always strong in our gardens, having resumed growth not long after Candlemas. Tansy gathered from the previous year's harvest is well suited for the

337

Eostara rites. For uses such as this it may be gathered with any magickal timing.

For those wishing to enter the realm of our Mother's mysteries, tansy may be combined with a ritual of purification when seeking to be placed within our Divine Mother's care. The dietary work should last throughout two fortnights: a full lunar cycle. From *The Master Book of Herbalism* we learn tansy "is used in women's rituals and, as such, shares its virtue of celebrating womanhood. It would be appropriate to give the live flowers to one's mother or another woman [who is] held in esteem."

❦ Tarragon ❦

Artemisia Cracunculus
Mars
Greene Herbe ... Herbe of Consecration ... Magickal Herbe
Invocatory: Lilith

LORE

The herbal history of tarragon has a wonderful association with dragons! The French called it *Herbe au Dragon* or herbe of the dragon and the English once called it "little dragon mugwort." Grieve in *A Modern Herbal* also writes that "the green leaves should be picked between Midsummer and Michaelmas [September 29]."

USAGE

Tarragon is the only herbe we know of associated with Lilith. Lilith is a most interesting feminine archetype, sometimes elevated to goddesshood. Occasionally appearing with Eve and Adam in artist's renderings of the Lovers card, she was the first independent woman! *Myths and Legends of All Nations* provides us with the story of Lilith:

> Created from the dust of the earth, (Lilith) had been one of the wives of Sammael (or Satan) but, being of a wild and passionate nature, had left her spouse and joined Adam. Lilith refused to be subservient and submissive to Adam on the ground that since both had issued from the dust, they were both equal.

Tarragon brings with it a magick which promotes compassion for

338

others but never at the inappropriate sacrifice of one's self. This Greene Herbe might be useful for women who are caretakers, helping them extend love and nurturing without becoming martyrs. We also recommend this herbe for women recovering from abusive situations, helping them reclaim their strength and independence. Tarragon is sometimes used in the consecration of chalices.

Teak

Tectona Grandis
Uranus
Religious Herbe

LORE

Larousse World Mythology tells of Mahavira, the final tirthamkara in the line of the Jain avatars, who sat beneath a teak (called *saka* in India) for two and a half days of meditation without moving a muscle of his body. Arising on the third day, he had reached enlightenment.

USAGE

Teak is an excellent wood for religious objects. The physical properties of the wood lend it readily to carving and endurance. The wood may be powdered and burned as an incense when one is seeking to learn more of the mysteries of the Universe through introspective disciplines, whether through meditation or divination.

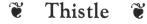

Thistle

Carduus sp.
Mars
Magickal Herbe

LORE

The old lore regarding the thistle is inconsistent with its modern magickal use. Perhaps running skyclad through the fields after being evicted from the Garden of Eden provided some sharp reminders of the nature of reality. In *A Modern Herbal* Grieve writes:

we read of the Thistle representing part of the primeval curse on the earth in general, and on man in particular, for *Thorns also and thistles shall it bring forth to thee.*

USAGE

The thistle represents the virtue of endurance and can be used magickally to strengthen one's ability to survive periods of stress, difficulty or, in herbal terms, to weather the storms of life. Thistles are sometimes used at the Autumn Equinox to provide the magick of survival to last throughout the fierce winter.

Thistles have been used in modern times in animal magick to provide healing and survival for the animals, both feral and domestic. A ritual of healing may be done for an animal, bringing it within a Circle which has a thistle bloom placed at each of the four directions.

❦ Thistle (Carline) ❦

Carlina Vulgaris
Mercury
Magickal Herbe

LORE

The following is from *A Modern Herbal*:

> The original name of this plant was Carolina, so called after Charlemagne, of whom legend relates that "a horrible pestilence broke out in his army and carried off many thousand men, which greatly troubled the pious emperor. Wherefore he prayed earnestly to God, and in his sleep there appeared to him an angel who shot an arrow from a crossbow, telling him to mark the plant upon which it fell, for with that plant he might cure his army of the pestilence." The herbe so miraculously indicated was this thistle *Carlina vulgaris*.

USAGE

The carline thistle may offer us a singular virtue: that of providing protection against diseases which can decimate a population. While it may not provide medical protection, it may, at the least, provide a divine grace which will help both those afflicted and those left behind.

❦ Thistle (Milk) ❦

Silybum Marianum
Moon
Religious Herbe
Also called: our lady's thistle

LORE

From *A Modern Herbal* we learn of an old belief which holds that "the milk-white veins of the leaves originated in the milk of the Virgin which once fell upon a plant of thistle."

USAGE

Although lore associates this herbe with the Virgin Mary, this variety of thistle may be used to work with the virginal or maiden aspect of the Goddess.

❦ Thistle (Scotch) ❦

Onopordon Acanthium
Mars
Also called: cotton thistle, wooly thistle

LORE

It is generally believed that this species is the symbol of the House of Stuart and is now the national emblem of Scotland.

❦ Thornapple ❦

Datura Stamonium
Jupiter
Visionary Herbe
Also called: datura

LORE

The following quote comes from *The Magickal & Ritual Use of Herbs*:

> The Algonquin peoples made a beverage known as "wusocca" which contained thornapple. This was used

during the rite of passage during which a boy became a man. "A type of violent madness would occur for about 20 days with a total loss of memory of their former life. When the boy regained consciousness, he would start adulthood forgetting that he was ever a child."

There is some belief that this herbe was proliferated throughout Europe by Gypsies as they emigrated from Asia. Old lore considers it an herbe used by witches in their spells. During the Burning Times thornapple growing in your garden might well have led to your persecution.

USAGE

Datura, as it is often called, is a potentially dangerous herbe to use (and, in many areas, a controlled substance). Any use must be with the greatest of care.

❦ Thyme ❦

Thymus Valgaris
Venus
Greene Herbe ... Herbe of Love ... Herbe of Protection ...
Magickal Herbe

LORE

Common thyme, according to *A Modern Herbal*, represented "activity, bravery and energy, and in the days of chivalry it was the custom for ladies to embroider a bee hovering over a sprig of thyme on the scarves they presented to their knights." If there is any herbe which represents being busy as a bee, it would be thyme.

It is uncertain whether its name is derived from its use by the Greeks as an incense or from the Greek word for courage. Both origins are consistent with the ancient use of this herbe.

USAGE

Thyme is a very friendly herbe for your garden devas and may be used to call upon the faerie folk. It carries with it the magick of delight and is an excellent herbe for those who take themselves too seriously. Practitioners can work with thyme to increase their courage, giving them power to meet that which confronts them.

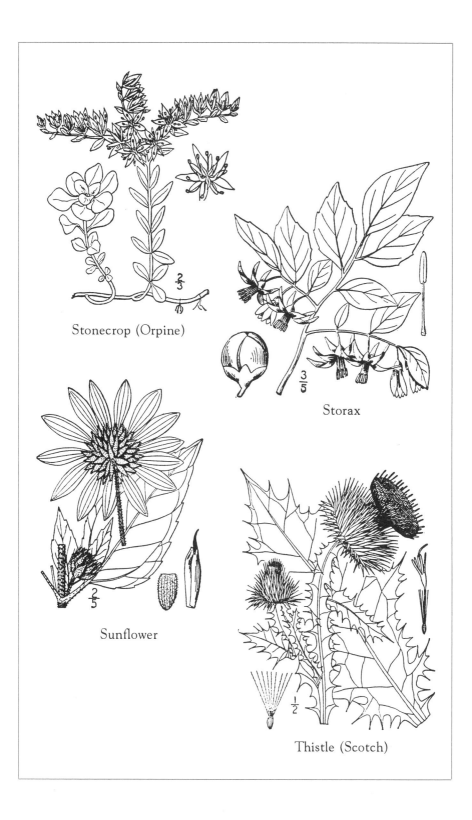

Stonecrop (Orpine)

$\frac{2}{3}$

Storax

$\frac{3}{5}$

Sunflower

$\frac{2}{5}$

Thistle (Scotch)

$\frac{1}{2}$

It can also be used to keep a light heart when working hard to achieve one's goals. Thyme is used to enhance the magick of pearls.

Thyme is gathered with marigolds, marjoram and wormwood for love divination on Saint Luke's Day (October 18).

From *A Modern Herbal* we learn Pliny said, "when burned, it puts to flight all venomous creatures." Even today thyme can be a valuable incense to protect against dangerous creatures, insects and reptiles.

❦ Thyme (Wild) ❦
Thymus Serpyllum
Venus
Funereal Herbe ... Herbe of Love ... Magickal Herbe

LORE

It is believed that the air and aura surrounding thyme are very pure. As we read in *A Modern Herbal*:

> It was looked upon as one of the fairies' flowers, tufts of thyme forming one of their favorite playgrounds.

Even the Romans recognized thyme's ability to elevate one's mood and dispel sorrow and melancholy.

Again, showing the interaction between life and death, it was once customary for young women to wear thyme (with mints and lavender), believing that it would help them find their true lover. But in Wales, wild thyme was planted upon graves and sometimes worn at funerals.

USAGE

The Master Book of Herbalism informs us that we may use thyme to "re-establish communion with those friends and relatives who have passed into death." This is achieved through divination or other forms of communication for the purpose of seeking counsel or sending love and blessings. Thyme may be a most useful herbe for Hallow's Eve.

Wild thyme and marjoram are said to keep milk from spoiling

during thunder. The old lore was that you laid them next to the milk, but this was before the days of refrigerators.

Growing various types of thyme in your gardens will encourage the devas to be lively. There is much magick to be found in the gardens when the thyme is in bloom.

🍏 Toadflax 🍏

Linaria Vulgaris
Mars, Pluto
Magickal Herbe
Also called: eggs and bacon, flaxweed, larkspur lion's mouth, pattens and clogs, rabbits

USAGE

Perhaps derived from the name, toadflax is somewhat associated with toads and with garden witches. The name actually originates in the flowers' resemblance to tiny toads. Toadflax can be quite toxic and may well have been used in medieval spell magick. It should not be used internally, but can be added to magickal formulas as one would invoke the power of elemental earth to strengthen the work at hand.

🍏 Tobacco 🍏

Nicotiana Tabacum
Mars
Religious Herbe
Invocatory: Yacatecutli

LORE

Tobacco is considered sacred by many peoples and its ceremonial use is widespread. It is used as an offering to the gods, smoked at council meetings, and the juice expressed to drink in the quest for visions. In *Larousse World Mythology* we discover that the Toba Indians of South America believe tobacco leaves came from the transformed ashes of a cannibal woman whom they had burned.

Also from *Larousse World Mythology* we learn that the elder magicians of the Jivaro peoples along the Amazon "use tobacco juice to reach a state of intoxication in which Earth appears to them in a vision and they can converse with her." *The Golden Bough* presents a similar religious custom that is found in Uganda: the priest, "in order to be inspired by his god, smokes a pipe of tobacco fiercely till he works himself into a frenzy; the loud excited tones in which he then talks are recognized as the voice of the god speaking through him."

Yacatecutli, a patron deity for travelers in Mexico, is given tobacco as an offering.

USAGE

If one is going to use tobacco as a sacred herbe, then its mundane use should be proscribed. The smoking of tobacco on extremely rare occasion produces a far more dramatic physiological response than one might expect. Tobacco has been corresponded to all four Knight cards of the minor arcana. On a more generic level, one might use tobacco when communicating with Mother Earth.

Trillium

Trillium Pendulum
Pluto
Magickal Herbe
Also called: bethroot, birthroot, ground lily, wake-robin

USAGE

The lovely trillium represents the spring season and, depending upon your climate, may be used to symbolize the Spring Equinox. Trilliums are oftentimes symbols of initiation.

They are sacred to women who are giving birth, offering them calm and hope. Trilliums are patron flowers for bards.

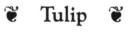

Tulip

Tulipa sp.
Venus
Magickal Herbe

LORE

From a source since forgotten (for which I apologize) I found a story from Persian myths in which the character Ferhad has his heart broken by his beloved. He abandons himself to the desert where he wishes his life to end. Each teardrop he sheds becomes a tulip.

USAGE

In light of the above lore, is it not curious that tulips are popular around Valentine's Day? They do not last so long as the far more popular roses, and they readily drop their petals.

Many experience the pain of a broken heart during their lifetime. Perhaps the tulip would be an appropriate flower to use as a healing herbe for these folk.

❦ Turmeric ❦

Curcuma Longa
Mercury
Greene Herbe ... Herbe of Protection ... Magickal Herbe

LORE

The shepherds of Nepal cook their rice in turmeric. Before they set out to herd their sheep high in the mountains, they daub the turmeric paste upon the chakra between their eyebrows. It is believed that this will provide blessings, success and protection when driving their sheep on long, perilous journeys through the mountain passes.

USAGE

I think we'd say that if it's good enough for the Nepalese, it's good enough for us. We recommend using turmeric to bring one through long and arduous journeys in safety. It might also be a most useful herbe to use when taking one's harvest to the market.

❦ Unicorn Root ❦

Aletris Farinosa
Uranus
Magickal Herbe ... Visionary Herbe
Also called: ague root, blazing star, stargrass, starwort

347

Within our Wiccan Tradition of Lothloriën we work with astral unicorns. These beautiful yet powerful creatures are not the products of our imagination; over the years they have more than demonstrated that they exist within the astral as real creatures. Unicorn root is used magickally by those who wish to work with unicorns as spiritual entities and is the patron herbe of The Rowan Tree Church.

Unicorn root brings a playful quality to one's magick. We have successfully integrated it into baby blessings and protective magickal work for infants. Also known as starwort, this herbe is ideal for those desiring some whimsical fantasy in their visionalizations.

❦ Unicorn Root (False) ❦
Chamaelirium Luteum
Pluto
Aphrodisiacal Herbe

USAGE

False unicorn root is used to treat impotence and is part of some pharmacopoeias devoted to herbal medicines. But it may also be used magickally to enhance one's sexual desire and call upon the sensuality of the unicorn: long associated with sexuality as well as with purity. It is an herbe appropriate for the Great Rite when one must explore that sexual magick as a solitary.

❦ Uva Ursi ❦
Arctostaphylos Uva-Ursi
Mars, Pluto
Scorpio
Religious Herbe
Also called: bearberry

USAGE

Commonly known as bearberry, uva ursi may be used to increase your intuitive and psychic abilities and skills. Small daily amounts taken as a spiritual tonic are recommended. Some Native American peoples include uva ursi in their ritual pipe-smoking mixtures. Some tribes use uva usi to train shamans in the development of their skills in divination and prophecy.

❦ Valerian ❦

Valeriana Officinalis
Mercury
Virgo, Aquarius
Herbe of Consecration ... Herbe of Protection ...
Herbe of Purification

LORE

Despite the distaste many have for its scent, valerian grows one of the sweetest scented of all flowers and was, in earlier times, highly valued. The root was placed with clothing and was even used as the base for perfumes.

Despite its reputation for being greatly loved by cats, we learn from *A Modern Herbal*:

> it has been suggested that the famous Pied Piper of Hamelin owed his irresistible power over rats to the fact that he secreted valerian roots about his person.

USAGE

Valerian is very cleansing and may be used to purify your ritual space. It is one of the herbes said to have been used by King Solomon when aspurging his temple.

Useful in consecrating thuribles or incense burners, you may also make an elixir of valerian to take daily (in modest doses) during periods of self-purification. For those fortunate enough to grow valerian in their gardens, all manner of wonderful magick can be worked with the blooms.

❧ Vervain ❧

Verbena Officinalis
Venus
Virgo, Libra
Aphrodisiacal Herbe ... Countermagick Herbe ... Fertility Herbe
... Herbe of Consecration ... Herbe of Immortality ... Herbe of
Love ... Herbe of Protection ... Herbe of Purification ...
Magickal Herbe ... Religious Herbe ... Visionary Herbe
Invocatory: Diana, Hermes, Medea
Also called: herba veneris, herb of grace, verbena

LORE

Vervain was one of the first herbes I learned of when beginning my studies of herbal magick over two decades ago. It was often referred to as a witch's herbe due to the large body of lore surrounding its attributes. My early affinity for vervain could have come from my first steps being tenuous and the fact that I was completely inexperienced. Albertus Magnus in his *Book of Secrets* offers a clue when he wrote that "infants bearing it shall be very apt to learn, and loving learning, and they shall be glad and joyous." And I definitely grew to love learning all I could about herbes.

Frequently referred to as verbena, we find that a great many cultures considered this a sacred herbe. The Greeks, Romans, Celts, Welsh and many other European peoples readily identified this herbe as magickal. The following quote comes from *A Modern Herbal*:

> The name Vervain is derived from the Celtic *ferfaen*, from *fer* (to drive away) and *faen* (a stone).... Another derivation is given by some authors from *Herba veneris*, because of the aphrodisiac qualities attributed to it by the Ancients. Priests used it for sacrifices, and hence the name *Herba Sacra*. The name *Verbena* was the classical Roman name for "altar-plants" in general, and for this species in particular. The Druids included it in their lustral water, and magicians and sorcerers employed it largely. It was used in various rites and incantations, and by ambassadors in making leagues. Bruised, it was worn round the neck as a charm against snake and other venomous bites as well as for general good luck. It was

thought to be good for the sight.

USAGE

Vervain may be used to enhance the dreaming process. We recommend including it when working a Dream Quest. Old folklore says it will help you dream of your future love but it is more useful when used ritually to expand your divinatory skills and abilities. Vervain may be used to consecrate and empower any of your ritual tools. The Pawnee used it to further their dreaming skills. Associated with the metallic element of mercury, storing a small glass vial of this heavy liquid will keep the magick of your vervain strong. Verbena is used with opals and agates.

By working with this herbe, we can come to better understand the mysteries of immortality. When consecrating your altar stone, there is no herbe better chosen than vervain. It is also used to consecrate magickal wands, chalices and thuribles, and it makes a wonderful aspurger.

Vervain has been used for a very long time to protect people against negative emotions and the feeling that life has become a burden. The Celts recognized this ability of verbena. Even today it is found in many spells and formulas for amulets which protect the practitioner against various types of negation both from within the person and from outside sources. Oftentimes it is recommended to reverse negative energy as well. We recommend that it be worn if one is performing an exorcism. Verbena is used in house and home blessings as well.

Many love spells and romantic magickal formulas include vervain. This may be due, in part, to its reputation as being able to empower any magick. In fact the Welsh call it *llysiaur hudol* or "the enchanting herbe." As well as being added to recipes to attract mates, help one find true love, achieve sexual fulfillment and work sexual magick, this herbe is sometimes used by brides to bring extra bliss to the first night. Vervain is held sacred to the goddess Diana and is corresponded with the Justice card.

It is said that ancient magicians in Persia gathered bunches of verbena to raise up to the newly risen Sun in preparation for a spiritual and magickal day. Even today we find a solar correspondence with the herbe; it is recommended that it be gathered at Midsummer with the previous year's dried vervain tossed into the

351

Midsummer fire.

This is an herbe of poets, singers and bards. Vervain is most potent if fresh cut and worn when performing. It increases the performer's skill and inspires the artistry. It is also a valuable herbe for students of any magickal path.

❦ Violets ❦

Viola Odorata
Venus
Funereal Herbe ... Herbe of Immortality ... Magickal Herbe
Invocatory: Io, Zeus

LORE

Violets are said to have originated from the nymph Io, a daughter of the river god Inachus. Ino (oftentimes related to Isis) and the god Zeus were developing a romance, when Hera (Zeus' primary other at that time) became so jealous that she cast a spell and changed Io into a heifer. Poor Io was left with grass to munch and a god who really loved women rather than cows. In his compassion, according to some versions, Zeus changed her not back into a young woman but into the violet.

"Violets, like Primroses, have been associated with death, especially with the death of the young. This feeling has been constantly expressed from early times." We also read in Mrs. Grieve's *A Modern Herbal* that "violets were mentioned frequently by Homer and Virgil...used by the Athenians 'to moderate anger,' to procure sleep and 'to comfort and strengthen the heart.' "

USAGE

One of the most difficult pains to ease is that of a parent who has lost a child. Violets are said to bring comfort to a grieving heart and are well suited for planting upon a child's grave. They are used within the rituals of death and dying or placed upon the altar whenever prayers are offered to keep the child's memory healthy and alive.

Violets also offer us the virtues of modesty, simplicity, serenity and peace, and they are a source of inspiration and good fortune for women. Although not so classified, we may use the blooms as a Greene Herbe by sprinkling them upon a salad.

Whether we use them as an oil or place the flowers in a small vase, there is much magick to be had in these simple flowers. They are often associated with the Spring Equinox and were once steeped in the milk of goats before being used as a cosmetic to increase a woman's beauty and appeal.

❦ Walnuts ❦

Juglans Nigra
Sun
Religious Herbe
Invocatory: Jupiter, Zeus

USAGE

Mythology describes a Golden Age when acorns were the food of humans and the gods, according to A *Modern Herbal*:

> lived upon Walnuts, and hence the name of *Juglans*, *Jovis glans*, or Jupiter's nuts.

USAGE

Walnuts provide us access to divine energy. There are many ways to integrate these Religious Herbes into our daily lives. Walnuts are readily used in cooking. For example, they can be chopped and used in place of ground beef for vegetarian chili at a ritual feast. They are a delicacy easily used when baking cakes, cookies or pies, as well as being offered just as they are. If we are all gods or goddesses, then walnuts are truly food for us as well.

But there's more. The extracted oil of walnuts is easy to obtain. This oil is excellent for conditioning a wooden wand or for treating the natural wood finishes of one's temple furniture or flooring.

❦ Watercress ❦

Nasturtium Officinale
Moon
Greene Herbe ... Herbe of Consecration ... Herbe of Protection
... Magickal Herbe ... Visionary Herbe

USAGE

This is a true herbe of water creatures; it is magickally symbolized by elementals called undines. Carrying it in a bit of red flannel will bring safety to those traveling in boats or flying across the waters. Watercress is believed by some practitioners to provide insight into the nature of elemental water.

Watercress eaten during the day is believed to help one's dreams be more precognitive, mystical or visionary. This herbe also promotes an understanding of the Chariot card and is used to consecrate ritual chalices and water containers.

We may work with this herbe to increase our compassion and understanding of the human condition. It may be made into an oil or balm to stimulate the third eye and bring balance into one's life. A few have corresponded this herbe with the twenty-third path of the Tree of Life.

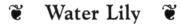

❦ Water Lily ❦

Nymphæa Odorata
Moon
Religious Herbe

LORE

Surya, the Hindu Sun god popular in India, is shown holding water lilies in two of his hands while, with the other two (he has four), he encourages us and bestows upon us his blessings.

USAGE

Not only do water lilies stir a sense of inner peace, but we can also use them to bring us light during times of darkness. They can ease those difficulties that are likely to keep us from seeing the light of our spiritual paths. Just as the water lily emerges from deep beneath the water's surface, so too must we emerge from within ourselves to bask in the radiance of the Sun.

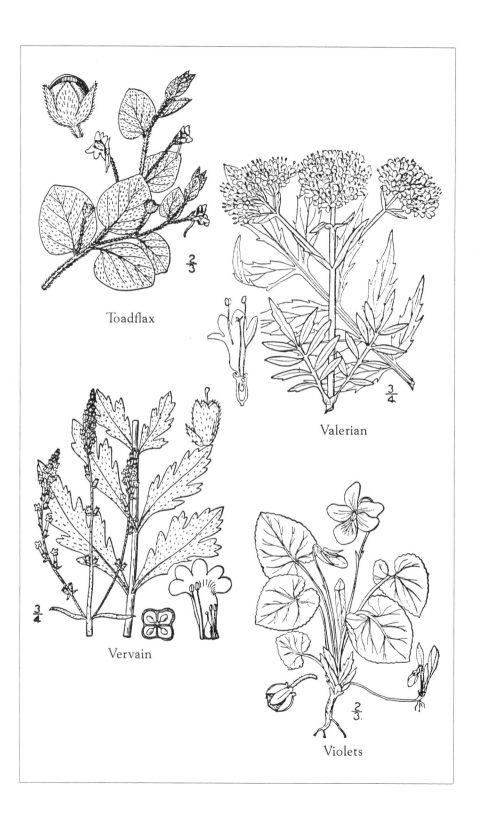

Toadflax

$\frac{2}{3}$

Valerian

$\frac{3}{4}$

Vervain

$\frac{3}{4}$

Violets

$\frac{2}{3}$

❦ Wheat ❦

Triticum sp.
Venus, Pluto
Leo
Fertility Herbe ... Greene Herbe ... Religious Herbe
Invocatory: Demeter, Siva

LORE

The creativeness of the gods is never to be doubted. From *Myths and Legends of All Nations* we learn about the goddess Cerridwen (sometimes spelled Kerridwen) who owns a magick cauldron in which she cooks an elixir which brings inspiration to all who taste it. A young man who is supposed to function as an assistant and stir the cauldron, named Gwion, gets in trouble when Cerridwen is cooking up a brew to bring good looks to the unfortunate Avaggdu. Gwion, with a characteristic boyish lack of self-control, drinks it himself. Knowing that he has incurred his Lady's wrath, he seeks to hide from her by shape-shifting into many creatures. At last, he thinks he will escape her by becoming a grain of wheat. But one doesn't fool with the goddess and she transforms herself into a hen, chases him about, catches him and eats him. She later births him and puts him in the sea.

Wheat is associated with many goddesses, including Demeter, an agricultural deity whose rulership included many grains. Demeter, sister of the Greek Zeus, is often shown holding wheat in one hand. Among the Slavs, Siva (sometimes spelled Ziva) was worshipped as the goddess of life and fertility. She is also depicted holding wheat. Prevalent among many peoples is the custom of gathering the last bunches which are called the "Mother of the Wheat" or "Wheat Mother" or other concept related to fertility worship.

Gerard believed that one variety of wheat would ensure that a woman be fertile and have sons (rather than daughters). An old Roman custom to promote fertility had the bride and groom eat wheat as part of their ceremony.

Frazer in *The Golden Bough* writes of the Moravian custom in which the last bunch of wheat is cut and given to a maiden who has been chosen as the Wheat Bride. She wears a wreath of wheat and it is generally held that she will marry before the next harvest. It is common in many cultures to braid the stalks of the last wheat into dollies and charms.

USAGE

It may be difficult for the magickal cook to think of that sack of white powder being a Religious Herbe, much less a Greene Herbe. Wheat has represented the food of life to peoples since the earli-est recorded history and it is a definite green before ripening into amber waves. Most of you already partake of this Fertility Herbe when you break your bread with friends or share ritual cakes or cookies. What would our Christian neighbors think to discover that their communion wafers are actually sacred to a fertility goddess?

🌱 Willow 🌱

Salix sp.
Moon, Saturn, Neptune
Funereal Herbe ... Herbe of Immortality ... Herbe of Protection
... Magickal Herbe ... Religious Herbe
Invocatory: Aino, Artemis, Circe, Diana, Hecate, Hera,
Hermes, Orpheus, Persephone

LORE

The weeping willow was one of the first sacred herbes of my childhood. At a very early age a forked branch was cut from the magnificent willow on our family farm and I was successful at my first dowsing. When my parents left Pine Lawn Farm they took willow cuttings, and a year later, when they purchased the house which is still their home, our family willow was given a new life. Just two years ago I asked my father to send me several cuttings which are now growing here at The Hermit's Grove. A fierce storm raged through my parents' town the following autumn bringing down their willows. But the tree lives on and I am very aware of its immortality representation. This virtue was long ago recognized by the Chinese because even the smallest piece of willow is able to bring forth another, living tree.

It is said that the Hebrew peoples, in Babylon while wandering on their long journey, came to a willow which reminded them of home. They hung their harps upon it and mourned the loss of their homeland. Graves writes in *The White Goddess* that "the willow was of great importance in the worship of Jehovah at Jerusalem, and the Great Day of the Feast of Tabernacles, a fire and water ceremony, was called the Day of Willows."

The willow is sacred to Hecate, Hermes and all deities of the Underworld. It is believed to be an herbe which will provide a safe journey into the Otherworld. Orpheus turned to the willow when passing through the Underworld to receive the virtue of eloquence. While in the gardens of Persephone, he placed his hand upon one of her magick willows to receive this gift. Graves places the willow as the letter *S*, or Saille, in the tree alphabet and writes the following in *The White Goddess*:

> The fifth tree is the willow, or osier, which in Greece was sacred to Hecate, Circe, Hera and Persephone, all Death aspects of the Triple Moon-goddess.... Its connection with witches is so strong in northern Europe that the words "witch" and "wicked" are derived from the same ancient word for willow, which also yields "wicker".... The Druidical human sacrifices were offered at the full of the Moon in wicker-baskets.... According to Pliny, a willow tree grew outside the Cretan cave where Zeus was born.... The wearing of the willow in the hat as a sign of the rejected lover seems to be originally a charm against the Moon-goddess's jealousy. The willow is sacred to her for many reasons....

Frazer writes that the Gypsy peoples of Romania bring the willow into their celebration of Green George, observed at the Spring Equinox (among other spring-oriented dates such as Easter Monday). Green George, according to *The Golden Bough* is a youth chosen to dress in green leaves, representing the Green Man. He offers grass to the animals to ensure plenty of food for the livestock "then he takes three iron nails, which have lain for three days and nights in water, and knocks them into the willow; after which he pulls them out and flings them into a running stream to propitiate the water spirits." This is believed to provide healing for the tribe during the coming year.

Old pagan lore of Finland connects the willow with the goddess Aino, whose myth is told in the entry for the birch. In the tale the willow arises out of her ribs and remains sacred to her.

USAGE

Another variety of willow, always a popular one during the spring season, is the pussy willow which was deemed ideal by the Druids for charms and protection. Even today there are many who believe a branch of the pussy willow offers the best of all ritual wands. There are many types of willow and they all make excellent magickal wands. Pussy willow cuttings are often included as altar decorations at Candlemas or Eostara, depending upon the climate.

Some legends maintain that Hera, who rose in prominence from being First Lady when Zeus ruled the pantheon to becoming a widely worshipped goddess in her own right, was born by a willow. Patroness of women everywhere, we may use willow to seek her patronage in all of the communication arts which were under her aegis. Those who do any public speaking might use willow to appeal to Orpheus or to Persephone in order to be granted eloquence. Willow is a wonderful herbe for bards.

As a Funereal Herbe, planting a willow during your lifetime is said to protect you when taking final leave of your body. The willow (or a direct descendant through a cutting) must be thriving at your death.

Graves calls the willow a tree of enchantment. Willow is the herbe to use with rock crystal to charge the stone and give it protective and healing virtues.

❦ Wisteria ❦

Wistaria Cinensis
Neptune
Aquarius
Magickal Herbe

USAGE

Wisteria is an herbe for those who devote time to reading and studying. Wearing the oil as a scent is believed to help one be a better student by promoting mental clarity and providing better retention. The flowers make a wonderful tea to use when preparing for an exam.

❦ Woad ❦

Ivatis Tinctoria
Mars, Saturn, Pluto
Religious Herbe

USAGE

Grieve believes that woad was readily found growing throughout the British Isles but that the extensive harvest of the plant led to a need to import it. For those who prefer dying their own ritual clothing, woad is a natural source of a beautiful blue color. Woad has a long history of use as a dye for clothing (and some say for facial designs) for ritual and ceremonial use.

❦ Woodruff ❦

Asperula Odorata
Venus, Mars
Herbe of Protection ... Religious Herbe

LORE

Woodruff is the singular herbe found in May wine, a festive drink used to celebrate the joyous return of spring. As we read in *A Modern Herbal*:

> In Germany, one of the favorite hockcups is still made by steeping the fresh sprigs in Rhine wine. This forms a specially delightful drink, known as *Maibowle*, and drunk on the first of May.

USAGE

Drawing upon the usage during the Middle Ages when woodruff was strewn in churches as a form of protection both against infestations of insects and also against evil, we may use this singularly scented herbe today to protect us against unwanted energies.

May wine can readily be purchased at most wine shops and remains a Beltane favorite of many peoples.

❦ Wormwood ❦

Artemisia Absinthium
Mars, Pluto
Herbe of Love ... Magickal Herbe ... Religious Herbe ...
Visionary Herbe
Invocatory: Artemis, Diana
Also called: artemisia, green ginger

LORE

The name *Artemisia* shows the long association with the Roman Diana and Greek Artemis. As Grieve has recorded in *A Modern Herbal*:

> In an early translation of the *Herbarium* of Apuleius we find: "Of these worts that we name Artemisia, it is said that Diana did find them and delivered their powers and leechdom to Chiron the Centaur, who first from these worts set forth a leechdom, and he named these worts from the name of Diana, Artemis, that is Artemisias."
>
> According to the Ancients, wormwood counteracted the effects of poisoning by hemlock, toadstools and the biting of the sea-dragon. The plant was of some importance among the Mexicans, who celebrated their great festival of the Goddess of Salt by a ceremonial dance of women, who wore on their heads garlands of wormwood.

USAGE

Wormwood is used to enhance prophecy and divination. It is associated with the Lovers card of the tarot and serves as a patron herbe of herbalists. In some versions of the myth, the goddess Artemis bestows this herbe upon the centaur, Chiron, healer of the gods, who uses it as one of his most important healing herbes.

Wormwood may be used to remove anger. Although such practices require a most thorough analysis of one's underlying motives and of social ethics. From *The Master Book of Herbalism* we learn that "for those who seek to vent their anger in a peaceful, creative means this herbe is appropriate to use. It is also used when a group works magick to stop war or to inhibit the enemy."

Grieve records an old love charm in *A Modern Herbal*:

On Saint Luke's Day, take marigold flowers, a sprig of marjoram, thyme, and a little wormwood; dry them before a fire, rub them to powder; then sift it through a fine piece of lawn, and simmer it over a slow fire, adding a small quantity of virgin honey, and vinegar. Anoint yourself with this when you go to bed, saying the following lines three times, and you will dream of your partner "that is to be":

> Saint Luke, Saint Luke, be kind to me,
> In dreams let me my true-love see.

❦ Yams ❦

Dioscorea sp.
Jupiter

LORE

Frazer writes in *The Golden Bough* of yams' connection to the sacrifice of the king. The king of Oneitsha is required to live within the walls of his palace unless a human sacrifice is being offered to the gods. There is an exception, however, for "at the Feast of Yams the king is allowed, and even required by custom, to dance before his people outside the high mud wall of the palace. In dancing he carries a great weight...on his back to prove that he is still able to support the burden and cares of state. Were he unable to discharge this duty, he would be immediately deposed and perhaps stoned."

❦ Yarrow ❦

Achillea Millefolium
Venus
Libra
Magickal Herbe ... Religious Herbe ... Visionary Herbe
Also called: carpenter's weed, milfoil, yarroway

LORE

Yarrow's ancient history is not consistent. Some maintain that it was first used by Achilles when healing his soldiers' wounds. Some say that it was a different Achilles, one who was a student of Chiron. Perhaps it is the same Achilles who appears under different guises. Mythology, over time, becomes an ever-complex weave of different layers of religious and cultural fabric which I hope to better understand in my next lifetime.

A prevalent herbe which grows naturally in most parts of the world, yarrow has some interesting lore. Grieve writes the following in A Modern Herbal:

> It was one of the herbs dedicated to the Evil One, in earlier days, being sometimes known as Devil's Nettle, Devil's Plaything, Bad Man's Plaything, and was used for divination in spells. Yarrow, in the eastern counties, is termed Yarroway, and there is a curious mode of divination with its serrated leaf, with which the inside of the nose is tickled while the following lines are spoken. If the operation causes the nose to bleed, it is a certain omen of success:
> Yarroway, Yarroway, bear a white blow,
> If my love love me, my nose will bleed now.
> An ounce of Yarrow sewed up in flannel and placed under the pillow before going to bed, having repeated the following words, brought a vision of the future husband or wife:
> Thou pretty herb of Venus' tree,
> Thy true name it is Yarrow;
> Now who my bosom friend must be,
> Pray tell thou me tomorrow.

USAGE

In the Orkney Islands yarrow is widely used for dispelling melancholy. Yarrow is an important herbe when healing someone burdened by troubled emotions, helping cleanse them of an unhealthy sorrow or a depression which has lasted too long. Albertus Magnus uses yarrow in combination with nettles to treat fear and self-negation.

Yarrow's associations with divination extend far beyond folk spells. In China yarrow stalks are gathered, the straightest collected for scattering when reading the I Ching. According to The Master Book of Herbalism, it is said that "the most prized yarrow is that which grows upon the burial site of Confucius."

Modern lore recommends waiting for the first yarrow bloom and using it to make a wish which should manifest prior to the harvest. The flowers are often included in rituals of union and are considered sacred to the Horned God.

❦ Yew ❦

Taxus Baccata
Saturn
Religious Herbe
Invocatory: Hecate, Mercury

LORE

One of the sacred trees of the British Isles, the yew is associated with Idho, the letter *I* in the tree alphabet. Grieve writes in *A Modern Herbal* that the tree was "favored by the Druids, who built their temples near these trees, a custom followed by the early Christians. The association of the tree with places of worship still prevails."

In *The White Goddess*, Graves describes this evergreen as "the death tree in all European countries, sacred to Hecate in Greece and Italy. At Rome, when black bulls were sacrificed to Hecate... they were wreathed in yew." Graves later associates the yew with the god Mercury.

USAGE

There are many ways to work with the sacred energies of the yew. Those fortunate to have outdoor ritual sites might plant one or more yew to provide their natural energy to all sacred events. The needles can be dried and powdered for incense. Internal use of yew should be avoided.

❦ Yohimbe ❦

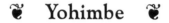

Coryanthe Yohimbe
Mars

LORE

The following comes from *The Magical & Ritual Use of Herbs*:

> Most of the Bantu-speaking tribes have traditionally used the inner shavings of the bark as a stimulant and aphrodisiac. It is only used when mate rituals occur. These orgy rituals have been known to last up to 10-15 days, with gradually increased doses.

USAGE

Miller recommends yohimbe as a sacramental herbe suitable for pagan rituals of union. It would be an excellent herbe to use for many rites of passage.

Yucca

Yucca sp.
Pluto
Religious Herbe

USAGE

The yuccas are, in some areas of South America, associated with the Earth Goddess. It is believed they have a connection with her spirit. If you grow one in your garden (some varieties can be grown indoors) use it to connect with the Mother.

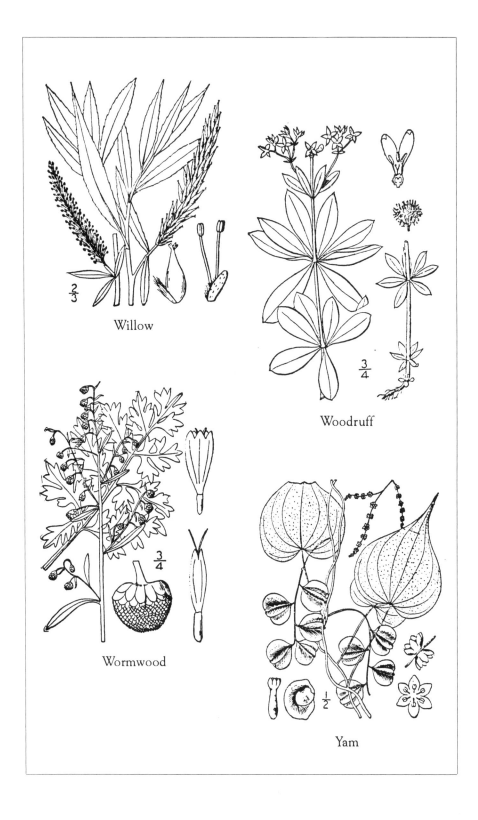

$\frac{2}{3}$

Willow

$\frac{3}{4}$

Woodruff

$\frac{3}{4}$

Wormwood

$\frac{1}{2}$

Yam

PART III

A Guide to Magickal Usage

Please do not treat this list as definitive. It has been developed as a convenient guide and handy reference. Undoubtedly, if we spent another year pouring over this manuscript and studying the individual herbes in this compendium, the list could be greatly expanded. It is provided for you to use as a starting point. You may add your own notes and create a wonderful reference tool for your magickal development.

Aces of tarot: lady's mantle

Use this herbe as an incense, drink it as a tea, or even sit near it when spending time learning what all four Aces have in common and how this information increases your interpretative skills.

agates: vervain

This herbe may be used to consecrate ritual tools or jewelry set with (or carved from) agate. Conversely, placing an agate in your jar of dried herbe may help preserve its magickal potency.

air: anemone (wood), bluebells, dandelion, hyacinth, olive

When working with elemental air in ritual, when calling upon the elemental creatures of air (the sylphs) or when bringing balance to your life by increasing the element of air, these herbes are most useful.

alcohol dependency: almond

This herbe may provide magickal assistance for those working to remain clean and sober. There are many ways to use it, ranging from cooking to making a magickal wand for strength and increased will power.

altar: acacia, flax, walnut

These herbes may be integrated into the construction of your altar. They may also impart their energy during the consecration of your altar or be used in providing it with proper maintenance and care in both worlds, caring for the wood and for your altar's aura at the same time.

altar cloths: flax, melilot, sandalwood

You might weave your cloths with flax, keep them in a drawer with sandalwood or use these herbes when laundering your altar cloths. You are only hemmed in by your imagination.

altar stones: vervain

It is common among those of us in The Tradition of Lothloriën to include altar stones as part of our ritual items. On our altar we have two pieces of petrified wood I purchased some fifteen years ago. They were sold as bookends, but since the day they came home with me, they have been kept on either side of the altar. One has been consistently worked as Yang, or solar energy, absorbing and holding that energy throughout at least five hundred ritual performances. The other represents the feminine counterpart within the Universe, its deep knothole a stunning symbol. Sitting upon the altar top we also keep a slice of petrified wood which functions, in many ways, as a pentacle. Set upon it during ritual is the chalice holding the herbal elixir which will be part of the Great Rite. Vervain may be used in the cleansing and consecration of your altar stones and as a wash when you do your cleaning and maintenance.

amber: anise seed, lotus

This petrified resin is believed to have an affinity with both of these herbes. The gemstones may be placed with your herbes or the herbes used to enhance the magick of your amber. Note that it is possible to purchase amber which is too coarse to be used for jewelry. These pieces can be shattered with a hammer, done while the stones are in a bag so as not to lose even a small piece. Amber provides one of the most powerful incenses and has a beautiful, pungent scent.

amethyst: cedar, hyssop

These herbes can be used to consecrate ritual tools or jewelry set with amethyst. Many work with amethyst crystals. Cedar or hyssop will help initiate a crystal or cluster of crystals for spiritual purposes. Conversely, placing an amethyst in your jars of dried herbes may help preserve their magick.

anger: violets, wormwood

Some use anger as a source of power. Some use anger as a means of justifying their need to be aggressive. Anger is a human condition, one not found among the devas. Those who wish to keep anger from interfering in a religious lifestyle may explore these herbes.

animal and pet magick: box, buckthorn (sea), carob, cassia, catnip, chickweed, columbine, corn, cypress, elder, gorse (golden), hellebore (black), henbane, houseleek, jack-in-the-pulpit, linden, loosestrife (purple), marshwort, moneywort, nightshade (woody), parsley, red clover, rowan, thistle

The realm of animal and pet magick is very broad. If you are someone who cares for animals, a person who shares your life with one or more creatures, please refer to these herbes and make notes which might apply to you. Some of these herbes work with animals in the most general way but some are associated with a particular species. One of our desires is to see someone research animal lore in the same manner we have studied herbe lore. We believe that animal rights could be furthered were rituals developed which called upon the powerful deities associated with a species.

aquamarine: lotus

The affinity between aquamarine and lotus seems almost artistic. If either the stone or the lotus is something you are close to, try working with both. The extracted oil of the lotus is an easy method of maintaining the spiritual energy within a set stone. A lotus pod could be fashioned to provide a safe place for the storage of a ring.

aspurger: aconite, asphodel, basil (sweet), broom, fennel, heather, hyssop, lavender, mints, rosemary, vervain

Generally, these are herbes which are considered handy when making your own aspurger. In its simplest form, it would be a slender bunch of herbes bound in some fashion. Whether you braid the herbes, wrap them with a piece of leather or use an elastic binder is a matter of personal choice. Because they are so closely linked with the aspurging of a sacred space, we believe that the water one aspurges around a Circle might be greatly enhanced with the addition of these herbes. Water in which one or more of these herbes has been steeped might be just what your ritual water chalice is wanting.

astral protection: basil (sweet), benzoin, frankincense, rue

These herbes are important for those who pursue skill within the astral. Some of them are said to provide protection or safety while your spirit is removed from your body. Some are said to improve your abilities.

astral temples: chervil, unicorn root

Too complex to discuss in this compendium, astral temples are frequently an essential part of the cosmology of a religious tradition, whether Christian, Buddhist, Wiccan or any denomination. Whether perceived as heaven or created as a specific place to meet with your loved ones following your death, these herbes are worth exploration. A more detailed discussion of astral temples may be found in *A Wiccan Bardo*.

astral work: anise seed, benzoin, catnip, cloves, cornflower, cucumber, damiana, elm, frankincense, hemp, horehound, mandrake, morning glory, peyote, rampion, Solomon's seal, tobacco

The herbes in this list are, in some manner, connected with activities we associate with the astral. Not only are they useful when journeying, they may be employed to improve the quality of any type of psychic work.

astrological transits: purslane

Even with a thorough understanding of astrology, periods such as these can be difficult. At your birth, the locations of the planets represented energy you related to in a very close way at your first moments as a separate entity. Paying attention to the transits, or passages of the planets in their orbits, to those points in the solar system which are yours can enable you to grow and learn, making your life more exciting and more rewarding. Working with your transits is like learning to go with the flow rather than working against it.

athame: aconite, ginger, hemlock, holly, mistletoe, nettles, nightshade (deadly), pimpernel

The athame is the ritual knife in modern witchcraft. It is

highly questionable whether our pagan ancestors would have used a blade as we do today: to carve sacred space out of the mundane, as a defense against our own weaknesses and distractions, and in many of the same uses as shamans, priest and priestesses have done throughout the ages.

athletic ability: stonecrop (orpine)

We see the body as no less an important ritual tool as your favorite chalice. It takes physical strength to hold a heavy sword at arms' length for ten minutes, it takes agility to dance in unison with the others of your group. In our tradition the body is treated as the temple for your soul. As a vessel for your own divinity, your body should be loved and respected. The neglect of one's body inevitably creates a decrease in one's magick.

Atlantis: angelica

We pay close attention to modern archaeological finds and even had the occasion to attend an important lecture on the myths and realities of Atlantis presented by a well-known scholar. Whether Atlantis first appeared when Pliny wrote about it or whether it was a reality is not worth debate. Even if it is but a legend, there is much power and wisdom associated with Atlantis which one can better understand with angelica.

automobiles: ash

The majority of herbal folklore evolved long before the first automobile went racing across the landscape at five miles per hour. I recommend making a protective amulet to keep someplace discreet within your vehicle. The amulet I made for a little, red German sports car in the 1970s is still working today in our truck.

Autumn Equinox: benzoin, caraway, corn, dogwood, honeysuckle, milkweed, myrrh, passion flower, rose, sage, thistle

There are a number of names for this date, when the days have shortened and nights increased until they are the same length. The Autumn Equinox is much more than the first day of fall; for many it is once again a major religious holiday. There are so many different ways to use these herbes in your rituals that I won't even begin to make suggestions.

aura: angelica

Of all the herbes we know, only angelica has an established reputation as being able to directly affect your aura. Certainly there are others as you will discover. But angelica alone has been documented in lore.

baby blessings: cedar, daisies, elfwort, flax, iris, milkweed, parsley, unicorn root

In The Rowan Tree Church a baby is blessed and introduced to the four elements and to the archetypes of the Divine Parents. Many traditions perform Wiccanings in which a baby is made Wicca much as a Christians baptize their children. Neither approach is better. You may, in fact, create your own traditions to celebrate the life of a baby. These herbes have a variety of backgrounds but all are of use.

balance: cumin, oak

The concept of keeping one's life in balance is quite widespread. It is usually easier to think about than it is to manifest. These two herbes help the overall process of getting us settled down and recognizing what we need for a healthy balance.

banishing: anise (star), asafoetida, birch, daffodil, juniper, rowan, rue, sage

Herbes associated with the act of banishing may be used to remove unwanted energy but they may also help remove energy which was good but no longer needed.

bards: beech, lachnanthes, mustard, senna, trillium, vervain, willow

The Bardic Tradition of Lothloriën has inspired me to list herbes which are important to bardic work. Bards not only keep stories and myths alive through their voices but they work with energy. The Rowan Tree Church, through Thomas Berkham's work, is establishing a bardic lineage which works to help keep our tradition well for future generations. These herbes would be of value for the bards of any tradition.

beauty: fern (maidenhair), heather, lovage

Will these herbes change the face which gazes back at you from the mirror? No, but they can give radiance to your inner beauty. When one relaxes and lets the inner light shine, it is beauty that none can deny. If you feel you are unattractive, these herbes will begin to bring change.

Beltane: almond, cinquefoil, cornflower, elder, frankincense, hawthorn, ivy, juniper, marsh marigold, meadowsweet, rose, woodruff

May Day remains an important festival even as we enter the twenty-first century. Who can resist the exuberance of nature, the lusty frolicking of the Mother's creatures? And who can deny that the sap is rising even within one's body. No matter how you spell Beltane, this time of the year is sacred.

betrothals and engagements: basil (bush), crowfoot, gorse (golden), hazel nut, southernwood

Some of these herbes have been part of lovely customs, integrated into the asking of another's hand or in offering a promise. Any of them may be used to make this a memorable and magickal event in your life.

bird magick: chickweed, columbine

Our winged friends are essential to the health of our gardens. We also have friends who work with birds as familiars and as totem creatures. These herbes will enhance any aspect of magick involving birds.

birth: lavender, trillium

These herbes may be used to increase the magick of giving birth, to bring sacred energy to the emergence of a new being from within your womb.

blessing, self: angelica

This is the herbe of choice when working any type of ritual or magick to provide blessings for your self.

blood: maguey

The ritual use of blood is far more common than one would guess from our literature. Even if one would not wish to use the maguey to induce the flow of blood, it could be burned as an offering during any ritual work involving blood.

Book of Shadows: beech, birch, cornflower, dogwood, holly, mulberry, sedge (papyrus)

These herbes may be used to protect the sacred words in your Book of Shadows or to consecrate it. Whether you use a loose-leaf notebook or bind your own book, the pages upon which you record your rituals and magickal information deserve the energy of these herbes.

boxes, storage: acacia

I can think of no person involved in magick who does not have special containers, whether for a tarot deck or for other tools. Acacia may be used in many ways with your storage box, chest or trunk so the ancient connection is made, transforming a simple storage box into a container for sacred items.

bravery: borage, fig, linden, poplar, thyme

There are many situations in life which call for the virtue of bravery. Although some see this word as synonymous with courage, others see them as different hues. For that reason they are treated as separate entries.

broom, ritual: broom, broom (butcher's)

With either of these herbes, you may fashion your own ritual broom. Made well and consecrated, this ritual tool can be used to sweep away all unwanted energy.

cakes, ritual: carob, cassia, oak

These herbes are among the best for inclusion in your ritual cakes. They have a natural magick which can be described as being divine food.

candle dressing: balm of Gilead, bay laurel, hazel nut, jasmine, lotus, patchouli

In our tradition, we coat a candle lightly with herbal oil, beginning at the center and working toward both ends. This process replaces any unwanted energy with the sacred purpose of the herbes being used. These herbes will enhance the general magick of a candle but may also be combined with herbes, not in this list, which are focused toward a specific magick.

Candlemas: almond, angelica, basil (sweet), bay laurel, benzoin, celery, heather, holly, ivy, myrrh, pine, willow

Also known as Imbolgh (with many variant spellings), modern remnants of a sacred holiday are found in Groundhog's Day, which recognizes the growing daylight and the return of the life forces.

candlesticks: almond

The association of almond with candlesticks allows us a more focused approach when we wish to consecrate and empower the candle holders to be used in our rituals.

cat magick: catnip, valerian

Catnip is associated with the feline goddesses. We know that cats love this herbe. It sets loose a whimsy within the cat, releasing the kitten-within, but there is also magick in these herbes. Not all cats are fond of valerian but it has a long history of working with feline energy.

cauldron: aconite, horehound

Both of these herbes will help transform your kettle into a cauldron, enhancing your ability to learn the deepest and most intense mysteries of the Universe.

celibacy: ivy, lavender, narcissus, pine

Celibacy is frequently dismissed in our culture, but abstinence as a means of using one's sexual energy toward other goals is recognized by many wise teachers. Those who are celibate (whether by choice or circumstance) might use these herbes to increase their self-control in maintaining their lifestyle or to better understand its spiritual value.

censers: lotus, olive, sage, valerian, vervain

Often called thuribles, these are the ritual tools designed to carry the burning incense around the Circle. Any of these herbes may be used in the consecration of a thurible. They may also be used to renew its energy.

chalcedony: peppermint

This pale, gray-blue quartz may be kept sacred by using pep-permint. Even a small piece may help you better work with this herbe's deva.

chalices: anise (star), benzoin, gourds, marsh marigold, tansy, tarragon, vervain, watercress

Ritual cups come in many styles and are found in many places. Whether it is a fine, bone china teacup from your grandmother or a wine goblet, a beautifully-crafted work of pottery from a fair or a true, antique chalice, these tools still need to set aside their pasts and become dedicated to ritual service. These herbes are all connected with the magick of chalices.

change: basil, benzoin, broom, catnip, elfwort, eyebright, storax

These herbes are all associated with the ability to bring about change. When faced with the necessity of making changes in your life, they can ease the process.

character, strength of: borage, fig, holly (sea), poplar, stonecrop (orpine)

These herbes will help build your personal character, helping you draw upon your inner strength. They will help you de-velop the quality of valor.

Chariot card: anise seed, balm, camphor, hyssop, parsley, water-cress

When studying the symbols within this card and learning how to harness your internal emotions (even when they wish to go in different directions), these herbes can help you gain insight which might otherwise escape you. Not being in control will leave your life in the hands of others.

child: daisies, elder, mugwort, mulberry, unicorn root

These herbes bring protection to your children. Some are said to work with babies but we feel that any of them will help a parent bring protection through magickal and spiritual work to bless any child.

clairvoyance: cornflower

This herbe increases your ability to divine or intuit information which requires the transcendence of distance.

concealment: alder

There are times we wish we were invisible, but are only able to blend in to our surroundings. This herbe will assist you.

concentration: cinnamon, cowslip, horehound

It is useful to know which herbes will help one's ability to stay mentally focused on a project and avoid distraction.

conception: catnip, marshmallow, mistletoe, rice, Saint John's wort, stitchwort

These Fertility Herbes are specifically associated with increasing the likelihood of becoming pregnant. Use them with wisdom.

cooperation: senna

How wonderful to know of an herbe which promotes the ability of people to get along and work together harmoniously. Senna deserves to grow in popularity.

copper: clover

The most common use of copper in ritual is in the pentacle but copper is frequently found in other tools and jewelry. The magick of clover works well with this metal.

courage: basil (sweet), borage, fig, poplar, thyme

These are herbes which give us an inner strength when facing a situation or person that is most challenging.

cup, ritual: aconite, amaranth, anise (star), apple, basil, blackberry, blessed thistle, butterbur, chaste tree, coriander, cornflower, dittany of Crete, elder, elfwort, horehound, mugwort

These herbes all lend themselves readily to the ritual cup, for the drink shared either with the ritual cakes or as the sacred elixir which represents the Great Rite.

Cups of tarot: benzoin

This refers to the suit in tarot. Benzoin, a most agreeable incense in many ways, will help you learn to distinguish this suit from the other three and learn of its mysteries.

death and dying, rituals of: aconite, alder, anemone (wood), asphodel, basil (bush), bluebells, camphor, chervil, chrysanthemum, coconut, dragon's blood, elder, elm, holly, iris, lotus,
marigold, myrrh, narcissus, nightshade (deadly), parsley, pennyroyal, rosemary, sandalwood, sycamore, tansy

These herbes are all associated with the rites of passage for
the beloved. Some are used as the beloved's body is dying.
Others are used at the ceremony which celebrates the beloved's union with the Universe and soothes the grief of those
left behind. We recommend reading about each herbe individually before making a selection.

death and dying, rituals for children: periwinkle, violets

These two herbes have specific lore which indicates their
magick is appropriate when the loss of a loved one is that of a
child.

Death card: basil (bush), nightshade (deadly)

This card appears when the degree of change asked of us is so
great it seems as if part of the old self must die. These herbes
help us understand the nature of death as an archetype and
as an essential process of renewal. Never forget the rising of
the Sun.

death, mysteries: aconite, banana

What an unlikely pair of herbes and yet both have much to
do with the spiritual nature of death. While they have different approaches, both herbes can guide you into an understanding of these mysteries.

decision making: calabar bean, cinnamon, sage, senna

These herbes may be used when one must arrive at a decision
based upon facts and data rather than through intuition and
divination.

depression: burnet (great), dodder, lavender, melilot, nettles,
peaches, pellitory, peony, pimpernel, purslane, sunflower, vervain, water lily, yarrow

Even though one might be receiving professional counseling

or be under the care of a doctor, these herbes are able to provide magickal assistance when treating fears or depression which leave us, in some way, dysfunctional.

devas: beech, columbine, cowslip, daisies, elder, elfwort, foxglove, goosefoots, hollyhock, lilac, lily-of-the-valley, milkweed, thyme, thyme (wild)

We might say that these herbes are deva friendly. Some have a history or lore indicating that they make communication between the world of plant energy and human energy easier. Most, if not all, will encourage the presence of more magickal energy about your gardens.

Devil card: asafoetida, bryony (white)

Often misunderstood, when this card appears in a reading it usually speaks of those situations, things or people to which you have placed yourself in bondage through your obsession. The Devil card is not, in any way, associated with the Christian devil but represents the concept found in the phrase bedeviling yourself.

dexterity: sunflower

Those who need to improve their dexterity may find sunflower a helpful magickal tonic. This stately flower, itself, demonstrates dexterity in the many ways it may be used.

diamonds: asafoetida, sandalwood

Until I saw the diamonds in the crown jewels in the Tower of London, I had no real appreciation for these stunning gems. Able to refract light as bright as a star, these herbes work well with this precious stone.

disagreements: coriander, olive, passion flower, pennyroyal

These herbes help sooth discord. They have the ability to promote peace and to help people find the common ground needed to settle differences in an amicable manner.

divination tools: flax, gum mastic, hemp, marigold, mugwort, palm, peppermint, vervain, yarrow

There are many forms of divination and a countless variety of tools and implements which may be used. Each of these herbes is, in some way, associated with tools of divination. We believe that any of them might be used to help you work with your tools or to consecrate them, allowing you to better divine information.

divorce: pepper (chili)

The religious lore of the chili pepper indicates that this herbe might help a person understand why the dissolution of a relationship or parting of the ways is best for all concerned.

dowsing: hazel nut, willow

Historically, these two herbal trees are cut as forked branches to provide a dowsing tool. We believe that their energy could be made available through other methods. The oil of the hazel or an infusion of willow might consecrate either the dowsing rod or the person doing the work.

dragons: tarragon

Did dragons ever exist? Were they once real? There are many who work with astral dragons in the same way that we work with astral unicorns. Tarragon has a strong association with dragons and may be used to establish a good relationship with one of these creatures. If you wish to consecrate or bless a statue of a dragon, there is no better herbe.

Drawing Down the Moon: chaste tree, pau d'arco, rose

There are books written on this process by which a Wiccan priestess or priest brings down into herself the divinity of the Universe as embodied by the Moon. These are the herbes which empower the process and make one an improved receptacle.

Drawing Down the Sun: blessed thistle, fenugreek, heliotrope, oxalis

In a very direct way, there are traditions which Draw Down the Sun with a magnifying glass, catching some flame from the Sun to light their temple flames. These herbes, so linked with the Sun, can help the magickal person bring the magick of the Sun into a ritual.

dream magick: anise seed, camphor, hops, lotus, mandrake, mugwort, peppermint, red clover, vervain

These herbes are connected with different aspects of dreaming. Dream magick is an important part of magickal training. These herbes should be studied individually to see how they might best benefit you.

eagles: columbine

With the popularity of Native American religions and myths, the eagle is a central image for many people. Columbine may be used in many ways to strengthen your connection to the eagle. Those who set out to find eagles to watch them flying free might work with columbine to better their chances of spotting this sacred bird.

earth: alder, clover, daisies, life-everlasting, toadflax

These herbes will help us understand the nature of elemental earth or increase (or balance) that element in our life. We may use them in our rituals if invoking earth as part of a cosmology and we might work with these herbes to establish communion with the elemental spirits of earth, often described as gnomes. Dryads, associated with trees, may also respond to these herbes.

Eights of tarot: elfwort, storax

The Eights represent change which is complex and transforming of the individual. The average person resents change, preferring to cling to the established past. In many decks the Eights are depicted as unpleasant but for the magickal person they are wonderful cards. These herbes can help you unlock their mysteries.

eldritch: elder, elfwort, flax, goosefoots, milkweed, rowan

There are no words which properly describe the astral world of the eldritch. While similar to the realm of faerie, there are differences which only one who has been there can understand.

elements, all four: bamboo, coconut, oak

While so many herbes have a more singular purpose, these have been clearly associated as relating to all four elements. If brought physically into a ritual, the possibilities are endless.

They may also be used to help you work with all four elements simultaneously.

elves: elfwort, flax

While faeries are frequently found dancing among the flowers, elves prefer their favored wooded areas. These herbes may be used to make an environment more friendly or to increase your ability to perceive an elven presence.

emeralds: rose, sandalwood

This beautiful green beryl is associated with two herbes. There is considerable lore and magick within all gemstones. That of the emerald is particularly potent and may be worked with either herbe.

emotional calm: agrimony, burnet (great), calamint, myrrh

These are not to be confused with the once popular herbal medicines used to treat hysteria. These herbes work within one's inner self to magickally affect your emotions.

emotional recovery: calamint, gentian, myrrh, pitcher plant, sage, tulip, yarrow

When recovering from an emotional trauma or a deep emotional pain, these herbes provide a spiritual source of healing.

Emperor card: blessed thistle, dragon's blood, patchouli

This fifth card of the major arcana (if we consider the Fool first) represents many aspects of discipline and mastery without a loss of sensitivity. These herbes work well with the Emperor card.

Empress card: bergamot, columbine, elder, heather, patchouli, sandalwood, rose

Often perceived as the maternal aspect of the goddess, the Empress offers us many mysteries associated with creativity. She extends a love into the world around her which is neither demanding nor demeaned by any conditions. These herbes will help you become more attuned with the meaning of this card.

Eostara: alder, almond, anemone, bistort, clover, dogwood, flax, gorse (golden), honeysuckle, iris, jack-in-the-pulpit, jasmine, lily, nettles, olive, rose, tansy, violets, willow

In many climates the Spring or Vernal Equinox coincides with birth, in colder climates it is the time when life emerges from within the earth through blossoms and the first flowers. No matter what name you use for this religious holiday, it seems everyone anticipates the return of spring. These herbes lend themselves to this energy whether used as flowers or made into herbal products such as wine or incense.

exorcism: daffodil, fumitory, mandrake, rue, vervain

To exorcise something is to remove all previous energy, to thoroughly cleanse or purge it particularly of unwanted, negative energies. Exorcism is frequently the first step in the consecration of a new ritual tool and any of these herbes may be used.

eyesight: clary, eyebright, larkspur, loosestrife (purple), marigold, panic grass, vervain

Although there are numerous remedial methods for healing our eyes, these herbes provide a magickal boost to the process. There is more than literal vision involved in our sense of sight; these herbes may also be used to improve our ability to see things clearly as they are, or to become more aware of the world around us through our eyes.

face painting: safflower, woad

Temporary decoration of one's face is a part of the ritual experience for many. Although these herbes may not be the easiest to work with, a diligent artist will find infinite reward in making her own herbal paints with these herbes.

faeries: alder, anemone (wood), beech, cowslip, daisies, elder, elm, foxglove, goosefoots, lily-of-the-valley, milkweed, rosemary, thyme, thyme (wild)

The realm of the faerie permeates many of our myths. Whether you believe in faerie folk as actual entities or see their existence as a spiritual energy which permeates the flowering gardens, these herbes will provide communion with their magick. Growing them in your gardens will encourage their wonderful magick to feel welcome.

faith: butterbur

Faith is not something we are born with, no matter what you might believe. It is not something which just *happens* to us, either. Solid faith, whether in the Universe or in your spiritual path, is something which evolves over time and requires work. Butterbur is an herbe which will help you during times when your faith feels shaken, when it is difficult to grasp just why events are moving in a direction beyond your understanding.

familiars: catnip, cypress, hellebore (black), rowan

Although catnip is strongly associated with our feline companions, it is important to dispel the stereotype that cats, alone, make good familiars. Among our circle of friends are people with birds, reptiles, dogs and a surprising variety of creatures with whom the role of familiar has been established. These herbes will help that relationship so that you become better connected through the astral and can share in one another's dreams.

family protection: avens, basil (sweet), fern (royal), snapdragon

These herbes are most useful in providing protection for your family and those with whom you share your household. Whether growing in your garden, hanging in a secreted amulet or given as gifts, their protective magick is available.

fasting: banana

One may use this herbal food during the transition when moving into a fast. We should never make a dramatic change from a normal diet to abstaining from all food. Our bodies prefer that we treat them more kindly. Spending time abstaining from all foods other than banana is a very useful period of spiritual work.

fertility goddesses: apple, cassia, chaste tree, coconut, corn, lily

It would seem that the vast majority of herbes are, in some manner, associated with the fertility of the Mother. These herbes have a specific association and may be used in Her honor.

fertility gods: apple, asafoetida, blessed thistle, fern (male), holly, red campion

These herbes work with the male aspect of the Universe which is healthy in attitude and nurturing to all creatures. Yet they also promote that sensual magick associated with the gods of fertility.

fidelity: caraway, ivy, rosemary

Associated with being faithful to one's partner, the herbes in this list may be given as a symbol of one's promise but may also be used to help strengthen one's resolve during those times when fidelity is more difficult to maintain.

financial protection: alfalfa

Folklore provides us with a strong link between alfalfa and its ability to protect your assets. It may be dried and placed with your stock portfolio or checkbook or included in a household amulet. I'm certain you can think of dozens of other ways to make use of this herbe.

fire: alder, basil (sweet), elder, fennel, mullein, myrrh, oak, olive, Saint John's wort

Its volatile nature makes fire a more difficult element to work with for many people. These herbes may be used to bring the energy of fire into your life or your rituals. They may also be used to understand the underlying nature of fire. The spirits of fire are, by many, called salamanders, which should not be confused with the amphibian variety.

fire protection: houseleek, mistletoe, Saint John's wort

While we may want elemental fire present in our ritual work, manifest fire is a tool which must be kept within its proper bounds. These herbes are said to protect us against unwanted fire, helping keep our homes and loved ones safe.

Fives of tarot: clover

The Fives have, generally, a reputation for representing changes which are difficult and often painful. The nature of the Fives is not to be avoided. Working with clover can help us embrace this manner of change, leading to a greatly improved position in life.

fluid condensers: eyebright, larkspur, loosestrife (purple)

Fluid condensers are described in detail in the section of this compendium entitled A Guide to the Usage of Magickal Herbes. Although most herbes might be used, these herbes work exceptionally well.

Fool card: anise (star), elfwort, mandrake, peppermint

While most people have a fondness for the Fool card, the majority of people are unable to make the leap of faith being taught us. These herbes can help us emulate the Fool when this type of change is needed, or they can be used to further understand the images of this card.

Fours of tarot: cedar

The Fours provide us with keys to understanding the role of structure in our lives, the value of a foundation. Cedar is the herbe of choice when studying these cards.

garden magick: chamomile

We know that all herbes bring magick to our gardens but chamomile is the herbe which brings magick to your entire garden. In addition to growing chamomile, you can use this herbe to cense or aspurge the perimeter of your garden to encourage a most magickal environment for your herbal friends.

generosity: benzoin

Not everyone finds it easy to be generous of the spirit or able to give gifts to those in need. This herbe helps open that part of the personality which is so necessary for spiritual health.

goals: balm, dill, ivy, lady's mantle, motherwort

Learning how to choose our goals with care and working to achieve them is essential for success in either the spiritual or the mundane world. These herbes will help you learn more about achieving your goals and are said to help one reach that desired end.

goddess as crone: chaste tree, holly, mandrake, pomegranate

Among the many herbes associated with the goddess, these have a particular affinity with the crone and may be used to understand her mysteries. This aspect of the goddess understands the role of death in our lives. She has experienced much but she is a survivor.

goddess as maiden: chaste tree, crowfoot, meadowsweet, narcissus, thistle (milk)

Long before the passing of so many years leading to her cronehood, the goddess began as the maiden. These herbes work with this energy. They may be brought into ritual when the maiden aspect is being invoked or used wisely by women who wish to keep the spark of the maiden fresh and vital even as they age gracefully.

goddess as mother: cinquefoil, cowslip, crowfoot, haricot, jasmine, marsh marigold, mugwort, palm, parsley, pomegranate, tansy, yucca

Only she who has given birth, so it is said, can truly understand the goddess in her aspect as mother. I would not disagree with that statement. These herbes may help us call upon this aspect of the goddess and they may help us gain some level of understanding of these mysteries.

goddess, love of the: balm, cowslip

These herbes may be used in several ways. You may work with them in order to feel the love which the goddess has for her children or you may use them in order to better express your love for her.

goddess worship: birch, chaste tree, corn, costmary, fern (maidenhair), marigold, meadowsweet, mulberry, peony, pomegranate, primrose, quince, rice, rowan, tansy, tobacco, yucca

This is a list of herbes which are, generically, associated with goddess worship. There are many practitioners who do not work with any specific personification or aspect of the goddess and these herbes will suit them well.

good fortune: apple, arrow root, basil (sweet), broom, cinnamon, cumin, dill, figwort (knotted), mistletoe, oak, oxalis, red clover

Almost everyone I know would like an increase of good luck and good fortune. These herbes will help us grow in ways so that we are more open to the benevolence of the Universe. They may be used, judiciously, upon infrequent occasion to provide a direct stimulus when we wish to manifest a change in the balance of our lives.

gossip: marigold

This herbe may be used either when one is the subject of gossip or if a person is working to bring a negative behavior pattern under control.

grave site planting: alder, anise (star), asphodel, basil (bush), bluebells, marjoram (wild), marshmallow, narcissus, parsley, periwinkle, thyme (wild), violets

One of the customs used to honor the deceased beloved is the planting of flowers or herbes upon the burial site. Each of these herbes has a history of this use and may be used not only for the magick of the beloved but also for the magick of those who remain behind.

Great Rite: alder, ash, coriander, cubeb, cyclamen, damiana, fern (male), fumitory, henna, holly (sea), kava kava, lemon, lovage, mandrake, marshmallow, marsh marigold, matico, millet, mistletoe, orchid, patchouli, rose geranium, saffron, savory, sesame, Solomon's seal, unicorn root (false), vervain, yohimbe

This long list of herbes is useful not only when working the Great Rite, bringing together archetypes of polarity, but in any form of sexual magick.

Green Man: holly

The Green Man is an image associated with the masculine aspect of fertility within nature. Holly may be used to call upon this energy. It can be worn by the man taking this role in your rituals or grown to keep this presence alive in your gardens.

grieving: bluebells, myrrh, periwinkle, sage, thyme (wild), violets

Not everyone has a religious belief system which allows them to deal with the death of a loved one. These herbes may be used to help a person deal with grief and come to understand the nature of death and its place in our lives. Working with these herbes will help a person see past their personal sense of loss and understand that the beloved's union with the Universe is a joyful thing.

grounding: flax

Flax is an herbe which will help people who are getting lost in the clouds or their imagination, bringing them gently back to earth so they may embrace reality.

Hallow's Eve: apple, dittany of Crete, fumitory, mullein, oak, pumpkin, sage

Called Samhain by many, this is the night which gives honor to death. In the myths of many cultures who recognize the divinity of nature, Mother Nature descends into the Underworld and we may commune with those who have gone before. These herbes have been associated with this important religious holiday and may be used throughout the ritual.

Handfasting cake: anise seed, coriander, cyclamen, orchid

These herbes may be integrated into the cake, itself or, in the case of orchid, placed as a decoration. Whether the cake is for a legal wedding, a ritual to celebrate or consecrate a relationship or a Handfasting, these herbes will enhance the magick of the occasion.

Handfastings: almond, anise seed, broom, caraway, coriander, crowfoot, ginkgo biloba, gorse (golden), ivy, lavender, marjoram (sweet), marjoram (wild), mistletoe, myrtle, orange, orchid, quince, rice, rose, rosemary, scullcap, southernwood, vervain, yarrow, yohimbe

There are many herbes associated with rituals of union. Add them to your bouquets, wear them as perfumes or oils, take a ritual bath with some of these herbes to start your day. Be creative, for this is a ceremony to be remembered. Your wedding or Handfasting can be made a very magickal event.

Hanged Man card: fern (bracken), lotus

Having placed the mundane activities of his life in suspension, the Hanged Man takes time for contemplation. These herbes may be used to help you make the necessary arrangements to set aside several days for solitude, completely removed from the world. They may also help you work with this card in order to achieve spiritual transformation.

happiness: anise seed, apple, olive, pimpernel, sunflower

Are there herbes which help a person increase their sense of happiness? Yes, and this is an important list of herbes to remember. You may use them for yourself or bestow their magick upon someone in your life.

healing: agrimony, anemone (wood), ash, balm of Gilead, betony (wood), blackberry, cherry (winter), clary, comfrey, elder, figwort (knotted), ginger, horehound, hyssop, jasmine, juniper, larkspur, panic grass, pau d'arco, peony

There are many forms of healing which work with the spiritual nature of the patient. Many people work forms of ritual healing, some work with the person's energy and some practitioners are skilled at psychic healing. Each of these herbes is capable of improving the quality of your work.

Hermit card: fern (maidenhair), lavender, narcissus

The epitome of the wise teacher, students seek out the Hermit because they recognize the light shining from his lantern. He has journeyed a lifetime, supported only by his staff. This staff is a close relative of a ritual wand. As such we see that the Hermit has had only his will and has not been able to depend upon others. These herbes may help you to manifest these qualities in your own life or to better understand this card.

Hierophant card: borage, cumin, lovage, periwinkle

Frequently misconstrued by people who see only the surface image, the Hierophant represents the wisdom of religions which serve large communities. His ritual items must be visible symbols even to those in the furthest seats. These herbes will help the card interpreter see the deeper meanings of this card. They will also benefit those who lead large, public rituals or who find themselves in the position of leadership.

highest ideals: angelica, coriander

In *the Charges of the Goddess*, variations of which are found in the majority of Wiccan traditions, we are told to "keep pure your highest ideals, strive ever toward them, let naught stop you nor turn you aside." How comforting to know there are herbes which will assist us in this process.

High Priestess card: camphor, ginger, iris, jasmine, pennyroyal, pomegranate, poppy

She has removed herself from many aspects of the world's distractions in order to more fully devote herself to her religious lifestyle. People will come to her. The mysteries associated with this card are among the most primary of the Universe and can be better learned with these herbes. They would also benefit anyone choosing to become more like the High Priestess (a quality which would benefit many men).

home blessing: basil (sweet), camphor, daffodil, eucalyptus, flax, fumitory, hollyhock, horehound, hyssop, juniper, lavender, mints, rowan, rue

These herbes may be used when cleaning your home, performing the initial house blessing or renewing its domestic magick. Growing them in your garden will surround your home with blessings. Censing or aspurging your home with them will increase the blessings as will using them in any manner you choose.

home protection: aloe, avens, basil (sweet), blackberry, camphor, coriander, cowslip, daffodil, daisy (ox-eye), dill, elder, fennel, mistletoe, nightshade (woody), rue, snapdragon

While these herbes may be used in combination with the previous list (and many herbes are found on both), these herbes are specifically known for their protective qualities.

hope: butterbur

There are times when our doubts and fears interfere with out ability to maintain a childlike sense of hope. This herbe will restore luster to your sense of hope.

Horned God: asafoetida, blessed thistle, bogbean, orchid, peony, red campion, savory, yarrow

These herbes are all associated with the Horned God, that male divine form representing the combination of animal fertility combined with divine wisdom and compassion.

horses: buckthorn (sea), linden, parsley, spikenard

Those who live with horses, who ride them or train them will find these herbes of value. One usage might be to include them in the water when washing your steed.

humility: narcissus, violets

A genuine sense of humility or modesty is, no matter what your religion, a virtue. These herbes help us avoid false modesty or the promotion of a humble image designed, in reality, to promote one's ego.

humor: chicory

Although this may be a short list, everyone can benefit from knowing of an herbe said to help increase one's sense of humor.

hypochondria: amaranth

Medical studies indicate a disturbing percentage of illness as being somewhat psychosomatic in origin. Almost every person experiences those times when we'd like to feel sorry for ourselves or invoke another's sympathy in order to avoid facing reality. Amaranth will help us take a more mature approach to life.

immortality, mysteries: amaranth, cassia, chervil, myrtle, tansy

Although your body is mortal and must someday become compost, the spirit or soul which resides within it during incarnation continues on. These herbes provide assistance in better recognizing one's immortality and the ensuing responsibility such knowledge implies.

impotence: unicorn root (false)

The causes of impotence are many. Working to treat this difficult problem may also be approached with ritual and spiritual work.

independence: tarragon

Tarragon may be used not only by those who need to become more independent but may impart an understanding of the true nature of independence.

initiation: asafoetida, basil (sweet), cherry, elfwort, heather, holly, pennyroyal, scullcap, sedge (sweet), trillium

These herbes are associated with various aspects of initiation and may be integrated into these important rites of passage as you choose.

ink: cornflower, dragon's blood

These herbes may be employed when making a magickal ink with which to write wishes or to scribe sacred words into your Book of Shadows.

inner peace: agrimony, benzoin, burnet (great), cinnamon, lavender, loosestrife (purple), olive, passion flower, violets, water lily

When working to increase your sense of serenity, to bring a more calm approach to the handling of life's uneven meter, these herbes will prove beneficial.

insight: celery, eyebright, honeysuckle, myrrh

These herbes will increase the gift of inner sight, helping us see beyond the surface of a situation.

inspiration: bay laurel, beech, cornflower, elfwort, fig, ginkgo biloba, hazel nut, horehound, jasmine, milkweed, mistletoe, narcissus, oak, pomegranate, sugar cane

When you wish to stimulate your sense of creativity and give it wings, work with these herbes. They will give you better access to your imagination and are useful in any form of creative or artistic endeavor.

intuition: uva ursi

This herbe may be used to increase one's intuitive perceptiveness or to more finely hone a skill which readily works for you.

iron: rue

While iron is not considered the most desirable metal for ritual tools, it is frequently found in cauldrons. We also have lovely wrought-iron hooks which hold hanging candles for the Dancing Circle in our gardens, where we hold rituals among the hawthorns.

job interviews: rosemary

Wearing a sprig of rosemary upon your lapel may not impress a prospective employer but you could use it as a Greene Herbe, bathe in it or use the oil as a refreshing, pleasing scent.

joy: angelica, anise (star), borage, burnet (great), butterbur, calamint, chicory, dill, eyebright, fenugreek, meadowsweet, melilot, motherwort, nettles, rose, rue, thyme, thyme (wild), vervain

These are wonderful herbes. They will help us maintain a more positive outlook on life, reflecting the natural joy of the world with an inner, healthy joy.

Judgement card: chervil, pomegranate

Having moved deep within yourself, perhaps even retreated from the world, you now emerge feeling reborn. Whether this is an event brought into your life by the Universe or something you seek, these herbes can help you achieve renewal.

Justice card: hyacinth, vervain

She cautions you to take your time and weigh all of the information objectively before attempting to take the sword of Justice in your hand. These herbes might help you understand that Justice is an Initiate, not simply a public official.

King Stag: cypress

The King Stag is a powerful, male archetype representing the presence of the masculine divinity in the forests. This herbe will help you explore this energy and might be of value for those hoping to see the male patriarch of a herd in person when exploring the woodlands.

knowledge: apple, dill

These herbes are said to increase your knowledge. They may be easily included as part of your regular diet.

Lammas: bilberry, caraway, corn, dogwood, fenugreek, frankincense, heather, hollyhock, millet, oak, strawberry, sunflower

When the tides of life shift and the harvest cycle begins, the holy day of Lammas is celebrated. There are many names for this religious festival. These herbes may be used in any traditional celebration of the harvest.

lapis lazuli: hyssop, pennyroyal

These herbes will keep the magick of your stone vital. A soft stone, oil of pennyroyal may be gently massaged into the stone in order to bring the magick into manifestation.

lead: nightshade (deadly)

Other than our leaded glass pieces, we haven't any rituals made with this metal. Those who find their treasures in antique shops may well work with tools made of lead. It is a worthy metal and has an affinity with this herbe.

limitations: elfwort

It is not always easy for us to transcend our limitations. Elfwort helps us reach beyond our grasp and consider goals we had previously thought unattainable.

loneliness: aloe, endive, iris, sunflower

These herbes are for those who feel they are without friends and are longing for companionship. They do not magickally make someone appear but they work a loving, internal change so that people will come your way, wanting to share life's experiences with you.

longevity: cassia, catsfoot, heather

No, these herbes won't help you defy death. Although they are said to prolong life, we believe they do more to help you improve the quality of your life, measuring it in fulfillment rather than in the number of your days.

love divination: butterbur, cinquefoil, marigold, marjoram (sweet), red clover, yarrow

There are many old customs which explain how herbes and divination can be used to foresee who your lover will be. I've always thought that knowing but still having to wait (divining does not change the timing of the Universe) would be unbearable and would rob one of the joy of surprise.

Lovers card: cinnamon, dragon's blood, elfwort, tarragon, wormwood

Although many perceive this card as dealing with issues of romance, those adept at tarot interpret this card as an indication of a person being unable to make an easy choice. Both options are appealing and there is no clear answer. When working with the Lovers card, these herbes will assist you. When facing a difficult choice in your own life you might combine this card with herbal magick to assist you in discerning which option is the best for you.

Magician card: cedar, elfwort, fenugreek, honeysuckle, horehound

Showing us the necessary tools in order to bring our ideas into manifestation, the Magician does his ritual work surrounded by nature. These herbes can assist you in learning to work a disciplined, well-balanced ritual without any loss of natural freedom so that you can manifest as well as the Magician.

manifestation: cinquefoil, frankincense, lotus

These herbes contain the magick of manifestation. In other words, using them in your ritual work will increase the likelihood that your work will be successful.

meditation and trance work: centaury, clary, cucumber, sandalwood, teak, watercress

These herbes will help you when working in a passive, receptive manner. They can be used to enhance setting aside your consciousness and ego in order to move deep within yourself to connect with your inner divinity.

meetings, business: dogwood, fig, nightshade (deadly), passion flower, rosemary, sage, senna, turmeric

These herbes may prove useful in any type of business dealing or meeting. We doubt that you will always be able to share a cup of herbal drink or cense your meeting place. Perhaps that is why brief cases were designed with many pockets. These herbes may be used at home before departing for an important conference or worn in an amulet.

memory: eyebright, rosemary, spikenard, willow

Now what you must do is remember to use these herbes!

men's mysteries: bean (kidney), blessed thistle, chestnut, mistletoe, pine, sedge (sweet), southernwood, thornapple

These herbes are well chosen for working in a circle of all men, learning to explore the masculine divinity of the Universe and understanding the nature of being male.

mental and nervous disorders: balm, chrysanthemum, dodder

Herbes are not a magickal cure for serious mental difficulties or nervous disorders, but whether dealing with one's own condition or that of a loved one, they may provide magickal comfort and understanding.

mental skills: balm, celery, chrysanthemum, cinnamon, dill, elfwort, eyebright, fenugreek, frankincense, horehound, jasmine, lady's mantle, lavender, mulberry, pitcher plant, sandalwood

There are many aspects of mental activity covered by these herbes, ranging from mental health to the ability to think clearly and keenly. If you wish to improve your mental acuity, use these herbes on a regular basis.

mercury: vervain

This herbe works with the element of mercury also known as quicksilver. If you use this metal, be careful as physical contact with it can be harmful.

Midsummer: cedar, cinquefoil, elder, fern (bracken), fern (male), flax, heather, hemp, larkspur, lavender, mugwort, mullein, oak, rose, Saint John's wort, vervain

Many celebrate this sabbat as Midsummer's Eve. This important turning point in our seasons has long held a mystique about it relating to the magick of twilight. On the shortest night it is believed we have greater access to the realm of nature spirits.

money: alfalfa, cedar, cumin, fern (bracken), hollyhock, lavender, moneywort

These herbes share a common lore based upon the belief that their use can help bring money or prosperity your way. We caution you that they can work but there is always a price to pay.

Moon card: elder, mugwort, peony

There is much magick afoot and if you're not careful, you will bring your fears into manifestation. Work with these herbes to make the energy of the Moon card work for you.

Moon god: juniper, panic grass

Modern neopagans are fairly steeped in the stereotype of the Sun as archetype of the male and Moon as archetype of the female. In a number of cultures the reverse is true. These herbes are associated with the lunar deity.

moonstone: cornflower, mugwort

This translucent feldspar is very popular in magickal jewelry. Representing inspiration and prophecy, its magick may be kept sacred with these herbes. When moonstones are kept with these herbes both herbes and stones grow in magick.

motorcycle: ash

Having spent over ten years and many thousands of miles with my motorcycle, it was a good feeling to recognize this herbe as being more than appropriate for herbal magick for bikers.

music: elder, gourds

Gourds make excellent musical instruments and elder may be used to bless all other types of instruments. Appealing to the Elder Mother might enhance one's musical ability. Hanging ritually adorned gourds in one's music room may encourage the spirits of music to take up residence in your home.

nightmare protection: mistletoe

Although there are a number of herbes said to bring protection during the dreaming time of the night, mistletoe is the singular herbe known to protect the sleeper against nightmares.

Nines of tarot: broom, catnip, jasmine

Nines are spiritual numbers, somewhat feminine in their essence. In the tarot they imply changes which are somewhat complex although not difficult to negotiate. These herbes will help you move through these changes or better understand these four cards.

oathmaking: garlic, lavender, scullcap, Solomon's seal

These herbes are all associated with the making of an oath, taking of vows, or giving of one's word in ways which should not be broken. These herbes make one's oath binding.

onyx: nightshade (deadly)

This form of chalcedony or agate is usually seen in black. A stabilizing stone, it is similar to working with the crone's own magick. This herbe works in correspondence with onyx, particularly the black varieties.

opals: vervain

An amorphous silica, the natural iridescence of opals catches one's imagination. Opals have a natural magick which intensifies one's being whether good or bad; vervain is a similar herbe. These two, opal and vervain, work well together.

opportunity: arrow root, endive

These herbes render us more able to recognize opportunities, helping us maintain an awareness of what is taking place around us and a healthy perspective of our place in the world.

oracles: bay laurel, cedar, cinnamon, oak, rowan

Working with an oracle is a slow process. It can take many years to develop the presence of an oracle. Very different than channeling, an oracle requires the creation of a sanctified temple which will sustain the passage of time. These herbes may be used in the consecration and maintenance of the temple, or they can be used in the rituals when the oracle is made active.

Otherworld: anise (star), asphodel, dittany of Crete, elder, elm, foxglove, lotus, pomegranate, rampion, willow

The Otherworld is somewhat similar in concept to that of the Underworld but there is a subtle difference which cannot be put into words. The Otherworld encompasses the realm of the eldritch and faerie whereas the Underworld, in mythology, has a closer connection with the space between lives. There is no boundary between the two. These herbes will help you learn of the Otherworld.

Pages of tarot: blessed thistle

When it is time to contemplate these four messengers of the court, this herbe will provide you with insight regarding their station in life and the way in which they will appear in a reading.

patience: balmony

There is no substitute for age and experience, but this herbe is singular in its ability to help a person be more patient with life. Balmony can help make the process of waiting a pleasant, creative time.

patron herbes

A patron herbe is one we feel might function almost like a guardian herbal spirit, a symbol of the higher ideals of a profession. The following is a list of patron herbes and those with whom they share an affinity. A patron herbe is, to the herbalist, what a totem animal is to the shaman.

> alchemists: lady's mantle, lily-of-the-valley
> animal keepers: gorse (golden), marshwort
> bards: trillium
> bird keepers: chickweed
> equestrians: linden, parsley
> fish keepers: parsley
> fishers: cinquefoil, houseleek, nettles, samphire
> gardeners: chamomile, coriander, life-everlasting
> gay men: cypress, hyacinth
> healers (physicians and medical people): mustard, peony
> herbalists: centaury, coltsfoot, cornflower
> lesbians: rose
> locksmiths: fern (moonwort), mistletoe
> seamstresses: flax
> snake keepers: poplar
> tailors: flax
> totem bears: jack-in-the-pulpit, quince
> veterinarians: marshwort
> Wiccans: periwinkle
> writers: beech

peace, social: coriander, olive

These herbes may be used when one is preparing for a social occasion or a gathering with the desire that all present get along well.

pearls: mugwort, myrrh, pennyroyal, sandalwood, thyme

Who could think concentric layers of nacre could be so beautiful? The soft glow of a pearl has seemed magickal to people from before recorded history. These herbes enhance the magick of pearls, which share some magickal similarities to opals. They have also been worn to represent the energy of unicorns.

pentacles: clover, ivy

In modern Wicca, the traditional pentacle is a round, copper disk. Many prefer wood, some use petrified wood, and others choose from a variety of materials ranging from pottery to wax. The pentacle, as a ritual tool, represents the principle of manifestation in the physical world. These herbes may be used in the consecration or maintenance of this disk.

Pentacles of tarot: ivy

In the tarot, pentacles are sometimes called coins even though the financial aspect of this suit is only a minor element. Pentacles teach us how to provide for ourselves and family, how to manage our resources and how to work within the world as a productive entity. Ivy is the herbe to use when studying this suit of the tarot.

peridot: narcissus

This silicate of magnesium and iron is a lovely, transparent yellow-green. It shares an affinity with narcissus. One interesting usage would be to plant a small peridot along with your bulbs.

perseverance: balmony, oak, thistle

No matter how much we long to achieve our goals and complete our projects, even with a strong will, we must keep at it until it is done. These herbes will help you persevere, improving your endurance and commitment.

playfulness: unicorn root

Even those who persevere and work hard need to balance their work ethic with recreational fun. This herbe will do wonders for those wanting to stimulate their whimsy.

poetic inspiration: bay laurel, vervain

These herbes are of particular value for poets, those who paint their images with words and meter.

polarities: pepper (chili)

In understanding the nature of the divine polarities, we often spend more time thinking of the Union, or Great Rite, forgetting to understand the mysteries involved in their being separate. This herbe will provide you with a fuller grasp of many aspects of these archetypes.

protection: alder, betony (wood), fennel

Although there are many Herbes of Protection, this list of herbes includes those which are very focused in their protective quality.

protection, possessions: caraway, dogwood, fern (royal), hyssop, marigold

When we wish to protect our property, the possessions we have acquired and cherish, these herbes provide additional spiritual insurance.

protection, travel: ash, cinquefoil, comfrey, fern (royal), mugwort, pimpernel, tobacco, turmeric

Magickal work to bring a traveler home safely, to protect one during all aspects of a journey, can be accomplished with any of the herbes in this list.

psychic attack: agrimony

A genuine psychic attack, one which is intentional, occurs far less often than one would believe from gathering gossip. For those rare occurrences, this is the herbe of choice. The more common form of psychic attack is feeling the energy created from another's images of anger, images which would do someone harm. Agrimony is an excellent herbe in these situations as well.

public speaking: willow

Standing in front of a room full of people and speaking is a difficult proposition for many people. This herbe will add magick to the process, providing not only comfort but also easing the flow of your words.

purification, rituals of: angelica, asafoetida, basil (sweet), camphor, fumitory, rosemary

This list of herbes offers you a selection when creating a ritual of purification, whether you are purifying an individual or a physical space.

quartz: damiana, jasmine, mugwort

This beautiful silicon dioxide is one of the more popular crystals in use. There are many ways its energy can be worked, several of which use quartz to focus energy. These herbes will keep your quartz clear. Small crystals of quartz also work well with these herbes.

Queens of tarot: myrrh

This herbe will help you understand the role this woman holds in her community. She is as strong as her partner, the King, but she has been trained in the spiritual arts and knows the importance of motherhood.

reincarnation: chervil, coriander, cyclamen, fennel, honeysuckle, marjoram (wild), mistletoe, myrrh, nightshade (deadly), pennyroyal

These herbes are all, in different ways, associated with the understanding of the nature of reincarnation and rebirth. Some of them will provide you with more control over the process and others will help you understand its mysteries.

relationships: caraway, clover, coriander, crowfoot, cyclamen, lavender, mandrake, myrtle, pepper (chili), quince, rice, rosemary, scullcap

These herbes are associated with that aspect of a relationship which involves making or keeping a commitment, whether the vows are formalized in ritual or exchanged privately as promises. We can also work with them to learn some of the lessons essential in being able to maintain a healthy relationship.

renewal: agrimony, basil (sweet), cherry

This list of herbes offers us a type of magick which will help us restore and refresh our energy.

resources: alfalfa, ammoniacum, broom, cedar, corn, cowslip, cumin, hollyhock, lavender, moneywort, oak, sandalwood

These herbes are said to help us learn the lessons necessary and make adjustments in our internal images and energy, which allow us to better attract the resources and possessions necessary to do our work. Some of them are said to contain the energy of abundance, which allows us to reward the self for work done well with gifts.

robes, ritual: flax, holly, hyssop, kamala, melilot, pomegranate, saffron, sunflower, woad

This list of herbes includes those which can be used as dye, those which can create the thread to be woven into fabric, and those which are ideal for consecrating and blessing your ritual robe.

rock crystal: willow

Pieces of rock crystal work well with willow, enhancing and deepening this herbe's magick. Willow may be used to enhance the divinatory quality of rock crystal.

romance: anise seed, balm, bay laurel, cinnamon, cloves, coriander, cyclamen, gorse (golden), heartsease, lavender, lemon, mandrake, myrtle, patchouli, tulip, vervain

If your magick is dealing with romantic issues, this is a list of herbes which you should consider individually.

romantic appeal: balm, cowslip, iris, lemon, lovage, mandrake, marigold, meadowsweet, orchid, parsley, patchouli, periwinkle, thyme (wild), vervain

These herbes are all said to assist in bringing romance into your life or to make you more sensually appealing to another.

rubies: rue

These very hard forms of alumina are among the more powerful of gems. Often seen as representing passion and used to help achieve goals, the ruby's energy remains focused with rue. A small ruby placed with rue for magickal purposes will keep the herbe's energy concentrated and fully charged until you release it in ritual.

sailing: pine

Pine's lore indicates that it would be an excellent herbe to use by those who love sailing and wish to work magick while on the water.

sapphire: cedar

Closely related to the ruby, sapphire is found in all colors but red. They help us establish a bond with the Universe and achieve our highest ideals. A sapphire and the herbe cedar work well together.

scrying: camphor

Camphor may be used to improve our ability to scry, regardless of the method you use. Whether the herbe is used to empower your tools or it is burned as incense during your scrying is a matter of choice.

security: apple, dogwood

The magick of these herbes may be used to provide us with improved spiritual security. They may also increase your general sense of being secure.

secrecy: dogwood, fern (bracken), hellebore (black), rose

These herbes allow us to move through a situation with far more discretion than would otherwise be available. While we may not literally be invisible, this magick may allow us to avoid detection and keep private that which should be secret.

self-confidence: celandine, chestnut, endive, frankincense, heliotrope, motherwort

These herbes are excellent when working to increase your sense of self. They can help improve one's self-esteem and help you feel as if you have more self-control in your life.

selfishness: benzoin

Someone who is prone to selfish behavior can make a healthy change by working with this herbe.

Seven of Cups: rose

This herbe may help you understand the need to look beyond your dreams. The Seven of Cups cautions you about good intentions and fantasies which are not backed up with action. Rose can help us look beyond the surface images of this card.

Sevens of tarot: benzoin

This herbe gives us access to the magick of the number seven as it unifies these four suits. A gently spiritual number, when worked well it represents a level of comfortable change which better unifies your spirit with the world around you.

sewing: flax

This herbe works well for seamstresses, tailors, dressmakers, costumers or anyone who works with needle and thread. One's needles might be consecrated with the oil of flax. As well, its lovely blue flowers may provide inspiration.

sexual abuse: myrrh, tarragon

These herbes are highly useful for someone who is recovering from any form of sexual abuse or incest.

shamanic journeying: anise seed, damiana, hemp, mescal, morning glory, peyote

These herbes are useful for trained shamans when they are journeying. Most are controlled substances and illegal to use but, in some areas of the world, are regarded as highly spiritual and treated with great respect.

shyness: chestnut

This herbe may be used by those who hold themselves back due to their discomfort. Chestnut can help a person overcome timidity.

silver: mugwort

Mugwort is the herbe of choice for working with anything made of silver. One method of linking these two energies is to rinse your silver tools in a mugwort wash after polishing them.

singers: mustard, vervain

These herbes give voice to the singer, increasing the quality of sound and providing the musician with a greater ability to work to improve her skills.

sleep: agrimony

Of all the herbes associated with sleeping and dreaming, agrimony is the one best known for its ability to promote a night of protected, good sleep.

snakes: alkanet

There are some varieties of snakes which can pose a danger to people and many others whose only threat is to a person's fears. This herbe is said to protect us against snakes.

solar rituals: celandine, chamomile, frankincense, heliotrope, olive, oxalis, peony, sunflower, vervain

The herbes in this list may be used in any rituals which are centered around the energy or mythologies of the Sun.

sorrow: calamint, daffodil, dodder, eyebright, thyme (wild)

These herbes work well for those suffering from melancholy and sorrow, those who are unable to bring light to their internal darkness.

spirit: ephedra

When the four elements of air, fire, water and earth are brought together in balance, the fifth element, or spirit, becomes manifest. Ritual work with this herbe will help us better understand the nature of spirit.

spirit guides: angelica

This herbe may be used by all who work with, or are seeking, communication with their spirit guides.

Star card: cloves

What helps her sustain her sense of freedom and inspiration is her willingness to pour the waters of her soul not only upon the manifest world but to also give to the waters of the unmanifest. Working with cloves to better manifest the Star card in your own life will show you that, truly, hope springs eternal.

storm: bay laurel, holly, houseleek, marjoram (wild), mugwort, oak, pennyroyal, rowan, Saint John's wort

These herbes are believed capable of protecting us and our homes from damage by lightning. They may be used for protection during any fierce storm. If you have a deep dread caused by loud thunder, these herbes might protect you against your own fears.

Strength card: angelica, bay laurel, catnip, rue, sage

She has neither rejected nor feared the primal passion from the animal nature of reality but has moved in balance with it. Patience has shown them how to work together. These herbes may help you balance your spiritual and incarnate selves.

studying: beech, cherry, dill, eyebright, fern (moonwort), fig (bo), spikenard, vervain, willow

These herbes provide important help for the student, whether working to learn a skill or pursue a degree. These herbes are most helpful for students of spiritual disciplines and religions, those working toward initiation.

success: aloe, benzoin, chamomile, frankincense, grapes, hollyhock, lady's mantle, mints, motherwort, oak, olive, orange, palm, parsley, rosemary

This is a list of herbes associated with success and victory. Each, in its own way, can provide magickal energy which will help you attain your goal.

Sun card: bay laurel, celandine, sunflower

Without any adult ego, joy is taken in the nature of reality. The youth does not boast of her accomplishment but, rather, radiates the miracle of life. It's wonderful when this card appears in a reading but we can use these herbes to work with the Sun card and learn how to better manifest it in our lives.

swords: pimpernel

This herbe works exceptionally well with a ritual sword. It may be used to consecrate this tool or to periodically renew its sacred power. It may also be used to enhance your understanding of this suit in the tarot.

Temperance card: dill, iris, parsley, sage

When you have the mysteries of the Universe as your foundation and seek neither the gratification of your ego nor the manipulation of reality, your life will seem to defy gravity. Work carefully with these herbes for temperance is a virtue often neglected in today's reality.

Tens of tarot: dittany of Crete

This herbe brings a more complete understanding of the Tens, which depict aspects of working a level of change that involves more than one person.

Threes of tarot: myrrh

The changes represented by the number three are well known. A three represents a natural change. Good things come in threes but sometimes deaths, also, seem to happen in threes. A three is a very natural number and represents a level of manifestation. This herbe may be used to help us understand these cards.

tin: hyssop

Although it is not one of the more popular metals, many of us have containers made of tin. This herbe has an affinity with tin and may be used to make items of tin more sacred.

tools, ritual: burnet (great), camphor, caraway, dragon's blood, fumitory, gum mastic, hyssop, Solomon's seal, vervain

This list of herbes offers a generic magick which is useful in consecrating or blessing any ritual tool.

topaz: frankincense, peppermint

One of the stones of the Apocalypse, this stone may be used to add magickal strength to these herbes and they, in turn, will work spiritually with topaz.

tourmaline: cinnamon

Cinnamon will work with any of the forms of tourmaline (there are many). The various colors of tourmaline have different properties but each can be enhanced with this herbe.

Tower card: eyebright

It's not a disaster at all, merely the destruction of your false sense of security. If you use the divine brightness of the lightning you will see further than ever before. Eyebright will help you understand that being jolted free of your complacency is not a bad thing.

turquoise: sandalwood

Composed of aluminum and copper, this stone has an affinity with sandalwood.

union, rituals of: almond, anise seed, broom, caraway, crowfoot, cyclamen

Although these rituals are frequently those of Handfasting, these herbes offer a magick for rituals of union which is far broader in its definition.

vessels, ritual: henbane, lotus

These herbes may be used in the magickal consecration of a ritual container which is to hold liquid for ritual use.

victory: celandine, ivy

When you desire to become the victor, either of these herbes may assist you in achieving that success.

violence: myrtle

Violence, domestic and otherwise, is a source of very dark, harmful energy. This herbe may assist you in learning to control your violent behavior. It may also be used by those who are subject to the violence of others. Ritual work to decrease the levels of violence in the world are enhanced with myrtle.

virility: bean (kidney), chestnut, cubeb, cumin, fern (male), ginkgo biloba, henna, hyacinth, jack-in-the-pulpit, mandrake, marshmallow, mistletoe, mushrooms, oak, orchid, savory, southernwood

This list of herbes includes those associated with male sexual energy or male sexual potency.

visualization: centaury, kava kava, mandrake, unicorn root

These herbes work specifically to increase one's effectiveness and skill of working with visualized images, no matter which senses are used in the creation of that magick.

wands: almond, ash, asphodel, bamboo, cedar, frankincense, hawthorn, holly, iris, mistletoe, rowan, vervain, walnut

Many of these herbes have provided people with wands capable of great magick. Any of them may be used to consecrate
or empower this tool which represents discipline and will.
They may also be used in the making of a ritual staff.

Wands of tarot: cedar

Cedar will help us understand the nature of wands, rods or
staves as they appear in the tarot. Cedar is frequently used as
an incense while laying out all the cards of this suit. The
lovely scent of cedar permeates the air, while the cedar helps
you discover a greater level of meaning in this suit.

water: alder, ash, birch, life-everlasting, watercress

Representing emotions and things spiritual, elemental water
has many similarities with the properties of physical water.
The elemental spirit is known as an undine. These herbes
help us commune with the undines, invoke elemental water,
or learn more of its mysteries.

Wheel of Fortune card: agrimony, horehound, magnolia, myrrh

When it seems as if your life is having its ups and downs and
things are going too quickly, these herbes will help you. The
Wheel of Fortune teaches us that we must be calm, for only
then can we truly discern the difference between opportunities and distractions.

Wheel of the Year: benzoin, honeysuckle, magnolia

The concept of the Wheel of the Year relates to the turning
of the seasons and of the cycle which moves through the
eight sabbats. These herbes will assist you in seeing how living
within the Wheel of the Year transforms your life and spiritual
progress into a process like a spiral.

will: dill, frankincense

These herbes help us to find more will power, to better develop a sense of resolve and to be able to sustain the energy
needed to follow through, thus bringing our word or commitment into manifestation.

wisdom: cassia, dittany of Crete, fern (moonwort), fig, fig (bo), fir, ginkgo biloba, hazel nut, larch, mulberry, mushrooms, myrrh, rosemary, rowan, sage, teak

All associated with the attainment of wisdom, these herbes bring an understanding of those things which often can only be learned through years of experience. They bring a deeper and more rewarding understanding of the meaning of life.

wish magick: bay laurel

Sometimes there is no magick as pure and simple as a mere wish. This herbe has a long history in wish magick and is one of the best to use.

wolf: fig, potato

Both of these herbal foods have a strong association with the wolf. Whether the wolf is your totem animal or you are doing magickal work to help save wolves in the wild, a creative magickal approach will benefit these sacred creatures. You may also work with these herbes to make a better connection with the wolf.

women's mysteries: cornflower, daisy (ox-eye), iris, jasmine, lime, maguey, mugwort, mullein, myrtle, pomegranate, primrose, rosemary, sage, tansy, tarragon, violets

These herbes are ideal for work when only women are present. Their magick allows an exploration and sharing of understanding of feminine divinity which only women can know.

World card: lovage, mandrake

She has the whole world in her hands, but only because she has a strong will, one kept in balance. Her life is lived within a balanced Circle and she has shed the garments of ego, clad only in her beliefs. This card holds the secrets which lead to achievement of one's goals and these herbes can help you come to know them.

writing: dogwood, dragon's blood

Those who appreciate the power and beauty of the written word, whether with letters or in a diary, may work with these herbes to bring magick to their art.

written skills: beech

We live in an era in which the written word (even when transmitted electronically) holds more power than at any previous time. The majority of priestesses and priests must develop some level of literary skill for modern Wicca is a literary craft. Beech will provide you with magickal support as you develop your arts.

Yule: blessed thistle, box, chamomile, cranberry, frankincense, holly, hyssop, ivy, mistletoe, rosemary

The wheel of the seasons turns at the Winter Solstice. Perceived as the time when the Sun is reborn, this is one of the most joyful holidays of nearly all religions. These herbes are used in rituals, placed as decorations, and help us connect with the magick of this season felt since ancient times.

Deities and Magickal Herbalism

Since earliest times certain herbes have been associated with specific deities. Some are believed to have first sprung from that divine being's blood, or emerged from within the divinity's belly or from its seed; while others are merely believed to be under that god or goddess's patronage.

We, as magickal practitioners, have many options in ritually using herbes to establish some level of spiritual communion with a deity. We may use the herbe as an offering, burn it as incense, dress our candles with it or drink it while chanting to the deity. Usage is only limited by your imagination. What bears mention is that there are many ways to use the invocatory aspects of an herbe.

One may use the herbe seeking the intercession of the deity, hoping that through our ritual work that divine personage will somehow look upon us with favor and grant the blessing we are seeking. Many of us were raised in a culture which used an image of Saint Christopher to help find a lost object. Today the same form of magick is used when invoking the recently created god Murray of Southern California who will help you find a parking space.

Another technique is to *invoke* the deity, a skill which requires extraordinary technical prowess not only with ritual but in matters of self-discipline, control of one's ego and in knowing the true nature of that divinity. Is it possible to burn an herbe of Hecate and see an actual image of her appearing in your temple and hear, with your body's ears, the sound of her words? Yes, it is possible but no, I would say that this is highly unlikely. Those with experience have learned that, to invoke a deity, one is more likely to encounter major changes in one's life because we are being touched with that energy. It is not the picture of the deity which is most likely to appear at that dramatic moment. It is more likely that the energy of what that divinity represents will permeate our lives and do so in a subtle fashion.

What follows is the list of deities found under the invocatory heading in the herbes section. These herbes may be used to establish a connection with the energy, personality or virtues of that deity. We apologize to these esteemed presences for the brevity with which they are described. We urge you to study these deities before working with their energies.

The Deities

Abellia (sometimes spelled Abellio): apple

He was a Celtic tree spirit or deity worshipped in some areas of the Pyrenees Mountains between Spain and France. Abellia was considered a tree-god and believed to reside within the apple.

Adonis: anemone, anemone (wood), frankincense, hellebore (false), myrrh, pomegranate

He was the Greek god known for his youthful good looks, who became one of Aphrodite's lovers. Ares, jealous and out of control, knows that Adonis loves to hunt so Ares shape-shifts into a boar and Adonis is killed while hunting.

Aesculapius: mustard

Aesculapius studied under the Greek centaur, Chiron. In some legends he is transformed into an owl or a boulder by Demeter after he reveals Persephone must stay in Hades because she has eaten the pomegranate. Rescued as a boy by Apollo, Aesculapius is known as a divine healer.

Aino: birch, willow

This Finnish goddess of beauty is sister of the divine bard Youkahainen. She becomes wife and consort of Wainamoinen, a famed singer and bard only after her future husband and her brother settle their differences with song.

Aitvarasm: corn

Aitvarasm is a Prussian domestic deity, somewhat impish and mischievous, who was invoked to bring good fortune and domestic protection. As he usually lived in an outbuilding (shed), food was set out for him.

Anemos: anemone (wood)

Greek god of the wind, Anemos may be invoked with the element of air. He may be called upon when you wish to stir the breeze or calm the wind.

Aphrodite: anemone (wood), apple, benzoin, myrrh, myrtle, parsley, pomegranate, quince, rose

Greek goddess of love and beauty, she was widely worshipped and had temples built in her honor. Sometimes believed born of the sea itself, other times said born of Zeus and Dione, Aphrodite was the wife of Hephaestus, considered unattractive. Not to be satisfied with him, she was involved with many gods and humans.

Apollo: anise seed, bay laurel, cypress, fenugreek, frankincense, hyacinth, lily-of-the-valley, orange, palm, sunflower

Greek god of the Sun, he also held music and poetry in his realm. The son of Zeus and twin brother of Artemis, he was a most important divinity. His worship spread and he was perceived in many different ways. In some temples he represented prophecy but in a few he represented death and destruction.

Artemis: almond, amaranth, daisy (ox eye), fir, willow, wormwood

Artemis is, perhaps, the most notable of the Greek Moon goddesses. Often considered virginal and depicted as a hunter, she is the daughter of Zeus and Leto, born on Delos with Apollo.

Athena: mulberry, oak, olive

Known as Atheme and Pallas Athene, she is the Greek goddess of wisdom, whose worship also spread widely.

Atlantis: angelica

This is the legendary island where knowledge was said to have been perfected. The myth was first reported by Pliny. In the legend, Atlantis is said to have sunk into the ocean.

Atropos: nightshade (deadly)

Of the three Greek Fates, she is the one who cuts the threads of life at death. Her sisters are Clotho, spinner of the fabric of the Universe and Lachesis, who disposes of lots.

Attis: almond

He is found in Phrygian myths and is a forerunner of Adonis. Attis, the son of the goddess Nana, conceived through virgin birth.

Atys (sometimes spelled Attis): ivy

He is a mythical Greek shepherd who meets a tragic end. Falling in love with the goddess Cybele his passion becomes so overwhelming that he castrates himself. He was sometimes honored during Cybele's Spring Equinox celebration.

Axo-mama: potato

The Potato Mother is a Peruvian fertility goddess and potato spirit.

Baal: frankincense

This ancient Canaanite Sun god was believed to have been imported from Babylon. The golden calf was one of his icons. Baal and his sister Anat are good friends with Astarte.

Bacchus: asclepias, asphodel, fig, grapes, ivy, orchid, rose

The famed Greek god of wine and good times is also known as Dionysus. His worshippers sought ecstasy through dance, music and hard drinking.

Balder: mistletoe

This solar deity of northern Europe was the second son of Odin and Frigg. Recognized primarily by the Norse, he often represents prophesy and wisdom.

Bast: catnip

Also known as Bubastis, this Egyptian deity is the cat-headed daughter of Isis and represents the goodness of the Sun's energy.

Bellona: nightshade (deadly)

The Roman goddess of war, she is a counterpart to Mars. She corresponds to the Greek Enyo. In some myths she is Mars' wife, in others his sister.

Bloddeuwedd: broom, hawthorn, meadowsweet, oak

She is a lesser European divinity associated with the hawthorn, femininity and fertility. She is often represented in festivals by the May Queen.

Bona Dea: myrtle

Also known as Fauna, wife of Faunus, she was worshipped only by women as a source of benevolence and protection.

Brahma: lotus

He is the creator god of the Hindu trinity. First of the trinity, he is depicted with four heads and four hands.

Cadmus: sage

The son of Agenor and Telephassa, he is considered the founder of Thebes. He is the brother of Europa. When she is carried off by a bull he consults the Oracle at Delphi.

Calypso: alder

The daughter of Atlas and lover of Odysseus in Greek mythology, she is a nymph who is invoked for her love of music.

Cardea: hawthorn

The consort of Janus, a lesser Roman deity, she was worshipped as the protector of children.

Centeotl: corn

This Aztec fertility goddess of agriculture and grains is sometimes equated with the concept of Mother Nature.

Ceres: chaste tree

She is an ancient Roman goddess of agriculture, similar to Greek Demeter and seen as her counterpart. Her festivals took place in April.

Cernunnos: asafoetida, red campion

He is an antlered, Celtic triple god who was worshipped in France and in parts of the British Isles.

Chiron: centaury, cornflower, wormwood

The son of Cronus and Philyra, he is the most famous of the centaurs. He is known for skills at healing and surgery, and is the patron of herbalists and healers.

Circe: mandrake, mullein, nightshade (deadly), willow

A Greek enchantress found in some of the mythical sagas, she loved to attract men with her magick and then turn them into swine.

Concordia: olive

She is a lesser Roman goddess who represents peace and harmony. There were several temples in her honor. She often represents the goddess as mother.

Consus: dogwood, sage

This ancient Roman god of agricultural harvests and commerce was honored at festivals following the autumn harvest.

Cronus (sometimes spelled Cronos): barley, orchid

The youngest son of Uranus and Gaea in the Greek pantheon, he was married to his sister Rhea and is the father of Zeus and Hera and of many of the greater Olympian deities. Cronus is the god who understands the passage of time.

Cybele: almond, ivy, myrrh, pine

This nature goddess was found in Asia Minor in ancient times. She emerges in ancient Greece as an aspect of the goddess Rhea. Cybele's celebration was at the Spring Equinox when a pine was brought into her sanctuary.

Cyparissus: cypress

The son of Telephus and grandson of Heracles, he is a Greek divinity who ran with the stag. He was a gay lover of Apollo.

Danu: meadowsweet

This goddess of India is also known as Diti. Diti represents the individuality of the human, the separation of human consciousness from the divine. She is sister to Aditi, the mother of worlds.

Daphne: bay laurel

A virtuous nymph in Greek mythology, she is lovely, a daughter of Peneus, but attracts Apollo. When she realizes that he will not say no, she is transformed into the bay laurel.

Delphi: bay laurel

This is the sacred site on Mount Parnassus in Greece, often claimed by different deities. It was at Delphi where Apollo was invoked through an oracle by his priestesses.

Demeter: barley, chaste tree, corn, frankincense, myrrh, penny-royal, poppy, sunflower, wheat

A Greek goddess of agriculture, corn and grains, she is the daughter of Cronus and Rhea, sister of Zeus, Poseidon, Hades, Hera and Hestia. Demeter has a number of divine offspring by more than one father, including Persephone and Plutus. She represents a bountiful harvest and was widely worshipped.

Deving Cerklicing: corn

This Latvian harvest deity brought blessings and fertility to the fields.

Diana: apple, balm, beech, jasmine, mandrake, mugwort, vervain, willow, wormwood

She is the Roman derivative of the Greek goddess Artemis and is the goddess of hunting and of chastity, worshipped with her brother Apollo. She represents the divinity of the Moon and Apollo of the Sun.

Dionysus: asphodel, grapes, ivy, rose

Also know as Bacchus, the son of Zeus and Semele and grand-son of Cadmus. Semele had a long-lasting lust for Zeus which culminated in her tricking him into appearing before her in all his power. When he visits her as thunder and lightning, she conceives but, about to be destroyed by the stormy power, Zeus snatches Dionysus away.

Donar: oak

Donar is the Germanic counterpart of the Norse god Thor. He was also known as Thunar. His sacred oak was known as *Donares eih*, or "the oak of Donar," according to Graves.

Dryope: poplar

She is the shepherdess nymph who caught Apollo's eye and later bore him a son. Known for her loveliness, Apollo se-duced her by appearing as a tortoise.

Embla: alder

The first human woman in Norse and Teutonic creation myths, she and her husband, Aske, are the equivalent of Adam and Eve.

Euphrosyne: eyebright

The daughter of Eurynome, an Oceanid, and Zeus, she is one of the Three Graces and represents joy.

Eurus: anemone (wood)

This is the name of the wind associated with the element of air and, in many modern Wiccan traditions, the east quarter of a ritual Circle.

Fagus: beech

Fagus is a Celtic tree spirit and divinity which resides within the beech. He was recognized by the Celts who lived in the Pyrenees.

Fides: bay laurel, corn, olive

This Roman goddess represented the ability to keep one's word or oath. She has some fertility attributes and is often shown with a wreath of olive leaves and carrying a basket of corn. A temple was built for her by Pompilius Numa.

Flora: cornflower, hawthorn

She is the Roman goddess of flowers, who was worshipped during the Floralia celebrated sometime around Beltane.

Freya (also known as Freyja): apple, cowslip, daisies, primrose

The Norse goddess of love and healing, she and Froh lead the Vanir, a race of deities. (The Aesir, the other race of gods were headed by Odin and Frigga).

Froh: apple

Froh is the god of fruitfulness who, with his sister Freya, is a great ruler. Sometimes spelled Freyr, he has sometimes been confused with Odin.

Gaea: apple, orange

The Greek earth goddess and mother of the Titans, she, with

Uranus, are the two oldest of the Greek pantheon. With Uranus, her offspring include Cronus and Rhea. As the primary mother of all, in modern times she has become equated with our planet's divine energy.

Ganymede: tansy

This Trojan prince and son of Heracles was brought to Mount Olympus by Zeus who disguised himself as an eagle.

Gwydion: ash

This legendary Druid and teacher of the gods in Celtic myths is one of the sons of Don, the fertility goddess worshipped as earth-mother by the Celts living on the British Isles.

Hades: corn, cypress, mints, narcissus

He is the Greek god of the Underworld which becomes known by his name. He is husband of Persephone. When the world was divided, his brother Poseidon was given the seas and Zeus the heavens.

Hathor: myrtle, sycamore

Also known as Athor, this important Egyptian deity is both daughter and mother of Ra. She is a goddess of love and beauty. Her realm was the sky, including the rising and setting of the Sun.

Hecate: aconite, almond, dandelion, garlic, hemlock, lavender, myrrh, willow, yew

She is a Greek triple goddess of the Underworld, sometimes called the "Lady of the Night," representing abundance, eloquence and often worshipped at a crossroads.

Helios: heliotrope

A Greek solar deity and son of Titans Hyperion and Thea and brother of Selene, his realm was the Moon.

Heng-O: cassia

A Chinese fertility goddess associated with the Moon, she was worshipped during the Han Dynasty.

Hera: apple, iris, orange, pomegranate, willow

She is the wife of Zeus in the Greek pantheon. A goddess of women, she was particularly the patroness of married women, protecting them in marriage. She and Zeus had a stormy marriage as she reacted to his philandering in ways not becoming a goddess.

Hercules: oak, poplar

The Roman equivalent of Heracles, he is a well-known mythical Greek hero. Born in Thebes of Zeus and Alcmene with his twin brother Iphicles (curiously, his twin brother had a different father), Hercules was known for strength and his deeds are legendary.

Hermes: anise seed, dittany of Crete, iris, lotus, mercury (dog's), oak, palm, storax, vervain, willow.

He is the son of Zeus and Maia (a Naid who was the eldest and most beautiful daughter of Atlas). The Greek equivalent of Mercury, Hermes is the messenger between the realm of the gods and the Underworld. Widely worshipped, his attributes are many.

Horus: horehound, lotus

Son of Osiris and Isis, he is an Egyptian solar god of light and of silence. Sometimes considered the same as Ra, Horus' worship spread, extending even to the Greeks and Romans as Harpocrates.

Hulda: flax

Northern Europes elf queen and feminine spirit, she is believed to have taught us spinning and sewing.

Hyacinthus: hyacinth

He was a youth so handsome that we was described as beautiful. He became a lover of Apollo. In modern times he is often a patron deity of gay men.

Hylde-Moer: elder

The feminine mother-spirit of elder trees, Hylde-Moer was recognized in parts of Britain and is probably Anglo-Saxon in origin.

Idun: apple

Wife of Bragi, she is the Teutonic goddess of youth and beauty. Through the apple, she is able to return again at spring as the maiden.

Indra: asclepias

A Hindu god of winds and storms, he is in some ways comparable to Zeus. Indra carries thunderbolts which he throws with his four arms. He is known for his ability to shape-shift at will. Originally very important, an equal of his twin brother Agni, his position slipped as time passed.

Io: violets

Io was a Greek mortal made immortal through Zeus' affection. Zeus, often taking the shape of a bull, changes Io into a cow but Hera drives her out of Greece. Zeus restores her to human form not without her becoming mother of his son, Epaphus.

Iris: iris

The Greek feminine counterpart to Hermes, she is the goddess of the rainbow, who conducts the departed to the Otherworld.

Isis: heather, horehound, lotus, narcissus

Egyptian goddess of both the earth and the Moon, she is both sister and consort of Osiris. Among the more widely worshipped Egyptian goddesses, her powers were considered limitless. Her realm included the earth, both land and sea, the heavens and the Underworld.

Itchita: beech

She is one of the three aspects of the Great Mother, a triple Goddess of Siberia. Itchita holds the secrets of the magick of beech which is also her home.

Iznagi: grapes, peaches

With his wife Izanami, they are the procreative couple of Japanese myths. He is recognized as a Shinto deity representing male sexuality.

Jove: marjoram (wild)

Another name for Jupiter, Jove is the Roman equivalent of Zeus. Originally the word *Jove* meant god but later became equated with his name. During the period when his worship was most prevalent, all other deities were secondary to him.

Juno: iris, myrrh

She was worshipped in Rome as queen of the heavens and is the wife of Jupiter. She corresponds to Hera. She is queen of the heavens. Her great festival was the first day of March.

Jupiter: ammoniacum, daisy (ox eye), gorse (golden), houseleek, marjoram (wild), oak, sage, walnuts

During his reign, he was the epitomy of divine essence, the Roman counterpart to Zeus. Married to Juno, Jupiter was worshipped in many temples and by a variety of names.

Kishimo-jin: pomegranate

Also known as Karitei-mo or Mother Hariti, she is the goddess mother of demons. In earlier myths she devours children and is feared. Later she becomes a Japanese fertility goddess and protector of children.

Krishna: basil (sweet)

He is a Hindu avatar who has since achieved the status of divinity. Part of the later Hindu myths, he is worshipped as a reincarnation of Vishnu.

Lakshmi: lotus

The wife of Vishnu, she is revered in India as the goddess of wealth and beauty. She is said to have been born of the foam of the sea.

Laukosargas: corn

This Baltic corn deity and agricultural spirit is guardian and protector of the fields and the harvest.

Leuce: poplar

Leuce was a Greek nymph who held Hades' heart for a time. He was so enamored of her that, following her death, he transformed her into a poplar.

Lilith: tarragon

An early woman in Hebrew myths, she is sometimes joined with Adam. She remains a feminine archetype of woman.

Loki: apple, storax

He is a Norse and Teutonic trickster who likes to play mischief, representing the destructive force of fire.

Luatiku: corn

This fertility goddess, both creator and Maize Mother, is revered by the Pueblos.

Lugeilan: coconut

Son of Aleulop, he is a Pacific sky god who brings wisdom to humans, including knowledge of death.

Mars: rue

The Roman god of war and counterpart to the Greek Ares, he is the father of Romulus and Remus, founding brothers of Rome.

Medea: aconite, vervain

Famed sorceress and goddess of the Greeks, she was the wife of Jason. Associated with witchcraft, she was able to escape by flying through the air.

Mercury: anise seed, mercury (dog's), storax, yew

He is the Roman god of commerce, comparable to the Greek Hermes. His festival was celebrated in May.

Michael: angelica

This human personification of the element of fire is depicted as angelic. The mythology surrounding this archangel is unclear although he later becomes one of the four magickal divinities associated with the four elements.

Minerva: alder, mulberry

The Roman goddess of wisdom, she is a counterpart to the Greek Athena. She represents evolved thinking processes and reason. Her festival was celebrated in March.

Mintha: mints

She was a Greek nymph who was transformed into a minor deity by Persephone after Mintha caught Hades' roving eye.

Mithra: corn, fig, lotus

A very ancient deity, he was a Persian god born of rock, carrying a torch and a sacred blade beneath a fig tree. He was a friend of the Sun.

Mut: benzoin

Mut is a Theban goddess and consort of Amun. She is a mother goddess, who became partnered with Amun.

Nuba: bamboo

A Sudanese sky god, he is the keeper of fruit-bearing seeds. He comes down to earth to offer his gifts to the earth.

Odin: apple, ash, cedar, mistletoe, oak

The primary god and creator in Norse and Teutonic mythology, he is comparable to Zeus. Among Germanic peoples he was known as Wotan or Wodin. A god of war, he was married to Frigga.

Odysseus: mullein

This legendary king of Ithaca and hero of Greek mythological sagas is a main character in the Trojan legends.

Orpheus: willow

He was a legendary Greek poet of pre-Homeric myths. Son of Oeagrus, king of Thrace and Calliope, muse of epic poetry, he was known for his skill with the lyre.

Osiris: acacia, dittany of Crete, heather, horehound, ivy, lotus

The Egyptian son of earth and sky, he was both brother and husband of Isis. One of the more widely worshipped Egyptian deities, he represented the principle of goodness and later became associated with both the Sun and Moon.

Paëthon: poplar

He is a lesser Greek solar deity.

Pan: asafoetida, blessed thistle, orchid, peony, red campion, savory

Pan was the primary deity and best known of satyrs. A woodland god skilled with pipes, Pan was later perceived as the primal force permeating all of nature.

Perkunas: oak

He was a Lithuanian god of thunder and storms, of Indo-European origin and related to the Russian thunder god, Perun.

Persephone: dittany of Crete, parsley, pomegranate, poppy, willow

Wife of the Greek Hades, she was the daughter of Demeter and Zeus. As did Hades, she represented both light and dark. On earth perceived as a virgin, in the Underworld she was a dreaded queen.

Perun: oak

A thunder deity of some Slavs and Russians, he is probably related to Perkunas.

Phyllis: almond

Beautiful and mythic daughter of King Sithon of ancient Greece, she is betrothed to Demophoön but comes to a tragic end.

Pluto: narcissus

The Roman equivalent of Hades, he is considered prince of the Underworld. He was known by many other names, including Dis, Orcus and Tartarus. He was also a god capable of bestowing wealth.

Pomona: apple

This Roman goddess's realm included all fruit trees. She was worshipped to obtain a plentiful harvest. She was said to be highly popular among male deities.

Poseidon: ash, olive, pine

The Greek god of seas, rivers and horses, he lived in a golden temple at the bottom of the sea with his wife, the queen Amphitrite, a Nereid. They had three children, Triton, Rhodos and Benthesikyme.

Priapus: asafoetida

He was worshipped in both Greece and Rome. Not quite a full deity, he was a lesser god of fertility and male sexuality.

Puck: bogbean

Puck was a folk spirit of the British Isles known for shape-shifting; he was a type of elf or pixie. Puck gained fame under Shakespeare and is sometimes considered another name for Robin Goodfellow.

Ra: frankincense

Ra is the self-created Egyptian god of the Sun. There are inconsistent stories of his origin. He is often represented as a hawk.

Rgl: barley

A lesser nature divinity or woodland spirit, he is recognized by the agrarian peoples of what is now Russia.

Rhea: myrrh, oak, pine

Wife of the Greek Cronus, she was a major goddess of fertility who was worshipped to bring bountiful fruits and harvests. Her priests were called Curetes. There is some confusion at times and she later becomes Cybele.

Robur: oak

He was a Celtic god of oak trees who was worshipped throughout Gaul and in the Pyrenees.

Sappho: rose

This famed Greek poetess was known for her love of women who lived around 600 B.C. She is sometimes invoked in women's rituals as a source for inspiration and is a patroness of women who love women.

Saturn: corn, fig, lavender, mandrake, myrrh, pomegranate

Husband of Ops, he is the Roman equivalent of Cronus. Originally a pre-Greek divinity, he was given one of the great festivals, the Saturnalia.

Sekhet: catnip

Egyptian daughter of Isis and sister of Bast, she has the head of a lion and represented the Sun's ferocity.

Shu: oak

The Egyptian counterpart to Hercules, he is the protector of creatures. He is the son of Ra and associated with the light of the Sun.

Siva: wheat

She is a Slavic fertility goddess who represented the bringing of life. Considered very powerful, she was a major deity.

Soma: asclepias

Soma was a Hindu creature and father of gods but in another manifestation is considered the Divine Moon.

Sri: coconut, lotus

Sri is another name for Lakshmi, an Indian goddess of fertility and beauty.

Svantevit: grapes

A male fertility deity of the southern Baltic region, he was often worshipped as a standing stone carved with four faces for the four cycles.

Tammuz: corn

Lover and husband of Ishtar, he was a Babylonian god who later evolved into Adonis. He was the god of vegetation who comes to life in the spring and dies at autumn.

Thlassi: apple

Teutonic god of winter, he is also associated with the Underworld.

Thor: birch, daisy (ox eye), houseleek, marjoram (wild), oak

Son of Odin and Jörd, he is god of heaven and earth. In other versions he is the son of Odin and Fjorgyn, a mountain goddess. Thor is the Norse god of thunder and storms. Thor is often comparable to Zeus.

Thoth: palm, storax

Thoth is god of communication and Egyptian god of the Underworld who kept records for the gods of the value of those entering the Underworld.

Thunar: oak

He is a Germanic version of Thor.

Ukemochi: corn, haricot, millet, rice

This major Shinto goddess of foods is sometimes considered a food goddess for she brings many foods to earth through her body.

Ulysses: mullein

Also known as Odysseus.

Uttu: apple, cucumber

Uttu is a Sumerian goddess found early in the creation myths. Enki, the creation father, joins with Nintu, Lady of the Land who gives birth to his daughter Nindurra, with whom he sires the goddess Uttu.

Veles: corn

This northern European agrarian god of fertility and good harvests was invoked when making oaths. She also guarded the flocks.

Venus: aloe, anemone (wood), apple, benzoin, fern (maidenhair), heather, maidenhair, marjoram (sweet), myrtle, parsley, quince, rose, sandalwood

The Roman goddess of love and beauty she is the counterpart of the Greek Aphrodite and mother of Cupid.

Vishnu: basil (sweet), jasmine, lotus

The second of three aspects of the Hindy trinity, he is the supreme male divine in Hindu mythology. In the Vedic system he was almost obscure but in the Brahmanic order he became very prominent. His wife is Lakshmi. Vishnu is depicted holding a lotus.

Yacatecutli: tobacco

An ancient deity still recognized in Mexico, he is a patron for travelers and was once venerated in magnificent festivals, including human sacrifice.

Zara-mama: corn

She is one of the Maize Mothers found throughout the western hemisphere. She is a Peruvian corn mother who represents the divine energy of the plant.

Zeus: almond, daisy (ox eye), linden, oak, olive, peppermint, sage, violets, walnuts

God of gods in the Greek pantheon, he is husband of Hera and counterpart of the Roman Jupiter. Son of Cronus and Rhea, Zeus was a fertility figure in that he fathered children by a startling assortment of goddesses and mortals. No wonder Hera felt out of control. Zeus is god of the sky and represents light.

Working With
Astrological Correspondences

The Planets

It was my good fortune to have been placed upon several paths all at once. During my years in training for the priesthood I was not only studying and practicing to become a Master Herbalist but I also received a sound astrological background. There are not many who are skilled equally in herbal work and astrology and I consider myself most fortunate. When wading through Culpeper, Paracelsus and Heindel, I was able to navigate their esoteric waters.

Astrological correspondences are usually confusing to people. In fact, they are a complex and sometimes arbitrary means of indicating patterns in the energies of herbes. Correspondences between herbes and planets were already in use during Hippocrates' life and continued to be expanded through the centuries. Culpeper is usually considered a definitive source, listing the associations which were preferred during his day. A trained physician (through apprenticeship to an apothecary) and astrologer, we may assume that he further developed the known correspondences of the day. Although some expansion of these lists of correspondences began during the late nineteenth century, it was in the late twentieth century that a major period of renewed research began. With the discovery of Pluto, we now had ten planets (astrologers like to call the Sun and Moon planets) but the entire system of planetary correspondences had historically been based upon the seven visible planets.

Due to the varying opinions of assorted authors, there may be several planets assigned to a particular herbe. Without knowledge of astrology, you are left to pick and choose as you will. When we have a preference, we have indicated it in the following tables. No author's system should be judged as more correct or as incorrect. With one person, an herbe's association of Mercury may be more relevant than its secondary association with Mars. In one person the herbe might stimulate the mental process but in another it

434

might be a stimulus to the physical activity. In that situation Mars is the more appropriate correspondence for the person with the stimulus to physical activity.

How do astrological correspondences work? An herbe can help provide the practitioner access to a planet's particular energy. If you want to bring more of the attributes associated with the planet Venus into your life, choose one or more of the herbes listed under Venus in the tables and work with them.

The tables can also be used by selecting herbes of a particular planet in order to strengthen or enhance the energy of that planet in your natal chart. This type of usage brings that planetary energy more directly into your life. It is similar to working with a spiritual tonic. You may also work with one or more herbes which correspond to a particular planet to gain an understanding of the nature of that energy. In astrology the planets represent different types of energy which becomes manifest in reality. However, the different zodiac signs are archetypes of personality and the different houses of a natal chart indicate the various areas of one's life in which the various planetary energies are focused.

At The Hermit's Grove, we work with these correspondences in conjunction with medical astrology as well as with herbes. Over many centuries much of the human anatomy and a great many of the afflictions have been given correspondences. The Sun, for example, is associated with the heart. Herbes of the Sun may be taken as a tonic to strengthen the heart in a holistic or magickal sense. Other herbes were corresponded with the Sun because they were known remedies for heart conditions.

Those practitioners who have a solid knowledge of astrology can work considerable magick, using their astrological knowledge and manifesting that energy through herbes and ritual in order to bring about emotional and psychological changes and healing. The study of astrological magick is too involved to be explored in any detail in this book, but we are providing limited generalized information so that even the novice practitioner may begin exploring this aspect of herbal magick.

Herbes of the Sun

In natal astrology the Sun governs the emanation of one's ego. Just as it does for our solar system, the Sun represents one's overall health and is vital in the interpretation of one's expansive nature.

The Sun's correspondences with anatomy include the heart. Many modern sources also assign the Sun with the front pituitary gland, thymus, spleen and thyroid. The Sun indicates the presence and function of oxygen within the body. Difficult transits of the natal chart or other afflictions (e.g. a difficult natal aspect) concerning the natal Sun may affect the health of the body's vital fluids. At least one modern author (Llewellyn George) also places the Sun with the right eye.

Many diseases arise out of low self-esteem or follow a crisis which results in the loss of one's self-image. Healing of such afflictions can be promoted by using herbes of the Sun.

By nature the herbes of the Sun are considered hot and dry. This does not mean they taste hot to the tongue and will never feel moist to the touch but, rather, refers to the intrinsic energy of these herbes. The basic nature of these herbes' energy might be described with the archetype Yang, expansive and radiant. Herbes of the Sun make excellent tonics.

Through working with solar herbes, the inner seed within one's spirit is more easily brought into manifestation. We are able to better recognize our role in life, attaining a healthy perspective of our place in the Universe. Just as the radiance of that star which lights our solar system is an emanation of its inner energy, so too does one's ego seek to shine brightly, frequently seeking to radiate and be recognized as a star among one's peers. Herbes of the Sun will help us recognize that one does not discard the ego in achieving spiritual wisdom. A more holistic approach would hold that one comes to bring it into harmony with those around us.

We may also work with herbes of the Sun in order to better understand the divine nature of manifest reality. Just as herbes are dependant upon the Sun's rays so, too, are our creative endeavors dependant upon a positive, divine radiance from our own inner self. There is nothing within our solar system which is not touched by the energy of the Sun. There is nothing within your life which is not touched by your own divinity nor affected by your ego. Solar herbes help open your view of life around you. They are able to assist you in avoiding the magnetic tug of incarnate reality which seeks to place one's ego upon the very altar of one's circle.

Using solar herbes in ritual will bring to light an understanding of those aspects of the human ego which seek to be divine. These herbes will guide your ego into manifesting its divinity and working in union with the Universe.

The virtues of solar herbes are that they endow the human spirit with the courage to seek one's highest ideals. They help those with low self-esteem begin to see the divinity held deep within. Solar herbes are capable of assisting those who are overly egocentric in bringing themselves back into balance. It is important to remember that strengthening one's self-image will add power to all aspects of that image, including your faults and foibles. Careful work within ritual requires being selective about one's self-image and embracing change, no matter how painful, so that your highest ideals may manifest bright and radiant. Solar herbes are useful for those who are working to visualize themselves as successful in the completion of a goal.

Good solar herbes include angelica, bay laurel, chamomile, eyebright and frankincense.

Herbes of the Moon

Astrologers look at the Moon's position in a natal chart to understand that part of one's being which is most vulnerable, which includes those emotions which we nurture and protect. Just as the Moon lights the dark of night and provides some of the most primal times for the hunt in earlier times, so too do we interpret the natal Moon to understand one's instinctive behavior which arises from the inner self.

The lunar correspondences with human anatomy include much of the brain and the rear pituitary. The left eye and the digestive system (the esophagus, stomach and hormones associated with the alimentary system) are also governed by the Moon. So, too, are the breasts, ovaries and the menstrual cycle in women. Most modern medical astrologers place the lymph system and the sympathetic nervous system with the Moon as well.

Lunar transits and the aspects of other planets to the natal Moon may indicate vulnerable health issues. Some of these conditions include difficulties with the menstrual cycle or could indicate problems with digestion. Diseases of the bladder, once placed with the Moon, have recently been found to be better associated with

Neptune. Many diseases which readily fluctuate (measles, small-pox, colic) cause the healer to watch the progress of the Moon as it interacts with the individual. Some illnesses, such as colds, arise when we are more vulnerable due to emotional stress or anxieties which threaten the health of one's subconscious.

By nature lunar herbes are cool and moist. They represent the feminine or Yin aspect of the Universe and may be worked in polarity with solar herbes. Lunar herbes promote a nurturing quality within the individual and work compatibly with the receptive aspects of one's being.

Brought into magickal work, herbes of the Moon interact with the images held within the subconscious, those which are easily empowered by our emotions. Lunar herbes are most useful when working with visualization through meditation, hypnosis or trance work. Herbes of the Moon, when introduced to these processes, will assist us in replacing a bad habit with positive, productive behavior.

Herbes of the Moon have the potential to give us access to childhood memories. It is important that one be prepared for knowledge that can be deeply disturbing. Unlocking these secret doors can be a painful and, possibly, traumatic experience. Although some of these memories may force us to face hidden demons, lunar herbes assist in treating those fears which hold us back from finding fulfillment in life.

Not everyone has access to a professional who is trained in guiding one into past and other life experiences. Some must rely upon self-hypnosis and forms of trance induction. Herbes of the Moon open the portals of time and allow us to move through the webs woven by our inner consciousness. Lunar herbes which are now also corresponded with Neptune are, generally, valuable for those who work within the astral and who journey beyond their bodies.

Just as the Moon governs so many of the cycles of nature and reality upon our planet, lunar herbes may offer us spiritual keys which allow us to adjust our lives to move with the natural ebb and flow of life. Herbes of the Moon will guide us into the mysteries which bring inner peace and contentment.

Herbes of the Moon may be combined with solar herbes to achieve a number of purposes. When one wishes to embrace the energy of a new Moon, a combination of equal portions of solar and lunar herbes may represent that conjunction, since at this time the Sun and Moon are at the same place in the sky (which is why we sometimes have eclipses). Another approach would be to perceive this mixture as symbolic of the union of polarities, the bringing together of Yin and Yang, Moon and Sun, or Goddess and God which may be used to give birth to the creative forces within one's self.

The green world of plants grows at night, having generated its fuel during the day from the radiant light of the Sun. It is against a starlit night that life is simpler, that we must see with our feelings rather than with our logic. Herbes of the Moon render us more sensitive and, used wisely, help us uncomplicate our lives so that fulfillment becomes a more realistic goal.

Herbes of the Moon include anise seed, ginger, jasmine, rowan and wintergreen.

Herbes of Mercury

Astrologers interpret the energy of natal Mercury as the way in which we use our five physical senses to gather information from the world around us. We make sense out of that information based upon the data that was collected earlier and stored in the brain. Just as Mercury (the deity) carries messages from the Underworld to the outer world so do our thoughts carry information between the inner and the outer worlds.

As one would expect, the planet Mercury is corresponded with much of the brain's activity, as well as with the nervous system and sensory nerves. These sensory nerves include those of sight, hearing, tactile nerves, and organs associated with the production of sound. The organs of taste are more likely to be associated with Venus (although this is open to question). The entire respiratory system and the thyroid are found corresponded with Mercury as well. Some practitioners include the hands, fingers and their dexterity under Mercury's realm while others place all movement with Mars. Astrologers, even medical astrologers, are not as consistent as one would expect.

Physiological conditions found under Mercury include one's mental alertness and predisposition to disorders of speech and/or of the nervous system. Impediments of speech, whether physiological or psychological, are often studied as afflictions of the natal Mercury. One's ability to remember things or to retrieve information from the bins of frequently misfiled data within one's mind are mercurial in nature.

By nature mercurial herbes are androgynous, neither Yin nor Yang, feminine nor masculine. They are dualistic in energy and are metaphorically dry. They represent an energy which moves quickly within the physiological and psychological systems.

The herbes of Mercury will, generally, stimulate and improve one's mental alertness. They help us better understand that which our physical body is perceiving. They allow us to better draw upon our memories and gain a more complete grasp of our present reality. These are useful herbes when one must turn to the processes of logic, when communication is a key element along the path to success. When one's mind seems all a-whirl, these herbes may help us find the needed facts among the internal chaos of emotion and illusion.

Students benefit from mercurial herbes, finding improvement in their comprehension and in an increased retention of information. We are able to stay more focused when reading a text. Herbes of Mercury are of value to those whose lives involve the written or spoken word. Authors and poets, those who write ritual verse and students who must express their comprehension on paper using their own words are among the many who will find benefit from using these herbes.

Used ritually, the herbes of Mercury can help us move our consciousness between the worlds. Those who wish to retrieve lost information from past civilizations, those seeking to hear the voices of the holy ones, those who seek to be a medium through which a spiritual being may speak, all will find their work enhanced with these herbes.

What does it mean to be psychic? It means bringing back information through one's spiritual sensitivity and translating it through the conduit of one's consciousness. Herbes of Mercury may help you move more easily between the inner and outer worlds when mixed in combination with herbes of the Moon. This mixture is ideal when one wishes to function in a spiritually receptive or intuitive manner.

The process of using one's psychic energy as an active principle involves taking the images within one's mind and projecting them to another being or location. A formula of herbes which combines herbes of Mercury with those of the Sun allows you to increase your conscious focus during these mental processes.

Many students express a desire to increase their levels of discipline. Creating a mixture of mercurial herbes with those of Saturn brings a mature magick to one's mental processes. This combination will help you avoid distraction and stay focused upon your work.

Herbes of Mercury include cedar, fennel, licorice, marjoram and sedge.

Herbes of Venus

We study Venus in a natal chart in order to interpret how the individual derives pleasure and fulfillment from the surrounding environment. This includes the appreciation of things of beauty both in the arts and from nature. Venus is interpreted to understand one's joy of living and may well include many issues surrounding romance. Venus is a planet with a passionate climate just as we are often passionate about our loves and our lives.

Venus' correspondences with anatomy include the throat, for Venus is the planet assigned as the ruler of Taurus. Through Venus' association with Libra, Venus is linked with the kidneys. As a planet which indicates one's aesthetic values, Venus is corresponded with the skin, cheeks and hair. Other anatomical aspects of Venus include the veins and tactile system (but not quite the same aspect of this function as assigned to Mercury). Modern astrology has added the thyroid, parathyroid and thymus.

Afflictions (aspects with other planets which cause the natal Venus to malfunction) of Venus can lead the native into dysfunctional sexual behavior which may lead to the contraction of venereal diseases. Other health issues corresponded with Venus include diseases of the urinary and/or reproductive systems. Many of these illnesses are induced by feelings of loneliness or despair. One's ability to find pleasure in life is essential for good health. Herbes of Venus will help strengthen this virtue.

By nature the herbes of Venus are feminine, gentle and relaxing.

They promote a loving aura about the individual which helps calm one's being so that one can settle down and enjoy the beauty of life. These herbes bring a warmth of spirit to one's being which enhances our ability to draw goodness from the world around us. They help us experience an improved inner balance and harmony.

Venusian herbes work with the energies of attraction. From one perspective they can make one feel more attractive which, in turn, increases natural beauty and increases our appeal to others. From another perspective they are able to help us attract those qualities, people or objects which appeal to our aesthetic sense.

Herbes of Venus may be combined with those of the Sun in order to stimulate a more likeable quality in our personality and make us more appealing to others. They make us more amiable and promote the type of personality which is found to be a pleasure in the lives of others. When combined with lunar herbes we become more sensitive to the beauty of our own inner, spiritual self. The interaction of herbes of the Moon with those of Venus helps one become comfortable with one's emotions, learning to work with them so that they become a source of goodness and fulfillment.

When combining venusian and mercurial herbes we may brighten a dour outlook, perk up a sense of humor and find we are better able to avoid nagging thought patterns. Herbes of Venus combined with those of Mars add a sense of romance about life. They can help us develop the ability to find fulfillment through one's labor. This mixture brings together the feminine and masculine polarities in a different manner than found in the solar-lunar balance.

Bringing herbes of Venus together with those of Jupiter may make the role of provider more pleasurable. This mixture may bring a sense of internal understanding to the process involved in working at a job to provide the resources needed for survival. This combination increases one's sense of generosity.

When herbes of Saturn are mixed with those of Venus we may gain access to the discipline needed to achieve success as an artist. This mixture should be used with care for Saturn's edge may be too difficult to handle for Venus' comfort.

The herbal combination of venusian and uranian herbes is particularly joyous in nature. Used wisely it can open one to the divine sparks of inspiration while finding enough pleasure in the process to follow a project through to completion. While herbes of Venus lend an aura of amiability and allow us the skills which make others comfortable, the addition of herbes of Uranus add an element of spontaneity, wit and charm.

Herbes of Venus can be combined with those of Neptune should you wish to expand your awareness and sensitivity within the astral. This is the type of energy which enhances our ability to see the divine light which radiates throughout all of nature, and allows you to feel bathed in that same natural beauty.

When working with the elderly or with the very young, herbes of Venus combined with herbes of Pluto can help us move beyond our personal identification with our peers in order to perceive reality from the perspective of a far different generation.

Workable herbes of Venus include birch, coltsfoot, elder, rose geranium and thyme.

Herbes of Mars

Astrologically, Mars describes the manner in which we bring our ideas and desires into manifestation through the exertion of physical activity. In a natal chart Mars is a key element to one's drive, agility and the nature of one's physical energy.

Anatomically this energy corresponds with the muscular system, motor nerves and the production of adrenalin. Astrologers look to Mars' placement in a natal chart to describe how an individual pursues many aspects of sexual fulfillment. Medical astrology includes the external sexual organs in the correspondence with Mars.

Diseases which induce a fever are sometimes associated with Mars, such as smallpox. We also find outbreaks of herpes in this correspondence. Due to the sexual nature of Mars' energy, sexually transmitted diseases correspond with Mars as well. Accidents caused by a lack of coordination are frequently timed with a transit by celestial Mars across a natal planet. Another condition associated with Mars is the general levels of energy or fatigue one may be dealing with at a particular time in life.

By nature the herbes of Mars are masculine in energy and are considered hot, dry and energetic. They frequently cause an increase in energy or heat, even if only in a metaphorical sense. They ought, generally, to be used with temperance. In excess they make it more difficult to control one's emotions. An excess of Mars' energy can lead to behavior patterns perceived as confrontational or argumentative.

The nature of Mars within the individual as a spiritual archetype is that of primal energy which arises from the animal nature. No matter how sublime the human spirit one must remember that, while incarnate, that divine spirit is housed within an animal body. Herbes of Mars work with the spiritual aspect of the primal, for the animal is no less divine. The spiritually wise will take joy in knowing the self to be both human and animal, while seeing neither as better than the other.

The herbes of Mars often function as tonics, enhancing one's overall physical health. They must be used wisely for they add energy to all facets of one's being, including one's discomfort or tendency toward being disagreeable.

A combination of solar herbes with those of Mars adds strength and forcefulness to one's personality. They can increase independence and purpose. It is good, however, to already have developed a sense of direction in one's life. When combined with an inner spiritual knowledge they help us better understand the underlying drive our species has for survival and self-preservation.

Combining herbes of Mars with those of the Moon is a mixture one should not take lightly. This formula may empower our emotions and should only be done when we know ourselves well. A lack of emotional understanding or self-control can be further imbalanced by this mixture.

If one needs to put more energy into generating income or being a better provider of resources, herbes of Mars can be combined with those of Jupiter. It might be useful to add herbes of Uranus as well, in order to keep this drive from becoming so strong one becomes overly serious about life. The mixture of martial herbes with uranian herbes adds a sense of fun to life and allows things to occur with an increased sense of delight and spontaneity.

Discipline and focus can be enhanced by combining herbes of Mars with those of Saturn. This mixture should be used for limited periods of time and balanced with periods during which recreation and pleasures are enjoyed.

Magickally we may combine herbes of Mars with those of Neptune in order to bring our dreams into manifestation. And we may combine martial herbes with herbes of Pluto to allow our deeper desires to surface and have expression.

A few good herbes of Mars (and there are many!) include basil, benzoin, germander, loosestrife, nettles and pine.

Herbes of Jupiter

We interpret Jupiter's natal chart position to help us understand where we need to expand our outlook in order to have increased access to resources. Jupiter, the first of the giant, gaseous planets gives off more energy than it receives. It is not surprising that this planet has represented concepts of generosity and benevolence to wise people for many thousands of years. Despite its turbulent atmosphere, it reflects the Sun brightly, shining in the night sky as if it were a beautiful, serene star. Working with (rather than against) a mature Jupiter energy in one's natal chart gives the individual more energy with which to approach life.

Anatomical correspondences include the storage of body fats, the pancreas, the liver, and the production of insulin including the entire adrenalin-producing system. As the ruling planet of Sagittarius, the thighs are also associated with Jupiter.

Among other facets of the human body, the arterial circulatory system is corresponded with Jupiter and, as a consequence, afflictions associated with this planet include arteriosclerosis. Other afflictions include diseases of the liver, strokes, complications of the sinuses and, according to some, extreme inflammation of the throat. Other conditions include a sense of depression such as when the good things of life seem out of reach or when financial worries are a great burden and no relief is believed available.

By nature the herbes of Jupiter are warm and moist. They promote an expansive quality to one's nature accompanied with a more positive outlook. They are good for the spiritual aspect of one's incarnate being and are masculine yet nurturing. Used wisely, herbes of Jupiter may promote moderation.

As so many often need, jovian herbes can help us increase our income, provided we make the appropriate changes in our philosophy of life so that we provide a balanced environment in which this resourcefulness can mature. Astrology teaches us that opportunities are present at all times in our life if we are aware of our environment and avoid becoming caught up in our personal travails. The ritual use of herbes of Jupiter can provide much assistance in this process, helping us open our minds to new ideas which will show us how and where to apply our energy. Herbes of Jupiter work well when the practitioner has a mature, responsible understanding of life. Should a person be functioning without maturity (wanting money to fix problems which are caused by financial irresponsibility), herbes of Jupiter point the way to make needed changes in ideals and priorities. Those who are greedy or selfish are almost never able to see these opportunities which the Universe is providing.

Herbes of Jupiter are able to teach us how to better treat our bodies, recognizing that our bodies are the temples for our divinity during this incarnation. Jovian herbes help you see that your body is a valuable resource and tool. These herbes assist us in maintaining these tools in order to have a productive and rewarding existence.

Those who pursue a religious understanding may incorporate these herbes to gain an understanding of the larger cycles in the evolution of the human species; allowing them to see the patterns which form as religious beliefs evolve over many thousands of years. Jovian herbes bring an understanding of the larger laws, those which are universal and apply to all beings. Herbes of Jupiter provide us insight regarding social customs. They help us understand the place of religious and magickal ritual in life as seen from the perspective of the divinity of the Universe.

Those who hold public office, whether as spiritual leaders or as public servants, would benefit from the herbes of Jupiter for they increase one's tactfulness and promote a compassionate understanding coupled with mature objectivity.

The combination of solar and jovian herbes would be excellent for any clergy person or for a professional entrusted with the emotional or psychological healing of another. This mixture helps promote the presence needed to encourage trust.

It is often advisable to add mercurial herbes to those of Jupiter as this helps bring into consciousness the intangible, philosophical growth one can achieve with jovian herbes. Some believe that this combination increases one's intuitive understanding of the great spiritual avatars whose words have shaped human destiny.

Combinations of herbes of Jupiter with those of Saturn provide the practitioner with a greater work ethic and maturity regarding one's career. They help one understand the discipline essential in order to achieve success.

When adding herbes of Uranus to those of Jupiter, one's ability to find delight in the simplest aspects of life is increased. This mixture is beneficial in keeping us from taking life too seriously.

Herbes of Jupiter can be added to those of Neptune but maturity and wisdom are needed to understand the reality of the information arriving through one's dreams and intangible senses. When one wishes to bring forth one's latent desires, adding herbes of Pluto to Jovian herbes can be beneficial.

Good herbes which bring forth the energy of Jupiter include avens, borage, dandelion, hyssop and sandalwood.

Herbes of Saturn

Although Saturn is regarded by many people as representative of undesirable energy and unpleasant experiences, the nature of Saturn's energy in a natal chart and in our lives provides us with the lessons required for our survival. The Universe is wise, recognizing that we do not learn and grow when things are easy but require occasional pruning if we are to become strong and endure. The lessons of Saturn teach us discipline and character.

In medical astrology, Saturn is associated with the hard structures within the body such as the skeletal system, the knees, joints and even the teeth. Saturn is further corresponded with the mineral salts needed by our bodies. Many (but not all) associate Saturn with the gall bladder and skin. Saturn is associated not with the sensory perception of sound but with the inner ear and the physical organs required for hearing.

Problems with hearing are considered a Saturn affliction, as are gallstones or stones in the kidney or bladder. Structural difficulties with one's joints (arthritis and rheumatism) or with one's bones are associated with Saturn (although accidents are more likely to correspond with a Mars transit). Among the many disparate diseases associated with Saturn are tuberculosis, gout, wasting diseases and palsy. Loss of memory is also considered Saturnian although not when it is part of the natural process of aging.

By nature the herbes of Saturn are binding, cold and without moisture. Herbes of Saturn help provide us with structure. You may think of them as helping crystalize one's ideas or goals. They can also be restrictive and help provide a clear focus. They keep us well grounded, preventing us from getting lost wandering in the clouds.

Some maintain that saturnian herbes are masculine. However, I perceive them as being beyond gender and in the realm of the crone or of Cronus which are, in their aged wisdom, interchangeable in many aspects. Whether you prefer considering these herbes as having a masculine or feminine energy matters little, for they help you touch the wisdom of the ages, that which is only understood when you have faced the mysteries of death and accepted the mortality of your flesh. Only then will you begin to understand the immortality of your spirit.

Saturnian herbes help us achieve maturity. They teach us patience and demonstrate that our attachment to things or our unhealthy dependencies upon people, attitudes or situations will hold us from achieving our dreams. Herbes of Saturn help us learn how to prune our lives down to what is important, to the bare essentials and, as a consequence, help us discover our inner strength.

If there is any planetary correspondence of herbes which teaches us the wisdom of making change it is that found through Saturn. These herbes help us let go gracefully so that we can begin moving forward with our lives. Saturnian herbes will help you recognize what is needed to transcend your limitations. The most important lessons in life can be better understood with these herbes.

As well as helping us develop structure in our own lives, they also provide an understanding of the essential qualities of structure, whether it is found in the manifestation of our earth or within the energy of the Universe. Magickal or ritual work aimed toward manifestation within physical reality may be enhanced with herbes of Saturn, but in the process you must be willing to accept any lessons the Universe believes you need.

A combination of herbes of Saturn with those of Uranus tempts the Universe and should be used only with care. Not only does this ask the Universe to take her pruning shears to our lives but to do so with the unpredictability of Uranus.

Herbes of Neptune, when combined with those of Saturn, may help us distinguish between reality and fantasy, between those dreams which we should pursue and those dreams which are for diversion and should be considered harmless fantasy. When combining herbes of Pluto with those of Saturn, careful ritual work may enable us to better perceive the wisdom of the ages.

Saturnian herbes which are favorites and also safe to use include arnica, comfrey, hellebore, ivy and Solomon's seal.

Herbes of Uranus

In astrology, Uranus helps us understand where to let go, and how to take chances and keep life fun. Often interpreted as that point in a natal chart where access to inspiration is found, the energy brought into a person's life during a transit of celestial Uranus can often be change for the sake of change. Healthy Uranus energy in one's life keeps it playful.

As the ruling planet of Aquarius, Uranus is associated with the circulatory system, and with the gasses contained within the blood and within the body's cells. Uranus is also corresponded with the pupils of one's eyes, the nervous system and the natural energy triggered by the impulses between nerves which communicate sensations. Uranus' correspondence includes the field of energy which is generated by the brain.

Medical conditions associated with Uranus include varicose veins, narcolepsy and difficulties which arise when one is too easily bored and requires an abnormal amount of stimulus. Some types of chemical imbalances and seizures, and many types of dysfunctional behavior, are associated with Uranus as well.

By nature the herbes of Uranus are androgynous, highly active, stimulating and dry. They promote alertness by keeping life a little off-balance and unpredictable. Uranian herbes stimulate one's sense of curiosity.

Working magickally with herbes of Uranus stimulates our imagination, helping us find ways to have fun while being productive and mature. They help provide play space for the child within.

These herbes are good for social situations, helping us enjoy the company of others by making it easier to explore other's interests. Events we might otherwise find dull and tedious can become more lively when we learn how to ask questions and treat each person as unique and interesting. Herbes of Uranus may be included in food served at a gathering for they work as a natural stimulant to the energy of a group, adding a cheery atmosphere to the situation.

When adding solar herbes to those of Uranus we learn to lighten up and not take our egos too seriously. They allow us to view life through a twinkling eye and balance serious work with time for the childlike quality of one's spiritual being.

A mixture of lunar and uranian herbes can help pry us loose from a mental rut, allowing us to be more spontaneous in our approach to life. This can be an exciting energy when one needs to have creativity and develop new ideas.

Inspiration is likely to be stimulated by the interaction of mercurial herbes with those of Uranus. They should be used judiciously for an excess of this combined energy can cause a person to be too easily distracted and lose all sense of focus.

Herbes of Mars combine well with those of Uranus and are useful when we have become staid and need to break free, when we need a creative manner to get a job done. They are also useful for those who have become burdened with feelings of guilt.

Herbes of Uranus mixed with those of Neptune create a good balance when one is a student of dreams, provided one has disciplined sleeping habits. They can help us move from passive dreaming to those realms of magick which occur when our conscious mind is at rest.

Adding herbes of Pluto to those of Uranus may be useful when dealing with individuals much younger than yourself or those of a venerable age who the Universe has entitled to live in a reality not consistent with that of society.

Among the herbes of Uranus we find allspice, elfwort, ginseng, spikenard and true unicorn root.

Herbes of Neptune

Neptune provides the astrologer with information about the nature of one's dreams and fantasies. The word *illusion* is often associated with the manifest energy of this giant planet.

Neptune's anatomical correspondences include the kidneys, bladder and urinary system. It is also corresponded with the pineal gland and the parathyroid. Fibrous nerves and the spinal canal are sometimes associated with Neptune by modern practitioners.

Infections within the kidney, bladder or related problems are associated with Neptune. Some types of chemical imbalances and difficulties in maintaining a grasp of reality are also associated with this illusive energy.

By nature herbes of Neptune are feminine and moist. They can be illusory and, if one does not stay grounded in reality, can actually hold one back in life. They help open us to our imagination and to our dreams.

Herbes of Neptune assist in working within the astral. They can help one let go of structured thinking and concrete mental images, allowing one to slip into *the dreaming*, as it is called by the Aborigine people of Australia. At the same time they have the ability to lead one into an illusion within astral work. Herbes of Neptune are best worked with when balanced with herbes that keep you grounded, providing a solid grasp of reality.

Many of the herbes of Neptune have been used in religious ceremonies, for they are capable of inducing divine visions. While it is tempting to dabble within the realm of visionary luxury, such practices require very infrequent use following extensive preparation of one's body. When used by the priests or priestesses of past times, such rites followed fasting, training and, frequently, abstinence from worldly contact and activity (including sexual pleasures).

Herbes of Pluto can be combined with those of Neptune but the effects are very subtle and easily missed by the average person.

Solar or mercurial herbes may increase one's awareness of these changes, those which help us touch our most secret dreams.

Good neptunian herbes include citrus, cypress, lotus, passion flower and willow.

Herbes of Pluto

Astronomers know the least about Pluto. Our space probes have barely begun to retrieve information from this most distant astrological planet from the Sun. Pluto's existence was verified in 1930 and it has taken astrologers considerable time to study Pluto and its transits. In natal astrology we interpret Pluto in order to describe aspects of the self which are the furthest removed from the light of our consciousness. Moving very slowly, Pluto's energy extends beyond the realm of the individual and has much to do with the way in which a generation (all those born while Pluto is in a given constellation) determines its own standards of behavior and morality.

Anatomical correspondences include the various organs of the reproductive system, among them the uterus, vagina, testicles, penis and related reproductive organs. Diseases and afflictions associated with Pluto are, obviously, those which may affect these organs. Sexual dysfunction may be indicated by planetary energy which creates conflicts with the natal Pluto as well. Other conditions which are considered connected with Pluto include impotency and, possibly, certain of the chemical imbalances which affect behavior.

By nature the herbes of Pluto are moist, potent and procreative in their energy. They are capable of easing the individual through a long-term transition.

The herbes of Pluto touch the abyss which exists within one's own soul. One of your own mysteries, deeply buried even from self-awareness, is a secret image of the person you would be if your dreams came true. Herbes of Pluto help bring about the procreation of these desires and can help us evolve into the reality of our desires. Never a quick process, it is an evolution one can perceive only when stepping back and looking at the changes made over a period of years.

These herbes provide us with access to some of the mysteries of the Universe as well. If we but let them, they will teach us about the ways in which a species seeks to preserve itself. They will also teach us that we will, indeed, return again to incarnate realities.

Herbes of Pluto can be combined with those of the Sun when one is seeking to create a new self-image in pursuit of the ideal of one's dreams. Lunar herbes can be combined with those of Pluto to help one become more sensitive to one's deepest desires and the underlying motives behind one's feelings. The herbes of Pluto can be combined with mercurial herbes when seeking to bring our deeper self to the surface, but we recommend a small amount of solar herbes be added to ensure being able to bring this information into the conscious mind.

Adding herbes of Pluto to those of Venus and/or Mars would increase one's lust for life and one's sensual desires. It may, however, also bring to the surface latent sexual desires. Combining herbes of Jupiter with those of Pluto can be most useful when one desires to create new ways in which to provide for one's self. Saturnian and plutonian herbes mix well if one seeks to learn more of the crone and her deeper mysteries. Combining herbes of Pluto with those of Uranus or of Neptune produce very subtle results which can be highly individualized if one has thorough ritual experience.

This exquisite blend of the spiritual nature of rebirth with the sexual needs of a species can be balanced through plutonian herbes. Through working with the herbes associated with Pluto we are able to gain access to some of the wisdom usually available only through age. These herbes help us bridge the differences between generations.

Plutonian herbes include asafoetida, damiana, eucalyptus, patchouli and toadflax.

Planetary Correspondences

This is an alphabetical listing of herbes grouped by planet. Herbes marked with an * in this and the subsequent lists of correspondences are those which have been assigned more than one planetary signature by various authors. Some Herbes are marked ** to denote the traditional planetary correspondence preferred by the

Master Herbalists of The Hermit's Grove.

Sun

acacia (*Acacia sp*)   *
almond (*Amygdalus communis*)   **
angelica (*Angelica archangelica*)
arum (*Arum maculatum*)   *
ash (*Fraxinus excelsior*)   **
bay laurel (*Laurus nobilis*)   **
bergamot (*Monarda didyma*)   *
birch (*Betula alba*)   *
broom (*Cytisus scoparius*)   *
burnet (great) (*Sanguisorba officinalis*)
butterbur (*Petasites vulgaris*)
butterbur (*Tussilago petasites*)
carob (*Jacaranda procera*)   *
catsfoot (*Antennaria dioica*)
celandine (greater) (*Chelidonium majus*)
centaury (*Erythræa centaurium*)
chamomile (*Anthemis nobilis*)   *
chamomile (*Anthemis matricaria*)
cinnamon (*Cinnamomum zeylanica*) *
crocus (*Crocus sativa*)
dwarf red rattle (*Pedicularis sylvatica*)
English sarsaparilla (*Smilax sp.*)
eyebright (*Euphrasia officinalis*)
false acacia (*Robinia pseudacacia*)
false saffron (*Carthamus tinctorius*) *
fern (bracken) (*Pteris aquilina*)   **
frankincense (*Boswellia thurifera*)
frostwort (*Helianthemum canadense*)
gnaphaliums (*Gnaphalium sp.*)
juniper (*Juniperus communis*)   *
life-everlasting (*Antennaria margaritaceum*)

locust (*Robinia pseudacacia*)
lovage (*Levisticum officinale*)
marigold (*Calendula officinalis*)
marsh marigold (*Caltha palustris*)   *
mayweed (*Anthemis cotula*)
mayweed (*Pyrethrum parthenium*)   *
mistletoe (*Viscum album*)   *
moss rose (*Helianthemum canadense*)
myrrh (*Commiphora myrrha*)   *
oats (*Avena sativa*)   *
olibanum (*Boswellia thurifera*)
olive (*Olea Europæa*)
peony (*Pæonia officinalis*)
pimpernel (*Anagallis arvensis*)   *
rice (*Oryza sativa*)
rock rose (*Helianthemum canadense*)
rosemary (*Rosmarinus officinalis*)
rue (*Ruta graveolens*)   **
safflower (*Carthamus tinctorius*)   *
saffron (*Crocus sativa*)
Saint Joan's wort (*Hypericum perforatum*)
Saint John's wort (*Hypericum perforatum*)
shepherd's knot (*Potentilla tormentilla*)
storax (*Liquidambar orientalis*)
sundew (*Drosera rotundifolia*)
sunflower (*Helianthus annus*)
tormentil (*Potentilla tormentilla*)
vine (*Vitis vinifera*)
walnut (*Juglans sp.*)

Moon

acanthus (*Acanthus sp.*)
adder's tongue (*Erythronium Americanum*)
adder's tongue (*Ophioglossum vulgatum*)
agar agar (*Gelidium amansii*)   *
American boxwood (*Cornus florida*)
anise seed (*Pimpinella anisum*)

anserina (*Galium aparine*)
ash (mountain) (*Sorbus americana*)
ash (mountain) (*Sorbus aucuparia*)
bamboo (*Bambusa vulgaris*)   *
boxwood (American) (*Cornus florida*)
burnet (small) (*Pimpinella saxifraga*)
cabbage (*Brassica oleracea*)
camphor (*Cinnamomum camphora*)

cashew (Anacardium occidentale) *
chickweed (Stellaria media)
clary (Salvia sclarea)
cleavers (Galium aparine)
coconut (Cocos nucifera)
coolwort (Tiarella cordifolia)
coriander (Coriandrum sativum) *
cucumber (Cucumis sativa)
dog rose (Rosa canina)
dog's tooth violet (Erythronium americanum)
dog's tooth violet (Erythronium dens canis)
dogwood (Piscidia erythrina) *
duckweed (Lens palustris)
eucalyptus (Eucalyptus globulus) *
flag (Iris versicolor)
fleur-de-lis (Iris pallida)
ginger (Zingiber officinale)
goose grass (Galium aparine)
hibiscus (white) (Hibiscus sp.)
holly (sea) (Eryngium maritimum)
holy herb (Eriodictyon glutinosum) *
iris (Iridaceæ sp.)
Irish moss (Chondrus crispus) *
lettuce (Lactuca sp.)
lilac (white) (Syringa vulgaris candida)
lily (madonna) (Lilium candidum)
loosestrife (Lysimachia sp.) **
milk thistle (Silybum marianum)
moonwort (Boptrychium lunaria)
mouse ear (Hieracium pilosella) *
myrrh (Commiphora myrrha) *
orris (Iris florentina)
orris (Iris pallida)
pau d'arco (Tahebuia altissima) **
poppy (Papaver sp.) *
privet (Ligustrum vulgare)

pumpkin (Cucurbita pepo)
purslane (Portulaca sp.)
Queen Elizabeth root (Iris florentina)
rattle grass (Rhinanthus sp.)
rhododendron (Rhododendron chrysanthrum)
rose (white) (Rosa sp. (alba))
rose (wild) (Rosa canina)
rowan (Sorbus americana)
rowan (Sorbus aucuparia)
saxifrage (Pimpinella saxifraga)
sea salt (Sal maritimum)
sedum (Sedum acre)
sedum (Sedum album)
sedum (Sedum telephium)
sesame (Sesamum sp.)
siegesbeckia (Siegesbeckia orientalis)
snowdrop (Galanthus nivalis)
squaw vine (Mitchella repens)
star anise (Illicum verum) *
star of Bethlehem (Ornithogalum umbellatum)
starweed (Stellaria media)
stonecrop (Sedum album)
tamarind (Tamarindus indica) *
tapioca (Jatropha manihot)
thistle (milk) (Silybum marianum)
turnip (Brassica rapa) **
veronica (Veronica sp.) *
wallflower (Cherranthus sp.)
watercress (Nasturtium officinale)
water lily (Nymphæa odorata)
wild celery (Apium graveolens)
willow (Salix alba) **
willos (Salix sp.) *
wintergreen (Gaultheria procumbens)
wintergreen (Pyrola minor)
yellow flag (Iris pseudoacorus)
yerba santa (Eriodictyon glutinosum) *

Mercury

agaric (Amanita muscaria) *
all heal (Valeriana officinalis)
almond (Amygdalus communis) *
anemone (Anemone pulsatilla)
azaleas (Azalea sp.)
balloon flower (Platycodon grandi-

florus)
bamboo (Bambusa vulgaris) *
bayberry (Myrica ceriferia)
bittersweet (Solanum dulcamara) *
buckwheat (Polygonum fagopyrum) *
calamint (Calamintha officinalis)

caraway (Carum carvi)
carrots (Daucus carota)
cascara (Rhamnus purshianus)
cassia (Cinnamomum cassia)
cedar (Cedrus atlanticus)   *
cedar (Thuja occidentalis)   *
celery (Apium graveolens)
Chinese lanterns (Physalis alkekengi)
cinquefoil (Potentilla reptans)   *
clover (Trifolium sp.)   **
coffee (Coffea arabica)   *
cranesbill (Geranium maculatum)
day lily (Lilium sp.)
dill (Peucedanum graveolens)
elecampagne (Inula helenium)   *
elfwort (Inula helenium)   *
fennel (Fœniculum vulgare)
fenugreek (Trigonella fœnum-græcum)
fern (Pteris aquilina)   *
fern (maidenhair) (Adiantum capillus-
    veneris)
five-leaf grass (Potentilla reptans)   *
flax (Linum usitatissimum)   *
gentian (Gentiana sp.)   *
geranium (scented) (Geranium)
goat's rue (Galega officinalis)
good Henry (Mercurialis annua)
gorse (Ulex europæus)   *
hare's foot (Pes leporinus)
hare's foot (Trifolium arvense)
hazel nut (Corylus avellana)
honeysuckle (Lonicera caprifolium)   *
honeywort (Cerinthe major)
horehound (Marrubium vulgare)
hound's-tongue (Cynoglossum offici-
    nale)   *
Jacob's ladder (Polemonium cœruleum)
lady's slipper (Cypripedium pubescens) *
lanterns (Physalis alkekengi)
lavender (Lavendula vera)
licorice (Glycyrrhiza glabra)

lignum vitae (Thuja occidentalis)   *
lily-of-the-valley (Convallaria magalis)
linseed (Linum usitatissimum)   *
mace (Myristica fragrans)
mandrake (Atropa mandragora)   **
marjoram (Origanum marjorana)   *
May lily (Convallaria magalis)
meadowsweet (Spiræa ulmaria)   *
melilot (Melilotus officinalis)
melilot (Trifolium melilotus)
mezereon (Daphne mezereum)   *
mountain grape (Berberis aquifolium)
mulberry (Morus nigra)
myrtle (Myrtus communis)
papyrus (Cyperus papyrus)
parsley (Carum petroselinum)   *
parsnips (Heracleum sphondylium)
parsnips (Pastinaca sativa)
pellitory (Anacyclus pyrethrum)   *
pellitory-of-the-wall (Parietaria offici-
    nalis)
pomegranate (Punica granatum)   *
potentilla (Potentilla sp.)   *
sassafras (Sassafras officinale)
savory (Satureia hortensis)
saw palmetto (Serrenoa serrulata)
sedge (Acorus calamus)
senna (Cassia acutifolia)
senna (bladder) (Colutea sp.)
southernwood (Artemisia abrotanum)
spurge (Euphorbia sp.)   **
starwort (Aster sp.)
tea (Camillia thea)
trefoil (Trifolium)   **
turmeric (Curcuma longa)
valerian (Valeriana officinalis)
white balsam (Gnaphalium poly-
    cephalum)
winter cherry (Physalis alkekengi)
woody nightshade (Solanum dul-
    camara)   *

Venus

alder (Alnus glutinosa)   *
alkanet (Alkanna tinctoria)
apple (Pyrus malus)   *
apple blossom (Pyrus malus)

apricot (Prunus armeniaca)   *
balm of Gilead (Commiphora opobal-
    samum)
beans (Phaseolus vulgaris)

bedstraw (*Galium verum*)
bergamot (*Monarda didyma*) **
birch (*Betula alba*) **
birthwort (*Aristolochia longa*)
bishop's weed (*Ægopodium poda-graria*)
bishop's weed (*Ammi majus*)
blackberry (*Rubus fructicosus*)
bleeding heart (*Dicentra spectabilis*)
blites (*Amaranthus blitus*)
bloodroot (*Sanguinaria canadensis*) *
boneset (*Eupatorium perfoliatum*)
buck's horn plantain (*Plantago coronopus*) *
bugle (*Ajuga reptans*) *
burdock (*Arctium lappa*)
burning bush (*Dictamnus albus*)
catnip (*Nepeta cataria*)
cherry (*Prunus serotina*)
cherry laurel (*Prunus laurocerosus*)
cherry (wild) (*Prunus virginiana*)
chickpease (*Cicer arietinum*)
clover (*Trifolium sp.*) *
cocoa (*Theobroma cacao*)
coltsfoot (*Tussilago·farfara*)
columbine (*Aquilegia vulgaris*)
cornflower (*Centaurea cyanus*) *
cowslip (*Primula veris*)
cudweed (*Gnaphalium sp.*)
currants (*Ribes vulgaris*) *
currants (*Vitis vinifera*)
daffodil (*Narcissus pseudo-narcissus*) **
daisies (*Bellis perennis*)
dittany (white) (*Dictamnus alba*)
dittany of Crete (*Dictamnus creticus*)
dog's mercury (*Mercurialis perennis*)
dropwort (*Spiræa filipendula*)
dwarf elder (*Sambucus ebulus*)
elder (*Sambucus nigra*)
fairy cups (*Primula veris*)
feverfew (*Chrysanthemum parthenium*)
figwort (*Scrophylaria sp.*)
fleabane (*Erigeron sp.*)
fleabane (*Inula dysenterica*)
fleabane (*Senecio vuilgaris*)
foxglove (*Digitalis purpurea*) **
fraxinella (*Dictamnus albus*)

gardenia (*Gardenia sp.*)
gelsemium (*Gelsemium nitidum*) *
geranium (*Geranium sp.*)
goldenrod (*Solidago sp.*)
golden seal (*Hydrastis canadensis*)
gooseberry (*Ribes grossularia*)
goose grass (*Galium aparine*)
gosmore (*Hypochœris sp.*)
goutweed (*Ægopodium podagraria*)
groundsel (*Senecio vuilgaris*)
heather (*Calluna vulgaris*)
heather (*Erica sp.*)
herb true-love (*Paris quadrifolia*) *
hibiscus (pink) (*Hibiscus sp.*)
hibiscus (red) (*Hibiscus sp.*)
hollyhock (*Althæa rosea*)
impatiens (*Impatiens aurea*) *
jewelweed (*Impatiens aurea*) *
kava kava (*Piper methysticum*) *
kidneywort (*Cotyledon umbilicus*) *
lady's mantle (*Alchemilla vulgaris*) *
lemon (*Citrus limonum*) *
lemon balm (*Melissa officinalis*)
lemongrass (*Cymbopogon citratus*)
lemon verbena (*Lippia citriodorata*)
lentils (*Lens esculenta*)
lilac (mauve) (*Syringa vulgaris*)
mallows (*Malva sp.*)
marshmallow (*Althea officinalis*)
mercury (dog's) (*Mercurialis perennis*)
mints (*Mentha sp.*)
monarda (*Monarda punctata*)
motherwort (*Leonurus cardiaca*)
mugwort (*Artemisia vulgaris*) *
orach (*Artiplex patula*)
orchid (*Orchis sp.*)
paris herb (*Paris quadrifolia*) *
peaches (*Prunus persica*) *
pear (*Pyrus communis*) *
pennyroyal (*Mentha pulegium*)
pennywort (*Hydrocotyle vulgaris*)
peppermint (*Mentha piperita*)
periwinkle (*Vinca sp.*) *
plantain (*Plantago major*) **
plum (*Prunus domestica*) *
primrose (*Primula vulgaris*)
quince (*Pyrus cydonia*) *
ragweed (*Senecio vuilgaris*)

457

rampion (Campanula rapunculus)
raspberry (Rubus idæus)
rose (Rosa sp.)
rose geranium (Pelargonium capitatum)
rose geranium (Pelargonium graveolens)
rose geranium (Pelargonium roseum)
sage (Salvia officinalis)   *
satyrium (Orchis sp.)
sea holly (Eryngium maritimum)
self-heal (Prunella vulgaris)
sicklewort (Diapensia iapponica)
silverweed (Potentilla anserina)
skirret (Sium sisarum)
soapwort (Saponaria officinalis)   **
sorrel (Rumex sp.)
sowbread (Cyclamen hederæfolium)   *
sow thistle (Sonchus sp.)
speedwell (Veronica sp.)   *
strawberry (Amaranthus blitus)

strawberry (Fragaria vesca)
sycamore (Ficus sycomorus.)
tansy (Tanacetum vulgare)
teasel (Dipsacus sylvestris)
teazle (Dipsacus sylvestris)
thyme (Thymus vulgaris)
thyme (wild) (Thymus serpyllum)
trefoil (Trifolium sp.)   *
turkey corn (Dicentra canadensis)
verbena (Verbena officinalis)
vervain (Verbena officinalis)
violets (Viola odorata)
wheat (Triticum sp.)   *
wild arrach (Artiplex patula)
wild cherry (Prunus virginiana)
wild thyme (Thymus serpyllum)
woodruff (Asperula odorata)   *
wood betony (Betonica officinalis)   *
wood sage (Teucrium scorodonia)
yarrow (Achillea millefoium)

Mars

abscess root (Polemonium reptans)
acacia (gum) (Acacia sp.)
alder (Alnus glutinosa)   *
all heal (Prunella vulgaris)
aloes (Aloe sp.)   *
American mandrake (Podophyllum peltatum)
anemone (wood) (Anemone nemorosa)
araroba (Andira araroba)
arsesmart (Polygnum hydropiper)   *
asarabacca (Asarum europæum)
asclepias (Asclepiadaceæ)   *
bamboo (Bambusa vulgaris)   *
barberry (Berberis vulgaris)
basil (Ocymum basilium)
bay laurel (Pimenta racemosa)
bearberry (Arctostaphpylos uva-ursi)   *
beech (Fagus sylvatica)   *
benzoin (Styrax benzoin)
betel (Piper betel)
bitter wood (Picræna excelsa)
black cress (Sisymbrium nigra)
black pepper (Piper nigrum)

blessed thistle (Carduus benedictus)
bloodroot (Sanguinaria canadensis)   *
bluebells (Hyacinthus nonscriptus)   *
brooklime (Veronica beccabunga)   **
broom (Cytisus scoparius)   **
bryony (Bryonia sp.)   *
buckthorn (Rhamnus sp.)   *
cashew (Anacardium occidentale)   *
castor (Ricinus communis)
cat thyme (Teucrium marum)
cayenne (Capsicum minimum)
chilies (Capsicum minimum)
chives (Allium schœnoprasum)
cinchona (Cinchona succirubra)
clematis (Clematis recta)   *
coriander (Coriandrum sativum)   *
cotton thistle (Onopordon acanthium)
crawley root (Corallorhiza odontorhiza)
crowfoot (Ranunculus sp.)
cubeb (Piper cubeba)
cumin (Cuminum cyminum)
cyclamen (Cyclamen hederæfolium)
daffodil (yellow) (Narcissus pseudo-

narcissus)
double rocket (Hesperis matronalis)
dragon's blood (Dæmomorops draco) *
dragon's claw (Corallorhiza odontorhiza)
dysentery bark (Simaruba officinalis)
ephedra (Ephedra vulgaris)
euphorbia (Euphorbia sp.)
eveweed (Hesperis matronalis)
fireweed (Erechtites hieracifolia)
flaxweed (Linaria vulgaris)   *
fleabane (blue) (Erigeron acris)
furze (Europæus)   *
garlic (Allium sativum)
gentian (Gentiana sp.)   *
germander (Teucrium sp.)
ginkgo biloba (Salisburia adiantifolia)
goat's thorn (Astragalus gummifer)   **
ground pine (Ajuga chamæpitys)   *
guarana (Paulinia cupana)   *
gum dragon (Dæmomorops draco)   *
gum thistle (Euphorbia resinifera)
hawthorne (Cratægus oxyacantha)
holly (Ilex aquifolium)   *
holy thistle (Carduus benedictus)
honeysuckle (Lonicera caprifolium)   *
hops (Humulus lupulus)   *
horseradish (Cochlearia armoracia)
horsetongue (Ruscus hippoglossum)
hyacinth (Hyacinthus sp.)
indigo (Indigofera tinctoria)
Jesuits' powder (Cinchona succirubra)
juniper (Juniperus communis)   *
lady's mantle (Alchemilla vulgaris)   *
larkspur (Delphimium consolida)
laurel (Kalmia latifolia)   *
leeks (Allium sp.)
litmus (Rocella tinctoria)
loosestrife (Lysimachia sp.)   *
lupine (Lupinus sp.)
madder (Rubia tinctorium)
male fern (Dryopteris felix-mas)   *
marjoram (Origanum marjorana)   *
masterwort (Imperatoria ostruthium)
mastic (gum) (Pistacia lentiscus)
mastic (thyme) (Thymus mastichina)
matico (Piper angustifolium)
mayapple (Podophyllum peltatum)

mayblossom (Cratægus oxycantha)
mustard (Brassica sp.)
nettles (Urtica dioica)
onion (Allium cepa)
papaw (custard apple) (Asimina trilo-
  bata)
paprika (Croton annum)
parsley (Carum petroselinum)   *
pau d'arco (Tecoma conspicua)   *
peppers (Piper sp.)
Peruvian bark (Cinchona succirubra)
pilewort (Ranunculus ficaria)
pine (Pinaceæ sp.)   *
pipsissewa (Chimaphila umbellata)
plantain (Plantago major)   *
poison ivy (Rhus toxicodendron)
prickly ash (Xanthoxylum americanum)
quassia (Picræna excelsa)
radish (Raphanus sativus)
red root (Ceanothus americanus)
rheumatism weed (Chimapila umbellata)
rhubarb (Rheum sp.)
rocket (Eruca satova)
rue (Ruta graveolens)   *
salep (Orchis sp.)   *
saltwort (Salsola kali)
sanicle (Sanicula europæa)   *
sarsaparilla (Smilax ornata)
savine (Sabina cacumina)
savine (Sabina juniperus)
shepherd's rod (Dipsacus pilosus)
simaruba (Simaruba officinalis)
simson (Erigeron acris)
smartweed (Polygnum hydropiper)   *
snapdragon (Antirrhinum magus)
soapwort (Saponaria officinalis)   **
sowbread (Cyclamen hederæfolium)   **
sowerweed (Oxyria reniformis)
spikenard (Inula conyza)
spurge (Euphorbia sp.)   **
squill (Urginea scilla)
tallow tree (Sapium salicifolium)
tarragon (Artemisia cracunculus)
thistle (Carduus sp.)
thistle (Scotch) (Onopordon acanthium)

thorn (Cratægus oxyacantha)
toadflax (Linaria vulgaris) *
tobacco (Nicotiana tabacum)
toothcress (Dentaria bulbiferia)
tragacanth (Astragalus gummifer) **
uva ursi (Arctostaphylos uva-ursi) *
water pepper (Polygonum hydropiper) *
water pimpernel (Veronica bec-
    cabunga) *
woad (Ivatis tinctoria) *

woodruff (Asperula odorata) **
wormseed (Chenopodium anthelmin-
    ticum)
wormwood (Artemisia absinthium) *
yellow bugle (Ajuga chamæpitys) **
yellow daffodil (Narcissus pseudo-nar-
    cissus)
yerba santa (Eriodictyon glutinosum)**
yohimbe (Coryanthe yohimbe)

Jupiter

agrimony (Agrimonia eupatoria)
alexander (Smyrnium olisatrum)
alfalfa (Medicago sativa)
apple (Pyrus malus) *
arrowhead (Sagittaria sagittifolia)
arrow root (Maranta arundinaceæ)
asclepias (Asclepiadaceæ) *
asparagus (Asparagus officinalis)
asphodel (Asphodelus ramosus)
avens (Geum urbanum)
balm (Melissa officinalis)
balm melissa (Melissa officinalis)
balmony (Chelone glabra) *
banana (Musa paradisiaca)
betony (Betonica officinalis) *
bilberry (Vaccinium myrtillus) *
bitter root (Apocynum androsæmifo-
    lium)
bladderwrack (Fucus vesiculosis) *
borage (Borago officinalis)
cardamom (Elettaria cardamomum)
carob (Jacaranda procera) *
chervil (Anthriscus cerefolium)
chestnut (Castanea vesca)
cinquefoil (Potentilla reptans) **
coneflower (Echinacea angustifolia) *
costmary (Tanacetum balsamita)
couch grass (Agropyrum repens)
currants (Ribes vulgaris) *
dahlias (Dahlia variabilis)
dandelion (Taraxacum officinale)
datura (Datura stamonium)
dock (Rumex sp.)
dog grass (Agropyrum repens)
echinacea (Echinacea angustifolia) *

eglantine (Rosa rubiginosa)
endive (Cichorium endivia)
fig (Ficus carica)
five-leaf grass (Potentilla reptans) *
gelsemium (Gelsemium nitidum) *
goat's beard (Tragopogon sp.)
grapes (Vitis vinifera)
hare's ear (Bupleura rotundifolia)
hart's tongue (Asplenium scolopen-
    drium)
henna (Lawsonia alba)
herb bennet (Geum urbanum)
hounds-tongue (Cynoglossum offici-
    nale) *
houseleek (Sempervivum tectorum)
hyssop (Hyssopus officinalis)
Indian corn (Zea mays) *
jack-in-the-pulpit (Arum triphyllum)
jasmine (Jasminum officinale)
knapweed (Centaurea scabiosa) *
larch (Pinus larix)
lime (Citrus acida)
liverwort (Anemone hepatica)
lungwort (Sticta pulmonaria)
magnolia (Magnolia virginiana)
maize (Zea mays)
maple (Acer sp.)
meadowsweet (Spiræa ulmaria) *
milkweed (Apocynum androsæmifo-
    lium)
millet (Panicum miliaceum)
mistletoe (Viscum album) *
moneywort (Lysimachia nummularia)
myrrh (English) (Cicufaria odorata)
oak (Quercus sp.)

papaw (melon tree) (*Carica papaya*)
pine (*Pinus picea*)
pinks (*Matthiola sp.*)
plantain fruit (*Musa paradisiaca*)
pleurisy root (*Asclepias tuberosa*)
potentilla (*Potentilla sp.*) *
quack grass (*Agropyrum repens*)
rose hips (*Rosa canina*)
rudbeckia (*Echinacea angustifolia*) *
sage (*Salvia officinalis*) **
salsafy (*Tragopogon porrifolius*)
sandalwood (*Santalum album*)
scabious (*Scabiosa sp.*)
scurvey grass (*Cochlearia officinalis*)
sedum (*Sedum sp.*)
slippery elm (*Ulmus fulva*)
sphagnum moss (*Sphagnum cymbifo-
lium*)

spinach (*Spinacia oleracea*)
spruce (*Pinus picea*)
succory (*Chichorium sp.*)
sumac (*Rhus sp.*)
swallow wort (*Asclepias sp.*)
swamp milkweed (*Asclepsias incarnata*)
sweet briar (*Rosa rubiginosa*)
sweet cicely (*Myrrhis odorata*)
tamarac (*Larix americana*)
tamarind (*Tamarindus indica*) *
thornapple (*Datura stramonium*)
tragacanth (*Astragalus gummifer*) *
wake robin (*Arum triphyllum*)
wild turnip (*Arum triphyllum*)
wood betony (*Betonica officinalis*) **
yams (*Dioscorea villosa*) *

Saturn

aconite (*Aconitum napellus*)
adderwort (*Polygonum bistortum*)
amaranthus (*Amaranthus sp.*)
arnica (*Arnica montana*)
arsesmart (*Polygnum hydropiper*) *
asclepias (*Asclepiadaceæ*) *
bamboo (*Bambusa vulgaris*) *
baneberry (*Actæa spicata*)
barley (*Hordeum sp.*)
beech (*Fagus sylvatica*) *
beets (*Beta hortensis*)
belladonna (*Atropa belladonna*)
bindweed (*Convolvulus sp.*)
bird's foot (*Ornithopus perusillus*)
bistort (*Polygonum bistorta*)
black hellebore (*Helleborus niger*)
black willow (*Salix nigra*) *
bluebells (*Hyacinthus nonscriptus*) *
bottle brush (*Equisetum sp.*)
box (*Buxus sempervirens*) *
bruisewort (*Symphytum officinale*)
buck's horn plantain (*Plantago
coronopus*) *
buckthorn (*Rhamnus sp.*) **
calabar bean (*Physostigma venenosum*)
campion (*Cucubalus sp.*)
cannabis (*Cannabis sativa*) *

carob (*Jacaranda procera*) *
Chinese sumach (*Rhus vernicifera*)
Christmas rose (*Helleborus niger*)
clematis (*Clematis recta*) *
cocculus (*Anamirta paniculata*)
comfrey (*Symphytum officinale*)
cornflower (*Centaurea cyanus*) *
cramp bark (*Viburnum opulus*)
cress (*Iberis amara*)
crosswort (*Galium cruciata*)
cypress (*Cupressus*) *
daffodil (*Narcissus pseudo-narcissus*) *
devil's claw (*Harpagophytum procumbens*)
devil's garters (*Convvovulus arvensis*)
dodder (*Cuscutua europæa*)
dracontium (*Dracontium fœtidum*)
dracontium (*Symplocarpus fœtiidus*)
elm (*Ulmus campestris*)
evening primrose (*Œnothera biennis*)
false saffron (*Carthamus tinctorius*) *
fern (*Pteris aquilina*) *
flax (*Linum usitatissimum*) *
fleabane (*Erigeron canadense*)
fleawort (*Erigeron canadense*)
fumitory (*Fumaria officinalis*)
gall oak (*Quercus infectoria*)

461

green hellebore (Veratrum viride)
guelder rose (Viburnum opulus)
hawkweed (Hieracium sp.)
heartsease (Viola tricolor)
hellebore (Helleborus niger)
hemlock (Conium maculatum)
hemp (Cannabis sativa)   *
henbane (Hyoscyamus niger)
holly (Ilex aquifolium)   *
horsetail (Equisetum sp.)
Irish moss (Chondrus crispus)   *
itch weed (Veratrum viride)
ivy (Hedera helix)
juniper (Juniperus communis)   *
knapweed (Centaurea scabiosa)   *
knapwort (Centaurea jacea)
knot grass (Illecebrum verticillatum)
laburnum (Cystisus laburnam)
lady's seals (Polygonatum multiflorum)
laurel (Kalmia latifolia)
liverwort (Peltigera canina)
marijuana (Cannabis sativa)   *
meadow saffron (Colchicum autumnale)
meadowsweet (Spiræa ulmaria)   *
mezereon (Daphne mezereum)   *
monkshood (Aconitum napellus)
morning glory (Convolvulus sp.)
mountain laurel (Kalmia latifolia)
mouse ear (Hieracium pilosella)   *
mullein (Verbascum thapsus)
musk (Hibiscus abelmoschus)   *
nightshade (Solanum sp.)
paddock pipes (Equisetum sp.)
pansies (Viola tricolor)
pau d'arco (Tecoma conspicua)   *
periwinkle (Vinca sp.)   *
phytolacca (Phytolacca decandra)
poke root (Phytolacca decandra)
pomegranate (Punica granatum)   *
poplar (Populus sp.)
poppy (Papaver sp.)   *
potato (Solanum tuberosum)
pussy willow (Salix nigra)   *

quebracho (Aspidosperma quebracho-blanco)
queen's delight (Stillengia sylvatica)
quince (Pyrus cydonia)   **
ragwort (Senecio jacobæs)
rattlesnake root (Polygala senega)
royal fern (Osmunda regalis)
rupturewort (Herniaria sp.)
sabadilla (Veratrum sabadilla)
safflower (Carthamus tinctorius)   *
sassy bark (Erythrophlœum guineense)
scammony (English) (Convolvulus sp.)
sciatica (Iberis sisymbrium)
scopolia (Scopola carniolica)
scullcap (Scutellaria galericulata)   *
senega (Polygala senega)
shave grass (Equisetum sp.)
shepherd's purse (Capsella bursa-pastoris)
skunk cabbage (Dracontium fœtidum)
skunk cabbage (Symplocarpus fœtidus)
smartweed (Polygnum hydropiper)   *
snake root (Aristolochia serpentaria)
snakeweed (Plantago major)
Solomon's seal (Polygonatum multiflorum)
squaw tea (Ephedra vulgaris)
strophanthus (Strophanthus kombé)
sumbul (Ferula sumbul)
tamarisk (Tamarix gallica)
thorough leaf (Bupleurum campestris)
thrift (Armeria maritima)
tree of heaven (Ailanthus glandulosa)
Virginia creeper (Vitis hederacea)
water gladiole (Butomus umbellatus)
water pepper (Polygonum hydropiper) *
water violet (Hottonia palustris)
water yarrow (Hottonia palustris)   *
wild snowball (Viburnum opulus)   *
witch hazel (Hamamelis virginiana)
woad (Ivatis tinctoria)   *
wolf's bane (Aconitum napellus)
yew (Taxus baccata)

Uranus

allspice (Pimento officinalis)

American valerian (Cypripedium pu-

462

bescens)
ash (Fraxinus excelsior) *
bittersweet (Solanum dulcamara) *
black willow (Salix nigra) *
bluebells (Hyacinthus nonscriptus) *
buttercup (Ranunculus bulbosus)
cacao (Theobroma cacoa)
cedar (Cedrus atlanticus) *
cedar (Thuja occidentalis) *
chicory (Cichorium intybus)
Chinese anise (Illicum verum) *
cinnamon (Cinnamomum zeylanica) **
cloves (Eugenia caryophyllata)
coca leaves (Erythroxylon coca)
coffee (Coffea arabica) *
elecampagne (Inula helenium) *
elfwort (Inula helenium) *
flax (Linum usitatissimum)
galbanum (Ferula galbaniflua)
guiacum (Guiacum officinale)
herb true-love (Paris quadrifolia) **
kola nuts (Kola vera)
lady's slipper (Cypripedium pubescens)*
lignum vitae (Thuja occidentalis) *
linseed (Linum usitatissimum) *

logwood (Haematooxylon campeachianum)
mandrake (Atropa mandragora) *
marsh marigold (Caltha palustris) *
nard (Nardostachys jatamansi)
nard (Valeriana jatamansi)
nutmeg (Myristica fragrans)
paris herb (Paris quadrifolia) *
pellitory (Anacyclus pyrethrum) *
pimpernel (Anagallis arvensis) *
pomegranate (Punica granatum) *
pussy willow (Salix nigra) *
soap tree (Quillaja saponaria)
Spanish chamomile (Anthemis nobilis) *
spikenard (Inula conyza) *
star anise (Illicum verum) *
teak (Tectona grandis)
tonka bean (Dipteryx odorata)
tonquin bean (Dipteryx odorata)
trailing arbutus (Epigæa repens)
true Unicorn root (Aletris farinosa)
wild carrot (Daucus carota)
woody nightshade (Solanum dulcamara) *

Neptune

adam and eve root (Orchis sp.)
adrue (Cyperus articulatus)
apricot (Prunus armeniaca) *
arbutus (Arbutus sp.) *
arum (Arum maculatum) *
ash (Fraxinus excelsior) *
balmony (Chelone glabra) *
bladderwrack (Fucus vesiculosis) *
bogbean (Menyanthes trifoliata)
brooklime (Veronica beccabunga) *
bugle (Ajuga reptans) *
bur marigold (Bidens tripartita)
cabbage tree (Andira inermis)
cannabis (Cannabis sativa) *
cowbane (cicuta virosa)
cuckoo-pint (Arum maculatum)
cypress (Cupressus) *
dropwort (Enanthe phellandrium)
glasswort (Salsola sp.)
hemp (Cannabis sativa) *

impatiens (Impatiens aurea) *
jewelweed (Impatiens aurea) *
kidneywort (Cotyledon umbilicus) *
lemon (Citrus limonum) *
lobelia (Lobelia inflata)
lotus (Nymphæa lotus)
mare's tail (Hippuris vulgaris)
marijuana (Cannabis sativa) *
marsh trefoil (Menyanthes trifoliata)
marshwort (Helosciadium nodiflorum)
melons (Cucumis sp.)
mescal (Anhalonium lewinii)
mugwort (Artemisia vulgaris) *
narcissus (Narcissus sp.)
opium poppies (Papaver somniferum)
orange (Citrus aurantium)
osier (Cornus sericea)
passion flower (Passiflora incarnata)
peaches (Prunus persica) *
pear (Pyrus communis) *

463

peyote (Lophophora diffusa)
pitcher plant (Sarracenia purpurea)
plum (Prunus domestica)   *
psilocybin (Psylocybe sp.)
samphire (Crithmum maritimum)
sanicle (Sanicula europæa)   *
sea fennel (Crithmum maritimum)
sea plantain (Plantago maritimo)
soapwort (Saponaria officinalis)   *
sphagnum moss (Sphagnum cymbifo-
    lium)
strawberry tree (Arbutus sp.)   *
water agrimony (Bidens tripartita)

water betony (Scrophularia aquatica)
water figwort (Scrophularia aquatica)
water hemlock (cicuta virosa)
water parsnip (Sium latifolia)
water pimpernel (Veronica bec-
    cabunga)   *
water plantain (Alisma plantago)
water yarrow (Hottonia palustris)   *
wild lettuce (Lactuca virosa)
wild snowball (Viburnum opulus)   *
willow (Salix sp.)   **
wisteria (Wistaria cinensis)
worm bark (Andira inermis)

Pluto

agar agar (Gelidium amansii)   *
agaric (Amanita muscaria)   *
alder (black) (Prinos verticillatus)
aloes (Aloe sp.)   *
angostura (Cusparia febrifuga)
arbutus (Arbutus sp.)   *
arrachs (Chenopodium sp.)
artichoke (Cynara scolymus)
asafoetida (ferula fœtida)
bearberry (Arctostaphpylos uva-ursi) *
bethroot (Trillium erectum)
bilberry (Vaccinium myrtillus)   *
black cohosh (Cimicifuga racemosa)
black root (Leptandra virginica)
blue cohosh (Caulophyllum thalictroides)
box (Buxus sempervirens)   *
bryony (Bryonia sp.)   *
buckwheat (Polygonum fagopyrum)   *
chaste tree (Agnus castus)
club moss (Lycopodium clavatum)
coneflower (Echinacea angustifolia)   *
corn (Zea mays)   *
damiana (Turnera aphrodisiaca)
dogwood (Piscidia erythrina)   *
dragon's blood (Dæmomorops draco) *
echinacea (Echinacea angustifolia)   *
eucalyptus (Eucalyptus globulus)   **
false unicorn root (Chamælarium
    luteum)
fern (male) (Dryopteris felix-mas)   *
fever bush (Barrya fremonti)
flaxweed (Linaria vulgaris)   *

foxglove (Digitalis purpurea)   **
gelsemium (Gelsemium nitidum)   *
globe artichoke (Cynara sclymus)
ground pine (Ajuga chamæpitys)   *
guarana (Paulinia cupana)   *
hops (Humulus lupulus)   *
kava kava (Piper methysticum)   *
mandrake (Atropa mandragora)   *
oats (Avena sativa)   **
patchouli (Pogostemon patchouli)
pau d'arco (Tahebuia altissima)   *
pine (Pinaceæ sp.)   *
potato (Solanum tuberosum)   *
redwood (Sequoia sp.)
rudbeckia (Echinacea angustifolia)   *
rye (Secale cereale)
salep (Orchis sp.)   *
scullcap (Scutellaria galericulata)   *
sequoia (Sequoia sp.)
strawberry tree (Arbutus sp.)   *
toadflax (Linaria vulgaris)   *
trillium (Trillium sp.)
turnip (Brassica rapa)   *
uva ursi (Arctostaphylos uva-ursi)   *
wake robin (Trillium pendulum)
wheat (Triticum sp.)   *
winter's bark (Drimys Winteri)
woad (Ivatis tinctoria)   *
wormwood (Artemisia absinthium)   *
yams (Dioscorea villosa)   *
yellow bugle (Ajuga chamæpitys)   *
yucca (Yucca sp.)

Signs of the Zodiac

There are many fewer correspondences between herbes and the signs of the zodiac than there are between herbes and planets. While this has been a source of frustration for some, this system of correspondences will undoubtedly grow over the next couple of generations. In the meantime we must recognize the scarcity of those practitioners who have a mastery of knowledge in both herbalism and astrology and ask that you be patient.

In working with these correspondences it is important to remember that *every* natal chart contains all twelve of these archetypes of personality. Our western culture encourages us to identify the self in terms of the Sun sign rather than accepting the self as a whole, a composite of many facets of personality.

Herbes of Aries

An independent personality, Aries represents that facet of personality which has the ability to take initiative and break new ground. Requiring more than the average amount of freedom, Aries abhors following established routines and needs encouragement to be creative.

This fiery personality corresponds with the head and face, the carotid arteries and the physiological process which moves adrenalin into the blood stream.

Diseases and conditions associated with Aries include sunburn, headaches and inflammations of the brain. Many inflammatory conditions and feverish illnesses are associated with Aries, including mumps, measles and smallpox. Problems associated with one's sense of balance are often corresponded with Aries. Diseases arising out of an aggressive attitude which is inconsiderate of others or is unwilling to be patient when patience is needed fall under Aries as well.

By nature the herbes of Aries are masculine, represent elemental fire and are dominant. They provide energy which can be used to take charge of one's life. They are considered hot and dry and may stimulate the energy of impulsiveness or impetuousness. Herbes of Aries are recommended for those who need a boost in their energy levels, for explorers and those with an inventive spirit. These herbes are better suited for the entrepreneur than they are the corporate employee.

Some of the herbes corresponded with Aries include blackberry, pepper (chili), juniper, lupine and marjoram.

Herbes of Taurus

Wanting to take time to stop and smell the flowers, Taurus seeks stability, believing that the wise approach is to take its time and build a foundation which is able to endure for more than a life-time. Taurus appreciates the finer things in life and appreciates the patience required to achieve them.

Taurus is associated with the throat and neck, including the thyroid, vocal cords and pharynx. Related physiological features such as the cervical vertebrae and jugular veins are typically included as well.

Conditions associated with Taurus include enlargement of, or problems with, the thyroid, swollen glands in one's throat, as well as other afflictions of the throat including laryngitis. Due to its somewhat sedentary nature, a tendency to carry too much weight, a vulnerability to colds and chills, and a mild tendency toward hypochondria can complicate the health of the Taurus nature of a natal chart. Other illnesses may develop because this personality is unyielding to new ways, and can be stubborn as a bull in resisting needed change.

By nature the herbes of Taurus are feminine, of elemental earth and can be of a stoic energy. They increase one's ability to enjoy the pleasures of life and can help one find fulfillment. Most people with strong Taurus energy enjoy singing (even though many feel their voices inadequate). Herbes of Taurus are excellent choices for all musicians. They can be used by any artistically creative person to help them settle down with a project and see it through to completion.

Among the herbes of Taurus are apple blossom, cumin, heather, lovage and monarda.

Herbes of Gemini

Gemini is known for its ability to see both sides of things. Gemini lets its thought processing have verbal expression, a process which can be disconcerting for some but is a source of delight for others.

Medical astrology places Gemini with the upper torso, particularly upper limbs and the pulmonary region including the rib cage and lungs, from the diaphragm to the clavicles. Gemini has a close correspondence with the process the body uses to take in oxygen, including the entire respiratory system. Seemingly nervous by disposition, Gemini includes the many aspects of the nervous system.

Afflicted conditions of Gemini include problems arising from having a low boredom threshhold with resulting nervousness. Inflammatory conditions of the respiratory tract or problems with the lungs, pneumonia and tuberculosis are included, as are problems arising from fluid around the lungs. Difficulties with the arms or fingers are considered by some to be under Gemini. A number of conditions readily aggravated by nervous tension such as asthma, neuralgia of the upper limbs or eczema are corresponded with Gemini.

By nature herbes of Gemini are active and dry. Associated with elemental air they are often considered masculine but are, in fact, more androgynous. There is a natural tension about them which, used wisely, can increase productivity and open-mindedness. Gemini herbes help keep one's mind open to other possibilities. The innate tendency to always see the other side of things can, if not matured, lead one to a negative mind-set. Herbes of Gemini are most useful for those involved in communication such as those who must interact frequently with the public.

Herbes of Gemini include dill, elecampagne, horehound, mulberry and senna.

Herbes of Cancer

The Cancer personality must learn to find security from within or else the shell it develops to avoid being hurt creates isolation. When this personality is out of sorts, it acts like a crab. Cancer is the most sensitive and vulnerable of the personality archetypes and tends to take things too personally. Yet there is none so giving and willing as the Cancer archetype to proffer care and help to others.

Cancer corresponds with the breasts. Its region of the body also includes the stomach, esophagus and upper alimentary system. Some correspond the pancreas and liver as well.

The Cancerian personality is prone to diseases arising from insecurity. Medical astrology includes tumors within the breasts as well as other lumpy growths, problems with digestion (including ulcers) and complications arising from the stresses of anxiety. Some sources place asthma with Cancer rather than with Gemini. Digestive disorders arising from stress, loss of appetite due to depression, and disorders which develop from clinging too tightly to people or to things are associated with Cancer.

By nature the herbes of Cancer are gentle and sensitive, feminine and of elemental water. They help one develop the ability to trust one's self and, in turn, trust others. Trust is not easy for the individual with planetary energy in Cancer, for early in life they tend to be too trusting and set themselves up for painful lessons. Herbes of Cancer can help deal with another difficulty: this personality tends to nurture old hurts and keep those pains alive as a source of security. Herbes of Cancer provide a nurturing condition so that a personality is more capable of letting go. These herbes are very useful for those in care-giving professions, whether medical or maternal.

Cancerian herbes include agrimony, duckweed, hyssop, liverwort and loosestrife.

Herbes of Leo

It is difficult for the Leo to resist basking in its own glory and yet its desire to please and entertain its audience can be a joy for many. Leo is eager to please but can find itself at the mercy of its friends, becoming dependant upon the approval of others in an attempt to hold its audience.

The heart and cardiac system are associated with Leo. Many include the corresponding region of the spine and some include the spleen. Less tangible but equally important is one's self-esteem.

Diseases associated with Leo include problems with the heart ranging from irregularities to major cardiovascular afflictions and heart attacks. Some include convulsions and cramps with Leo but this is not a standard correspondence. Many illnesses arise when one's ego is in pain or feels that it has suffered an unfair personal attack. These conditions also correspond with Leo.

By nature the herbes of Leo are of elemental fire, masculine, dominant and expansive. They may be used to help the Leo personality understand that approval comes from within and that the stage should be shared with others. Those who are timid and shy may benefit from herbes of Leo. People who find they must appear before others, whether for business or at a social engagement, can increase their self-confidence. Performers needing to bolster their Leo nature can integrate these herbes into their lives as well.

Some herbes of Leo include angelica, bay laurel, eyebright, peony and sage.

Herbes of Virgo

Virgo is not everyone's favorite personality but those of us who have learned how to utilize it wouldn't trade it for any other. Virgo learns quickly in order to be more efficient and productive in dealing with life. This ability to perceive even meticulous details can be a blessing or can create an uncomfortable, picky lifestyle.

This practical sign of the zodiac is associated with the lower regions of the alimentary system. Some include the spleen in this association along with other organs within the abdomen.

Virgo is usually, in some manner, tense. It cannot avoid an ever-present, intense scrutiny either of itself or of others. Tension frequently leads to disruption of the lower intestines and colon: many Virgos are prone to colitis and diarrhea as a result of stress. Virgo's sense of detail makes it very unforgiving in its judgement of itself (not to mention others) and the resulting anxiety and tension may also lead to ulcers or diverticulitis. The slightest disturbance within one's body does not escape Virgo's sensitive nature. An unhealthy Virgo personality can become a skilled hypochondriac.

By nature the herbes of Virgo are of elemental earth, feminine but controlled. Those prone to guilt will benefit from the herbes of Virgo which help one set boundaries and recognize what is appropriate responsibility and when to let others be responsible for their own activities. It pains a Virgo deeply to see people create difficulties for themselves. Virgo has an overwhelming desire to be helpful but this urge will often be perceived as meddling. Herbes of Virgo can bring about an understanding of the proper balance when offering help or advice. Used ritually, they can help a person maintain perspective when dealing with criticism, helping them avoid defensive behavior when that response works against the situation. Herbes of Virgo are ideal for teachers for Virgo is a born teacher.

Among the herbes of Virgo are cedar, gentian, lavender, myrtle and valerian.

Herbes of Libra

Represented with the scales as its symbol, Libra is known for its ability to listen objectively, weigh carefully and then offer balanced advice. When the issues at hand are personal, however, the scales are easily tipped by others' behavior for Libra believes life should be shared and can be overly reactionary. Libra is not a solitary personality.

Libra corresponds with the kidneys and bladder including the urinary system. Many consider the skin (the largest organ of the body) also under Libra and some also correspond Libra with the lumbar region of the back.

Problems with the lower back (particularly those resulting in pain) are associated with Libra. Kidney and bladder infections or obstructions of these organs, as well as incontinence, are often corresponded with Libra. Diseases which arise out of extreme mood swings are often indicative of afflicted Libra planets. Although I have found at least one author who considers abortion a condition associated with Libra, the necessity of an abortion under these circumstances is a symptom. The actual condition has to do with behavior (e.g. arising from the fear of being without a relationship which led to the acceptance of a bad relationship).

By nature herbes of Libra are balancing. They are masculine but gentle. Of elemental air, they can help us maintain a sense of proportion in life. They may be used to counter feelings of possessiveness or jealousy, helping one understand what is necessary for a healthy relationship. Libran herbes are most suitable for those who must remain detached and objective in order to evaluate a situation and provide balanced, fair advice.

Among the herbes of Libra are bergamot, primrose, rose geranium, verbena and yarrow.

Herbes of Scorpio

Scorpio is generally considered the most intense of the personality archetypes, capable of quickly moving from the extreme of the celibate spiritually sublime to that of primal animal lust and gutter humor. Scorpio is an idealistic personality in an imperfect world which may lead to a dissatisfaction regarding life and is often the underlying motivation for its Scorpionic humor.

Anatomically, Scorpio is corresponded with the procreative sexual organs. Those organs associated with reproduction of the species which also provide sexual ecstasy are in the realm of Scorpio. We found that some authors place the red blood cells here as well.

Conditions associated with this zodiacal sign include sexual dysfunction, difficulties associated with conception, infertility, diseases of the reproductive organs and, according to at least one twentieth century author, diseases of the bone marrow. This water sign can be tempestuous and is known for attempting to dominate others. An out-of-balance Scorpio personality creates stress which can weaken one's system, leading toward illness. The Scorpionic personality encounters stress from its pursuit of extremes and its expectation of an ideal world. Intensely private, public exposure or the loss of its privacy can cause this personality to become vulnerable to disease.

By nature herbes of Scorpio are passionate. Many herbes of Scorpio are able to enhance one's sexual energy. These herbes are of elemental water, but water which is heating and intensely energized. We may work with these herbes to develop comfort with our mortality and to come to terms with the reality of human imperfection. Used wisely they will teach one patience and help one understand that perfection is never achieved. Rather, perfection is a process which unfolds over many lives.

Scorpionic herbes include basil, bloodroot, guarana, patchouli and uva ursi.

Herbes of Sagittarius

Requiring mental and physical stimulation, Sagittarius seeks constant challenge. Without temperance it becomes overly competitive. This fiery personality wants life to be thrilling. Anyone born with planets in Sagittarius requires exercise in order to maintain good health and well-being. This feisty personality is daring, seeking freedom and education. The wisdom Sagittarius hungers for is that lasting freedom, one which is never achieved without discipline. Sagittarius' challenge is learning the patience required by a disciplined approach.

Sagittarius is said to rule the thighs and hips. It needs to walk or run, skate or ride bicycle, dance or just be in motion. The sciatic nerves are associated with Sagittarius as well as the liver and hepatic system.

Afflictions to Sagittarius are corresponded with hepatitis or other problems with the liver. Poorly developed Sagittarian planets can result in frequent accidents caused by a lack of coordination. Stress is often caused by perceiving a loss of freedom and incorrectly placing the blame upon others. Some associate goiter problems with Sagittarius. Difficulties with the legs and hips, including rheumatism and sciatica are listed here as well.

By nature Sagittarian herbes are stimulating to one's mind and spirit. They are of elemental fire and are masculine, outgoing and strengthening. They are useful for anyone on a quest, providing the fuel necessary to pursue one's goal until it has been attained. These are useful herbes for anyone needing to use the body as a tool, getting it out and putting it in motion. Herbes of Sagittarius urge the spirit to explore life beyond the security of one's home, traveling and exploring the world.

Among the herbes of Sagittarius are coneflower, dandelion, hyssop, oak and sumac.

Herbes of Capricorn

Capricorn represents the nature of structure which is needed to achieve long-term goals. This personality likes stability, wanting to be certain each foot is placed solidly as it climbs up the spiral path to reach the goal at top of the mountain.

Anatomical correspondences include the knees and those bones of the lower limbs. The entire skeletal system, including the teeth, are also placed with Capricorn. Most sources place the body's joints and some correspond hair with Capricorn as well.

Difficulties with one's joints are associated with Capricorn as are problems with one's teeth or other dental concerns. The need for orthopedic devices is placed here as well. Capricorn afflictions include fractures, broken bones and dislocations. Diseases of the bone, including rickets and osteoporosis are included. Diseases of the skin and/or hair are Capricornian in correspondence as well. Some consider Hansen's disease appropriate for this list.

By nature Capricornian herbes promote patience and persever-ance. They help us understand our limitations and the need for structure in our lives. They contain the essence of elemental earth and are feminine in quality. These herbes can be used to help us endure. They can also help us crystallize our goals so that we may embrace the work needed to achieve them.

Herbes of Capricorn include aconite, bindweed, comfrey, laurel and woad.

Herbes of Aquarius

Constantly distracted by its pervasive sense of curiosity, the Aquarius is perceived as being forgetful and ever tardy. When well balanced, Aquarians are known for their sense of childlike delight. This inquisitive nature leads the Aquarius personality into many social situations, for few archetypes of personality are so good with social skills and making friends.

Aquarius has been corresponded with the circulatory or vascular systems within the body. Less widely accepted are associations with the legs, shins and ankles.

My professional experience has verified one Aquarian condition: persons with strong Aquarius planets in their natal charts are, in fact, prone to varicose veins. Other conditions associated with this sign of the zodiac include arteriosclerosis or other circulatory problems. The phrase cold hands, warm heart seems written for Aquarians. Difficulties with the lower limbs such as swelling or cramps are included here. A minority of sources include several other afflictions such as rheumatic fever, paralysis and problems with eyesight.

By nature herbes of Aquarius promote social interaction but some provide the means to keep the Aquarian's elemental air grounded and focused upon making progress in life. Some of these herbes are stimulants, for this personality can be far more inflexible than would be expected. Other herbes stimulate the quality of elemental air, helping blow away the cobwebs of gloom which surround some Aquarians.

Among the herbes of Aquarius are found buttercup, mandrake, spikenard, anise (star) and wisteria.

Herbes of Pisces

Sometimes feeling adrift in a sea of sensory and intuitive impressions, the Pisces personality is among the most visionary and creative. Until it achieves maturity and with it an understanding of the underlying structure of reality, its life may be subject to its insecurities and worries. Yet few have so warm a heart as the Pisces.

Anatomically, Pisces is corresponded with the feet and toes. The urinary system, including the kidneys and bladder, are Piscean by nature as well. Some authors assign the hepatic system, which includes the liver, to Pisces. There are times in which a lack of vitality may be indicated by afflictions to this sign of the zodiac.

Afflictions associated with Pisces include difficulties with one's feet, such as bunions, corns, or swelling. Gout, external ulcers and boils and abscesses are corresponded with Pisces as well. There are subtle currents of distrust which flow through the unmatured Pisces personality. When severe, these can become manifest as paranoia. The inability to feel secure keeps the Piscean personality from being productive, caught by its feelings of uncertainty. When strongly out of balance, this part of one's being can become so inert that it feels it is sinking to the bottom. A Pisces so out of balance is often prone to escapist behavior.

By nature the herbes of Pisces are feminine, gentle and of elemental water. They stimulate creativity and enhance the ability to use daydreaming skills toward productive manifestation. They may increase one's sensitivity and some of these herbes must be used only when the personality has first been stabilized and grounded.

474

Piscean herbes promote the imagination and help a person unfold wondrous artistic imagery which has been latent. Many of these herbes provide comfort for the anxieties of Pisces and may help dispel its fears.

Herbes of Pisces include dogwood, lobelia, passion flower, pussy willow and wild lettuce.

Zodiacal Correspondences

Herbes marked with an * in this and the subsequent lists of correspondences are those which have been assigned more than one signature by various authors. Some Herbes are marked ** to denote the traditional zodiacal correspondence preferred by the Master Herbalists of The Hermit's Grove.

Aries

betony (wood) *(Betonica officinalis)*
blackberry *(Rubus fructicosus)*
blessed thistle *(Carduus benedictus)*
cowslip *(Primula veris)*
fairy cups *(Primula veris)*
juniper *(Juniperus communis)*
loosestrife *(Lysimachia sp.)*
lupine *(Lupinus sp.)*
marjoram *(Origanum marjorana)*
pepper (chili) *(Capsicum minimum)*
plantain *(Plantago major)*

Taurus

apple blossom *(Pyrus malus)*
balm of Gilead *(Commiphora opobal-samum)*
clover *(Trifolium pratense)*
cumin *(Cuminum cyminum)*
figwort *(Scrophularia sp.)*
heather *(Calluna vulgaris)*
hibiscus (red) *(Hibiscus sp.)*
lovage *(Levisticum officinale)*
monarda *(Monarda punctata)*
roses (pink) *(Rosa sp.)*
roses (red) *((Rosa sp. (rubra))*

Gemini

balloon flower *(Platycodon grandi-florus)*
bamboo *(Bambusa vulgaris)*
dill *(Peucedanum graveolens)*
dragon's blood *(Dæmomorops draco)*
elecampagne *(Inula helenium)*
elfwort *(Inula helenium)*
gum thistle *(Euphorbia resinfera)*
horehound *(Marrubium vulgare)*
lady's seals *(Polygonatum multiflorum)*
lily-of-the-valley *(Convallaria magalis)*
meadowsweet *(Spiræa ulmaria)*
mulberry *(Morus nigra)*
senna (bladder) *(Colutea sp.)*
Solomon's Seal *(Polygonatum multi-florum)*
spurge *(Euphorbia sp.)*
spurge *(Euphorbia resinfera)*

Cancer

adder's tongue (*Erythronium americanum*)
agrimony (*Agrimonia eupatoria*)
alder (black) (*Prinos verticillatus*)
alder (*Alnus glutinosa*) **
balm (*Melissa officinalis*)
daisies (*Bellis perennis*)

duckweed (*Lens palustris*)
honeysuckle (*Lonicera caprifolium*)
hyssop (*Hyssopus officinalis*) **
jasmine (*Jasminum officinale*)
liverwort (*Anemone hepatica*)
loosestrife (*Lysimachia sp.*) **
sundew (*Drosera rotundifolia*)

Leo

agaric (*Amanita muscaria*) *
angelica (*Angelica archangelica*)
bay laurel (*Laurus nobilis*)
borage (*Borago officinalis*)
celandine (greater) (*Chelidonium majus*)
eyebright (*Euphrasia officinalis*)
goat's rue (*Galega officinalis*)
hawthorn (*Cratægus oxyacantha*)
marigold (*Calendula officinalis*)
motherwort (*Leonurus cardiaca*)
oats (*Avena sativa*)

peony (*Pæonia officinalis*)
rue (*Ruta graveolens*)
rye (*Secale cereale*)
saffron (*Crocus sativus*)
sage (*Salvia officinalis*)
Saint Joan's wort (*Hypericum perforatum*)
Saint John's wort (*Hypericum perforatum*)
thorn (*Cratægus oxyacantha*)
wheat (*Triticum sp.*)

Virgo

cascara (*Rhamnus purshianus*)
cedar (*Thuja occidentalis*)
cinquefoil (*Potentilla reptans*)
fern (maidenhair) (*Adiantum capillus-veneris*)
five-leaf grass (*Potentilla reptans*)
gentian (*Gentiana sp.*)
lanterns (*Physalis alkekengi*)

lavender (*Lavendula vera*)
lignum vitae (*Thuja occidentalis*)
myrtle (*Myrtus communis*)
potentilla (*Potentilla reptans*)
sassafras (*Sassafras officinale*)
valerian (*Valeriana officinalis*) **
verbena (*Verbena officinalis*) *

Libra

bergamot (*Monarda didyma*)
catnip (*Nepeta cataria*)
columbine (*Aquilegia vulgaris*)
herb true-love (*Paris quadrifolia*)
hollyhock (*Althæa rosea*)
horsetongue (*Ruscus hippoglossum*)
kidneywort (*Cotyledon umbilicus*)

paris herb (*Paris quadrifolia*)
primrose (*Primula vulgaris*)
rose geranium (*Pelargonium graveolens*)
vervain (*Verbena officinalis*) **
yarrow (*Achillea millefolium*)

Scorpio

agaric (*Amanita muscaria*) **

arrachs (*Chenopodium sp.*)

basil (Ocymum basilium)
bearberry (Arctostaphylos uva-ursi)
bloodroot (Sanguinaria canadensis)
fireweed (Erechtites hieracifolia)
foxglove (Digitalis purpurea)
guarana (Paulinia cupana)

hops (Humulus lupulus)
horseradish (Cochlearia armoracia)
patchouli (Pogostemon patchouli)
snapdragon (Antirrhinum magus)
uva ursi (Arctostaphylos uva-ursi)

Sagittarius

alexander (Smyrnium olisatrum)
arrowhead (Sagittaria sagittifolia)
centaury (Erythræa centaurium)
coneflower (Echinacea angustifolia)
dandelion (Taraxacum offinale)
datura (Datura stamonium)
echinacea (Echinacea angustifolia)
goat's thorn (Astragalus gummifer)

houseleek (Sempervivum tectorum)
hyssop (Hyssopus officinalis)   *
Indian corn (Zea mays)
maize (Zea mays)
oak (Quercus sp.)
sage (Salvia officinalis)
sumac (Rhus sp.)
tragacanth (Astragalus gummifer)

Capricorn

aconite (Aconitum napellus)
bindweed (Convolvulus sp.)
comfrey (Symphytum officinale)
dracontium (Symplocarpus fœtidus)
elm (Ulmus capestris)
Irish moss (Chondrus crispus)
laurel (Kalmia latifolia)

liverwort (Peltigera canina)
monkshood (Aconitum napellus)
moss (Lycopodiaceæ)
poke root (Phytolacca decandra)
skunk cabbage (Symplocarpus fœtidus)
woad (Ivatis tinctoria)

Aquarius

anise (star) (Illicum verum)
buttercup (Ranunculus bulbosus)
cloves (Eugenia caryophyllata)
lady's slipper (Cypripedium pubescens)
mandrake (Atropa mandragora)

pitcher plant (Sarracenia purpurea)
spikenard (Inula conyza)
valerian (Valeriana offcinalis)
wisteria (Wistaria cinensis)

Pisces

alder (common) (Alnus glutinosa)   *
bladderwrack (Fucus vesiculosis)
cannabis (Cannabis sativa)
dogwood (Piscidia erythrina)
hemp (Cannabis sativa)
lobelia (Lobelia inflata)
marshwort (Helosciadium nodiflorum)
moss (sea water) (Chondrus crispus)

passion flower (Passiflora incarnata)
pussy willow (Salix nigra)
seaweed (Fucus sp.)
sphagnum moss (Sphagnum cymbifo-
lium)
turnip (Brassica rapa)
wild lettuce (Lactuca virosa)

Herbal Correspondences

The following is a list of the herbes in this compendium and additional herbes presented in alphabetical order. Herbes marked with an * in this list of correspondences are those which have been assigned more than one planetary signature by various authors. Some Herbes are marked ** to denote the traditional planetary correspondence preferred by the Master Herbalists of The Hermit's Grove.

abscess root (*Polemonium reptans*)		Mars
acacia (*Acacia sp.*)	**	Mars
acacia (*Acacia sp*)	*	Sun
acanthus (*Acanthus sp.*)		Moon
aconite (*Aconitum napellus*)		Saturn
adam and eve root (*Orchis sp.*)		Neptune
adder's tongue (*Erythronium americanum*)		Moon
adder's tongue (*Ophioglossum vulgatum*)		Moon
adderwort (*Polygonum bistortum*)		Saturn
adrue (*Cyperus articulatus*)		Neptune
agar agar (*Gelidium amansii*)	**	Pluto
agar agar (*Gelidium amansii*)	*	Moon
agaric (*Amanita muscaria*)	**	Pluto
agaric (*Amanita muscaria*)	*	Mercury
agrimony (*Agrimonia eupatoria*)		Jupiter
alder (*Alnus glutinosa*)	*	Venus
alder (*Alnus glutinosa*)	*	Mars
alder (black) (*Prinos verticillatus*)		Pluto
alexander (*Smyrnium olisatrum*)		Jupiter
alfalfa (*Medicago sativa*)		Jupiter
alkanet (*Alkanna tinctoria*)		Venus
all heal (*Prunella vulgaris*)		Mars
all heal (*Valeriana officinalis*)		Mercury
allspice (*Pimento officinalis*)		Uranus
almond (*Amygdalus communis*)	**	Sun
almond (*Amygdalus communis*)	*	Mercury
aloes (*Aloe sp.*)	*	Mars
aloes (*Aloe sp.*)	*	Pluto
amaranthus (*Amaranthus sp.*)		Saturn
American boxwood (*Cornus florida*)		Moon
American mandrake (*Podophyllum peltatum*) . .		Mars
American valerian (*Cypripedium pubescens*) . . .		Uranus
anemone (*Anemone pulsatilla*)		Mercury
anemone (wood) (*Anemone nemorosa*)		Mars

478

angelica *(Angelica archangelica)*		Sun
angostura *(Cusparia febrifuga)*		Pluto
anise seed *(Pimpinella anisum)*		Moon
anise (star) *(Illicum verum)*	*	Moon
anise (star) *(Illicum verum)*	*	Uranus
anserina *(Galium aparine)*		Moon
apple *(Pyrus malus)*	*	Venus
apple *(Pyrus malus)*	*	Jupiter
apple blossom *(Pyrus malus)*		Venus
apricot *(Prunus armeniaca)*	*	Venus
apricot *(Prunus armeniaca)*	*	Neptune
araroba *(Andira araroba)*		Mars
arbutus *(Arbutus sp.)*	*	Neptune
arbutus *(Arbutus sp.)*	*	Pluto
arnica *(Arnica montana)*		Saturn
arrachs *(Chenopodium sp.)*		Pluto
arrowhead *(Sagittaria sagittifolia)*		Jupiter
arrow root *(Maranta arundinaceæ)*		Jupiter
arsesmart *(Polygnum hydropiper)*	*	Mars
arsesmart *(Polygnum hydropiper)*	*	Saturn
artichoke *(Cynara scolymus)*		Pluto
arum *(Arum maculatum)*	*	Sun
arum *(Arum maculatum)*	*	Neptune
asafoetida *(ferula fœtida)*		Pluto
asarabacca *(Asarum europæum)*		Mars
asclepias *(Asclepiadaceæ)*	*	Mars
asclepias *(Asclepiadaceæ)*	*	Jupiter
asclepias *(Asclepiadaceæ)*	*	Saturn
ash *(Fraxinus excelsior)*	**	Sun
ash *(Fraxinus excelsior)*	*	Uranus
ash *(Fraxinus excelsior)*	*	Neptune
ash (mountain) *(Sorbus americana)*		Moon
ash (mountain) *(Sorbus aucuparia)*		Moon
asparagus *(Asparagus officinalis)*		Jupiter
asphodel *(Asphodelus ramosus)*		Jupiter
avens *(Geum urbanum)*		Jupiter
azaleas *(Azalea sp.)*		Mercury
balloon flower *(Platycodon grandiflorus)*		Mercury
balm *(Melissa officinalis)*		Jupiter
balm melissa *(Melissa officinalis)*		Jupiter
balm of Gilead *(Commiphora opobalsamum)* . . .		Venus
balmony *(Chelone glabra)*	*	Jupiter
balmony *(Chelone glabra)*	*	Neptune
bamboo *(Bambusa vulgaris)*	*	Moon
bamboo *(Bambusa vulgaris)*	*	Mars
bamboo *(Bambusa vulgaris)*	*	Saturn
bamboo (for pipes) *(Bambusa vulgaris)*	*	Mercury
banana *(Musa paradisiaca)*		Jupiter

baneberry (Actæa spicata) . . . .   Saturn
barberry (Berberis vulgaris) . . . .   Mars
barley (Hordeum sp.) . . . .   Saturn
basil (bush) (Ocymum minimum) . . . .   Mars
basil (sweet) (Ocymum basilium) . . . .   Mars
bayberry (Myrica ceriferia) . . . .   Mercury
bay laurel (Laurus nobilis) . . . . **   Sun
bay laurel (Pimenta racemosa) . . . .   Mars
beans (Phaseolus vulgaris) . . . .   Venus
bearberry (Arctostaphpylos uva-ursi) . . . . **   Pluto
bearberry (Arctostaphpylos uva-ursi) . . . . *   Mars
bedstraw (Galium verum) . . . .   Venus
beech (Fagus sylvatica) . . . . *   Mars
beech (Fagus sylvatica) . . . . *   Saturn
beets (Beta hortensis) . . . .   Saturn
belladonna (Atropa belladonna) . . . .   Saturn
benzoin (Styrax benzoin) . . . .   Mars
bergamot (Monarda didyma) . . . . **   Venus
bergamot (Monarda didyma) . . . . *   Sun
betel (Piper betel) . . . .   Mars
bethroot (Trillium erectum) . . . .   Pluto
betony (Betonica officinalis) . . . . *   Jupiter
bilberry (Vaccinium myrtillus) . . . . *   Jupiter
bilberry (Vaccinium myrtillus) . . . . *   Pluto
bindweed (Convolvulus sp.) . . . .   Saturn
birch (Betula alba) . . . . *   Sun
birch (Betula alba) . . . . **   Venus
bird's foot (Ornithopus perusillus) . . . .   Saturn
birth root (Trillium pendulum) . . . .   Pluto
birthwort (Aristolochia longa) . . . .   Venus
bishop's weed (Ægopodium podagraria) . . . . . .   Venus
bishop's weed (Ammi majus) . . . .   Venus
bistort (Polygonum bistorta) . . . .   Saturn
bitter root (Apocynum androsæmifolium) . . . . .   Jupiter
bittersweet (Solanum dulcamara) . . . . *   Mercury
bittersweet (Solanum dulcamara) . . . . *   Uranus
bitter wood (Picræna excelsa) . . . .   Mars
blackberry (Rubus fructicosus) . . . .   Venus
black cohosh (Cimicifuga racemosa) . . . .   Pluto
black cress (Sisymbrium nigra) . . . .   Mars
black hellebore (Helleborus niger) . . . .   Saturn
black pepper (Piper nigrum) . . . .   Mars
black root (Leptandra virginica) . . . .   Pluto
blackthorn (Prunus spinosa) . . . .   Mars
black willow (Salix nigra) . . . . *   Saturn
black willow (Salix nigra) . . . . *   Uranus
bladderwrack (Fucus vesiculosis) . . . . *   Jupiter
bladderwrack (Fucus vesiculosis) . . . . *   Neptune

bleeding heart *(Dicentra spectabilis)*			Venus
blessed thistle *(Carduus benedictus)*			Mars
blites *(Amaranthus blitus)*			Venus
bloodroot *(Sanguinaria canadensis)*		*	Venus
bloodroot *(Sanguinaria canadensis)*		*	Mars
bluebells *(Hyacinthus nonscriptus)*		*	Mars
bluebells *(Hyacinthus nonscriptus)*		*	Saturn
bluebells *(Hyacinthus nonscriptus)*		*	Uranus
blue cohosh *(Caulophyllum thalictroides)*			Pluto
bogbean *(Menyanthes trifoliata)*			Neptune
boneset *(Eupatorium perfoliatum)*			Venus
borage *(Borago officinalis)*			Jupiter
bottle brush *(Equisetum sp.)*			Saturn
box *(Buxus sempervirens)*		*	Saturn
box *(Buxus sempervirens)*		*	Pluto
boxwood (American) *(Cornus florida)*			Moon
brooklime *(Veronica beccabunga)*		**	Mars
brooklime *(Veronica beccabunga)*		*	Neptune
broom *(Cytisus scoparius)*		*	Sun
broom *(Cytisus scoparius)*		**	Mars
bruisewort *(Symphytum officinale)*			Saturn
bryony *(Bryonia sp.)*		**	Mars
bryony *(Bryonia sp.)*		*	Pluto
buck's horn plantain *(Plantago coronopus)*		*	Venus
buck's horn plantain *(Plantago coronopus)*		*	Saturn
buckthorn *(Rhamnus sp.)*		*	Mars
buckthorn *(Rhamnus sp.)*		**	Saturn
buckwheat *(Polygonum fagopyrum)*		*	Mercury
buckwheat *(Polygonum fagopyrum)*		*	Pluto
bugle *(Ajuga reptans)*		*	Venus
bugle *(Ajuga reptans)*		*	Neptune
burdock *(Arctium lappa)*			Venus
bur marigold *(Bidens tripartita)*			Neptune
burnet (great) *(Sanguisorba officinalis)*			Sun
burnet (small) *(Pimpinella saxifraga)*			Moon
burning bush *(Dictamnus albus)*			Venus
butterbur *(Petasites vulgaris)*			Sun
butterbur *(Tussilago petasites)*			Sun
buttercup *(Ranunculus bulbosus)*			Uranus
cabbage *(Brassica oleracea)*			Moon
cabbage tree *(Andira inermis)*			Neptune
cacao *(Theobroma cacoa)*			Uranus
calabar bean *(Physostigma venenosum)*			Saturn
calamint *(Calamintha officinalis)*			Mercury
camphor *(Cinnamomum camphora)*			Moon
campion *(Cucubalus sp.)*			Saturn
cannabis *(Cannabis sativa)*		*	Saturn
cannabis *(Cannabis sativa)*		*	Neptune

caraway (*Carum carvi*)		Mercury
cardamom (*Elettaria cardamomum*)		Jupiter
carob (*Jacaranda procera*)	*	Sun
carob (*Jacaranda procera*)	*	Jupiter
carob (*Jacaranda procera*)	*	Saturn
carrots (*Daucus carota*)		Mercury
cascara (*Rhamnus purshianus*)		Mercury
cashew (*Anacardium occidentale*)	*	Moon
cashew (*Anacardium occidentale*)	*	Mars
cassia (*Cinnamomum cassia*)		Mercury
castor (*Ricinus communis*)		Mars
catnip (*Nepeta cataria*)		Venus
catsfoot (*Antennaria dioica*)		Sun
cat thyme (*Teucrium marum*)		Mars
cayenne (*Capsicum minimum*)		Mars
cedar (*Cedrus atlanticus*)	*	Mercury
cedar (*Cedrus atlanticus*)	*	Uranus
cedar (*Thuja occidentalis*)	*	Mercury
cedar (*Thuja occidentalis*)	*	Uranus
celandine (greater) (*Chelidonium majus*)		Sun
celery (*Apium graveolens*)		Mercury
centaury (*Erythræa centaurium*)		Sun
chamomile (*Anthemis nobilis*)	*	Sun
chamomile (*Anthemis matricaria*)		Sun
chaste tree (*Agnus castus*)		Pluto
cherry (*Prunus serotina*)		Venus
cherry laurel (*Prunus laurocerosus*)		Venus
cherry (wild) (*Prunus virginiana*)		Venus
chervil (*Anthriscus cerefolium*)		Jupiter
chestnut (*Castanea vesca*)		Jupiter
chickpease (*Cicer arietinum*)		Venus
chickweed (*Stellaria media*)		Moon
chicory (*Cichorium intybus*)		Uranus
chilies (*Capsicum minimum*)		Mars
Chinese anise (*Illicum verum*)	*	Uranus
Chinese lanterns (*Physalis alkekengi*)		Mercury
Chinese sumach (*Rhus vernicifera*)		Saturn
chives (*Allium schœnoprasum*)		Mars
Christmas rose (*Helleborus niger*)		Saturn
cinchona (*Cinchona succirubra*)		Mars
cinnamon (*Cinnamomum zeylanica*)	**	Uranus
cinnamon (*Cinnamomum zeylanica*)	*	Sun
cinquefoil (*Potentilla reptans*)	**	Jupiter
cinquefoil (*Potentilla reptans*)	*	Mercury
clary (*Salvia sclarea*)		Moon
cleavers (*Galium aparine*)		Moon
clematis (*Clematis recta*)	*	Mars
clematis (*Clematis recta*)	*	Saturn

clove (*Eugenia caryophyllata*) . . . .   Uranus
clover (*Trifolium sp.*) . . . . ** Mercury
clover (*Trifolium sp.*) . . . . * Venus
club moss (*Lycopodium clavatum*) . . . .   Pluto
coca leaves (*Erythroxylon coca*) . . . .   Uranus
cocculus (*Anamirta paniculata*) . . . .   Saturn
cocoa (*Theobroma cacao*) . . . .   Venus
coconut (*Cocos nucifera*) . . . .   Moon
coffee (*Coffea arabica*) . . . . * Mercury
coffee (*Coffea arabica*) . . . . * Uranus
coltsfoot (*Tussilago farfara*) . . . .   Venus
columbine (*Aquilegia vulgaris*) . . . .   Venus
comfrey (*Symphytum officinale*) . . . .   Saturn
coneflower (*Echinacea angustifolia*) . . . . * Jupiter
coneflower (*Echinacea angustifolia*) . . . . * Pluto
coolwort (*Tiarella cordifolia*) . . . .   Moon
coriander (*Coriandrum sativum*) . . . . * Moon
coriander (*Coriandrum sativum*) . . . . * Mars
corn (*Zea mays*) . . . . * Pluto
cornflower (*Centaurea cyanus*) . . . . * Venus
cornflower (*Centaurea cyanus*) . . . . * Saturn
costmary (*Tanacetum balsamita*) . . . .   Jupiter
cotton thistle (*Onopordon acanthium*) . . . . . .   Mars
couch grass (*Agropyrum repens*) . . . .   Jupiter
cowbane (*cicuta virosa*) . . . .   Neptune
cowslip (*Primula veris*) . . . .   Venus
cramp bark (*Viburnum opulus*) . . . .   Saturn
cranesbill (*Geranium maculatum*) . . . .   Mercury
crawley root (*Corallorhiza odontorhiza*) . . . . .   Mars
cress (*Iberis amara*) . . . .   Saturn
crocus (*Crocus sativa*) . . . .   Sun
crosswort (*Galium cruciata*) . . . .   Saturn
crowfoot (*Ranunculus sp.*) . . . .   Mars
cubeb (*Piper cubeba*) . . . .   Mars
cuckoo-pint (*Arum maculatum*) . . . .   Neptune
cucumber (*Cucumis sativa*) . . . .   Moon
cudweed (*Gnaphalium sp.*) . . . .   Venus
cumin (*Cuminum cyminum*) . . . .   Mars
currants (*Ribes vulgaris*) . . . . * Venus
currants (*Ribes vulgaris*) . . . . * Jupiter
currants (*Vitis vinifera*) . . . .   Venus
cyclamen (*Cyclamen hederæfolium*) . . . .   Mars
cypress (*Cupressus*) . . . . * Saturn
cypress (*Cupressus*) . . . . * Neptune
daffodil (*Narcissus pseudo-narcissus*) . . . . ** Venus
daffodil (*Narcissus pseudo-narcissus*) . . . . * Saturn
daffodil (yellow) (*Narcissus pseudo-narcissus*) . .   Mars
dahlias (*Dahlia variabilis*) . . . .   Jupiter

daisies (Bellis perennis)		Venus
damiana (Turnera aphrodisiaca)		Pluto
dandelion (Taraxacum officinale)		Jupiter
datura (Datura stamonium)		Jupiter
day lily (Lilium sp.)		Mercury
devil's claw (Harpagophytum procumbens)		Saturn
devil's garters (Convvovulus arvensis)		Saturn
dill (Peucedanum graveolens)		Mercury
dittany of Crete (Dictamnus creticus)		Venus
dittany (white) (Dictamnus alba)		Venus
dock (Rumex sp.)		Jupiter
dodder (Cuscutua europæa)		Saturn
dog grass (Agropyrum repens)		Jupiter
dog rose (Rosa canina)		Moon
dog's mercury (Mercurialis perennis)		Saturn
dog's tooth violet (Erythronium americanum) . .		Moon
dog's tooth violet (Erythronium dens canis) . . .		Moon
dogwood (Piscidia erythrina)	**	Moon
dogwood (Piscidia erythrina)	*	Pluto
double rocket (Hesperis matronalis)		Mars
dracontium (Dracontium fœtidum)		Saturn
dracontium (Symplocarpus fœtiidus)		Saturn
dragon's blood (Dæmomorops draco)	*	Mars
dragon's blood (Dæmomorops draco)	*	Pluto
dragon's claw (Corallorhiza odontorhiza)		Mars
dropwort (Enanthe phellandrium)		Neptune
dropwort (Spiræa filipendula)		Venus
duckweed (Lens palustris)		Moon
dwarf elder (Sambucus ebulus)		Venus
dwarf red rattle (Pedicularis sylvatica)		Sun
dysentery bark (Simaruba officinalis)		Mars
echinacea (Echinacea angustifolia)	*	Jupiter
echinacea (Echinacea angustifolia)	*	Pluto
eglantine (Rosa rubiginosa)		Jupiter
elder (Sambucus nigra)		Venus
elecampagne (Inula helenium)	*	Mercury
elecampagne (Inula helenium)	*	Uranus
elfwort (Inula helenium)	*	Mercury
elfwort (Inula helenium)	*	Uranus
elm (Ulmus campestris)		Saturn
endive (Cichorium endivia)		Jupiter
English sarsaparilla (Smilax sp.)		Sun
ephedra (Ephedra vulgaris)		Mars
eucalyptus (Eucalyptus globulus)	**	Pluto
eucalyptus (Eucalyptus globulus)	*	Moon
euphorbia (Euphorbia sp.)		Mars
evening primrose (Œnothera biennis)		Saturn
eveweed (Hesperis matronalis)		Mars

eyebright *(Euphrasia officinalis)* . . . . Sun
fairy cups *(Primula veris)* . . . . Venus
false acacia *(Robinia pseudacacia)* . . . . Sun
false saffron *(Carthamus tinctorius)* . . . . * Sun
false saffron *(Carthamus tinctorius)* . . . . * Saturn
false unicorn root *(Chamælarium luteum)* . . . . Pluto
fennel *(Fœniculum vulgare)* . . . . Mercury
fenugreek *(Trigonella fœnum-græcum)* . . . . . . Mercury
fern (bracken) *(Pteris aquilina)* . . . . ** Sun
fern (bracken) *(Pteris aquilina)* . . . . * Mercury
fern (bracken) *(Pteris aquilina)* . . . . * Saturn
fern (maidenhair) *(Adiantum capillus-veneris)* . . Mercury
fern (male) *(Dryopteris felix-mas)* . . . . * Mars
fern (male) *(Dryopteris felix-mas)* . . . . * Pluto
fern (moonwort) *(Boptrychium lunaria)* . . . . . Moon
fern (royal) *(Osmunda regalis)* . . . . Saturn
fever bush *(Barrya fremonti)* . . . . Pluto
feverfew *(Chrysanthemum parthenium)* . . . . . . Venus
fig *(Ficus carica)* . . . . Jupiter
figwort *(Scrophylaria sp.)* . . . . Venus
fireweed *(Erechtites hieracifolia)* . . . . Mars
five-leaf grass *(Potentilla reptans)* . . . . * Mercury
five-leaf grass *(Potentilla reptans)* . . . . * Jupiter
flag *(Iris versicolor)* . . . . Moon
flax *(Linum usitatissimum)* . . . . * Mercury
flax *(Linum usitatissimum)* . . . . * Saturn
flax *(Linum usitatissimum)* . . . . * Uranus
flaxweed *(Linaria vulgaris)* . . . . * Mars
flaxweed *(Linaria vulgaris)* . . . . * Pluto
fleabane *(Erigeron sp.)* . . . . Venus
fleabane *(Erigeron canadense)* . . . . Saturn
fleabane *(Inula dysenterica)* . . . . Venus
fleabane *(Senecio vuilgaris)* . . . . Venus
fleabane (blue) *(Erigeron acris)* . . . . Mars
fleawort *(Erigeron canadense)* . . . . Saturn
fleur-de-lis *(Iris pallida)* . . . . Moon
foxglove *(Digitalis purpurea)* . . . . ** Pluto
foxglove *(Digitalis purpurea)* . . . . * Venus
frankincense *(Boswellia thurifera)* . . . . Sun
fraxinella *(Dictamnus albus)* . . . . Venus
frostwort *(Helianthemum canadense)* . . . . Sun
fumitory *(Fumaria officinalis)* . . . . Saturn
furze *(Europæus)* . . . . * Mars
galbanum *(Ferula galbaniflua)* . . . . Uranus
gall oak *(Quercus infectoria)* . . . . Saturn
gardenia *(Gardenia sp.)* . . . . Venus
garlic *(Allium sativum)* . . . . Mars
gelsemium *(Gelsemium nitidum)* . . . . * Venus

gelsemium (Gelsemium nitidum)	*	Jupiter
gelsemium (Gelsemium nitidum)	*	Pluto
gentian (Gentiana sp.)	*	Mercury
gentian (Gentiana sp.)	*	Mars
geranium (Geranium sp.)		Venus
geranium (scented) (Geranium)		Mercury
germander (Teucrium sp.)		Mars
ginger (Zingiber officinale)		Moon
ginkgo biloba (Salisburia adiantifolia)		Mars
glasswort (Salsola sp.)		Neptune
globe artichoke (Cynara sclymus)		Pluto
gnaphaliums (Gnaphalium sp.)		Sun
goat's beard (Tragopogon sp.)		Jupiter
goat's rue (Galega officinalis)		Mercury
goat's thorn (Astragalus gummifer)	**	Mars
goldenrod (Solidago sp.)		Venus
golden seal (Hydrastis canadensis)		Venus
good Henry (Mercurialis annua)		Mercury
gooseberry (Ribes grossularia)		Venus
goose grass (Galium aparine)	**	Moon
goose grass (Galium aparine)	*	Venus
gorse (Ulex europæus)	*	Mercury
gosmore (Hypochœris sp.)		Venus
goutweed (Ægopodium podagraria)		Venus
grapes (Vitis vinifera)		Jupiter
green hellebore (Veratrum viride)		Saturn
ground pine (Ajuga chamæpitys)	*	Mars
ground pine (Ajuga chamæpitys)	*	Pluto
groundsel (Senecio vuilgaris)		Venus
guarana (Paulinia cupana)	*	Mars
guarana (Paulinia cupana)	*	Pluto
guelder rose (Viburnum opulus)		Saturn
guiacum (Guiacum officinale)		Uranus
gum dragon (Dæmomorops draco)	*	Mars
gum mastic (Pistacia lentiscus)		Mars
gum thistle (Euphorbia resinifera)		Mars
hare's ear (Bupleura rotundifolia)		Jupiter
hare's foot (Pes leporinus)		Mercury
hare's foot (Trifolium arvense)		Mercury
hart's tongue (Asplenium scolopendrium)		Jupiter
hawk weed (Hieracium sp.)		Saturn
hawthorn (Cratægus oxyacantha)		Mars
hazel nut (Corylus avellana)		Mercury
heartsease (Viola tricolor)		Saturn
heather (Calluna vulgaris)		Venus
heather (Erica sp.)		Venus
hellebore (black) (Helleborus niger)		Saturn
hellebore (false) (Adonis autumnalis)		Saturn

hellebore (green) (*Veratrum viride*)		Saturn
hemlock (*Conium maculatum*)		Saturn
hemp (*Cannabis sativa*)	*	Saturn
hemp (*Cannabis sativa*)	*	Neptune
henbane (*Hyoscyamus niger*)		Saturn
henna (*Lawsonia alba*)		Jupiter
herb bennet (*Geum urbanum*)		Jupiter
herb true-love (*Paris quadrifolia*)	**	Uranus
herb true-love (*Paris quadrifolia*)	*	Venus
hibiscus (pink) (*Hibiscus sp.*)		Venus
hibiscus (red) (*Hibiscus sp.*)		Venus
hibiscus (white) (*Hibiscus sp.*)		Moon
holly (*Ilex aquifolium*)	*	Mars
holly (*Ilex aquifolium*)	*	Saturn
hollyhock (*Althæa rosea*)		Venus
holly (sea) (*Eryngium maritimum*)		Moon
holy herb (*Eriodictyon glutinosum*)	*	Moon
holy thistle (*Carduus benedictus*)		Mars
honeysuckle (*Lonicera caprifolium*)	*	Mercury
honeysuckle (*Lonicera caprifolium*)	*	Mars
hops (*Humulus lupulus*)	*	Mars
hops (*Humulus lupulus*)	*	Pluto
honeywort (*Cerinthe major*)		Mercury
horehound (*Marrubium vulgare*)		Mercury
horseradish (*Cochlearia armoracia*)		Mars
horsetail (*Equisetum sp.*)		Saturn
horsetongue (*Ruscus hippoglossum*)		Mars
hounds-tongue (*Cynoglossum officinale*)	*	Mercury
hounds tongue (*Cynoglossum officinale*)	*	Jupiter
houseleek (*Sempervivum tectorum*)		Jupiter
hyacinth (*Hyacinthus sp.*)		Mars
hyssop (*Hyssopus officinalis*)		Jupiter
impatiens (*Impatiens aurea*)	*	Venus
impatiens (*Impatiens aurea*)	*	Neptune
Indian corn (*Zea mays*)	*	Jupiter
indigo (*Indigofera tinctoria*)		Mars
iris (*Iridaceæ*)		Moon
Irish moss (*Chondrus crispus*)	*	Moon
Irish moss (*Chondrus crispus*)	*	Saturn
itch weed (*Veratrum viride*)		Saturn
ivy (*Hedera helix*)		Saturn
jack-in-the-pulpit (*Arum triphyllum*)		Jupiter
Jacob's ladder (*Polemonium cœruleum*)		Mercury
jasmine (*Jasminum officinale*)		Jupiter
Jesuits' powder (*Cinchona succirubra*)		Mars
jewelweed (*Impatiens aurea*)	*	Venus
jewelweed (*Impatiens aurea*)	*	Neptune
juniper (*Juniperus communis*)	*	Sun

juniper (*Juniperus communis*) . . . . * Mars
juniper (*Juniperus communis*) . . . . * Saturn
kava kava (*Piper methysticum*) . . . . * Venus
kava kava (*Piper methysticum*) . . . . * Pluto
kidneywort (*Cotyledon umbilicus*) . . . . * Venus
kidneywort (*Cotyledon umbilicus*) . . . . * Neptune
knapweed (*Centaurea scabiosa*) . . . . * Jupiter
knapweed (*Centaurea scabiosa*) . . . . * Saturn
knapwort (*Centaurea jacea*) . . . . Saturn
knot grass (*Illecebrum verticillatum*) . . . . Saturn
kola nuts (*Kola vera*) . . . . Uranus
laburnum (*Cystisus laburnam*) . . . . Saturn
lady's mantle (*Alchemilla vulgaris*) . . . . * Venus
lady's mantle (*Alchemilla vulgaris*) . . . . * Mars
lady's seals (*Polygonatum multiflorum*) . . . . . . Saturn
lady's slipper (*Cypripedium pubescens*) . . . . . * Mercury
lady's slipper (*Cypripedium pubescens*) . . . . . * Uranus
lanterns (*Physalis alkekengi*) . . . . Mercury
larch (*Pinus larix*) . . . . Jupiter
larkspur (*Delphimium consolida*) . . . . Mars
laurel (*Kalmia latifolia*) . . . . * Mars
laurel (*Kalmia latifolia*) . . . . Saturn
lavender (*Lavendula vera*) . . . . Mercury
leeks (*Allium sp.*) . . . . Mars
lemon (*Citrus limonum*) . . . . * Venus
lemon (*Citrus limonum*) . . . . * Neptune
lemon balm (*Melissa officinalis*) . . . . Venus
lemongrass (*Cymbopogon citratus*) . . . . Venus
lemon verbena (*Lippia citriodorata*) . . . . Venus
lentils (*Lens esculenta*) . . . . Venus
lettuce (*Lactuca sp.*) . . . . Moon
licorice (*Glycyrrhiza glabra*) . . . . Mercury
life everlasting (*Antennaria margaritaceum*) . . . Sun
lignum vitae (*Thuja occidentalis*) . . . . * Mercury
lignum vitae (*Thuja occidentalis*) . . . . * Uranus
lilac (mauve) (*Syringa vulgaris*) . . . . Venus
lilac (white) (*Syringa vulgaris candida*) . . . . . . Moon
lily (madonna) (*Lilium candidum*) . . . . Moon
lily-of-the-valley (*Convallaria magalis*) . . . . . . Mercury
lime (*Citrus acida*) . . . . Jupiter
linseed (*Linum usitatissimum*) . . . . * Mercury
linseed (*Linum usitatissimum*) . . . . * Uranus
litmus (*Rocella tinctoria*) . . . . Mars
liverwort (*Anemone hepatica*) . . . . Jupiter
liverwort (*Peltigera canina*) . . . . Saturn
lobelia (*Lobelia inflata*) . . . . Neptune
locust (*Robinia pseudacacia*) . . . . Sun
logwood (*Haematooxylon campeachianum*) . . . . Uranus

loosestrife *(Lysimachia sp.)* . . . . ** Moon
loosestrife *(Lysimachia sp.)* . . . . * Mars
lotus *(Nymphæa lotus)* . . . . Neptune
lovage *(Levisticum officinale)* . . . . Sun
lungwort *(Sticta pulmonaria)* . . . . Jupiter
lupine *(Lupinus sp.)* . . . . Mars
mace *(Myristica fragrans)* . . . . Mercury
madder *(Rubia tinctorium)* . . . . Mars
magnolia *(Magnolia virginiana)* . . . . Jupiter
maidenhair fern *(Adiantum capillus-veneris)* . . . Mercury
maize *(Zea mays)* . . . . Jupiter
male fern *(Dryopteris felix-mas)* . . . . * Mars
male fern *(Dryopteris felix-mas)* . . . . * Pluto
mallows *(Malva sp.)* . . . . Venus
mandrake *(Atropa mandragora)* . . . . ** Mercury
mandrake *(Atropa mandragora)* . . . . * Uranus
mandrake *(Atropa mandragora)* . . . . * Pluto
maple *(Acer sp.)* . . . . Jupiter
mare's tail *(Hippuris vulgaris)* . . . . Neptune
marigold *(Calendula officinalis)* . . . . Sun
marigold (marsh) *(Caltha palustris)* . . . . . . * Sun
marigold (marsh) *(Caltha palustris)* . . . . . . * Uranus
marijuana *(Cannabis sativa)* . . . . * Saturn
marijuana *(Cannabis sativa)* . . . . * Neptune
marjoram *(Origanum marjorana)* . . . . ** Mercury
marjoram *(Origanum marjorana)* . . . . * Mars
marshmallow *(Althea officinalis)* . . . . Venus
marsh marigold *(Caltha palustris)* . . . . * Sun
marsh marigold *(Caltha palustris)* . . . . * Uranus
marsh trefoil *(Menyanthes trifoliata)* . . . . . . Neptune
marshwort *(Helosciadium nodiflorum)* . . . . . . Neptune
masterwort *(Imperatoria ostruthium)* . . . . . . Mars
mastic (gum) *(Pistacia lentiscus)* . . . . Mars
mastic (thyme) *(Thymus mastichina)* . . . . . . Mars
matico *(Piper angustifolium)* . . . . Mars
mayapple *(Podophyllum peltatum)* . . . . Mars
mayblossom *(Cratægus oxycantha)* . . . . Mars
May lily *(Convallaria magalis)* . . . . Mercury
mayweed *(Anthemis cotula)* . . . . Sun
mayweed *(Pyrethrum parthenium)* . . . . * Sun
meadow saffron *(Colchicum autumnale)* . . . . . Saturn
meadowsweet *(Spiræa ulmaria)* . . . . * Mercury
meadowsweet *(Spiræa ulmaria)* . . . . * Jupiter
meadowsweet *(Spiræa ulmaria)* . . . . * Saturn
melilot *(Melilotus officinalis)* . . . . Mercury
melilot *(Trifolium melilotus)* . . . . Mercury
melons *(Cucumis sp.)* . . . . Neptune
mercury (dog's) *(Mercurialis perennis)* . . . . . . Saturn

mescal (Anhalonium lewinii)		Neptune
mezereon (Daphne mezereum)	*	Mercury
mezereon (Daphne mezereum)	*	Saturn
milkweed (Apocynum androsæmifolium)		Jupiter
millet (Panicum miliaceum)		Jupiter
mints (Mentha sp.)		Venus
mistletoe (Viscum album)	*	Sun
mistletoe (Viscum album)	*	Jupiter
monarda (Monarda punctata)		Venus
moneywort (Lysimachia nummularia)		Jupiter
monkshood (Aconitum napellus)		Saturn
moonwort (Boptrychium lunaria)		Moon
Mormon tea (Ephedra vulgaris)		Mars
morning glory (Convolvulus sp.)		Saturn
moss (club) (Lycopodium clavatum)		Pluto
moss (Irish) (Chondrus crispus)	*	Moon
moss (Irish) (Chondrus crispus)	*	Saturn
moss rose (Helianthemum canadense)		Sun
motherwort (Leonurus cardiaca)		Venus
mountain grape (Berberis aquifolium)		Mercury
mountain laurel (Kalmia latifolia)		Saturn
mouse ear (Hieracium pilosella)	*	Moon
mouse ear (Hieracium pilosella)	*	Saturn
mugwort (Artemisia vulgaris)	*	Venus
mugwort (Artemisia vulgaris)	*	Neptune
mulberry (Morus nigra)		Mercury
mullein (Verbascum thapsus)		Saturn
musk (Hibiscus abelmoschus)	*	Saturn
mustard (Brassica sp.)		Mars
myrrh (Commiphora myrrha)	*	Sun
myrrh (Commiphora myrrha)	*	Moon
myrrh (English) (Cicufaria odorata)		Jupiter
myrtle (Myrtus communis)		Mercury
narcissus (Narcissus sp.)		Neptune
nard (Nardostachys jatamansi)		Uranus
nard (Valeriana jatamansi)		Uranus
nettles (Urtica dioica)		Mars
nightshade (Solanum sp.)		Saturn
nutmeg (Myristica fragrans)		Uranus
oak (Quercus sp.)		Jupiter
oats (Avena sativa)	**	Pluto
oats (Avena sativa)	*	Sun
olibanum (Boswellia thurifera)		Sun
olive (Olea europæa)		Sun
onion (Allium cepa)		Mars
opium poppies (Papaver somniferum)		Neptune
orach (Artiplex patula)		Venus
orange (Citrus aurantium)		Neptune

orchid (*Orchis sp.*)	Venus
orris (*Iris florentina*)	Moon
orris (*Iris pallida*)	Moon
osier (*Cornus sericea*)	Neptune
paddock pipes (*Equisetum sp.*)	Saturn
pansies (*Viola tricolor*)	Saturn
papaw (custard apple) (*Asimina trilobata*)	Mars
papaw (melon tree) (*Carica papaya*)	Jupiter
paprika (*Croton annum*)	Mars
papyrus (*Cyperus papyrus*)	Mercury
paris herb (*Paris quadrifolia*) . . . . *	Venus
paris herb (*Paris quadrifolia*) . . . . *	Uranus
parsley (*Carum petroselinum*) . . . . *	Mercury
parsley (*Carum petroselinum*) . . . . *	Mars
parsnips (*Heracleum sphondylium*)	Mercury
parsnips (*Pastinaca sativa*)	Mercury
passion flower (*Passiflora incarnata*)	Neptune
patchouli (*Pogostemon patchouli*)	Pluto
pau d'arco (*Tahebuia altissima*) . . . . **	Moon
pau d'arco (*Tahebuia altissima*) . . . . *	Saturn
pau d'arco (*Tecoma conspicua*) . . . . *	Mars
pau d'arco (*Tecoma conspicua*) . . . . *	Saturn
peaches (*Prunus persica*) . . . . *	Venus
peaches (*Prunus persica*) . . . . *	Neptune
pear (*Pyrus communis*) . . . . *	Venus
pear (*Pyrus communis*) . . . . *	Neptune
pellitory (*Anacyclus pyrethrum*) . . . . *	Mercury
pellitory (*Anacyclus pyrethrum*) . . . . *	Uranus
pellitory-of-the-wall (*Parietaria officinalis*)	Mercury
pennyroyal (*Mentha pulegium*)	Venus
pennywort (*Hydrocotyle vulgaris*)	Venus
peony (*Pæonia officinalis*)	Sun
peppermint (*Mentha piperita*)	Venus
peppers (*Piper sp.*)	Mars
periwinkle (*Vinca sp.*) . . . . *	Venus
periwinkle (*Vinca sp.*) . . . . *	Saturn
Peruvian bark (*Cinchona succirubra*)	Mars
peyote (*Lophophora diffusa*)	Neptune
phytolacca (*Phytolacca decandra*)	Saturn
pilewort (*Ranunculus ficaria*)	Mars
pimpernel (*Anagallis arvensis*) . . . . *	Sun
pimpernel (*Anagallis arvensis*) . . . . *	Uranus
pine (*Pinaceæ sp.*) . . . . *	Mars
pine (*Pinaceæ sp.*) . . . . *	Pluto
pine (*Pinus picea*)	Jupiter
pinks (*Matthiola sp.*)	Jupiter
pipsissewa (*Chimaphila umbellata*)	Mars
pitcher plant (*Sarracenia purpurea*)	Neptune

plantain (*Plantago major*)	**	Venus
plantain (*Plantago major*)	*	Mars
plantain (fruit) (*Musa paradisiaca*)		Jupiter
pleurisy root (*Asclepias tuberosa*)		Jupiter
plum (*Prunus domestica*)	*	Venus
plum (*Prunus domestica*)	*	Neptune
poison ivy (*Rhus toxicodendron*)		Mars
poke root (*Phytolacca decandra*)		Saturn
pomegranate (*Punica granatum*)	*	Mercury
pomegranate (*Punica granatum*)	*	Saturn
pomegranate (*Punica granatum*)	*	Uranus
poplar (*Populus sp.*)		Saturn
poppy (*Papaver sp.*)	*	Moon
poppy (*Papaver sp.*)	*	Saturn
potato (*Solanum tuberosum*)		Saturn
potato (*Solanum tuberosum*)	*	Pluto
potentilla (*Potentilla sp.*)	*	Mercury
potentilla (*Potentilla sp.*)	*	Jupiter
prickly ash (*Xanthoxylum americanum*)		Mars
primrose (*Primula vulgaris*)		Venus
privet (*Ligustrum vulgare*)		Moon
psilocybin (*Psylocybe sp.*)		Neptune
pumpkin (*Cucurbita pepo*)		Moon
purslane (*Portulaca sp.*)		Moon
pussy willow (*Salix nigra*)	*	Saturn
pussy willow (*Salix nigra*)	*	Uranus
quack grass (*Agropyrum repens*)		Jupiter
quassia (*Picræna excelsa*)		Mars
quebracho (*Aspidosperma quebracho-blanco*) . .		Saturn
Queen Elizabeth root (*Iris florentina*)		Moon
queen's delight (*Stillengia sylvatica*)		Saturn
quince (*Pyrus cydonia*)	**	Saturn
quince (*Pyrus cydonia*)	*	Venus
radish (*Raphanus sativus*)		Mars
ragweed (*Senecio vuilgaris*)		Venus
ragwort (*Senecio jacobæs*)		Saturn
rampion (*Campanula rapunculus*)		Venus
raspberry (*Rubus idæus*)		Venus
rattle grass (*Rhinanthus sp.*)		Moon
rattlesnake root (*Polygala senega*)		Saturn
red root (*Ceanothus americanus*)		Mars
redwood (*Sequoia sp.*)		Pluto
rheumatism weed (*Chimapila umbellata*)		Mars
rhododendron (*Rhododendron chrysanthrum*) . .		Moon
rhubarb (*Rheum sp.*)		Mars
rice (*Oryza sativa*)		Sun
rocket (*Eruca satova*)		Mars
rock rose (*Helianthemum canadense*)		Sun

rose (*Rosa sp.*)		Venus
rose geranium (*Pelargonium capitatum*)		Venus
rose geranium (*Pelargonium graveolens*)		Venus
rose geranium (*Pelargonium roseum*)		Venus
rose hips (*Rosa canina*)		Jupiter
rosemary (*Rosmarinus officinalis*)		Sun
rose (white) (*Rosa sp. (alba)*)		Moon
rose (wild) (*Rosa canina*)		Moon
rowan (*Sorbus americana*)		Moon
rowan (*Sorbus aucuparia*)		Moon
royal fern (*Osmunda regalis*)		Saturn
rudbeckia (*Echinacea angustifolia*)	*	Jupiter
rudbeckia (*Echinacea angustifolia*)	*	Pluto
rue (*Ruta graveolens*)	**	Sun
rue (*Ruta graveolens*)	*	Mars
rupturewort (*Herniaria sp.*)		Saturn
rye (*Secale cereale*)		Pluto
sabadilla (*Veratrum sabadilla*)		Saturn
safflower (*Carthamus tinctorius*)	*	Sun
safflower (*Carthamus tinctorius*)	*	Saturn
saffron (*Crocus sativa*)		Sun
sage (*Salvia officinalis*)	**	Jupiter
sage (*Salvia officinalis*)	*	Venus
Saint Joan's wort (*Hypericum perforatum*)		Sun
Saint John's wort (*Hypericum perforatum*)		Sun
salep (*Orchis sp.*)	*	Mars
salep (*Orchis sp.*)	*	Pluto
salsafy (*Tragopogon porrifolius*)		Jupiter
saltwort (*Salsola kali*)		Mars
samphire (*Crithmum maritimum*)		Neptune
sandalwood (*Santalum album*)		Jupiter
sanicle (*Sanicula europæa*)	*	Mars
sanicle (*Sanicula europæa*)	*	Neptune
sarsaparilla (*Smilax ornata*)		Mars
sarsaparilla (English) (*Smilax sp.*)		Sun
sassafras (*Sassafras officinale*)		Mercury
sassy bark (*Erythrophlœum guineense*)		Saturn
satyrium (*Orchis sp.*)		Venus
savine (*Sabina cacumina*)		Mars
savine (*Sabina juniperus*)		Mars
savory (*Satureia hortensis*)		Mercury
saw palmetto (*Serrenoa serrulata*)		Mercury
saxifrage (*Pimpinella saxifraga*)		Moon
scabious (*Scabiosa sp.*)		Jupiter
scammony (English) (*Convolvulus sp.*)		Saturn
sciatica (*Iberis sisymbrium*)		Saturn
scopolia (*Scopola carniolica*)		Saturn
scullcap (*Scutellaria galericulata*)	*	Saturn

scullcap (*Scutellaria galericulata*) . . . . *   Pluto
scurvy grass (*Cochlearia officinalis*) . . . .   Jupiter
sea fennel (*Crithmum maritimum*) . . . .   Neptune
sea holly (*Eryngium maritimum*) . . . .   Venus
sea plantain (*Plantago maritimo*) . . . .   Neptune
sea salt (*Sal maritimum*) . . . .   Moon
sedge (*Acorus calamus*) . . . .   Mercury
sedum (*Sedum sp.*) . . . .   Jupiter
sedum (*Sedum acre*) . . . .   Moon
sedum (*Sedum album*) . . . .   Moon
sedum (*Sedum telephium*) . . . .   Moon
self-heal (*Prunella vulgaris*) . . . .   Venus
senega (*Polygala senega*) . . . .   Saturn
senna (*Cassia acutifolia*) . . . .   Mercury
senna (bladder) (*Colutea sp.*) . . . .   Mercury
sequoia (*Sequoia sp.*) . . . .   Pluto
sesame (*Sesamum sp.*) . . . .   Moon
shave grass (*Equisetum sp.*) . . . .   Saturn
shepherd's knot (*Potentilla tormentilla*) . . . . . .   Sun
shepherd's purse (*Capsella bursa-pastoris*) . . . .   Saturn
shepherd's rod (*Dipsacus pilosus*) . . . .   Mars
sicklewort (*Diapensia iapponica*) . . . .   Venus
siegesbeckia (*Siegesbeckia orientalis*) . . . .   Moon
silverweed (*Potentilla anserina*) . . . .   Venus
simaruba (*Simaruba officinalis*) . . . .   Mars
simson (*Erigeron acris*) . . . .   Mars
skirret (*Sium sisarum*) . . . .   Venus
skunk cabbage (*Dracontium fœtidum*) . . . . . .   Saturn
skunk cabbage (*Symplocarpus fœtidus*) . . . . .   Saturn
slippery elm (*Ulmus fulva*) . . . .   Jupiter
smartweed (*Polygnum hydropiper*) . . . . *   Mars
smartweed (*Polygnum hydropiper*) . . . . *   Saturn
snake root (*Aristolochia serpentaria*) . . . .   Saturn
snakeweed (*Plantago major*) . . . .   Saturn
snapdragon (*Antirrhinum magus*) . . . .   Mars
snowdrop (*Galanthus nivalis*) . . . .   Moon
soap tree (*Quillaja saponaria*) . . . .   Uranus
soapwort (*Saponaria officinalis*) . . . . **   Venus
soapwort (*Saponaria officinalis*) . . . . *   Mars
soapwort (*Saponaria officinalis*) . . . . *   Neptune
Solomon's seal (*Polygonatum multiflorum*) . . . .   Saturn
sorrel (*Rumex sp.*) . . . .   Venus
southernwood (*Artemisia abrotanum*) . . . . . .   Mercury
sowbread (*Cyclamen hederæfolium*) . . . . **   Mars
sowbread (*Cyclamen hederæfolium*) . . . . *   Venus
sowerweed (*Oxyria reniformis*) . . . .   Mars
sow thistle (*Sonchus sp.*) . . . .   Venus
Spanish chamomile (*Anthemis nobilis*) . . . . . . *   Uranus

speedwell *(Veronica sp.)* . . . . *	Venus
sphagnum moss *(Sphagnum cymbifolium)* . . . . *	Jupiter
sphagnum moss *(Sphagnum cymbifolium)* . . . . *	Neptune
spikenard *(Inula conyza)* . . . . *	Mars
spikenard *(Inula conyza)* . . . . *	Uranus
spinach *(Spinacia oleracea)*	Jupiter
spruce *(Pinus picea)*	Jupiter
spurge *(Euphorbia sp.)* . . . . *	Mercury
spurge *(Euphorbia hortense)* . . . . *	Mars
squaw tea *(Ephedra vulgaris)*	Mars
squaw vine *(Mitchella repens)*	Moon
squill *(Urginea scilla)*	Mars
star anise *(Illicum verum)* . . . . *	Moon
star anise *(Illicum verum)* . . . . *	Uranus
star of Bethlehem *(Ornithogalum umbellatum)* .	Moon
starweed *(Stellaria media)*	Moon
starwort *(Aster sp.)*	Mercury
stonecrop *(Sedum album)*	Moon
storax *(Liquidambar orientalis)*	Sun
strawberry *(Amaranthus blitus)*	Venus
strawberry *(Fragaria vesca)*	Venus
strawberry tree *(Arbutus sp.)* . . . . *	Neptune
strawberry tree *(Arbutus sp.)* . . . . *	Pluto
strophanthus *(Strophanthus kombé)*	Saturn
succory *(Chichorium sp.)*	Jupiter
sumac *(Rhus sp.)*	Jupiter
sumbul *(Ferula sumbul)*	Saturn
sundew *(Drosera rotundifolia)*	Sun
sunflower *(Helianthus annus)*	Sun
swallow wort *(Asclepsias sp.)*	Jupiter
swamp milkweed *(Asclepsias incarnata)*	Jupiter
sweet briar *(Rosa rubiginosa)*	Jupiter
sweet cicely *(Myrrhis odorata)*	Jupiter
sycamore *(Ficus sycomorus.)*	Venus
tallow tree *(Sapium salicifolium)*	Mars
tamarac *(Larix americana)*	Jupiter
tamarind *(Tamarindus indica)* . . . . *	Moon
tamarind *(Tamarindus indica)* . . . . *	Jupiter
tamarisk *(Tamarix gallica)*	Saturn
tansy *(Tanacetum vulgare)*	Venus
tapioca *(Jatropha manihot)*	Moon
tarragon *(Artemisia cracunculus)*	Mars
tea *(Camillia thea)*	Mercury
teak *(Tectona grandis)*	Uranus
teasel *(Dipsacus sylvestris)*	Venus
teazle *(Dipsacus sylvestris)*	Venus
thistle *(Carduus sp.)*	Mars
thistle (carline) *(Carlina vulgaris)*	Venus

thistle (cotton) (*Onopordon acanthium*)	Mars
thistle (gum) (*Euphorbia resinifera*)	Mars
thistle (milk) (*Silybum marianum*)	Moon
thistle (Scotch) (*Onopordon acanthium*)	Mars
thistle (sow) (*Sonchus sp.*)	Venus
thorn (*Cratægus oxyacantha*)	Mars
thornapple (*Datura stramonium*)	Jupiter
thorough leaf (*Bupleurum campestris*)	Saturn
thrift (*Armeria maritima*)	Saturn
thyme (*Thymus vulgaris*)	Venus
thyme (wild) (*Thymus serpyllum*)	Venus
toadflax (*Linaria vulgaris*) . . . . *	Mars
toadflax (*Linaria vulgaris*) . . . . *	Pluto
tobacco (*Nicotiana tabacum*)	Mars
tonka bean (*Dipteryx odorata*)	Uranus
tonquin bean (*Dipteryx odorata*)	Uranus
toothcress (*Dentaria bulbifera*)	Mars
tormentil (*Potentilla tormentilla*)	Sun
tragacanth (*Astragalus gummifer*) . . . . **	Mars
tragacanth (*Astragalus gummifer*) . . . . *	Jupiter
trailing arbutus (*Epigæa repens*)	Uranus
tree of heaven (*Ailanthus glandulosa*)	Saturn
trefoil (*Trifolium sp.*) . . . . **	Mercury
trefoil (*Trifolium sp.*) . . . . *	Venus
trillium (*Trillium sp.*)	Pluto
true unicorn root (*Aletris farinosa*)	Uranus
turkey corn (*Dicentra canadensis*)	Venus
turmeric (*Curcuma longa*)	Mercury
turnip (*Brassica rapa*) . . . . **	Moon
turnip (*Brassica rapa*) . . . . *	Pluto
unicorn root (true) (*Aletris farinosa*)	Uranus
uva ursi (*Arctostaphylos uva-ursi*) . . . . *	Mars
uva ursi (*Arctostaphylos uva-ursi*) . . . . *	Pluto
valerian (*Valeriana officinalis*)	Mercury
verbena (*Verbena officinalis*)	Venus
veronica (*Veronica sp.*) . . . . *	Moon
vervain (*Verbena officinalis*)	Venus
vine (*Vitis vinifera*)	Sun
violets (*Viola odorata*)	Venus
Virginia creeper (*Vitis hederacea*)	Saturn
wake robin (*Arum triphyllum*)	Jupiter
wake robin (*Tillium pendulum*)	Pluto
wallflower (*Cherranthus sp.*)	Moon
walnut (*Juglans sp.*)	Sun
water agrimony (*Bidens tripartita*)	Neptune
water betony (*Scrophularia aquatica*)	Neptune
watercress (*Nasturtium officinale*)	Moon
water figwort (*Scrophularia aquatica*)	Neptune

water gladiole *(Butomus umbellatus)* . . . . Saturn
water hemlock *(cicuta virosa)* . . . . Neptune
water parsnip *(Sium latifolia)* . . . . Neptune
water lily *(Nymphæa odorata)* . . . . Moon
water pepper *(Polygonum hydropiper)* . . . . * Mars
water pepper *(Polygonum hydropiper)* . . . . * Saturn
water pimpernel *(Veronica beccabunga)* . . . . . * Mars
water pimpernel *(Veronica beccabunga)* . . . . . * Neptune
water plantain *(Alisma plantago)* . . . . Neptune
water violet *(Hottonia palustris)* . . . . Saturn
water yarrow *(Hottonia palustris)* . . . . * Saturn
water yarrow *(Hottonia palustris)* . . . . * Neptune
wheat *(Triticum sp.)* . . . . ** Pluto
wheat *(Triticum sp.)* . . . . * Venus
white balsam *(Gnaphalium polycephalum)* . . . . Mercury
wild arrach *(Artiplex patula)* . . . . Venus
wild carrot *(Daucus carota)* . . . . Uranus
wild celery *(Apium graveolens)* . . . . Moon
wild cherry *(Prunus virginiana)* . . . . Venus
wild lettuce *(Lactuca virosa)* . . . . Neptune
wild snowball *(Viburnum opulus)* . . . . * Saturn
wild snowball *(Viburnum opulus)* . . . . * Neptune
wild turnip *(Arum triphyllum)* . . . . Jupiter
willow *(Salix sp.)* . . . . ** Neptune
willow *(Salix sp.)* . . . . * Moon
willow (white) *(Salix alba)* . . . . ** Moon
winter cherry *(Physalis alkekengi)* . . . . Mercury
wintergreen *(Gaultheria procumbens)* . . . . Moon
wintergreen *(Pyrola minor)* . . . . Moon
winter's bark *(Drimys Winteri)* . . . . Pluto
wisteria *(Wistaria cinensis)* . . . . Neptune
witch hazel *(Hamamelis Virginiana)* . . . . Saturn
woad *(Ivatis tinctoria)* . . . . * Mars
woad *(Ivatis tinctoria)* . . . . * Saturn
woad *(Ivatis tinctoria)* . . . . * Pluto
wolf's bane *(Aconitum napellus)* . . . . Saturn
wood betony *(Betonica officinalis)* . . . . ** Jupiter
wood betony *(Betonica officinalis)* . . . . * Venus
woodruff *(Asperula odorata)* . . . . ** Mars
woodruff *(Asperula odorata)* . . . . * Venus
wood sage *(Teucrium scorodonia)* . . . . Venus
woody nightshade *(Solanum dulcamara)* . . . . . * Mercury
woody nightshade *(Solanum dulcamara)* . . . . . * Uranus
worm bark *(Andira inermis)* . . . . Neptune
wormseed *(Chenopodium anthelminticum)* . . . . Mars
wormwood *(Artemisia absinthium)* . . . . * Mars
wormwood *(Artemisia absinthium)* . . . . * Pluto
yams *(Dioscorea villosa)* . . . . * Jupiter

yams (*Dioscorea villosa*) . . . . * Pluto

yarrow (*Achillea millefoium*) . . . . Venus

yellow bugle (*Ajuga chamæpitys*) . . . . ** Mars

yellow bugle (*Ajuga chamæpitys*) . . . . * Pluto

yellow daffodil (*Narcissus pseudo-narcissus*) . . . Mars

yellow flag (*Iris pseudoacorus*) . . . . Moon

yerba santa (*Eriodictyon glutinosum*) . . . . ** Mars

yerba santa (*Eriodictyon glutinosum*) . . . . * Moon

yew (*Taxus baccata*) . . . . Saturn

yohimbe (*Coryanthe yohimbe*) . . . . Mars

yucca (*Yucca sp.*) . . . . Pluto

Common Names

The following list contains common names of herbes matched with the corresponding name that is used in this compendium.

adderwort: bistort
ague root: unicorn root
anise chervil: chervil
aniseed: anise seed
anthemis: chrysanthemum
artemisia: wormwood
arum: jack-in-the-pulpit
asphodel: asphodel
ayegreen: houseleek
balm melissa: balm
balsam tree: balm of Gilead
basil thyme: calamint
bead tree: azadirachta
bear's foot: lady's mantle
bearberry: uva ursi
beggarweed: dodder
belladonna: nightshade (deadly)
bellflower: red campion
bethroot: trillium
bindweed: morning glory
birthroot: trillium
bishopswort: betony (wood)
bittersweet: nightshade (woody)
blazing star: unicorn root
blue rocket: aconite
blue cap: cornflower
bluebottle: cornflower
bluet: cornflower
bog rhubarb: butterbur
bog: beech
boke: beech
bowstick: pau d'arco
boy's love: southernwood
brake fern: fern (bracken)
bramble: blackberry
brameberry: blackberry
bridewort: meadowsweet
British myrrh: chervil
broom: gorse (golden)

buckbean: bogbean
butterdock: butterbur
calamus: sedge (sweet)
call me to you: heartsease
campanula: red campion
campanula: rampion
candlewick plant: mullein
carpenter's weed: yarrow
catmint: catnip
cayenne: pepper (chili)
Chinese anise: anise (star)
Chinese lanterns: cherry (winter)
Christmas rose: hellebore (black)
church steeples: agrimony
cinnamon root: spikenard
clove root: avens
colewort: avens
compass plant: rosemary
corn cockle: red campion
cotton thistle: thistle (Scotch)
cowslip: marsh marigold
crowfoot: anemone (wood)
cuckoo-pint: jack-in-the-pulpit
daggers: iris (yellow)
datura: thornapple
devil plant: basil (bush)
devil's dung: asafoetida
devil's herb: nightshade (deadly)
donnersbart: houseleek
dun daisy: daisy (ox-eye)
easter flower: anemone
eggs and bacon: toadflax
elecampagne: elfwort
elf dock: elfwort
English mercury: goosefoots
faggio: beech
fagos: beech
fairy caps: foxglove
fairy thimbles: foxglove

fairy's glove: foxglove
female fern: fern (bracken)
field daisy: daisy (ox-eye)
five-leaf grass: cinquefoil
flaxweed: toadflax
flixweed: mustard
folks' glove: foxglove
food of the gods: asafoetida
friar's cowl: jack-in-the-pulpit
furze: gorse (golden)
goldens: daisy (ox-eye)
gowans: daisy (ox-eye)
great fleabane: spikenard
green ginger: wormwood
ground lily: trillium
gum arabic: acacia
gyrotheca: lachnanthes
haws: hawthorn
hellweed: dodder
herb bennet: avens
herb of grace: vervain
herba veneris: vervain
holy tree: azadirachta
horse heal: spikenard
huckleberry: bilberry
hummingbird tree: balmony
hypericum: Saint John's wort
Indian lilac tree: azadirachta
ipe roxo: pau d'arco
jacinth: bluebells
Jacob's ladder: lily-of-the-valley
Jacob's sword: iris (yellow)
Jew's myrtle: broom (butcher's)
John's bread: carob
Jupiter's beard: houseleek
Jupiter's nut: chestnut
king's clover: melilot
king's spear: asphodel
kneeholy: broom (butcher's)
lad's love: southernwood
Lady of the Meadow: meadowsweet
lady's seals: Solomon's seal
larkspur lion's mouth: toadflax
lemon balm: balm
linseed: flax
love-lies-bleeding: amaranth
male lily: lily-of-the-valley
marsh trefoil: bogbean

maudlinwort: daisy (ox-eye)
May lily: lily-of-the-valley
mayblossom: hawthorn
meadow anemone: anemone
mercury goosefoot: goosefoots
milfoil: yarrow
moho-moho: matico
monkshood: aconite
moon daisy: daisy (ox-eye)
moonwort: fern (moonwort)
mountain balm: calamint
mountain mint: calamint
musk root: sumbul
naughty man's cherries: nightshade
 (deadly)
olibanum: frankincense
our lady's thistle: thistle (milk)
paint root: lachnanthes
pasque flower: anemone
pattens and clogs: toadflax
pearl barley: barley
pellitory: chrysanthemum
pellote: mescal
peyote: mescal
pot marigold: marigold
potentilla: cinquefoil
pyrethrum: chrysanthemum
Queen of the Meadow: meadowsweet
quickbeam: rowan
rabbits: toadflax
red root: lachnanthes
royal staff: asphodel
Saint Mary's seal: Solomon's seal
Saint Joan's wort: Saint John's wort
salep: orchid
satyrion root: orchid
scarlet berry: nightshade (woody)
sea fennel: samphire
sloe: blackthorn
snakehead: balmony
snakeweed: bistort
sorcerer's violet: periwinkle
sowbread: cyclamen (ivy-leafed)
spirea: meadowsweet
star anise: anise (star)
starchwort: jack-in-the-pulpit
stargrass: unicorn root
starwort: unicorn root

stellaria: lady's mantle
sticklewort: agrimony
stinging nettles: nettles
styrax: benzoin
sweet broom: broom (butcher's)
sweet cicely: chervil
sweet clover: melilot
sweet fern: chervil
synkefoyle: cinquefoil
taheebo: pau d'arco
thorn: hawthorn
trefoil: clover
turtle bloom: balmony
umbrella plant: butterbur
velvet flower: amaranth
verbena: vervain
wake robin: jack-in-the-pulpit
wake-robin: trillium

water fern: fern (royal)
water trefoil: bogbean
way bennet: avens
whortleberry: bilberry
wild pansy: heartsease
wild rye: avens
wild sunflower: elfwort
wind flower: anemone
wind flower: anemone (wood)
witches' gloves: foxglove
wood sorrel: oxalis
wood bells: bluebells
wooly thistle: thistle (Scotch)
yarroway: yarrow
yellow flag: iris (yellow)
yellow iris: iris (yellow)
yerba soldado: matico

Bibliography

It is difficult to feel certain that every book from which I have gained information is included in this list. After twenty years of study and work as an herbalist some references undoubtedly have slipped through. Many of the following books have since been made available in newer editions with other publishers. What follows are the books in our research library which have been invaluable, those which are highly recommended and which we consider essential.

Best, Michael R., and Frank H. Brightman, eds. *The Book of Secrets of Albertus Magnus.* New York: Oxford University Press, 1973.

Beyerl, Rev. Paul. *Amulet Making.* Hermit's Grove Coursenote Series.

———. *The Holy Books of the Devas.* Palm Springs, CA: IGOS Publishing, 1993.

———. *The Master Book of Herbalism.* Custer, WA: Phoenix Publishing, Inc., 1984.

———. *A Wiccan Bardo.* England: Prism-Unity Press, 1989.

Crow, W. B. *The Occult Properties of Herbs.* New York: Samuel Weiser, Inc., 1969.

Culpeper, Nicholas. *Culpeper's Complete Herbal.* Bucks, England: W. Foulsham & Co. Ltd.

Emboden, Willia. *Narcotic Plants.* New York: Macmillan Publishing Co., 1979.

Farrar, Janet and Stewart. *Eight Sabbats for Witches.* Custer, WA: Phoenix Publishing, Inc., 1981.

Frazer, Sir James. *The Golden Bough.* New York: Macmillan Company, 1950.

Gerard, John. *The Herbal or General History of Plants.* New York: Dover Publishing, 1975.

Graves, Robert. *The White Goddess.* New York: Farrar, Straus and Giroux, 1948.

Grieve, Mrs. M. A. *Modern Herbal (2 vol.).* New York: Dover Publishing, 1971.

Grimal, Pierre, ed. *Larousse World Mythology.* New York: Excalibur Books, 1981.

Hartmann, Franz. *Occult Science in Medicine.* New York: Samuel Weiser Inc., 1975.

Hurley, Phillip. *Herbal Alchemy.* Santa Fe: Lotus Press, 1977.

Huson, Paul. *Mastering Herbalism.* New York: Stein and Day, 1975.

Junius, Manfred M. *Practical Handbook of Plant Alchemy.* New York: Inner Traditions International, 1985.

Miller, Richard Alan. *The Magical & Ritual Use of Herbs.* New York: Destiny Books, 1983.

Robinson, Herbert Spencer and Knox Wilson. *Myths and Legends of All Nations.* Totowa, NJ: Littlefield, Adams & Co., 1976.

Smith, Stephen R. *Wylundt's Book of Incense.* York Beach, ME: Samuel Weiser, 1989.

Additional Reference Sources

In addition to the books we used as reference in our research, there are many other books which are of interest. What follows is only a partial list of books kept in our library. Many of these authors are highly reputable. Some of them, we believe, meet our requirements to be considered Master Herbalists. Most of the following books are important references for herbal studies or further work in related fields. We use many of these books for reference when teaching astrological prognostics or astrological herbalism. Some of these books contain extensive lore and magickal properties but we were unable to verify their historical authenticity. In other cases, an author's material was found to be derivative (e.g. from Frazer). A number of these books do not, in our opinion, contain authentic historical lore but are still of interest. A title's inclusion in this list does *not* mean it has our recommendation. Some of these books require a sense of humor and many grains of salt. If you wish a thorough understanding of herbal lore, many of the following books belong in your library in addition to the titles listed in the bibliography. Investigate them on your own and select those which suit your personal taste and style.

Albertus, Frater. *Alchemist's Handbook.* York Beach, ME: Samuel Weiser, 1987.

Beyerl, Rev. Paul. *Colour Therapy.* Hermit's Grove Coursenote Series.

———. *Dream Magick.* Hermit's Grove Tapes or Coursenote Series.

———. *Gardening: The Magickal Approach.* Hermit's Grove Coursenote Series.

———. *Gems and Minerals: A Compendium.* Hermit's Grove Coursenote Series.

———. *Painless Astrology.* California: IGOS Publishing, 1993.

Boland, Maureen & Bridget. *Old Wives' Lore for Gardeners.* New York: Farrar, Straus and Giroux, 1976.

Buckland, Raymond. *Secrets of Gypsy Love Magick.* St. Paul, MN: Llewellyn Publishing, 1990.

Birren, Faber. *The Symbolism of Color.* New Jersey: Citadel Press, 1988.

Cabot, Laurie. *Love Magic.* New York: Delta Books, 1992.

Clark, Linda. *The Ancient Art of Color Therapy.* Connecticut: Devin-Adair Co., 1977.

Cornell, H. L. *Encyclopaedia of Medical Astrology.* New York: Samuel Weiser, 1979.

Culpeper, Nicholas. *Astrological Judgement of Diseases.* Tempe, AZ: American Federation of Astrology, 1959.

Cunningham, Scott. *Earth, Air, Fire & Water.* St. Paul, MN: Llewellyn Publishing, 1991.

———. *Earth Power.* St. Paul, MN: Llewellyn Publishing, 1985.

———. *Encyclopedia of Magical Herbs.* St. Paul, MN: Llewellyn Publishing, 1989.

———. *The Magic of Incense, Oils & Brews.* St. Paul, MN: Llewellyn Publishing, 1986.

———. *Magical Aromatherapy.* St. Paul, MN: Llewellyn Publishing, 1989.

———. *Magical Herbalism.* St. Paul, MN: Llewellyn Publishing, 1982.

Cunningham & Harrington. *The Magical Household.* St. Paul, MN: Llewellyn Publishing, 1987.

Däath, Heinrich. *Medical Astrology.* Santa Fe: Sun Publishing, 1992.

Darling, Harry F. *Essentials of Medical Astrology.* Arizona: American Federation of Astrology, 1981.

Dunwich, Gerina. *The Secrets of Love Magick.* New Jersey: Citadel Press, 1992.

Galadriel, Lady. *Incenses & Oils.* Georgia: Moonstone Publishing, 1986.

Gamache, Henri. *The Magic of Herbs*. New York: Original Publishing, 1985.

George, Llewellyn. *Improved Perpetual Planetary Hour Book*. St. Paul, MN: Llewellyn Publishing, 1975.

Greer, Mary K. *The Essence of Magic*. California: Newcastle Publishing, 1993.

Hawken, Paul. *The Magic of Findhorn*. New York: Bantam Books, 1976.

Heindel, Max. *Astro-Diagnosis*. California: Rosicrucian, 1929.

Hopman, Ellen Evert. *Tree Medicine, Tree Magic*. Custer, WA: Phoenix Publishing, Inc., 1991.

Huson, Paul. *Mastering Herbalism*. New York: Stein and Day, 1975.

Jo & James. *The Color Book*. Colorado: Castle Rising, 1980.

Morrison, Sarah L. *The Modern Witch's Spellbook*. New Jersey: Citadel Press, 1971.

Morwyn. *Green Magic*. Pennsylvania: Whitford Press, 1994.

Muir, Ada. *The Healing Herbs of the Zodiac*. St. Paul, MN: Llewellyn Publishing, 1974.

Nagle, C. A. *Magical Charms, Potions and Secrets for Love*. Minneapolis: Marlar Publishing, 1972.

Ouseley, S. G. J. *Colour Meditations*. England: L. N. Fowler & Co., 1976.

Petulengro, Leon. *Herbs, Health & Astrology*. Connecticut: Keats Publishing, 1977.

Rago, Linda Ours. *The Herbal Almanac*. Washington, D.C.: Starwood Publishing Inc., 1992.

Riva, Anna. *Golden Secrets of Mystic Oils*. California: International Imports, 1978.

Rose, Jeanne. *Herbs & Things*. New York: Grosset & Dunlap, 1972.

Slater, Herman. *Magickal Formulary*. New York: Magickal Childe, 1988.

Telesco, Patricia. *The Victorian Flower Oracle*. St. Paul, MN: Llewellyn Publishing, 1994.

Thompson, Janet. *Magical Hearth*. York Beach, ME: Samuel Weiser, 1995.

Tierra, Michael. *Planetary Herbology*. Santa Fe: Lotus Press, 1988.

Tompkins & Bird. *The Secret Life of Plants*. New York: Avon Books, 1973.

Vinci, Leo. *Incense*. Northamptonshire, England: Aquarian Press, 1983.

Worth, Valerie. *The Crone's Book of Words*. St. Paul, MN: Llewellyn Publishing, 1986.

Wright, Elbee. *Book of Legendary Spells*. Minneapolis: Marlar Publishing, 1974.

Zalewski, C. L. *Herbs in Magic and Alchemy*. Dorset, England: Prism-Unity, 1990.

For additional information about The Rowan Tree Church or The Tradition of Lothloriën, send a self-addressed stamped business-sized envelope to: The Rowan Tree Church, P. O. Box 0691, Kirkland, WA 98083-0691. Please note that our former Minneapolis address is listed in hundreds of resource directories but is no longer our primary mailing address.

For a copy of The Hermit's Grove catalog (a listing of dried herbes available by mail) and a sample issue of *The Hermit's Lantern*, if you live in North America, please send $3.00 U.S. payable to The Hermit's Grove. If you live outside North America, please send $5.00 in U.S. funds. Send your request (we do not need an envelope) to: The Hermit's Grove, 9724 - 132nd Ave. NE, Kirkland, WA 98033. Visiting The Hermit's Grove may be arranged but is *by appointment only*. Please contact us by mail for further information.

Index

510

512

516

517

525